Frommer's®

P9-CAO-991

Guatemala
1st Edition

by Eliot Greenspan

WITHDRAWN

Here's what the critics say about Frommer's:

"Amazingly easy to use. Very portable, very complete."

—*Booklist*

"Detailed, accurate, and easy-to-read information for all price ranges."
—*Glamour Magazine*

"Hotel information is close to encyclopedic."

—*Des Moines Sunday Register*

"Frommer's Guides have a way of giving you a real feel for a place."
—*Knight Ridder Newspapers*

Wiley Publishing, Inc.

Published by:

Wiley Publishing, Inc.

111 River St.
Hoboken, NJ 07030-5774

ISBN: 978-0-470-04730-9

Editor: Anuja Madar
Production Editor: Suzanna R. Thompson
Cartographer: Andrew Murphy
Photo Editor: Richard Fox
Anniversary Logo Design: Richard Pacifico
Production by Wiley Indianapolis Composition Services

Front cover photo: Antigua: Entrance to arch
Back cover photo: View of Lake Atitlán

For information on our other products and services or to obtain technical support, please contact our Customer Care Department within the U.S. at 800/762-2974, outside the U.S. at 317/572-3993 or fax 317/572-4002.

Wiley also publishes its books in a variety of electronic formats. Some content that appears in print may not be available in electronic formats.

Manufactured in the United States of America

5 4 3 2 1

Contents

List of Maps

Acknowledgments

I'd like to tip my hat and extend my thanks to Jennifer Reilly and Anuja Madar. I'd also like to thank Timoteo Pertz and Jim Shapiro for plenty of behind-the-scenes work on the phone, keyboards, and World Wide Web.

An Invitation to the Reader

In researching this book, we discovered many wonderful places—hotels, restaurants, shops, and more. We're sure you'll find others. Please tell us about them, so we can share the information with your fellow travelers in upcoming editions. If you were disappointed with a recommendation, we'd love to know that, too. Please write to:

Frommer's Guatemala, 1st Edition
Wiley Publishing, Inc. • 111 River St. • Hoboken, NJ 07030-5774

An Additional Note

Please be advised that travel information is subject to change at any time—and this is especially true of prices. We therefore suggest that you write or call ahead for confirmation when making your travel plans. The authors, editors, and publisher cannot be held responsible for the experiences of readers while traveling. Your safety is important to us, however, so we encourage you to stay alert and be aware of your surroundings. Keep a close eye on cameras, purses, and wallets, all favorite targets of thieves and pickpockets.

About the Author

Eliot Greenspan is a poet, journalist, and travel writer who took his backpack and typewriter the length of Mesoamerica before settling in Costa Rica in 1992. Since then, he has worked steadily as a travel writer, freelance journalist, and translator, and has continued his travels in the region. He is the author of *Frommer's Belize, Frommer's Cuba, Frommer's Costa Rica,* and *Costa Rica For Dummies,* as well as the Venezuela chapter in *Frommer's South America.* When not traveling or writing, Eliot plays mandolin, sings, and performs with Los Flying Borracho Brothers.

Other Great Guides for Your Trip:

Frommer's Belize

Frommer's Costa Rica

Frommer's Mexico

Frommer's Panama

Frommer's Star Ratings, Icons & Abbreviations

Every hotel, restaurant, and attraction listing in this guide has been ranked for quality, value, service, amenities, and special features using a **star-rating system.** In country, state, and regional guides, we also rate towns and regions to help you narrow down your choices and budget your time accordingly. Hotels and restaurants are rated on a scale of zero (recommended) to three stars (exceptional). Attractions, shopping, nightlife, towns, and regions are rated according to the following scale: zero stars (recommended), one star (highly recommended), two stars (very highly recommended), and three stars (must-see).

In addition to the star-rating system, we also use **seven feature icons** that point you to the great deals, in-the-know advice, and unique experiences that separate travelers from tourists. Throughout the book, look for:

Finds	Special finds—those places only insiders know about
Fun Fact	Fun facts—details that make travelers more informed and their trips more fun
Kids	Best bets for kids and advice for the whole family
Moments	Special moments—those experiences that memories are made of
Overrated	Places or experiences not worth your time or money
Tips	Insider tips—great ways to save time and money
Value	Great values—where to get the best deals

The following **abbreviations** are used for credit cards:

AE	American Express	DISC	Discover	V	Visa
DC	Diners Club	MC	MasterCard		

Frommers.com

Now that you have this guidebook to help you plan a great trip, visit our website at **www.frommers.com** for additional travel information on more than 3,500 destinations. We update features regularly to give you instant access to the most current trip-planning information available. At Frommers.com, you'll find scoops on the best airfares, lodging rates, and car rental bargains. You can even book your travel online through our reliable travel booking partners. Other popular features include:

- Online updates of our most popular guidebooks
- Vacation sweepstakes and contest giveaways
- Newsletters highlighting the hottest travel trends
- Online travel message boards with featured travel discussions

The Best of Guatemala

Guatemala's charms are as varied as the riotous colors woven into its famed fabrics. From the Maya ruins of Tikal and the colonial splendor of Antigua—both exquisitely preserved through the centuries—to the breathtaking natural beauty of Lake Atitlán and Semuc Champey, there are a range of destinations and attractions here to please just about any type of traveler. I've been visiting Guatemala for more than 20 years, and I continue to discover new places and have new experiences that add to my own personal "best of" list. On my most recent trip, I visited the Kan' Ba cave, one of the newest attractions in Guatemala. I had to wade in the river to get to the cave, and when the water got too deep, I put my candle (my only source of light) in my mouth and swam. Not every "best of" place or experience on this list is quite as adventurous, but if you're looking for the best hotels or restaurants to suit a certain style, taste, or budget, or trying to figure out the "must-see" destinations for your trip, the lists below should help you narrow down your choices and fine-tune your itinerary.

1 The Best Purely Guatemalan Experiences

- **Enjoying the Holy Week Festivities in Antigua:** Semana Santa, or Holy Week, is celebrated with both fervor and style in Antigua. In fact, the Holy Week celebrations are arguably the most beautiful and elaborate in all of the Americas, and rival even the most famous ones in Europe. Massive processions weave slowly through the cobblestone streets over painstakingly gorgeous *alfombras,* or carpets, made of fine colored sawdust and flower petals. The air is thick with incense smoke, and the small city is a spectacle for a solid week. See chapter 5.
- **Touring the Towns & Villages around Lake Atitlán:** While Lake Atitlán is exceedingly beautiful in and of itself, the true charm of the lake is its ability to let you visit a half-dozen or more lakeshore towns via local water-taxi services. The water taxis run regular routes throughout the

day, stopping at the villages of Santiago de Atitlán, San Pedro de la Laguna, San Marco, San Antonio Palopó, and more. You can hop on and off the taxis at your whim, and stay as long as you like before heading on to the next place or back home to your hotel. See chapter 6.
- **Paying Your Respects to Maximón:** A syncretic saint worshiped by Guatemala's Maya and Catholic alike, Maximón is the bad boy of the religious pantheon. Maximón apparently responds well to gifts, and has very specific tastes, so be sure to bring some rum or a cigar as an offering. Many towns across Guatemala have a carved idol of Maximón, or San Simon, although only a few really keep the practice of his daily worship alive. The towns with the most elaborate Maximón rituals and traditions include

The Best of Guatemala

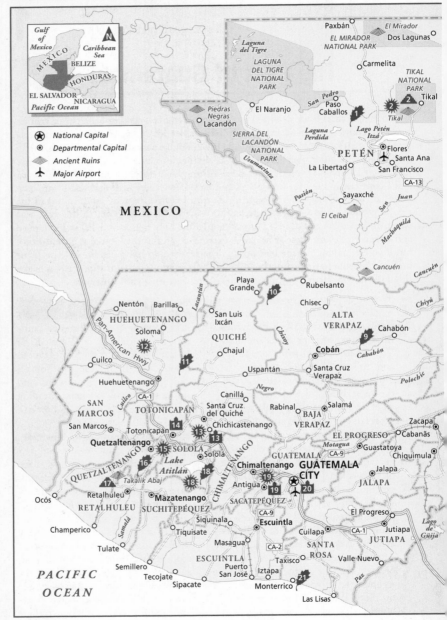

Río Azul
RÍO AZUL NATIONAL PARK
Belize City
Belize
Belmopan
Yaxhá
Melchor de Mencos
BELIZE
Mopán
Ixkun
Poptún
San Luis
Gulf of Honduras
Modesto Méndez
Sarstún
Bahía de Amatique
CA-13
Livingston
El Golfete
Río Dulce
Puerto Barrios
IZABAL
Sánto Tomás de Castilla
El Estor
Lago Izabal
Morales
Motagua
Los Amates
CA-9
Quiriguá
ZACAPA
La Unión
Copán
CHIQUIMULA
HONDURAS
Esquipulas
EL SALVADOR

0   40 mi
0   40 km

THE BEST PURELY GUATEMALAN EXPERIENCES

Enjoying the Holy Week Festivities in Antigua **19**
Touring the Towns and Villages Around Lake Atitlán **18**
Paying Your Respects to Maximón **18**
Shopping at the Chichicastenango Market **13**
Studying Spanish and Staying With a Local Family **15, 18, 19**
Watching the Sunrise From the Top of a Pyramid in Tikal **2**
Cheering On Riders in the "Drunken Horse Race" **12**

THE BEST OF NATURAL GUATEMALA

Lake Atitlán **18**
Semuc Champey **9**
Parque Nacional Laguna de Lachuá **10**
Volcán Santa María **16**
Nebaj & the Ixil Triangle **11**
El Petén **1**
Río Dulce **5**
Los Siete Altares **4**
Tortuguerio Monterrico **21**

THE BEST MAYA ARCHAEOLOGICAL SITES

Tikal **2**
Yaxhá **3**
Copán **7**
Quiriguá **6**
Takalik Abaj **17**

THE BEST CHURCHES, CONVENTS & MONASTERIES

Catedral Metropolitana **20**
Iglesia San Francisco **20**
Convento de las Capuchinas **19**
Iglesia La Merced **19**
Iglesia de Santo Tomás **13**
Iglesia de San Andés Xecul **14**
La Basilica **8**

Santiago de Atitlán and Zunil. See chapters 6 and 7, respectively.

- **Shopping at the Chichicastenango Market:** Guatemala's Maya people are world-famous for their incredible arts and crafts, which they sell predominantly at local and regional open-air markets. These markets are held in the central plazas of the country's towns and cities. The twice-weekly market in Chichicastenango is the largest and most famous of these open-air markets, with hundreds of stands selling everything from handicrafts and flowers to household goods and furniture. See p. 173.

- **Studying Spanish & Staying with a Local Family:** Studying Spanish in a foreign country is all the rage, and Guatemala is the perfect place to do it. In addition to the wonderful surroundings and bargain prices, the Guatemalan accent is one of the cleanest and easiest to master. All of Guatemala's major tourist destinations have Spanish schools, each of which offers the option of living with a local family while you study. See the various destination chapters, as well as chapter 2, for more information.

- **Watching the Sunrise from the Top of a Pyramid in Tikal:** A visit to Tikal is a remarkable experience on its own, but my favorite way to start a visit here is by catching the sunrise from the top of one of the pyramids. In addition to the ruins and sunrise, the surrounding jungle comes to life with the cries of howler monkeys and the frenzied activity and calls of awakening birds. See chapter 8.

- **Cheering On Riders in the "Drunken Horse Race":** The tiny highland Maya town of Todos Santos Chuchumatán holds one of the equestrian world's oddest races every November 1. The town's "Drunken Horse Race" is a daylong event that involves equal parts drinking and racing. The last rider (who's highly intoxicated) left on his horse is declared the winner. Riders fall, and numerous riders and spectators end up lying in an unconscious stupor along the streets and walkways of the small town. It's hilarious, nerve-racking, and sad all at the same time. See chapter 7.

2 The Best of Natural Guatemala

- **Lake Atitlán (Western Highlands):** Whether or not you agree with Aldous Huxley that Atitlán is the "most beautiful lake in the world," you would be hard pressed to not be at least slightly impressed. Formed thousands of years ago in the crater of a massive volcano and surrounded today by several other towering volcanoes, Lake Atitlán is stunning. The road that circumnavigates much of the lake actually follows the rim of the extinct crater, and the views on high end, and those from the lakeshore and the many boats plying its waters, are fabulous. See chapter 6.

- **Semuc Champey (Alta Verapaz):** Semuc Champey is a series of stepped waterfalls and pools that actually sit on top of a raging underground river in a narrow forested canyon. It's often described as the most beautiful spot in all of Guatemala, and in addition to swimming in the pools, there's great hiking here. The spots where the Cahabón River enters and then exits its underground tunnel are jaw-dropping in their power and fury. The surrounding area is also full of caves that are worth exploring. See p. 228.

- **Parque Nacional Laguna de Lachuá (Alta Verapaz):** The deep turquoise of Lake Lachuá may have you wondering if you're staring at the Caribbean Sea. All around the lake, lush rainforests are home to an amazing array of tropical flora and fauna. See p. 228.

- **Volcán Santa María (outside Quetzaltenango):** Not only is Volcán Santa María an imposing sight and exhilarating climb, the view from the summit peers down into the crater of its very active sister volcano, Santiaguito. It's about a 3- to 4-hour hike to the summit. Camping is allowed, and many enjoy spending the night up here, although it can get cold and windy. See chapter 7.
- **Nebaj & the Ixil Triangle (Northern Quiché Province):** This remote area was once ground zero in the government's oppressive civil war campaign against indigenous populations suspected of supporting leftist rebels. Today, it's the best place to go deep into the Guatemalan highlands for a glimpse into the country's timeless rural life and landscape. Numerous towns can be visited by hiking centuries-old dirt paths and trails. See chapter 7.
- **El Petén (Northeastern Guatemala):** The Petén province is a massive region comprised primarily of virgin tropical rainforest, and is home to many of the country's major archaeological sites and Maya ruins. The bird-watching is top-notch, and you can see a host of other species of tropical flora and fauna on a guided hike

through one of the natural parks or nature reserves. See chapter 8.

- **Río Dulce (Lago Izabal Region):** The Río Dulce, or Sweet River, runs from a narrow opening at one end of Lago Izabal all the way down to the Caribbean Sea. Along the way it passes through lush tropical lowland rainforest, as well as one gorgeous narrow canyon. In addition, hot springs bubble from underground, creating hot pools where you can stop and soak. Boat trips between the villages of Fronteras and Livingston are popular. See chapter 10.
- **Los Siete Altares (Livingston):** The name of this place translates as "The Seven Altars." Each of these altars is, in fact, a beautiful jungle waterfall. The falls are set in a steady progression in a narrow forest canyon and fed by a gentle river. The final waterfall is the largest, with a deep pool for swimming. This spot was chosen as a location for the filming of an early "Tarzan" movie. See p. 249.
- **Tortuguerio Monterrico (Monterrico):** This turtle protection project is a great place to learn about the life cycle of giant sea turtles. If you're lucky enough to be here when the turtle eggs are hatching, you can take part in their weekly raffle, wherein participants are assigned a hatchling, and the quickest hatchling to the sea wins its sponsor a prize. If the turtle hatchlings aren't in season, you can still see iguanas and caimans and hike the nature trail. See p. 267.

3 The Best Maya Archaeological Sites

- **Tikal (El Petén):** In my opinion, Tikal is the most impressive of all the ancient Maya ceremonial cities. Not only is the site massive and meticulously excavated and restored, it's set in the midst of a lush and lively tropical jungle. The peaks of several temples

poke through the dense rainforest canopy, toucans and parrots fly about, and the loudest noise you'll hear is the guttural call of howler monkeys. In its heyday, the city probably covered as many as 65 sq. km (25 sq. miles) and supported a population of more than 100,000. See "Tikal" in chapter 8.

- **Yaxhá (El Petén):** This Classic-period Maya city was recently put on the map when CBS chose it as a site for its reality show *Survivor*. While little has been excavated, this remains the third-largest Maya ceremonial city in Guatemala, behind Tikal and El Mirador. See chapter 8.
- **Copán (Honduras):** It's not technically in Guatemala, but Copán is just a few quick miles over the Honduran border. A big and beautifully restored Maya city, Copán is renowned for its impressive quantity and variety of stone carvings, which can be seen on stelae, individual sculptures, architectural adornments, and one massive stairway of a major pyramid. The new Museum of Maya Sculpture contains probably the best collection of original Maya ceremonial stone art in all of Mesoamerica. Back at the archaeological site, you can walk through some

newly dug tunnels that reveal the Maya technique of building new temples over existing ones. See chapter 9.

- **Quiriguá (En Route to Puerto Barrios):** While overall this archaeological site is pretty small, it's home to an impressive collection of large, carved stelae and stones. The tallest stela here is 10m (35 ft.) tall and weighs more than 65 tons. It's the tallest Maya stela yet discovered. Almost as interesting are the massive stones with complex hieroglyphic carvings. See p. 261.
- **Takalik Abaj (Northwest of Retalhuleu):** This little-known ruin is a hidden gem. Dating from the pre-Classic period, it's one of the oldest ceremonial and trade cities to be excavated in Guatemala. Perhaps its greatest claim to fame, however, is the fact that there's a lovely lodge located on the grounds of the archaeological site, combining ecotourism and archaeological preservation in an interesting symbiosis. See p. 274.

4 The Best Churches, Convents & Monasteries

- **Catedral Metropolitana (Guatemala City):** It took a long time to build this church, some 86 years, but the elegant main cathedral of Guatemala City has stood the test of time and weathered the effects of some major earthquakes. Today, the most impressive aspect of this church is its facade, which is both big and bold. However, the interior holds a treasure-trove of religious art and icons. Fronting the Plaza Mayor, this is a great place to start any tour of downtown Guatemala City. See p. 108.
- **Iglesia San Francisco (Guatemala City):** This church isn't quite as old as other more famous Catholic churches in the country, but it has arguably the most impressive main altar—a massive work of carved wood that's almost 92m (300 ft.) tall. See p. 108.

- **Convento de las Capuchinas (Antigua):** Life was pretty difficult and austere for the nuns at this Capuchin convent, but today the grounds and buildings are some of the most pastoral and picturesque in all of Antigua. The large and sprawling complex was abandoned in the wake of the 1776 earthquake, but the damage was relatively minor. The view from the rooftop is not to be missed. See p. 128.
- **Iglesia La Merced (Antigua):** In a city awash in Catholic churches, convents, and monasteries, Iglesia La Merced reigns supreme. It's no small coincidence—nor small honor—that the principal procession of the Holy Week celebrations leaves from this church. The ornate baroque facade is painted bright yellow and white, and

the interior is full of art and sculptures. The ruins of the attached convent are also worth a visit. See p. 129.

- **Iglesia de Santo Tomás (Chichicastenango):** Dating back to 1540, this modest church serves simultaneously as a place for Catholic worship and ancient Maya rituals. The exterior steps, which possess a privileged perch over the town of Chichicastenango, are believed to represent the 18 months of the Maya calendar. Today, these steps are constantly in use as an altar for Maya prayer and offerings. It was in the attached convent that the oldest known version of the Popol Vuh was discovered. See p. 174.
- **Iglesia de San Andrés Xecul (outside of Quetzaltenango):** The brilliantly painted ornate facade of this church, located in a small town in the Western Highlands, is easily the most psychedelic in the entire country. The facade features the prominent figures of jaguars mixed with religious iconography. Be sure to come in the afternoon, when the sun directly hits the church's front. See p. 185.
- **La Basílica (Esquipulas):** This is the most famous religious site in Guatemala, and the only church in the country to earn the honor of being named a Basilica. More than one million pilgrims from around the world come to the 1758 church to pay their respects to the famous statue of the "Black Christ." See p. 235.

5 The Best Outdoor Adventures

- **Mountain Biking the Rural Back Roads:** The back roads and dirt paths of rural Guatemala are perfect for fat tire explorations. Whether you choose to take a ridge ride between small villages or a more technically challenging ascent or descent of a volcano, there is something for all ability levels. **Old Town Outfitters (© 502/5399-0440;** www.bikeguatemala.com) is my favorite operator, and has excellent guides and equipment, and a wide range of tours and trips. See chapter 5.
- **Climbing an Active Volcano:** Guatemala's mountainous terrain is predominantly volcanic, and many of these volcanoes are still active. There's nothing as primal as climbing the flanks of an active volcano or peering down into an erupting crater. Both of these experiences are possible on a climb to the summit of **Pacaya** volcano. Many tours take you close enough to actually feel the heat of fresh lava. Once Pacaya's whetted your appetite, there are numerous other volcanoes here to scale, including **Santa María, Tajumulco, Agua,** and **Acatenango.** See chapters 5 and 7, respectively.
- **Swinging through the Treetops on a Canopy Tour:** Zip-trekking is becoming all the rage, and offers a different way to experience the rich wonders of the tropical rainforest. If you visit Tikal, don't miss the opportunity to take a trip with the **Canopy Tour Tikal (© 502/7926-4270;** www.canopytikal.com). See chapter 8.
- **Exploring the Underworld:** Many of Guatemala's volcanic mountains are riddled with caves. The ancient Maya considered caves holy sites that served as passageways to the next world. The caves of **Lanquin** and **Candelaria** are popular tourist destinations, but my favorite cave adventure is a tour into the depths of **Kan' Ba.** This cave has a small river running through it, and the spelunking here is a mix of hiking, wading, and swimming. The entrance to the cave is a large opening where the river exits

and forms a gentle jungle waterfall. See chapter 9.

- **Rafting on the Cahabón River:** The Alta Verapaz region is rapidly becoming the center of Guatemala's growing adventure tourism industry, and the raging rapids of the Cahabón River are part of the reason. After it exits the natural marvel of Semuc Champey, the Cahabón has both class III and class IV sections that are perfect for whitewater rafting. Single-day adventures and multiday tours are available. Contact **Aventuras Turísticas** (© 502/ 7951-4213; www.aventurasturisticas. com), or see chapter 9 for more details.

- **Landing a Marlin or Sailfish:** Although a relative newcomer to the world of international offshore game-fishing, Guatemala is fast creating quite a buzz. The waters off Guatemala's Pacific coast are excellent for sportfishing year-round, and big game fish are being hauled in at a record pace. If you want to reel 'em in, contact **The Great Sailfishing Company** (© 877/763-0851 in the U.S. and Canada, or 502/7832-1991; www.greatsailfishing.com), or **Parlama Sport Fishing** (© 502/ 5704-4254 or 502/7832-2578; www. parlama.com). See chapter 11.

6 The Best Shopping & Markets

- **Ron Zacapa Centenario:** While I spend a lot of time waxing poetic over the beauty and quality of Guatemala's arts and crafts, it's worth emphasizing how special this 23-year-old dark rum is. Whether you think you like rum or not, any aficionado of fine spirits should pick up a bottle of this amazingly smooth brew. See p. 116.

- **In Nola** (Guatemala City; © 502/ 2367-2424): This is the place in Guatemala City for textiles and just about any other arts-and-crafts item. The large store is beautifully laid out, service is excellent, and the prices are fair. You won't find the bargains you might be able to negotiate at the informal markets, but you won't be taken to the cleaners either. See p. 115.

- **Carlos Woods Arte Antiguo y Contemporáneo** (Guatemala City; © 502/ 2366-6883): This is the finest art gallery in Guatemala City, with an excellent variety of modern and historical works. The rooms here are well-lit and beautifully designed, making a visit a pure pleasure whether or not you're looking to buy. See p. 114.

- **Nim Po't** (Antigua; © 502/7832-2681; www.nimpot.com): A massive indoor space with a soaring ceiling houses this local craft and textile cooperative warehouse. Textiles, woodcarvings, and ceramic wares from across the country are available here. The quality varies greatly, but if you know what to look for, you can find some fine works without having to venture into the farther reaches of rural Guatemala. See p. 141.

- **Joyería del Angel** (Antigua; © 502/ 7832-3189): Antigua has a glut of high-end jewelry stores selling locally produced wares. However, this shop has the most interesting and unique pieces that you'll ever see in one place in this town. It's worth checking their clearance rack, as they periodically try to update their stock. See p. 140.

- **Wer** (Antigua; © 502/7832-7161): Give yourself some time to wander through the many rooms of art in this contemporary gallery, set up in the rambling space of a converted colonial-era home. More than 100 Guatemalan artists are represented here. See p. 139.

- **Chichicastenango's Market** (Chichicastenango; no phone): There's a reason this twice-weekly open-air market is so famous. The abundance and variety of wares for sale and the somewhat controlled frenzy of the entire operation are not to be missed. You may find better bargains and products around the country, but you'll never see so much in one place at one time. See p. 173.
- **San Francisco El Alto Market** (San Francisco El Alto; no phone): Local cognoscenti swear that the Friday market in San Francisco El Alto is even better than the one in Chichi. It's certainly a great market, and if you know what you're looking for, and how to bargain, you might even do better here than in Chichi. See p. 186.
- **Q'eqchi' Women's Craft Cooperative** (on the Río Dulce; no phone): The Caribbean lowlands are a particularly barren zone for die-hard shoppers. This small shop is the exception to the rule. You can only get to this humble cooperative by boat, but all of the tour operations in Livingston and Río Dulce stop here. See p. 252.

7 The Best High-End Hotels

- **Real InterContinental** (Zona 10, Guatemala City; ✆ **502/2379-4446;** www.interconti.com): There's a host of high-end business class hotels in Guatemala City, but this one tops them all in terms of rooms, amenities, facilities, location, and service. The InterContinental sits on a very busy corner of the Zona Viva, with shops, restaurants, bars, and more just steps away in every direction. See p. 95.
- **Casa Santo Domingo** (Antigua; ✆ **502/7820-1220;** www.casasanto domingo.com.gt): You can sometimes get lost on the extensive grounds of this fabulous hotel. In addition to the fine rooms, excellent service, and colonial-era ambience, this place features museum-quality collections of art and artifacts, as well as a large amphitheater. The whole complex sits on, and is integrated into, the ruins of an old convent. See p. 131.
- **Posada del Angel** (Antigua; ✆ **502/ 7832-5303;** www.posadadelangel. com): With just five beautiful rooms, this place gives you intimacy with your luxury, and is consistently considered one of the top hotels in the entire country. I like the second-floor suite, with its own private rooftop terrace. See p. 133.
- **Mesón Panza Verde** (Antigua; ✆ **502/ 7832-1745;** www.panzaverde.com): This elegant and artistic Antigua hotel is actually listed in the "moderate" price category in this book, thanks to the inclusion of several excellent midrange rooms. However, the large suites and superb service easily make this one of Guatemala's top luxury options. The old building is loaded with artwork and interesting architectural details, and there's a wonderful, mazelike rooftop terrace with panoramic views. The restaurant (below) is one of the best in the country. See p. 132.
- **Hotel Atitlán** (Finca San Buenaventura, Panajachel; ✆ **502/7762-1441;** www.hotelatitlán.com): This fabulous hotel is set on the shores of Lake Atitlán, with a stunning view of the lake and its surrounding volcanoes. Beautiful rooms, lush gardens, ample amenities, impeccable service, and a great restaurant make this a complete package. See p. 153.

- **Casa Palopó** (Carretera a San Antonio Palopó, Lake Atitlán; ℂ **502/ 7762-2270**; www.casapalopo.com): Artwork and interesting design touches abound in this boutique hotel, which is perched high on a hillside overlooking Lake Atitlán. The vibe here is hip, intimate, refined, and romantic, and the place is perfect for couples. (Honeymooners should seriously consider it.) The restaurant is excellent. See p. 167.
- **La Lancha Resort** (Lago Petén Itzá, Petén; ℂ **800/746-3743** in the U.S., or ℂ/fax 502/7928-8331 in Guatemala; www.lalanchavillage.com): Set on a steep hillside overlooking the lake, this is the plushest hotel near Tikal. The rooms at this Francis Ford Coppola regional resort (he has two others in Belize) are decorated with style, featuring furniture and artwork from around the world. The food is also excellent, taking local cuisine as its inspiration and adding creative touches and refined twists. See p. 220.
- **Hotel Villa Caribe** (Livingston; ℂ **502/2334-1818** or 502/7947-0072; www.villasdeguatemala.com): My favorite rooms here are the individual bungalows, which are what earns this hotel a spot in this exclusive group. These rooms have air-conditioning, cable television, and minibars, which the other rooms lack. However, every room here has a private balcony with a commanding view of the Río Dulce river mouth and the Caribbean Sea. See p. 252.

8 The Best Midrange Hotels

- **Otelito Casa Santa Clara** (Zona 10, Guatemala City; ℂ/fax **502/2339- 1811**; www.otelito.com): With only 12 rooms, this exceedingly hip hotel stands out from all the large, high-rise, business-class monsters that dominate this downtown neighborhood. Each room is slightly different, but a sense of refined, minimalist design is felt in the decor throughout. In addition to the intimate setting and trendy vibe, they also have an excellent in-house fusion restaurant. See p. 98.
- **Casa Azul** (Antigua; ℂ **502/7832- 0961**; www.casazul.guate.com): While most of the boutique hotels in Antigua seek to mimic the city's colonial splendor in their design and decor, Casa Azul has gone for a more modern and eclectic style. The hotel is just a half-block from the Plaza Mayor, making it one of the best located hotels in the city. See p. 134.
- **Hotel Dos Mundos** (Panajachel; ℂ **502/7762-2078**; www.hoteldos mundos.com): The spacious rooms here are one of my top choices in Panajachel. Although the hotel is located right in the center of Calle Santander, the rooms are set back from the street in a quiet garden area, giving you easy access to all the action and peace and quiet at the same time. See p. 154.
- **Bambú Hotel & Restaurant** (Santiago de Atitlán; ℂ **502/7721-7332**; www.ecobambu.com): The two private lakefront bungalows are the best rooms in the house, and probably the best rooms in all of Santiago de Atitlán, so be sure to try and book one of these. Better still is that they're the same price as those in the larger building, which are set back from the water's edge. Even if you don't get one of the private bungalows, you'll be

plenty happy at this excellent hotel. See p. 165.

• **Villa Sumaya** (San Marcos La Laguna, Lake Atitlán; ✆ **502/5617-1209;** www.villasumaya.com): This lakefront boutique hotel is also a yoga and meditation retreat center. The individual cabins are wonderful, and the grounds and gardens are beautiful. If you want an isolated getaway on Lake Atitlán, whether to seek spiritual or physical enlightenment, this is a great choice. See p. 169.

• **Casa Mañen** (Quetzaltenango; ✆ **502/ 7765-0786;** www.comeseeit.com): This is my favorite hotel in Quetzaltenango. The rooms are all decorated with a range of local arts and craft works, the service is excellent, and the owners are very knowledgeable about the various local tour options. The large rooftop terrace offers wonderful panoramic views of the city. See p. 187.

• **Las Cumbres** (Zunil; ✆ **502/5399-0029**): This hotel is built on top of steam vents fed by underground sulfur hot springs, and some of the rooms come with their own private natural steam bath. All of the rooms have a natural hot-spring-fed Jacuzzi, and there are common steam baths and saunas for all to enjoy. Other amenities include a squash court and small gym. See p. 188.

• **Portal de la Fe** (Esquipulas; ✆ **502/ 7943-4124;** www.portaldelafehotel. com): This should be the top choice for anyone coming to Esquipulas to pay their respects to the "Black Christ." This new hotel offers free Wi-Fi throughout, and is a definite step up from the other options around town in the same price range. See p. 236.

• **Hacienda San Lucas** (south of Copán Ruinas, Honduras; ✆/fax **504/**

651-4495; www.haciendasanlucas. com): This converted farm and ranch offers a sense of refinement and creative flare you won't find anywhere else in the Copán area. The hotel is set on a hillside across from and overlooking the Copán archaeological site. In addition, there's a secondary Maya site, Los Sapos, right on the grounds, as well as excellent hiking and horseback-riding trails. As if all this weren't enough, the restaurant is one of the best in Copán. See p. 244.

• **Catamaran Island Hotel** (Fronteras, Río Dulce; ✆ **502/5902-0831;** www. catamaranisland.com): Whenever I come to the Río Dulce area, I book one of this hotel's private bungalows built out over the water. I love sitting on my private balcony with a book, listening to the river lap against the support posts below me. At night, you'll usually be mingling with hotel guests and some itinerant cruising sailors who tie up at the hotel's dock or anchor just offshore. See p. 257.

• **Amatique Bay Resort and Marina** (4km/2½ miles east of Puerto Barrios, on the Bahia de Amatique; ✆ **502/ 7948-1800;** www.amatiquebay.net): This gets my vote as the best beach resort in the country. The rooms are large, and the grounds and facilities trump any other beach hotel in Guatemala. See p. 260.

• **Hotel Utz Tzaba** (west of Monterrico, on the road to Itzapa; ✆ **502/5318-9452;** www.utz-tzaba.com): There are tons of good hotels set right on the beach along Guatemala's Pacific coast, and this is one of the few worth seeking out. The rooms are relatively simple, but they're modern and clean, and the beach is just steps away. See p. 268.

9 The Best Budget Hotels

- **Posada Belén** (Zona 1, Guatemala City; ✆ **866/864-8283** in the U.S. and Canada, or 502/2253-4530 in Guatemala; www.posadabelen.com): You'll feel at home in this long-standing family-run hotel. The rooms are charming and beautifully done, and the converted home is filled with a wealth of art and Maya artifacts. Although it's near the heart of the city's colonial center, it's on a quiet street, away from the hustle and bustle. These folks have an excellent in-house tour operation. See p. 102.
- **Posada Asejemenou** (Antigua; ✆ **502/7820-2670**; asjemenou1@yahoo.com): The entrance to this pretty budget hotel is practically underneath the iconic Santa Catalina arch in Antigua. Rooms are kept immaculately clean, and there's a convivial hostel-like vibe to the whole operation. The antique tile floors and worn wood furniture remind you that you really are in the colonial heart of town. The attached restaurant specializes in thin-crust pizzas and other Italian fare. See p. 135.
- **Hotel Posada La Merced** (Antigua; ✆ **502/7832-3197** or 502/7832-3301; www.merced-landivar.com): As the name implies, this popular hotel is just around the corner from beautiful La Merced church. The friendly and welcoming staff is a real plus. Those looking for longer stays can book the fully equipped apartments. Interior courtyard areas and communal kitchen lend themselves to a friendly vibe. See p. 135.
- **Hotel Primavera** (Panajachel; ✆ **502/7762-2052**; www.primaveratitlan.com): I enjoy the neatly varnished wood and slightly European feel to this place. Some of the rooms feature large, bay windows overlooking Calle Santander. If you land room no. 9, you're in for a real budget treat, as it comes with its own private stairway, entrance, and balcony. See p. 155.
- **Hotelito El Amanacer Sak'cari** (San Pedro La Laguna; ✆ **502/7721-8096**; www.hotelsakcari.com): The rooms here lack something in the way of style and personality, but for less than Q150 ($20/£11) for a double, you can enjoy the sunrise from a hammock stretched out on the veranda of one of the second-floor units. See p. 161.
- **La Casa del Mundo** (Jaibalito, Lake Atitlán; ✆ **502/5218-5332**; www.lacasadelmundo.com): Set atop an isolated rocky outcropping jutting into Lake Atitlán, this hotel offers a few rooms with shared bathrooms that are a real steal (even the private bathrooms are a bargain), with stupendous views of the lake. A lakeside fire-heated Jacuzzi and several open-air terraces make this place really special. See p. 168.
- **Casa Doña Mercedes** (Quetzaltenango; ✆ **502/5569-1630**; www.geocities.com/guest_house_mercedes): In a town with a glut of budget lodgings, this one stands out for its friendly service, immaculate rooms, and central location. See p. 187.
- **Hotel Santana** (Flores, Petén; ✆/fax **502/7926-0262** or 502/7926-0491; www.santanapeten.com): This lakefront hotel is the best budget choice on the island of Flores. In fact, it might just be the best hotel on the island itself, regardless of price. All of the rooms come with private balconies with wonderful views. See p. 216.
- **Casa Alcazar Victoria** (Cobán; ✆ **502/7952-1388**; http://hoteles.aventurasturisticas.com): I love the rustic yet refined feel of the rooms in this beautiful colonial home. All of the rooms

are different. Those on the second floor are my favorite, with high ceilings featuring exposed wood beams. Throughout the hotel there are eye-catching artistic touches. The owners have a couple other hotels in town, as well as the best adventure tour operation in the region. See p. 231.

- **La Casa de Café** (Copán Ruinas, Honduras; ✆ **504/651-4620;** www.casadecafecopan.com): Although a few blocks outside of the "downtown" area, this is my favorite budget option in Copán Ruinas. The personable hosts make you feel right at home. Each day starts off with a delicious breakfast and coffee in the lush garden. See p. 245.
- **La Casa Rosada** (Livingston; ✆ **502/7947-0303;** www.hotelcasarosada.com): Set on the waterfront in Livingston, the individual bungalows feature cheerful design touches, with brightly painted furniture, architectural accents, and sea shell decorations. You'll have to use one of several communal bathrooms and showers, but these are just steps away and kept spotless. Moreover, the restaurant and in-house tour operation are great. See p. 253.

10 The Best Restaurants

- **Tamarindos** (Zona 10, Guatemala City; ✆ **502/2360-2815**): The chef at this trendy Zona Viva restaurant is wowing Guatemala City with her eclectic fusion cooking. It's easy to overdo or miscalculate when combining ingredients and techniques from various world cuisines, but Tamarindos hits all the right notes. The menu is very long, and touches many bases, with culinary influences from Asia, Italy, and many places in between. Be sure to ask about daily specials, as this is where the chef really shines. See p. 104.
- **Kacao** (Zona 10, Guatemala City; ✆ **502/2237-4188** or 502/2377-4189): This popular restaurant takes Guatemalan cuisine and polishes it up a bit. The cooking is fairly traditional, with signature dishes from around the country, but the service, ambience, and presentation are far more refined than you'll find at almost any other place specializing in Chapin cuisine. Although they do a brisk lunch business, I prefer to come for dinner, when the thatch roof is illuminated by candles and other strategically placed lighting. See p. 104.
- **Ambia** (Zona 14, Guatemala City; ✆ **502/2322-3232**): It's worth the effort to find this slightly out-of-the-way restaurant. The fusion cuisine is heavily influenced by a range of Asian styles, but you can also get hearty steaks and some delicious lamb. See p. 107.
- **Mesón Panza Verde** (Antigua; ✆ **502/7832-1745;** www.panzaverde.com): Don't come to Antigua without having a meal at Mesón Panza Verde. The Swiss chef ventures somewhat from his Continental roots, incorporating local ingredients into many of his dishes. The results are always superb. Tables are spread around various rooms, hallways, and open-air spaces in this elegant boutique hotel, and several nights a week there's live jazz to accompany your meal. See p. 136.
- **Welten** (Antigua; ✆ **502/7832-0630** or 502/7832-6967; www.weltenrestaurant.com): I like to grab a poolside table in the back courtyard of this long-standing Antiguan restaurant. The Continental cuisine isn't as creative or adventurous as many of the restaurants listed in this section, but it is consistently well-prepared.

The service is top-notch and the ambience delightful. See p. 136.

- **Hotel Atitlán** (Panajachel; ✆ **502/ 7762-1441**): With a burning fireplace, wood furniture, and ornate table settings and decor, this is easily the most elegant and refined restaurant in or around Panajachel. When the weather is nice, you can grab one of the outdoor tables, which have a good view of the lake and volcanoes. Luckily, the cuisine and service here live up to the ambience and surroundings. The Sunday brunch is quite renowned. See p. 156.

- **Royal Paris** (Quetzaltenango; ✆ **502/ 7761-1942**): While this is certainly the best restaurant in Quetzaltenango, the name is slightly misleading. Sure there are some French dishes on the menu, but there are also curries, vegetarian options, and simple sandwiches on home-baked whole wheat bread. There are also regular movie nights during the week, and live music most weekends. See p. 189.

- **La Luna** (Flores; ✆ **502/7926-3346**): If you find yourself in Flores, be sure to find your way to this restaurant. The eclectic decor varies from room to room, but like the food, it's consistently creative and tasteful. See p. 217.

- **Casa D'Acuña** (Cobán; ✆ **502/ 7951-0482**): The beautiful garden courtyard setting is enough to earn it a place on this list, but the excellent chefs do their part as well. The long menu includes pizzas, pastas, and typical Mexican cuisine. Your best bet is to get a nice steak or fresh grilled fish. See p. 232.

- **Hacienda San Lucas** (south of Copán Ruinas on the road to Los Sapos ruins; ✆/fax **504/651-4495**): The house specialty is a fire-roasted chicken smothered in a spicy *adobo* sauce, which the owners claim is based on ancient Maya recipes. I can't imagine the Maya ate this well, but you certainly should. The open-air setting by lamplight is very romantic. See p. 245.

- **La Casa Rosada** (Livingston; ✆ **502/ 7947-0303**): On any given night, the regularly changing menu at this cozy restaurant might feature a Thai-influenced stir-fry or shrimp gumbo. However, I often end up ordering the local *tapado*, a seafood stew cooked in coconut milk, which is as good as any in the area. See p. 254.

- **Taberna El Pelícano** (Monterrico; ✆ **502/5584-2400**): The fresh grilled fish is always dependable at this beach restaurant, but they also have a large menu with some unexpected twists, including excellent pastas thanks to their Italian chef, and a rich goulash thanks to the European owner. See p. 269.

11 The Best of Guatemalan Nightlife

- **La Bodeguita del Centro** (Guatemala City; ✆ **502/2221-4904**): This bohemian downtown bar has almost nightly programming that includes poetry readings, improvised theater pieces, and concerts of folk, jazz, and even hard-core punk. See p. 117.

- **Trovajazz** (Guatemala City; ✆ **502/ 2334-1241**): The compact pedestrian mall area of Cuatro Grados Norte is chock-full of clubs, bars, and discos, and this is consistently my favorite. There's live music most nights, and the ambience is relaxed and convivial. See p. 118.

- **Tequila Bar** (Antigua; ✆ **502/5501- 2680**): You'd better like tequila and mescal if you stop in here, and if you do, you're in luck. Little more than a hole in the wall, this place stocks little else than a wide range of high-end and hard-to-find tequilas and mescals. You even have to do a quick shot of house tequila just to get in the door. See p. 143.

- **Circus Bar** (Panajachel; © 502/7762-2056): This place is an institution in Panajachel, and for good reason. A "circus" theme dominates the decor, live music takes the stage most nights, and a friendly mix of locals, expatriates, and tourists populate the bar. See p. 157.

- **Salón Tecún** (Quetzaltenango; © 502/7761-2832): While there are always plenty of people in the crowded interior of this popular Xela bar, the most happening scene is usually at the large picnic-style tables out front. In a university and language school town with lots of clubs and bars, this is consistently the place to see and be seen. See p. 189.

- **Moonlight at Tikal** (Tikal; no phone): Standing atop of Temple IV under the full moon with nothing but the sound of crickets and howler monkeys remains one of my favorite after-dark memories of Guatemala. While this isn't officially open to the public, if you're staying at one of the hotels right outside the archaeological site at Tikal, you can sometimes receive permission to visit the site after dark. Be sure to ask your hotel if this is possible, and check on the current security situation. See p. 207.

- **Ubafu** (Livingston; no phone): The Garífuna people of Livingston are direct descendants of escaped African slaves, and this local bar swings nightly to the beat of ancient rhythms mixed with the modern forms of *punta* rock and reggae. Local bands beat out the rhythms on handmade drums and hollowed-out turtle shells. See p. 255.

12 The Best of Guatemala Online

- **http://lanic.utexas.edu/la/ca/guatemala**: Hosted by the University of Texas Latin American Studies Department, this site houses a vast collection of information about Guatemala.

- **www.visitguatemala.com**: This is the official site of the Guatemala Tourism Commission (INGUAT).

- **www.revuemag.com**: This is an excellent English-language monthly magazine geared toward tourists and expatriates. The entire magazine, as well as past issues, is available online.

- **www.xelawho.com**: A slightly irreverent English-language magazine produced in Quetzaltenango and directed at the town's large population of foreign-language students, this site has honest reviews and a wealth of useful information.

2

Planning Your Trip to Guatemala

Guatemala is a land of many colors and cultures. Its many ruins attest to the architectural prowess of both the Maya and the Spanish conquistadors. A trip to Guatemala can focus on the art and culture, natural beauty, ancient archaeology, or a combination of the above. You can partake in adventure sports, spend some time brushing up on your Spanish, or lend a hand as a volunteer.

Some like to travel independently, while others are more comfortable booking a package tour. Guatemala is a country that's easier to navigate with a guide and organized transport for at least some legs of your trip. Whatever your interests or travel style, this chapter will provide you with all the tools and information necessary to plan and book your trip.

Guatemala sits at the northwestern tip of Central America. It's bordered by Mexico to the north, Belize and the Caribbean Sea to the east, Honduras and El Salvador to the southeast, and the Pacific Ocean to the southwest. The country covers an area of 100,000 sq. km (just more than 40,000 sq. miles), which is slightly smaller than the state of Tennessee. Almost two-thirds of the country is covered by mountains, most of which are volcanic. There are some 33 named volcanoes in Guatemala. Of these, quite a few are active, including Volcán Pacaya, Volcán Santiaguito, and Volcán Fuego.

Aside from a few major urban areas, the country is predominantly rural and densely populated. Most visitors stick close to a well-defined tourist trail that encompasses Guatemala City, Antigua, Lake Atitlán, and the Western Highlands, with a side trip to Tikal and the Petén. Those with more time, or a more adventurous spirit, are starting to explore the Atlantic Lowlands, Pacific coast, and the central region, which includes Las Verapaces and El Oriente.

1 The Regions in Brief

GUATEMALA CITY Set on a high, broad plateau and surrounded by volcanic peaks, Guatemala City is the largest (really the only) metropolitan city in the country. With a population of more than three million, the city is a sprawling, congested, confusing, and polluted urban center. Guatemala City has a small but vibrant arts and nightlife scene, as well as some of the finest hotels and restaurants in the country. The city sits at an elevation of 1,469m (4,897 ft.) above sea level, and enjoys moderate temperatures year-round. Home to the country's principal international airport and bus connections to every corner of the country, Guatemala City serves as a de facto transportation hub for most, if not all, visitors.

ANTIGUA This small colonial city lies just 40km (25 miles) southwest of Guatemala City. For a couple hundred years, it was the nation's capital, until a series of devastating earthquakes forced its evacuation. Like its neighbor and the current capital, Antigua is also set in a valley surrounded by towering volcanic mountain peaks. However, the Antigua valley is much, much smaller. The entire colonial city is little more than 10 blocks by 10 blocks, with a bit more modern urban sprawl around the edges. The city is one of the most well-preserved examples of a colonial city in the Americas. The colonial core of Antigua is a living museum, with rough cobblestone streets and restored colonial-era buildings, mixed in with a few newer constructions that maintain the colonial style and feel. Combined with this living museum are a host of actual museums, and the ruined and restored examples of grand churches, convents, and monasteries. From Antigua, the **Agua and Fuego volcanoes** are clearly visible.

LAKE ATITLAN   Lake Atitlán is technically part of the Western Highlands, but for the purposes of this book, and in the minds of most travelers, it is a world unto itself. Lake Atitlán is a beautiful mountain lake that is actually the filled-in crater of a massive volcano. It's hard to imagine this, since today, several more volcanoes rise from around the shores and tower over the lake. More than 16km (10 miles) across at its widest point, Lake Atitlán has a series of small villages and a few major towns lining its shores. While roads connect all of these towns (in many cases they are rough dirt and gravel), the main means of transportation between the various towns and villages is by boat and boat taxi. The main town and gateway to Lake Atitlán is **Panajachel,** which sits on the northern shore of the lake. Other major towns include **Santa Catarina Palopó** and **San Antonio Palopó** to the east of Panajachel, and **Santiago de Atitlán** and **San Pedro La Laguna** across the lake to the south.

The Lake Atitlán region was severely affected by Hurricane Stan in October 2005, and the damage caused is still palpable, especially in Panajachel and Santiago de Atitlán. Landslides, flooding, and overflowing rivers plagued several communities around the lake, and nearby, you can see their muddy scars on the mountains and hillsides.

THE WESTERN HIGHLANDS   The area to the west and northwest of Guatemala City is widely referred to as the Western Highlands, or Altiplano (the "Highlands" in Spanish). This is the heart of Guatemala's rural Maya population. Following the collapse of the major Maya empires of the Petén and lowland coastal regions, many fled in small groups and family units to Altiplano. Today, the Western Highlands are populated with a dense patchwork of small, rural farming communities spread around the rough, steep, mountainous region. The towns and cities of **Chichicastenango, Quetzaltenango,** and **Huehuetenango** serve as central market and commercial centers for the smaller surrounding communities. The Western Highlands are home to Guatemala's greatest artisans, and are the best place in the country to purchase a wide array of arts, crafts, carvings, and textile products. Perhaps the most famous place to buy these goods is the twice-weekly market held in Chichicastenango. Those looking for a taste of the real rural Maya Altiplano should visit the village of **Nebaj** and the surrounding area, known as the **Ixil Triangle.**

THE PETEN   The Petén, or El Petén, is Guatemala's largest and least populated province. It occupies the entire northeastern section of the country, and borders Mexico to the north and Belize to the east. It's an area of lush primary tropical rainforest, within which lies an immense natural wealth of flora and fauna, as well as many of Mesoamerica's most amazing archaeological treasures. In 1990, the government of Guatemala officially established the **Maya Biosphere Reserve,** a tract of 1 million hectares (2.5 million acres) that includes most of the Petén province. Moreover, the Maya Biosphere Reserve adjoins the neighboring **Calakmul Biosphere Reserve** in Mexico and the **Río Bravo Conservation Area** in Belize, comprising a joint protected area of more than 2 million hectares (5 million acres).

The only major population centers of note in El Petén are the sister cities of Santa Elena and Flores. In addition to the world-renowned ruins of **Tikal,** visitors to the Petén can visit the archaeological sites of **Yaxhá, El Ceibal, El Mirador,** and **Uaxactún,** to name just a few.

CENTRAL GUATEMALA The central section of Guatemala comprises the general area east of Guatemala City, before the Atlantic Lowlands. This is perhaps the country's fastest-growing tourist destination, and includes the **Alta Verapaz** and **Baja Verapaz** regions, as well as **El Oriente,** or the "East." Just over the border in Honduras lie the fabulous Maya ruins of **Copán,** which are often included as a stop on a more complex itinerary through Guatemala. Las Verapaces (the plural for the combined Alta Verapaz and Baja Verapaz) is a rich highland region with numerous opportunities to go whitewater rafting or cave exploring. It's also home to several of Guatemala's most stunning natural areas, including the pools and waterfalls of Semuc Champey and the turquoise splendor of Lake Lachuá.

To the south and east of Las Verapaces lies El Oriente. Most visitors come here to visit the town of Esquipulas. Housed in the impressive Basilica of Esquipulas is the famous statue of the "Black Christ." Believed to have magical, curative, and wish-giving powers, the church and its Christ attract more than one million pilgrims a year.

ATLANTIC LOWLANDS The common name for this region is a gross misnomer—Guatemala actually borders the Caribbean Sea. However, most Guatemalan maps, books, and tourist information sources refer to this region as the Atlantic coast or Atlantic lowlands, and the highway is officially known as La Carretera al Atlántico (the Atlantic Highway). That quibble aside, this is a beautiful and often neglected part of Guatemala. The region really begins around **Lago Izabal,** the largest freshwater lake in the country. From Lago Izabal, the **Río Dulce (Sweet River)** runs gently down to the sea. Along the way it passes through rich primary forests, several nature reserves, and beautiful steep-walled canyons.

Another primary attraction on the Caribbean coast is the small Garífuna village of **Livingston.** The Garífuna are a unique race born of the intermarriage between escaped slaves and Carib Indians. Livingston, which is known as La Buga in the local Garífuna language, is only accessible by boat. The rainforests around Livingston are great for birdwatching and wildlife-viewing.

Located just off the Atlantic Highway are the Maya ruins of **Quiriguá,** which contain some wonderful examples of carved monumental stelae and stone rocks.

PACIFIC SLOPE Below the mountain chains that run the length of Guatemala, from Mexico down to El Salvador, the land gently slopes off and flattens out before meeting the Pacific Ocean. This is a hot and steamy agricultural region with large sugar cane, pineapple, and banana plantations. Spread throughout this agricultural land are several lesser-known Maya and pre-Maya ruins. Of these, **Takalik Abaj** and **Finca El Baúl** are worth a visit by anyone truly interested in ancient Mesoamerican archaeology. In general, the beaches of Guatemala's Pacific coast have dark sand, rough surf, and little development. Given the length of this coastline, there are few developed beach destinations and resorts. If you expect the same kind of beach experience offered throughout the Caribbean, or even the rest of Central America and Mexico, you will be disappointed. The most popular beach town on the Pacific coast is **Monterrico,** which has a handful of small hotels and resorts. The nearby port towns of **Puerto Quetzal, Iztapa,** and **Puerto San José** are beginning to earn reputations as **sportfishing** centers, with excellent opportunities to land marlin, sailfish, and other deep-sea game fish just offshore.

2 Visitor Information

The Guatemalan Tourism Commission (INGUAT), 7a Av. 1-17, Zona 4, Guatemala City (www.visitguatemala.com), is the principal informational and promotional arm of the Guatemalan government. You can call them toll-free from the United States and Canada at ℂ **800/ 464-8281,** or directly in Guatemala at ℂ **502/2421-2854.** They can send you a basic information package, though most of the same information is available on their website. Once you land in Guatemala, INGUAT has an information booth inside the airport, open Monday through Friday from 6am until 9pm, and Saturday and Sunday from 8am until 8pm. The booth supplies maps and brochures, and will often make a call for you if you need a last-minute hotel or car rental reservation. INGUAT also maintains offices or information booths at several of the major tourist destinations

Destination Guatemala: Red Alert Checklist

- Take the address and phone number of your country's embassy or consulate with you.
- Make any restaurant or travel reservations that need to be booked in advance prior to leaving home.
- Did you find out your daily ATM withdrawal limit? Did you check with your bank to see if your credit or debit card will work in Guatemala?
- While many of Guatemala's ATMs will work fine with five- and six-digit PINs, some will only accept four-digit PINs. Before traveling, it's wise to change your PIN to avoid any unexpected hassles in getting cash.
- Do you know your credit card PINs?
- Save time by checking in at the e-ticket kiosk at the airport. Have the credit card you bought your ticket with or your frequent-flier number.
- If you purchased traveler's checks, record the check numbers and store the documentation separately from the checks.
- Pack your camera, an extra set of camera batteries, and enough film.
- Have a safe, accessible place to store money.
- Bring emergency drug prescriptions and extra glasses and/or contact lenses.
- Leave a copy of your itinerary with someone at home.
- Stop the newspaper and mail delivery, and leave a set of keys with someone reliable.
- Take measurements for those people you plan to buy clothes for on your trip.

around the country. Wherever these exist, they are listed in the corresponding sections throughout the book.

In addition to INGUAT's official website, you'll be able to find a wealth of Web-based information on Guatemala with a few clicks of your mouse. See "The Best of Guatemala Online" in chapter 1 for some helpful suggestions on where to begin your online search.

3 Entry Requirements & Customs

For information on how to get a passport, go to "Passports" in the "Fast Facts: Guatemala" section, later in this chapter. The websites listed provide downloadable passport applications, as well as the current fees for processing passport applications. For an up-to-date, country-by-country listing of passport requirements around the world, go to the "Foreign Entry Requirement" Web page of the U.S. State Department at **http://travel. state.gov**.

ENTRY REQUIREMENTS

Citizens of the United States, Canada, Great Britain, all European Union nations, Ireland, Australia, and New Zealand may visit Guatemala for a maximum of 90 days. No visa is necessary, but you must have a valid passport.

It's possible to extend your tourist visa, but the process is slightly tedious. To do so, you must go to the **Immigration Office**, 7a Av. 1-17, Zona 4, Guatemala City (© **502/2361-8476**), which is in the INGUAT building in Zona 4. The process involves presenting several authenticated documents and photocopies. Moreover, these documents will need a lawyer's stamp or a notarization from your embassy. The whole process can take as long as a week, and cost between Q75 and Q375 ($10–$50/ £5.25–£26). This hassle is meant to discourage "resident tourists." Your best bet, if you wish to visit Guatemala for longer than your original 90-day visa, is to leave the country for either Mexico or Belize for 72 hours, and return under a new visa.

If you need a visa or have other questions about Guatemala, you can contact any of the following Guatemalan embassies or consulates: in the **United States,** 2220 R St. NW, Washington, DC 20008 (© **202/ 745-4952;** www.guatemala-embassy.org); in Canada, 130 Albert St., Suite 1010, Ottawa, Ontario K1P 5G4 (© **613/233- 7188**); and in **Great Britain,** 13 Fawcett St., London, England SW10 9HN (© **020/7351-3042**). There are no Guatemalan embassies in Australia or New Zealand, but you could try contacting the

Coming & Going

In 2006, Guatemala entered into an immigration and border control treaty with El Salvador, Honduras, and Nicaragua. This agreement, which allows free travel between the countries to all nationals of these signatory nations, creates a single 90-day entry visa for foreign visitors. What this means is that if you travel between these four countries, your total stay cannot exceed 90 days without seeking an extension from the immigration authorities in the country you are visiting as the 90-day period expires. If you want to "renew" your Guatemalan visa by exiting the country for 72 hours and then returning on a new tourist visa, it must be to a country not covered in this agreement.

> **Tips** **Passport Savvy**
>
> Allow plenty of time before your trip to apply for a passport; processing normally takes 3 weeks but can take longer during busy periods (especially spring). Keep in mind that if you need a passport in a hurry, you'll pay a higher processing fee. When traveling, safeguard your passport in an inconspicuous, inaccessible place like a money belt, and keep a copy of the critical pages with your passport number in a separate place. If you lose your passport, visit the nearest consulate or embassy of your native country as soon as possible for a replacement. Children of all ages need an official passport to enter Guatemala.

embassy in **Japan,** 38 Kowa Building 9F, no. 905, 4-12-24 Nishi Azabu Minato-Ku, Tokyo 106-0031 (© **81/(03)3400-1830;** www.embassy-avenue.jp).

MEDICAL REQUIREMENTS

For information on medical requirements and recommendations, see "Health & Safety" on p. 30.

CUSTOMS
What You Can Bring into Guatemala

Visitors to Guatemala may bring any and all reasonable goods and belongings for personal use during their stay. Cameras, computers, and electronic equipment, as well as fishing and diving gear for personal use, are permitted duty-free. Customs officials in Guatemala seldom check arriving tourists' luggage.

What You Can Take Home from Guatemala

It's illegal to take any pre-Columbian artifact from Guatemala, whether you bought or discovered it, or whether it was given to you.

Returning **U.S. citizens** who've been away for at least 48 hours are allowed to bring back $800 worth of merchandise duty-free once every 30 days. You'll pay a flat rate of duty on the next $1,000 worth of purchases. Any dollar amount beyond that is subject to duties at whatever rates apply. On mailed gifts, the duty-free limit is $200. Be sure to keep your receipts or

purchases accessible to expedite the declaration process. *Note:* If you owe duty, you are required to pay on your arrival to the U.S.—either by cash, personal check, government or traveler's check, or money order (in some locations, Visa or MasterCard are accepted).

To avoid paying duty on foreign-made personal items you owned before your trip, bring along a bill of sale, insurance policy, jeweler's appraisal, or receipts of purchase. Or, you can register items that can be readily identified by permanently affixed serial number or marking—laptop computers, cameras, CD players—with Customs before you leave. Take the items to the nearest Customs office, or register them with Customs at the airport from which you're departing. You'll receive, at no cost, a Certificate of Registration, which allows duty-free entry for the life of the item.

With some exceptions, you cannot bring fresh fruits and vegetables into the United States. For specifics on what you can bring back, download the invaluable free pamphlet *Know Before You Go,* online at **www.cbp.gov** (click on "Travel," and then on "Know Before You Go! Online Brochure"). Or contact the **U.S. Customs & Border Protection (CBP),** 1300 Pennsylvania Ave. NW, Washington, DC 20229 (© **877/287-8667**), and request the pamphlet.

For a clear summary of **Canadian** rules, write for the booklet *I Declare,* issued by the

Canada Border Services Agency (© 800/ 461-9999 in Canada, or 204/983-3500; www.cbsa-asfc.gc.ca). Canada allows its citizens a C$750 exemption, and you're allowed to bring back duty-free one carton of cigarettes, 1 can of tobacco, 40 imperial ounces of liquor, and 50 cigars. In addition, you're allowed to mail gifts to Canada valued at less than C$60 a day, provided they're unsolicited and don't contain alcohol or tobacco. (Write on the package "Unsolicited gift, under $60 value.") All valuables should be declared on the Y-38 form before departure from Canada, including serial numbers of valuables you already own, such as expensive foreign cameras. *Note:* The $750 exemption can only be used once a year and only after an absence of 7 days.

U.K. citizens returning from a **non-E.U. country** have a Customs allowance of: 200 cigarettes, 50 cigars, or 250 grams of smoking tobacco; 2 liters of still table wine; 1 liter of spirits or strong liqueurs (over 22% volume), or 2 liters of fortified wine, sparkling wine, or other liqueurs; 60cc (ml) perfume; 250cc (ml) of toilet water; and £145 worth of all other goods, including gifts and souvenirs. People under 17 cannot have the tobacco or alcohol allowance. For more information, contact HM Customs & Excise at © 0845/ 010-9000 (from outside the U.K., 020/ 8929-0152), or consult their website at www.hmce.gov.uk.

The duty-free allowance in **Australia** is A$400 or, for those under 18, A$200. Citizens can bring in 250 cigarettes or 250 grams of loose tobacco, and 1,125 milliliters of alcohol. If you're returning with valuables you already own, such as foreign-made cameras, you should file form B263. A helpful brochure available from Australian consulates or Customs offices is *Know Before You Go.* For more information, call the **Australian Customs Service** at © 1300/363-263, or log on to www.customs.gov.au.

The duty-free allowance for **New Zealand** is NZ$700. Citizens over 17 can bring in 200 cigarettes, 50 cigars, or 250 grams of tobacco (or a mixture of all three if their combined weight doesn't exceed 250 grams); plus 4.5 liters of wine and beer or 1.125 liters of liquor. New Zealand currency does not carry import or export restrictions. Fill out a certificate of export, listing the valuables you are taking out of the country. That way, you can bring them back without paying duty. Most questions are answered in a free pamphlet available at New Zealand consulates and Customs offices, *New Zealand Customs Guide for Travellers, Notice no. 4.* For more information, contact **New Zealand Customs,** The Customhouse, 17–21 Whitmore St., Box 2218, Wellington (© 04/473-6099 or 0800/428-786; www.customs.govt.nz).

4 Money

The unit of currency in Guatemala is the *quetzal.* In October 2006, there were approximately 7.6 *quetzales* to the American dollar, but because the *quetzal* does fluctuate, you can expect this rate to change. In this book, we have used the rate of Q1 to 13¢ and 7p. To check the very latest exchange rates visit **www.oanda. com/convert/classic**.

The *quetzal* is theoretically divided into 100 *centavos.* However, because of

their insignificant value, you will rarely see or have to handle *centavos.* If you do, there are coins in denominations of 1, 5, 10, 25, and 50 *centavos.* There are also 1 *quetzal* coins, which are quite common and handy.

There are paper notes in denominations of 1, 5, 10, 20, 50, and 100 *quetzales.* This can be a bit of a problem for travelers, since the bill with the largest denomination is worth only around US$13 (£7).

The Quetzal, the U.S. Dollar, the Euro & the British Pound

Quetzal	US$	Euro €	UK£
1	0.13	0.10	0.07
5	0.65	0.52	0.35
10	1.35	1.05	0.71
25	3.35	2.62	1.76
50	6.65	5.23	3.52
100	13.35	10.47	7.05
250	33.35	26.17	17.62
500	66.65	52.34	35.24
1,000	133.35	104.70	70.45
2,500	333.35	261.71	176.15

If your ATM card doesn't work and you need cash in a hurry, **Western Union** (℃ 502/2360-1737 in Guatemala; www. westernunion.com) has numerous offices around Guatemala City and in several major towns and cities around the country. It offers secure and rapid, although pricey, money-wire and telegram service. A $100-wire costs around $15, and a $1,000-wire costs around $50.

EXCHANGING MONEY

You can change money at all banks in Guatemala. Most charge a very slight service fee. Given the fact that banks handle money exchanges, there are very few exchange houses in Guatemala, although you may run across one here or there. In general, there is little variation in the exchange rate offered at banks and exchange houses.

Hotels will often exchange money as well; there usually isn't much of a line, but they might shave a few *centavos* off the exchange rate. *Warning:* Be very careful when leaving a bank. Criminals are often looking for foreigners who have just withdrawn or exchanged cash.

Most airport taxis, shuttles, and major hotels will accept dollars upon your arrival, so it's not absolutely essential to exchange money before traveling to Guatemala. **BanQuetzal** (℃ 502/2347-5081; www.banquetzal.com.gt) in the airport exchanges dollars and some European currencies, and will cash traveler's checks. It's open Monday through Friday from 6am to 8pm, and Saturday through Sunday from 6am to 6pm. However, if you arrive outside of this bank's hours, or want to avoid any delay at the airport bank or ATMs, you might consider exchanging at least some money—just enough to cover airport incidentals and transportation to your hotel—before you leave home (though don't expect the exchange rate to be ideal). You can exchange money at your local American Express or Thomas Cook office or at your bank. American Express also dispenses traveler's checks and foreign currency via www.americanexpress.com or ℃ 800/807-6233, but they'll charge a $15 order fee and additional shipping costs. American Express cardholders should dial ℃ 800/221-7282; this number accepts collect calls, offers service in several foreign languages, and exempts Amex gold and platinum cardholders from the 1% fee.

ATMs

The easiest and best way to get cash away from home is from an ATM (automated teller machine). The **Cirrus** (© 800/424-7787; www.mastercard.com) and **PLUS** (© 800/843-7587; www.visa.com) networks span the globe; look at the back of your bank card to see which network you're on, then call or check online for ATM locations at your destination. Be sure you know your personal identification number (PIN) and daily withdrawal limit before you depart. *Note:* Remember that many banks impose a fee every time you use a card at another bank's ATM, and that fee can be higher for international transactions (up to $5 or more) than for domestic ones (where they're rarely more than $2). In addition, the bank from which you withdraw cash may charge its own fee. To compare banks' ATM fees within the U.S., use **www.bank rate.com**. For international withdrawal fees, ask your bank.

You can use your credit card to receive cash advances at ATMs. Keep in mind that credit card companies protect themselves from theft by limiting maximum withdrawals outside their home country, so call your credit card company before you leave home. Also remember that you'll pay interest from the moment of your withdrawal, even if you pay your monthly bills on time.

ATMs are fairly common throughout Guatemala, particularly in Guatemala City and Antigua, and at most major tourist destinations around the country. You'll find them at almost all banks and most shopping centers. Still, make sure you have some cash at the start of your trip; never let yourself run totally out of spending money, and definitely stock up on funds before heading to any of the more remote destinations in the country. Outside the more popular destinations, it's still best to think of your ATM card as a backup measure, because machines are not nearly as readily available or dependable as you might be accustomed to, and you might encounter compatibility problems.

While many of Guatemala's ATMs will work fine with five- and six-digit PINs, some will only accept four-digit PINs. Before traveling, it's wise to change your PIN to avoid any unexpected hassles in getting access to quick cash.

TRAVELER'S CHECKS

Traveler's checks are something of an anachronism from the days before the ATM made cash accessible at any time. Given the fees you'll pay for ATM use at banks other than your own, however, you might be better off with traveler's checks if you're withdrawing money often.

You can buy traveler's checks at most banks. **American Express** offers denominations of $20, $50, $100, $500, and (for cardholders only) $1,000. You'll pay a service charge ranging from 1% to 4%. By phone, you can buy traveler's checks by calling © 800/807-6233. American Express card holders should dial © 800/221-7282; this number accepts collect calls, offers service in several foreign languages, and exempts Amex gold and platinum cardholders from the 1% fee.

Tips Small Change

When you change money, try to get some smaller bills and 1 *quetzal* coins. Petty cash will come in handy for tipping and public transportation. Even though the largest bill is not very valuable by Western standards, many taxi drivers and small shop owners have trouble making change for a 100 *quetzales* bill. Consider keeping the change separate from your larger bills so that it's readily accessible and you'll be less of a target for theft.

Tips Dear Visa, I'm Off to Tikal!

Some credit card companies recommend that you notify them of any impending trip abroad so that they don't become suspicious of foreign transactions and block your charges. If you don't call your credit card company in advance, you can still call the card's toll-free emergency number (see "Fast Facts: Guatemala" on p. 68) if a charge is refused—provided you remember to carry the phone number with you. Perhaps the most important lesson here is to carry more than one card so you have a backup.

Visa offers traveler's checks at Citibank locations nationwide, as well as at several other banks. The service charge ranges between 1.5% and 2%; checks come in denominations of $20, $50, $100, $500, and $1,000. Call © **800/732-1322** for information. AAA members can obtain Visa checks for a $9.95 fee (for checks up to $1,500) at most AAA offices or by calling © **866/339-3378**. **MasterCard** also offers traveler's checks. Call © **800/223-9920** for a location near you.

Foreign currency traveler's checks are useful if you're traveling to one country or to the euro zone; they're accepted at locations where dollar checks may not be, such as bed-and-breakfasts, and they minimize the currency conversions you'll have to perform while you're on the go. **American Express, Thomas Cook, Visa,** and **MasterCard** offer foreign currency traveler's checks. You'll pay the rate of exchange at the time of your purchase (so it's a good idea to monitor the rate before you buy), and most companies charge a transaction fee per order (and a shipping fee if you order online).

If you do choose to carry traveler's checks, keep a record of their serial numbers separate from your checks in the event that they are stolen or lost. You'll get a refund faster if you know the numbers.

CREDIT CARDS

Credit cards are another safe way to carry money. They also provide a convenient record of all your expenses, and generally offer relatively good exchange rates. You

can also withdraw cash advances from your credit cards at banks or ATMs, provided you know your PIN. If you don't know yours, call the number on the back of your credit card and ask the bank to send it to you. It usually takes 5 to 7 business days, though some banks will provide the number over the phone if you provide some personal information. Keep in mind that many banks now assess a 1% to 3% "transaction fee" on **all** charges you incur abroad (whether you're using the local currency or U.S. dollars). But credit cards still may be the smart way to go when you factor in things like exorbitant ATM fees and the higher exchange rates and service fees you'll pay with traveler's checks. All major credit cards are accepted in Guatemala, although MasterCard and Visa will give you the greatest coverage, while American Express and Diners Club are slightly less widely used and accepted.

Because credit card purchases are dependent upon phone verifications, some hotels and restaurants in more remote destinations do not accept them. Moreover, some add on a 5% to 10% surcharge for credit card payments. Always check in advance if you're heading to a more remote corner of Guatemala.

To report a lost or stolen **American Express** card from inside Guatemala, you can call © **0800/012-3211**, or call © **336/393-1111** collect in the U.S.; for **MasterCard,** © **800/999-1480**, or call © **636/722-7111** collect in the U.S.; for **Visa,**

What Things Cost in Guatemala	Quetzal	US$	UK£
Taxi from the airport to Guatemala City	45.00–75.00	6.00–10.00	3.15–5.25
Shuttle from airport to downtown Guatemala City	30.00–60.00	4.00–8.00	2.10–4.20
Local taxi ride	15.00–75.00	2.00–10.00	1.05–5.25
Shuttle from Guatemala City to Antigua	75.00–90.00	10.00–12.00	5.25–6.30
Round-trip flight between Guatemala City and Tikal/Flores	1,700.00	225.00	119.00
Double room, expensive	600.00–900.00	80.00–120.00	42.00–63.00
Double room, moderate	338.00–600.00	45.00–80.00	23.66–42.00
Double room, inexpensive	150.00–338.00	20.00–45.00	10.50–23.66
Dinner for one without wine, expensive	250.00	33.00	17.50
Dinner for one without wine, moderate	115.00	15.00	8.05
Dinner for one, inexpensive	70.00	9.35	4.90
Bottle of Gallo beer	10.00–20.00	1.35–2.65	0.70–1.40
Bottle of Coca-Cola	5.00–10.00	0.65–1.35	0.35–0.70
Cup of coffee	3.00–5.00	0.40–0.65	0.20–0.35
Gallon of premium gas	26.00	3.46	1.82
Admission to most museums	10.00–15.00	1.35–2.00	0.70–1.05
Admission to Tikal National Park	50.00	6.65	3.50
Exit tax	225.00	30.00	15.75

🕾 **800/999-0115,** or call 🕾 **410/581-9994** collect in the U.S.; and for **Diners Club,** call 🕾 **502/2338-6801,** or call collect to 🕾 **303/799-1504.** When you contact your bank or issuing company, it might be able to wire you a cash advance off your credit card immediately; in many places, it can deliver an emergency credit card in 1 or 2 days. Odds are that if your wallet is gone, the police won't be able to recover it for you, but your credit card company or insurer might require a police report number, so file a police report anyway (after you cancel your credit cards).

5 When to Go

The tourist high season runs December through March, coinciding with the winter months in most northern countries. It also coincides with Guatemala's dry season. Throughout this season, and especially around the Christmas and Easter holidays, hotels can be booked solid well in advance, so be sure to have a reservation, especially in the more popular tourist spots. Easter and Holy Week are major holidays in Guatemala and in Antigua specifically. Hotels in Antigua are booked solid as much as a year in advance.

In general, the best time of year to visit weather-wise is in December and January, when everything is still green from the rains, but the sky is clear. If you want to avoid the crowds, I recommend traveling during "shoulder" periods, near the end or beginning of the rainy season, when the weather is still pretty good. *Note:* Some of the country's rugged roads become downright impassable without four-wheel-drive during the rainy season.

CLIMATE

Guatemala is a tropical country and has distinct wet and dry seasons. However, some regions are rainy all year, and others are very dry and sunny for most of the year. Temperatures vary primarily with elevations, not with seasons: On the coasts it's hot all year, while up in the mountains and highlands, it can be quite cool at night and in the early morning, before the sun heats things up, any time of year. At the highest elevations (3,500–4,000m/11,500–13,120 ft.), frost is common.

Generally, the **rainy season** (or *invierno*, winter) is May through October. The **dry season** (or *verano*, summer) runs from November to April. Along the Pacific Coast, the dry season lasts several weeks longer than in other places. Even in the rainy season, days often start sunny, with rain falling in the afternoon and evening. On the Atlantic coast, the weather is less predictable, and you can get rain year-round, though this area gets less rain in July and August than the rest of the country. The rainforests of the Petén get the heaviest rainfall, and the rainy season here lasts at least until mid-November. The chart below is for Guatemala City, which has similar temperatures to Antigua, Lake Atitlán, and Chichicastenango. Conditions are different in the Petén, Central Highlands, and both the Atlantic and Pacific coasts.

Average Minimum/Maximum Temperature & Precipitation for Guatemala City

	Jan	Feb	Mar	Apr	May	June	July	Aug	Sept	Oct	Nov	Dec
Min. Temp. (°F/°C)	54/12	54/12	57/14	57/14	61/16	61/16	61/16	61/16	61/16	61/16	57/14	55/13
Max. Temp. (°F/°C)	73/23	77/25	81/27	82/28	84/29	81/27	79/26	79/26	79/26	75/24	73/23	72/22
Precipitation (in.)	.31	.12	.52	1.22	5.98	10.79	7.99	7.80	9.09	6.81	.91	.31

HOLIDAYS

Because Guatemala is a predominantly Roman Catholic country, most of its holidays are church-related. The biggies are Christmas, New Year's, and Easter, which are all celebrated for several days. Keep in mind that Holy Week (Easter week) is a major holiday time in Guatemala. Government offices and banks are closed on official holidays, transportation services are reduced, and stores and markets might also close.

Official holidays in Guatemala include **January 1** (New Year's Day), Thursday and Friday of Holy Week, **June 30** (Armed Forces Day), **July 1** (Day of Celebration), **August 15** (Virgen de la Asunción), **September 15** (Independence Day), **October 20** (Commemoration of the 1944 Revolution), **November 1** (All Saints' Day), **December 24** and **25** (Christmas), and **December 31** (New Year's Eve).

GUATEMALA CALENDAR OF EVENTS

Most of the events listed here might better be considered a tradition, more than an event—there's not, for instance, a Virgen de la Asunción PR Committee that readily dispenses information. In many cases, I've given a more detailed description of the events listed below in the appropriate destination chapters throughout the book. Beyond that, your best bet for detailed information is to call the **Guatemalan Tourism Commission (INGUAT)** at © 800/ 464-8281 in the U.S. or 1500 in Guatemala; or visit www.visitguatemala.com. Alternatively, you can contact hotels where the event or festivities take place.

January

El Cristo Negro, Esquipulas. Pilgrims from across the world converge on the Basilica in this small city in El Oriente to pay their respects to the statue of the "Black Christ." January 15.

April

Holy Week. Religious processions are held in cities and towns throughout the country. Colorful carpets line the streets of Antigua in preparation for the processions, while in Quetzaltenango there's a live reenactment of the Passion and Crucifixion of Christ. Week before Easter.

July

La Fiesta Nacional Indígena de Guatemala, Cobán. This is one of Mesoamerica's greatest celebrations of Maya culture. The city of Cobán features a steady stream of street fairs, concerts, parades, and parties. This is celebrated for 2 solid weeks in late July, sometimes extending into early August.

August

Fiesta de la Virgen de la Asunción, celebrated countrywide. The Virgin of the Assumption is the patron saint of Guatemala City and, by extension, the entire nation. There are celebrations, parades, and small fairs across the country, but the largest celebrations are held in Guatemala City. August 15.

September

Guatemala's Independence Day, celebrated all over the country. This is a national holiday. Major cities and most towns and villages have parades and public concerts. September 15.

November

Día de los Muertos (All Saints' Day), celebrated countrywide. The most famous celebration is the "drunken horse race" in the mountain town of Todos Santos. Guatemalans also fly giant, colorful kites to communicate with the dead in the village of Santiago Sacatepéquez. In the rest of the country, the celebrations may not be as elaborate or ritualized as in Mexico, but most Guatemalans take some time this day to remember the dead with flowers and trips to the cemeteries. November 1.

National Garífuna Day, Livingston. Although the official celebration day is November 26, the local Garífuna population in Livingston pulls out all the stops for a solid week of partying around the actual date. Garífuna from neighboring Honduras, Belize, and Nicaragua often come to help in the celebration. Garífuna food and dancing are available all over town. There are parades and street parties. November 26.

December

Quema del Diablo (Burning the Devil), celebrated countrywide. Huge bonfires fill the streets throughout the country as trash, tires, old furniture, and effigies of Satan are burned in a symbolic ritual cleansing. December 7. **Fiesta de Santo Tomás, Chichicastenango.** The patron saint of this highland city is celebrated with fireworks, parades, and a massive street fair. One of the highlights is the dance of the Palo Volador, or "flying pole," in which a team of acrobats dive from a high pole and are slowly lowered while spiraling outward, attached only by a rope to their ankles. The festivities build for several days leading up to the main festival day of December 21.

6 Travel Insurance

Check your existing insurance policies and credit card coverage before you buy travel insurance. You may already be covered for lost luggage, canceled tickets, or medical expenses.

The cost of travel insurance varies widely, depending on the cost and length of your trip, your age and health, and the type of trip you're taking, but expect to pay between 5% and 8% of the vacation itself. You can get estimates from various providers through **InsureMyTrip.com.** Enter your trip cost and dates, your age, and other information for prices from more than a dozen companies.

TRIP-CANCELLATION INSURANCE Trip-cancellation insurance will help retrieve your money if you have to back out of a trip or depart early, or if your travel supplier goes bankrupt. Permissible reasons for trip cancellation can include sickness, natural disasters, and the State Department declaring a destination unsafe for travel. (Insurers usually won't cover vague fears, though, as many travelers discovered when they tried to cancel their trips in Oct 2001.) In this unstable world, trip-cancellation insurance is a good buy if you're purchasing tickets well in advance—who knows what the state of the world, or of your airline, will be in 9 months. Insurance policy details vary, so read the fine print—and make sure that your airline is on the list of carriers covered in case of bankruptcy. A good resource is **"Travel Guard Alerts,"** a list of companies considered high-risk by Travel Guard International (see website below). Protect yourself further by paying for the insurance with a credit card. By law, consumers can get your money back on goods and services not received if you report the loss within 60 days after the charge is listed on your credit card statement.

Note: Many tour operators, particularly those offering trips to remote or high-risk areas, include insurance in the total trip cost or can arrange insurance policies through a partnering provider, which is a convenient and often cost-effective way for the traveler to obtain insurance. Make sure the tour company is a reputable one, however, and be aware that some experts suggest you avoid buying insurance from the tour company you're traveling with. They contend it's more secure to buy from a "third party" than to put all your money in one place.

For more information, contact one of the following recommended insurers: **Access America** (© 866/807-3982; www.accessamerica.com); **Travel Guard International** (© 800/826-4919; www.travelguard.com); **Travel Insured International** (© 800/243-3174; www.travelinsured.com); and **Travelex Insurance Services** (© 888/457-4602; www.travelex-insurance.com).

MEDICAL INSURANCE For travel overseas, most health plans (including Medicare and Medicaid) do not provide coverage, and the ones that do often require you to pay for services upfront and reimburse you only after you return

> **Tips   Quick ID**
>
> Tie a colorful ribbon or piece of yarn around your luggage handle, or slap a distinctive sticker on the side of your bag. This makes it less likely that someone will mistakenly pick it up. And, if your luggage gets lost, it will be easier to find.

home. Even if your plan does cover overseas treatment, most out-of-country hospitals make you pay your bills upfront, and send you a refund only after you've returned home and filed the necessary paperwork with your insurance company. As a safety net, you may want to buy travel medical insurance, particularly if you're traveling to a remote or high-risk area where emergency evacuation is a possible scenario. If you require additional medical insurance, try **MEDEX Assistance** (© **410/453-6300;** www.medex assist.com) or **Travel Assistance International** (© **800/821-2828;** www.travel assistance.com; for general information on services, call the company's Worldwide Assistance Services, Inc., © **800/777-8710**).

LOST-LUGGAGE INSURANCE   On domestic flights, checked baggage is covered up to $2,500 per ticketed passenger. On international flights (including U.S. portions of international trips), baggage coverage is limited to approximately $9.10 per pound, up to approximately $635 per checked bag. If you plan to check items more valuable than what's covered by the standard liability, see if your homeowner's policy covers your valuables, get baggage insurance as part of your comprehensive travel-insurance package, or buy Travel Guard's "BagTrak" product. Don't buy insurance at the airport, where it's usually overpriced. Be sure to take any valuables or irreplaceable items with you in your carry-on luggage, because many valuables (including books, money, and electronics) aren't covered by airline policies.

If your luggage is lost, immediately file a lost-luggage claim at the airport, detailing the luggage contents. Most airlines require that you report delayed, damaged, or lost baggage within 4 hours of arrival. The airlines are required to deliver luggage, once found, directly to your house or destination free of charge.

7 Health & Safety

STAYING HEALTHY

Staying healthy on a trip to Guatemala is predominantly a matter of being a little cautious about what you eat and drink, and using common sense. Know your physical limits, and don't overexert yourself. Respect the tropical sun and protect yourself from it. Limit your exposure to the sun, especially during the first few days of your trip and, thereafter, from 11am to 2pm. Use a sunscreen with a high protection factor, and apply it liberally. Remember that children need more protection than adults do. I recommend buying and drinking bottled water or soft drinks everywhere you travel in Guatemala. Those wishing to really stay on the side of caution should avoid any drinks with ice in them, as well as any raw fruits or vegetables that may have been washed in unsafe water. In general, fruits and vegetables that are peeled—bananas, oranges, avocados—are safe. The sections below deal with specific health concerns in Guatemala.

BEFORE YOU GO

No specific vaccines are required for traveling to Guatemala. That said, many doctors recommend vaccines for Hepatitis A and B, as well as up-to-date booster shots for tetanus.

In most cases, your existing health plan will provide the coverage you need, but double-check; you might want to buy **travel medical insurance** instead. (See the section on insurance, above.) Bring your insurance ID card with you when you travel.

If you suffer from a chronic illness, consult your doctor before your departure. For conditions such as epilepsy, diabetes, or heart problems, wear a **MedicAlert identification tag** (© **800/825-3785;** www.medicalert.org), which will immediately alert doctors to your condition and give them access to your records through MedicAlert's 24-hour hot line.

Pack **prescription medications** in your carry-on luggage, and carry prescription medications in their original containers. Also, bring along copies of your prescriptions in case you lose your pills or run out, and carry the generic name of prescription medicines in case a local pharmacist is unfamiliar with the brand name. And don't forget an extra pair of contact lenses or prescription glasses.

Contact the **International Association for Medical Assistance to Travelers (IAMAT;** © **716/754-4883** or 416/652-0137 in Canada; www.iamat.org) for tips on travel and health concerns in the countries you're visiting and lists of local, English-speaking doctors. The U.S. **Centers for Disease Control and Prevention** (© **800/311-3435;** www.cdc.gov) provides up-to-date information on health hazards by region or country, and offers tips on food safety. The website **www.tripprep.com**, sponsored by a consortium of travel medicine practitioners, may also offer helpful advice on traveling abroad. You can find listings of reliable overseas clinics at the **International Society of Travel Medicine** (www.istm.org).

GENERAL AVAILABILITY OF HEALTHCARE

Guatemala's public healthcare system is overburdened, under-funded, and outdated. Massive strikes in the sector during 2006 only exacerbated the problem. Throughout the book, I've listed the nearest public hospital and, when available, private hospital or clinic. Still, when you're in Guatemala, your hotel or local embassy will be your best source of information and aid in finding emergency care or a doctor who speaks English. Most state-run hospitals and walk-in clinics around the country have emergency rooms that can treat most conditions. However, I highly recommend that you seek out a specialist recommended by your hotel or embassy if your condition is not life-threatening and can wait for treatment until you reach one of them.

COMMON AILMENTS

TROPICAL ILLNESSES Your chance of contracting any serious tropical disease in Guatemala is slim, especially if you stick to the well-worn tourist destinations. However, malaria and dengue fever both exist in Guatemala, so it's a good idea to know what they are.

Malaria is found in rural areas across the country, particularly in the lowlands on both coasts and in the Petén. There is little to no chance of contracting malaria in Guatemala City or Antigua. Malaria prophylaxes are available, but several have side effects, and others are of questionable effectiveness. Consult your doctor regarding what is currently considered the best preventive treatment for malaria. Be sure to ask whether a recommended drug will cause you hypersensitivity to the sun. Because malaria-carrying mosquitoes usually come out at night, you should do as much as possible to avoid being bitten after dark. If you are in a malarial area, wear long pants and long sleeves, use insect repellent, and either sleep under a mosquito net or burn mosquito coils (similar to incense, but with a pesticide).

Of greater concern is **dengue fever,** which has had periodic outbreaks in Latin America since the mid-1990s. Dengue fever is similar to malaria, and is spread by an aggressive daytime mosquito. This mosquito actually seems to prefer populated areas, and dengue has occurred throughout the country. Dengue is also known as "bone-break fever" because it is usually accompanied by severe body aches. The first infection with dengue fever will make you very sick but should cause no serious damage. However, a second infection with a different strain of the dengue virus can lead to internal hemorrhaging and could be life-threatening.

Many people are convinced that taking B-complex vitamins daily will help prevent mosquitoes from biting you. I don't think the American Medical Association has endorsed this idea yet, but I've run across it in enough places to think that there might be something to it.

If you develop a high fever accompanied by severe body aches, nausea, diarrhea, or vomiting during or shortly after a visit to Guatemala, consult a physician as soon as possible.

AMOEBAS, PARASITES, DIARRHEA & OTHER INTESTINAL WOES

Guatemala suffers from periodic outbreaks of **cholera,** a severe intestinal disease whose symptoms include severe diarrhea and vomiting. However, these outbreaks usually occur in predominantly rural and very impoverished areas. Your chances of contracting cholera while you're in Guatemala are very slight.

Other food and waterborne illnesses can mimic the symptoms of cholera and are far more common. These range from simple traveler's diarrhea to salmonella. Even though you've been careful to buy

bottled water, order your *licuado en leche* (fruit shakes made with milk rather than water), and drink your soft drink warm (without ice cubes—which are made from water, after all), you still might encounter some intestinal difficulties. Most of this is just due to tender northern stomachs coming into contact with slightly more aggressive Latin American intestinal flora. In extreme cases of diarrhea or intestinal discomfort, it's worth taking a stool sample to a lab for analysis. The results will usually pinpoint the amoebic or parasitic culprit, which can then be readily treated with available over-the-counter medicines.

Except in the most established and hygienic of restaurants, it's also advisable to avoid ceviche, a raw seafood salad, especially if it has any shellfish in it. It could be home to any number of bacterial critters.

In the event you experience any intestinal woe, staying well-hydrated is the most important step. Be sure to drink plenty of bottled water, as well as some electrolyte-enhanced sports drinks, if possible.

RIPTIDES   Most of Guatemala's Pacific coast beaches have riptides: strong currents that can drag swimmers out to sea. A riptide occurs when water that has been dumped on the shore by strong waves forms a channel back out to open water. These channels have strong currents. If you get caught in a riptide, you can't escape the current by swimming toward shore; it's like trying to swim upstream in a river. To break free of the current, swim parallel to shore and use the energy of the waves to help you get back to the beach.

BEES, SNAKES & BUGS   Although Guatemala has Africanized bees (the notorious "killer bees" of fact and fable), scorpions, spiders, and several species of venomous snakes, your chances of being bitten are minimal, especially if you refrain from sticking your hands into hives or under rocks in the forest. If you know that you're allergic to bee stings, consult your doctor before traveling. Snake sightings, much less snakebites, are very rare. Moreover, the majority of snakes in Guatemala are nonpoisonous. If you do encounter a snake, stay calm, don't make any sudden movements, and don't try to handle it. As recommended above, avoid sticking your hand under rocks, branches, and fallen trees.

Scorpions, black widow spiders, tarantulas, bullet ants, and other biting insects can all be found in Guatemala. In general, they are not nearly the danger or nuisance most visitors fear. Watch where you stick your hands, and shake out your clothes and shoes before putting them on to avoid any unpleasant and painful surprises.

WHAT TO DO IF YOU GET SICK AWAY FROM HOME

Any foreign embassy or consulate can provide a list of area doctors who speak English. If you get sick, consider asking your hotel staff or concierge to recommend a local doctor—even his or her own. You can also try the emergency room at a local hospital. Many hospitals also have walk-in clinics for emergency cases that are not life-threatening; you may not get immediate attention, but you won't pay the high price of an emergency room visit. We list hospitals and emergency numbers under "Fast Facts: Guatemala" (p. 68), "Fast Facts: Guatemala City" (p. 90), and "Fast Facts: Antigua" (p. 123).

STAYING SAFE

Guatemala still bears the wounds and ongoing effects of its brutal 30-year civil war. Guatemala is a violent country, with gross civil injustice, extreme economic hardship, and frequent public unrest and protests. The police and judicial systems are far outmatched by the levels of crime and violence. However, most of this crime and violence is internal. Most of the popular tourist areas have a strong police presence, and the situation has improved in recent years. A specialized branch of the police force, POLITUR, has been created especially to deal with tourists and crimes against tourists. That said, robberies and pickpocketing are the greatest problem facing most tourists in Guatemala. Crowded markets, public buses, and busy urban areas are the prime haunts of criminals and pickpockets. Never carry a lot of cash or wear very valuable jewelry. Men should avoid having wallets in your back pockets, and

Avoiding "Economy Class Syndrome"

Deep vein thrombosis, or as it's know in the world of flying, "economy-class syndrome," is a blood clot that develops in a deep vein. It's a potentially deadly condition that can be caused by sitting in cramped conditions—such as an airplane cabin—for too long. During a flight (especially a long-haul flight), get up, walk around, and stretch your legs every 60 to 90 minutes to keep your blood flowing. Other preventative measures include frequent flexing of the legs while sitting, drinking lots of water, and avoiding alcohol and sleeping pills. If you have a history of deep vein thrombosis, heart disease, or another condition that puts you at high risk, some experts recommend wearing compression stockings or taking anticoagulants when you fly; always ask your physician about the best course for you. Symptoms of deep vein thrombosis include leg pain or swelling, or even shortness of breath.

women should keep tight grips on your purses. (Keep it tucked under your arm.) Thieves also target gold chains, cameras and video cameras, prominent jewelry, and nice sunglasses. Be sure not to leave valuables in your hotel room.

Rental cars generally stick out, and are easily spotted by thieves. Don't ever leave anything of value in a car parked on the street, not even for a moment. Also be wary of solicitous strangers who stop to help you change a tire or bring you to a service station. Although most are truly good Samaritans, there have been reports of thieves preying on roadside breakdowns. Public intercity buses are also frequent targets of stealthy thieves. Never check your bags into the hold of a bus if you can avoid it. If this can't be avoided, when the bus makes a stop, keep your eye on what leaves the hold. If you put your bags in an overhead rack, be sure you can see the bags at all times. Try not to fall asleep. For more information on car and road safety, see "Getting Around: By Car," later in this chapter.

The local Maya people are very uneasy about having their picture taken. Many, in the more touristy areas, have parlayed this into a means of earning a few *quetzales* by charging to have their picture taken. In the more rural areas, a rude or disrespectful foreign shutterbug can earn the strong and sometimes vocal disdain of the local population. Always ask permission before taking photographs of people.

Political gatherings to protest current economic and social conditions are not uncommon. The most common form that will affect any tourist is road and highway blockades. There's really little you can do to avoid this; however, a fair amount of patience and some compassion will ease the bother and lower your stress levels. Many of these protests and blockades are announced in advance in the newspapers. If you have an important flight or connection, and you have a long ride to the airport, ask your hotel to check on any alerts, and be sure to leave plenty of time for your drive to the airport.

ECOTOURISM
The International Ecotourism Society (TIES) defines ecotourism as "responsible travel to natural areas that conserves the environment and improves the well-being of local people." You can find eco-friendly travel tips, statistics, touring companies, and associations—listed by destination under "Travel Choice"—at the TIES website, www.ecotourism.org. **Ecotravel.com** is a part online magazine and part eco-directory that lets you search for touring companies in several categories (water-based, land-based, spiritually oriented, and so on). Also check out **Conservation International** (www. conservation.org) which, with *National Geographic Traveler,* annually presents the **World Legacy Awards** (www.wlaward. org) to those travel tour operators, businesses, organizations, and places that have made a significant contribution to sustainable tourism.

8 Specialized Travel Resources

TRAVELERS WITH DISABILITIES
Although Guatemala does have a law mandating Integral Attention to Persons with Disabilities, and a few non-governmental organizations are addressing the needs of the country's disabled population, there are relatively few handicapped-accessible buildings or vehicles in the country. In most cities, sidewalks are narrow, crowded, and uneven. Few hotels offer wheelchair-accessible accommodations, and there are no public buses thus equipped. In short, it can be difficult for a person with disabilities to get around Guatemala. Still, most disabilities shouldn't stop anyone from traveling. There are more

options and resources out there than ever before.

Many travel agencies offer customized tours and itineraries for travelers with disabilities. **Flying Wheels Travel** (© 507/451-5005; www.flyingwheelstravel.com) offers escorted tours and cruises that emphasize sports and private tours in minivans with lifts. **Access-Able Travel Source** (© 303/232-2979; www.access-able.com) offers extensive access information and advice for traveling around the world with disabilities. **Accessible Journeys** (© 800/846-4537 or 610/521-0339; www.disabilitytravel.com) caters specifically to slow walkers and wheelchair travelers and their families and friends.

Organizations that offer assistance to travelers with disabilities include **Moss-Rehab** (www.mossresourcenet.org), which provides a library of accessible-travel resources online; the **American Foundation for the Blind** (AFB; © 800/232-5463; www.afb.org), a referral resource for the blind or visually impaired that includes information on traveling with Seeing Eye dogs; and **Society for Accessible Travel & Hospitality** (SATH; © 212/447-7284; www.sath.org; annual membership fees: $45 adults, $30 seniors and students), which offers a wealth of travel resources for all types of disabilities and informed recommendations on destinations, access guides, travel agents, tour operators, vehicle rentals, and companion services. **AirAmbulanceCard.com** is now partnered with SATH and allows you to pre-select top-notch hospitals in case of an emergency for $195 a year ($295 per family), among other benefits.

For more information specifically targeted to travelers with disabilities, the community website **iCan** (www.icanonline.net/channels/travel) has destination guides and several regular columns on accessible travel. Also check out the quarterly magazine *Emerging Horizons* (www.emerginghorizons.com; $14.95 per year, $19.95 outside the U.S.); and *Open World* magazine, published by SATH (see above; $13 per year, $21 outside the U.S.).

GAY & LESBIAN TRAVELERS

Guatemala is a largely Catholic, socially conservative Central American nation, and in general terms the nation is considerably homophobic. Public displays of same-sex affection are rare, and violence against prominent gay and lesbian activists is not unheard of. For these reasons, the local gay and lesbian communities are pretty discreet. For good, comprehensive information on the current situation for gay men, check out the site **Gay Guatemala** (www.gayguatemala.com), which appears in both English and Spanish. Information on the lesbian scene, and specifically lesbian clubs and bars, is much harder to come by. While Guatemala City has something of a gay and lesbian scene, and several bars and clubs cater to this clientele (see "The Gay & Lesbian Scene" in chapter 4), the situation gets radically worse outside of the capital. The more touristy and cosmopolitan destinations of Antigua, Panajachel, and Quetzaltenango can be considered somewhat gay and lesbian friendly; however, the overall reality is rather challenging for gays and lesbians in Guatemala.

The International Gay and Lesbian Travel Association (IGLTA; © 800/448-8550 or 954/776-2626; www.iglta.org) is the trade association for the gay and lesbian travel industry, and offers an online directory of gay- and lesbian-friendly travel businesses; go to their website, and click on "Members."

Many agencies offer tours and travel itineraries specifically for gay and lesbian travelers. **Above and Beyond Tours** (© 800/397-2681; www.abovebeyondtours.com) is the exclusive gay and lesbian tour operator for United Airlines. **Now, Voyager** (© 800/255-6951; www.nowvoyager.com) is a well-known San

Francisco–based, gay-owned and -operated travel service. **Olivia Cruises & Resorts** (© **800/631-6277;** www.olivia. com) charters entire resorts and ships for exclusive lesbian vacations, and offers smaller group experiences for both gay and lesbian travelers. (In 2005, tennis great Martina Navratilova was named Olivia's official spokesperson.)

Gay.com Travel (© **800/929-2268** or 415/644-8044; www.gay.com/travel or www.outandabout.com), is an excellent online successor to the popular *Out & About* print magazine. It provides regularly updated information about gay-owned, gay-oriented, and gay-friendly lodging, dining, sightseeing, nightlife, and shopping establishments in every important destination worldwide. It also offers trip-planning information for gay and lesbian travelers for more than 50 destinations along various themes, ranging from "Sex & Travel" to "Vacations for Couples."

The following travel guides are available at many bookstores, or you can order them from any online bookseller: *Spartacus International Gay Guide* (Bruno Gmünder Verlag; www.spartacusworld. com/gayguide) and *Odysseus: The International Gay Travel Planner* (Odysseus Enterprises Ltd.), both good, annual, English-language guidebooks focused on gay men; and the *Damron* guides (www. damron.com), with separate, annual books for gay men and lesbians.

SENIOR TRAVEL

Mention the fact that you're a senior when you make your travel reservations. Although all the major U.S. airlines except America West have canceled their senior discount and coupon book programs, many hotels still offer lower rates for seniors. In most cities, people over the age of 60 qualify for reduced admission to theaters, museums, and other attractions, as well as discounted fares on public transportation.

Members of **AARP** (formerly known as the American Association of Retired Persons), 601 E St. NW, Washington, DC 20049 (© **888/687-2277;** www.aarp. org), get discounts on hotels, airfares, and car rentals. AARP offers members a wide range of benefits, including *AARP: The Magazine* and a monthly newsletter. Anyone over 50 can join.

Many reliable agencies and organizations target the 50-plus market. **Elderhostel** (© **877/426-8056;** www.elder hostel.org) arranges study programs for those aged 55 and older (and a spouse or companion of any age) in the U.S. and in more than 80 countries around the world, including Guatemala. Most courses last 5 to 7 days in the U.S. (2–4 weeks abroad), and many include airfare, accommodations in university dormitories or modest inns, meals, and tuition. **ElderTreks** (© **800/741-7956;** www. eldertreks.com) offers small group tours to off-the-beaten-path or adventure-travel locations, restricted to travelers 50 and older. ElderTreks usually has at least one trip per year touching down in Guatemala.

Recommended publications offering travel resources and discounts for seniors include: the quarterly magazine *Travel 50 & Beyond* (www.travel50andbeyond. com); *Travel Unlimited: Uncommon Adventures for the Mature Traveler* (Avalon); *101 Tips for Mature Travelers,* available from Grand Circle Travel (© **800/221-2610** or 617/350-7500; www.gct.com); and *Unbelievably Good Deals and Great Adventures That You Absolutely Can't Get Unless You're Over 50* (McGraw-Hill), by Joann Rattner Heilman.

FAMILY TRAVEL

If you have enough trouble getting your kids out of the house in the morning, dragging them thousands of miles away may seem like an insurmountable challenge. But family travel can be immensely rewarding, giving you new ways of seeing the world through the eyes of children.

Hotels in Guatemala often give discounts for children under 12, and children under 3 or 4 are usually allowed to stay for free. Discounts for children and the cutoff ages vary according to the hotel, but in general, don't assume that your kids can stay in your room for free.

Hotels offering regular, dependable babysitting service are few and far between. If you'll need a babysitter, make sure that your hotel offers the service, and be sure to ask whether the babysitters are bilingual. In many cases, they are not. This is usually not a problem with infants and toddlers, but it can cause problems with older children.

To locate accommodations, restaurants, and attractions that are particularly kid-friendly, refer to the "Kids" icon throughout this guide.

Recommended online family travel sites include **Family Travel Forum** (www. familytravelforum.com), a comprehensive site that offers customized trip planning; **Family Travel Network** (www.family travelnetwork.com), an award-winning site that offers travel features, deals, and tips; **Traveling Internationally with Your Kids** (www.travelwithyourkids. com), a comprehensive site offering sound advice for long-distance and international travel with children; and **Family Travel Files** (www.thefamilytravelfiles. com), which offers an online magazine and a directory of off-the-beaten-path tours and tour operators for families.

All children, no matter how young, will need a valid passport to enter Guatemala. By law, minors under 18 need no special permission to enter or leave Guatemala. However, I recommend that adults traveling with children who are not your own carry documented permission from the parent or guardian of record.

WOMEN TRAVELERS

For lack of better phrasing, Guatemala is a typically "macho" Latin American nation. Misogyny and violence against women, while not rampant, are part of the social fabric. Women should be careful walking alone at night throughout the country. More and more hotels are ratcheting up security measures for women traveling alone on business or for pleasure. Some are even offering secure "women only" floors, with the added perk of spa services. So far, the **Radisson Hotel & Suites** (p. 99) in Guatemala City is the only hotel in the country with a specific "women only" floor, but they just may be in the vanguard, so feel free to ask before booking.

Check out the award-winning website **Journeywoman** (www.journeywoman. com), a "real life" women's travel information network where you can sign up for a free e-mail newsletter and get advice on everything from etiquette and dress to safety; or the travel guide *Safety and Security for Women Who Travel* by Sheila Swan and Peter Laufer (Travelers' Tales, Inc.), offering common-sense tips on safe travel.

AFRICAN-AMERICAN TRAVELERS

The Internet offers a number of helpful travel sites for African-American travelers. **Black Travel Online** (www.blacktravel online.com) posts news on upcoming events and includes links to articles and travel-booking sites. **Soul of America** (www.soulofamerica.com) is a comprehensive website with travel tips, event and family-reunion postings, and sections on historically black beach resorts and active vacations.

Agencies and organizations that provide resources for black travelers include: **Rodgers Travel** (© 800/825-1775; www. rodgerstravel.com), a Philadelphia-based travel agency with an extensive menu of tours in destinations worldwide, including heritage and private-group tours; the **African American Association of Innkeepers International** (℃ 877/422-5777; www.africanamericaninns.com), which provides information on member B&Bs in the U.S., Canada, and the Caribbean; and **Henderson Travel & Tours** (℃ 800/327-2309 or 301/650-5700; www.hendersontravel.com), which has specialized in trips to Africa since 1957. For more information, check out the following collections and guides: *Go Girl: The Black Woman's Guide to Travel & Adventure* (Eighth Mountain Press), a compilation of travel essays by writers including Jill Nelson and Audre Lorde, with some practical information and trip-planning advice; *The African American Travel Guide* by Wayne Robinson (Hunter Publishing; www.hunter publishing.com), with details on 19 North American cities; *Steppin' Out* by Carla Labat (Avalon), with details on 20 cities; *Travel and Enjoy Magazine* (℃ 866/266-6211; www.travelandenjoy. com; subscription $38 per year), which focuses on discounts and destination reviews; and the more narrative *Pathfinders Magazine* (℃ 877/977-PATH; www. pathfinderstravel.com; subscription $15 per year), which includes articles on everywhere from Rio de Janeiro to Ghana as well as information on upcoming ski, diving, golf, and tennis trips.

STUDENT TRAVEL

If you're a student planning to travel outside the U.S., you'd be wise to arm yourself with an **International Student Identity Card (ISIC)**, which offers substantial savings on rail passes, plane tickets, and entrance fees. It also provides you with basic health and life insurance and a 24-hour help line. The card is available for $22 from **STA Travel** (℃ 800/781-4040 in North America; www.sta.com or

www.statravel.com), the biggest student travel agency in the world. If you're no longer a student but are still under 26, you can get an **International Youth Travel Card (IYTC)** for the same price and from the same people. This card entitles you to some discounts (but not on museum admissions). *Note:* In 2002, STA Travel bought competitors **Council Travel** and **USIT Campus** after they went bankrupt. It's still operating some offices under the Council name, but it's owned by STA. **Travel CUTS** (℃ 800/667-2887 or 416/614-2887; www.travel cuts.com) offers similar services for both Canadians and U.S. residents. Irish students may prefer to turn to **USIT** (℃ 01/602-1600; www.usitnow.ie), an Ireland-based specialist in student, youth, and independent travel.

SINGLE TRAVELERS

Many people prefer traveling alone. Unfortunately, the solo traveler is often forced to pay a premium price for the privilege of sleeping alone. On package vacations, single travelers are often hit with a "single supplement" to the base price. To avoid it, you can agree to room with other single travelers on the trip, or you can find a compatible roommate before you go from one of the many roommate locator agencies.

GAP Adventures (℃ 800/708-7761 in North America, or 44/870-999-0144 in the United Kingdom; www.gapadventures. com) is an adventure tour company with a good range of regular and varied tours in Guatemala. As a policy, they do not charge a single supplement and will try to pair a single traveler with a compatible roommate.

For more information, check out Eleanor Berman's 2003 edition of *Traveling Solo: Advice and Ideas for More Than 250 Great Vacations* (Globe Pequot), a guide with advice on traveling alone, either solo or as part of a group tour.

9 Planning Your Trip Online

SURFING FOR AIRFARES

The "big three" online travel agencies, **Expedia.com, Travelocity.com,** and **Orbitz.com,** sell most of the air tickets on the Internet. (Canadian travelers should try Expedia.ca and Travelocity.ca; U.K. residents can go for Expedia.co.uk and Opodo.co.uk.). **Kayak.com** is also gaining popularity and uses a sophisticated search engine (developed at MIT). Each has different business deals with the airlines and may offer different fares on the same flights, so it's wise to shop around. Expedia, Kayak, and Travelocity will also send you **e-mail notification** when a cheap fare becomes available to your favorite destination. Of the smaller travel-agency websites, **SideStep** (www.sidestep.com) has gotten the best reviews from Frommer's authors. The website (with optional browser add-on) purports to "search 140 sites at once," but in reality only beats competitors' fares as often as other sites do.

Also remember to check **airline websites,** especially those for low-fare carriers such as Southwest, JetBlue, AirTran, WestJet, or Ryanair, whose fares are often misreported or simply missing from travel agency websites. Even with major airlines, you can often shave a few bucks from a fare by booking directly through the airline and avoiding a travel agency's transaction fee. But you'll get these discounts only by **booking online:** Most airlines now offer online-only fares that even their phone agents know nothing about. For the websites of airlines that fly to your desired location in Guatemala, see the "Getting There" information in the appropriate chapter.

Great **last-minute deals** are available through free weekly e-mail services provided directly by the airlines. Most of these are announced on Tuesday or Wednesday and must be purchased online. Most are only valid for travel that weekend, but some (such as Southwest's) can be booked weeks or months in advance. Sign up for weekly e-mail alerts at airline websites, or check mega-sites that compile comprehensive lists of last-minute specials, such as **Smarter Travel** (smartertravel.com). For last-minute trips, **site59.com, lastminutetravel.com** in the U.S., and **lastminute.com** in Europe often have better air-and-hotel package deals than the major-label sites.

If you're willing to give up some control over your flight details, use what is called an **"opaque" fare service** like **Priceline** (www.priceline.com; www.priceline.co.uk for Europeans) or its smaller competitor **Hotwire** (www.hotwire.com). Both offer rock-bottom prices in exchange for travel on a "mystery airline" at a mysterious time of day, often with a mysterious change of planes en route. The mystery airlines are all major, well-known carriers—and the possibility of being sent from Philadelphia to Chicago via Tampa is remote; the airlines' routing computers have gotten a lot better than they used to be. Your chances of getting a 6am or 11pm flight, however, are still pretty high. Hotwire tells you flight prices before you buy; Priceline usually has better deals than Hotwire, but you have to play their "name our price" game. If you're new at this, the helpful folks at **BiddingForTravel** (www.biddingfortravel.com) do a good job of demystifying Priceline's prices and strategies. Priceline and Hotwire are great for flights within North America and between the U.S. and Europe, but for flights to other parts of the world, consolidators will almost always beat their fares. *Note:* In 2004, Priceline added non-opaque service to its roster. You now have the option to pick exact flights, times, and airlines from a list of offers—or opt to bid on opaque fares as before.

SURFING FOR HOTELS

Shopping online for hotels is generally done one of two ways: by booking through the hotel's own website, or through an independent booking agency (or a fare-service agency like Priceline; see below). These Internet hotel agencies have multiplied in mind-boggling numbers as of late, competing for the business of millions of consumers surfing for accommodations around the world. This competitiveness can be a boon to consumers who have the patience and time to shop and compare the online sites for good deals—but shop they must, for prices can vary considerably from site to site. And keep in mind that hotels at the top of a site's listing may be there for no other reason than that they paid money to get the placement.

Of the "big three" sites, **Expedia** offers a long list of special deals and "virtual tours" or photos of available rooms so you can see what you're paying for (a feature that helps counter the claims that the best rooms are often held back from bargain-booking websites). **Travelocity** posts unvarnished customer reviews and ranks its properties according to the AAA rating system. **Trip Advisor** (www.tripadvisor.com) is another excellent source of unbiased user reviews of hotels around the world. While even the finest hotels can inspire a misleadingly poor review from a picky or crabby traveler, the body of user opinions, when taken as a whole, is usually a reliable indicator.

Other reliable online booking agencies include **Hotels.com** and **Quikbook.com.** An excellent free program, **TravelAxe** (www.travelaxe.net) can help you search multiple hotel sites at once, even ones you may never have heard of—and conveniently lists the total price of the room, including the taxes and service charges. Another booking site, **Travelweb** (www.travelweb.com), is partly owned by the hotels it represents (including the Hilton, Hyatt, and Starwood chains), and is therefore plugged directly into the hotels' reservations systems—unlike independent online agencies, which have to fax or e-mail reservation requests to the hotel, a good portion of which get misplaced in the shuffle. More than once, travelers have arrived at the hotel, only to be told that they have no reservation. To be fair, many of the major sites are undergoing improvements in service and ease of use, and Expedia will soon be able to plug directly into the reservations systems of many hotel chains—none of which can be bad news for consumers. In the meantime, it's a good idea to **get a confirmation number** and **make a printout** of any online booking transaction.

Your best bet in Guatemala might be negotiating directly with the hotels themselves, especially the smaller hotels. In this day and age, almost every hotel in Guatemala has e-mail, if not its own website, and you'll find the contact information right here. However, be aware that response times might be slower than you'd like, and many of the smaller hotels might have some trouble communicating back and forth in English.

In the opaque website category, **Priceline** and **Hotwire** are even better for hotels than for airfares; through both, you're allowed to pick the neighborhood and quality level of your hotel before paying. Priceline's hotel product even covers Europe and Asia, though it's much better at getting five-star lodging for three-star prices than at finding anything at the bottom of the scale. On the downside, many hotels stick Priceline guests in their least desirable rooms. Be sure to go to the BiddingForTravel website (see above) before bidding on a hotel room on Priceline; it features a fairly up-to-date list of hotels that Priceline uses in major cities. For both Priceline and Hotwire, you pay

Frommers.com: The Complete Travel Resource

For an excellent travel-planning resource, we highly recommend **Frommers. com** (www.frommers.com), voted Best Travel Site by *PC Magazine*. We're a little biased, of course, but we guarantee that you'll find the travel tips, reviews, monthly vacation giveaways, bookstore, and online-booking capabilities to be thoroughly indispensable. Special features include our popular **Destinations** section, where you can access expert travel tips, hotel and dining recommendations, and advice on the sights to see in more than 3,500 destinations around the globe; the **Frommers.com Newsletter**, with the latest deals, travel trends, and money-saving secrets; and our **Travel Talk** area featuring **Message Boards**, where Frommer's readers post queries and share advice, and where our authors sometimes show up to answer questions. Once you finish your research, the **Book a Trip** area can lead you to Frommer's preferred online partners' websites, where you can book your vacation at affordable prices.

upfront, and the fee is nonrefundable. *Note:* Some hotels do not provide loyalty program credits or points or other frequent-stay amenities when you book a room through opaque online services.

SURFING FOR RENTAL CARS

For booking rental cars online, the best deals are usually found at rental-car company websites, although all the major online travel agencies also offer rental-car reservations services. Priceline and Hotwire work well for rental cars, too; the only "mystery" is which major rental company you get, and for most travelers the difference between Hertz, Avis, and Budget is negligible.

TRAVEL BLOGS & TRAVELOGUES

More and more travelers are using travel web logs, or **blogs,** to chronicle their journeys online. You can search for blogs about Guatemala at **Travelblog.com** or post your own travelogue at **Travelblog. org.** For blogs that cover general travel news and highlight various destinations, try **Writtenroad.com** or Gawker Media's snarky **Gridskipper.com.** For more literary travel essays, try Salon.com's travel section (**Salon.com/Wanderlust**), and **Worldhum.com,** which also has an extensive list of other travel-related journals, blogs, online communities, newspaper coverage, and bookstores.

10 The 21st-Century Traveler

INTERNET ACCESS AWAY FROM HOME

Travelers have any number of ways to check e-mail and access the Internet on the road. Of course, using your own laptop— or even a PDA (personal digital assistant) or electronic organizer with a modem— gives you the most flexibility. But even if you don't have a computer, you can access

your e-mail and your office computer from cybercafes.

WITHOUT YOUR OWN COMPUTER

In Guatemala, you'll readily find cybercafes in most cities and towns, and every major tourist destination. Heck, there are even cybercafes in Livingston and Monterrico.

Although there's no definitive directory for cybercafes—these are independent businesses, after all—three places to start looking are at **www.cybercaptive.com** and **www.cybercafe.com**.

Aside from formal cybercafes, most **hotels** have at least one computer with Internet access. However, I recommend you avoid **hotel business centers** unless you're willing to pay exorbitant rates.

Most major airports now have **Internet kiosks** scattered throughout their gates. These kiosks, which you'll also see in shopping malls, hotel lobbies, and tourist information offices around the world, give you basic Web access for a per-minute fee that's usually higher than cybercafe prices. The kiosks' clunkiness and high prices, however, mean you should avoid them whenever possible.

To retrieve your e-mail, ask your **Internet Service Provider (ISP)** if it has a Web-based interface tied to your existing e-mail account. If your ISP doesn't have such an interface, you can use the free **mail2web** service (www.mail2web.com) to view and reply to your home e-mail. For more flexibility, you may want to open a free, Web-based e-mail account with **Yahoo! Mail** (http://mail.yahoo.com). (Microsoft's Hotmail is another popular option, but Hotmail has severe spam problems.) Your home ISP may be able to forward your e-mail to the Web-based account automatically.

If you need to access files on your office computer, look into a service called **GoToMyPC** (www.gotomypc.com). The service provides a Web-based interface for you to access and manipulate a distant PC from anywhere—even a cybercafe—provided your "target" PC is on and has an always-on connection to the Internet (as with Road Runner cable). The service offers top-quality security, but if you're worried about hackers, use your own laptop rather than a cybercafe computer to access the GoToMyPC system.

WITH YOUR OWN COMPUTER

In Guatemala, only the most upscale and technologically savvy hotels, cafes, and retailers are signing on as Wi-Fi (wireless fidelity) "hot spots," from where you can get high-speed connection without cable wires, networking hardware, or a phone line (see below). You can get Wi-Fi connection one of several ways. Many laptops sold in the last year have built-in Wi-Fi capability (an 802.11b wireless Ethernet connection). Mac owners have their own networking technology, Apple AirPort. For those with older computers, you can plug in an 802.11b/**Wi-Fi card** (around $50). You sign up for wireless access service, much like you do for cellphone service, through a plan offered by one of several commercial companies that have made wireless service available in airports, hotel lobbies, and coffee shops, primarily in the U.S. (followed by the U.K. and Japan). **T-Mobile Hotspot** (www.t-mobile.com/hotspot) serves up wireless connections at more than 1,000 Starbucks coffee shops nationwide. **Boingo** (www.boingo.com) and **Wayport** (www.wayport.com) have set up networks in airports and high-class hotel lobbies. IPass providers (see below) also give you access to a few hundred wireless hotel lobby setups. Best of all, you don't need to be staying at the Four Seasons to use the hotel's network; just set yourself up on a nice couch in the lobby. (Pricing policies can be byzantine, but in general you pay around $30 a month for unlimited access, and prices are dropping as Wi-Fi access becomes more common.) To locate other hot spots that provide **free wireless networks** in cities around the world, go to **www.personaltelco.net/index.cgi/WirelessCommunities**.

For dial-up access, most business-class hotels throughout the world offer dataports for laptop modems, and a few thousand hotels in the U.S. and Europe now offer free high-speed Internet access using an Ethernet network cable. You can bring your own cables, but most hotels rent them for around $10. **Call your hotel in advance** to see what your options are.

In addition, major Internet Service Providers (ISPs) have **local access numbers** around the world, allowing you to go online by placing a local call. Check your ISP's website or call its toll-free number and ask how you can use your current account away from home and how much it will cost.

The **iPass** network also has dial-up numbers around the world. You'll have to sign up with an iPass provider, who will then tell you how to set up your computer for your destination(s). For a list of iPass providers, go to www.ipass.com and click on "Individuals Buy Now." One solid provider is **i2roam** (*©* **866/811-6209** or 920/235-0475; www.i2roam.com).

Guatemala uses standard U.S.-style two- and three-prong electric outlets with 110-volt AC current, and standard U.S.-style phone jacks. Wherever you go, bring a **connection kit** of the right power and phone adapters, a spare phone cord, and a spare Ethernet network cable—or find out whether your hotel supplies them to guests.

USING A CELLPHONE

The three letters that define much of the world's **wireless capabilities** are GSM (Global System for Mobiles), a big, seamless network that makes for easy cross-border cellphone use throughout Europe and dozens of other countries worldwide. In the U.S., T-Mobile, AT&T Wireless, and Cingular use this quasi-universal system; in Canada, Microcell and some Rogers customers are GSM; and all Europeans and most Australians use GSM.

If your cellphone is on a GSM system, and you have a world-capable multiband phone such as many Sony Ericsson, Motorola, or Samsung models, you can make and receive calls across civilized areas around much of the globe, from Andorra to Uganda. Just call your wireless operator and ask for "international roaming" to be activated on your account. Unfortunately, per-minute charges can be high—usually $1.50 to $4 in Guatemala.

In Guatemala, there are several competing cellphone companies and networks.

Digital Photography on the Road

Many travelers these days are taking vacation photographs with digital cameras. Not only are they left relatively unscathed by airport X-rays, but with digital equipment you don't need to lug around armloads of film. In fact, you don't even need to carry your laptop to download the day's images and make room for more. With a **media storage card,** sold by all major camera dealers, you can store hundreds of images in your camera. These "memory" cards come in different configurations—from memory sticks to flash cards to secure digital cards—and different storage capacities. (The more megabytes of memory, the more images a card can hold.) They range in price from $30 to more than $200. (**Note:** Each camera model works with a specific type of storage card, so you'll need to determine which one is compatible with your camera.) When you get home, you can print the images on your own color printer; take the storage card to a camera store, drugstore, or chain retailer; or use an online service such as **Snapfish** (www.snapfish.com) to develop the images for about 25¢ a shot. You can also put together a spiffy high-quality album of all your photos at **MyPublisher.com** for less than $1 a page.

Online Traveler's Toolbox

Veteran travelers usually carry some essential items to make their trips easier. Following is a selection of handy online tools to bookmark and use.

- **Airplane Seating & Food:** Find out which seats to reserve and which to avoid (and more) on all major domestic airlines at www.seatguru.com. And check out the type of meal (with photos) you'll likely be served on airlines around the world at www.airlinemeals.net.
- **Foreign Languages for Travelers** (www.travlang.com): Learn basic terms in more than 70 languages, and click on any underlined phrase to hear what it sounds like.
- **Weather Forecasts: Intellicast** (www.intellicast.com) and **weather.com** (www.weather.com) give weather forecasts for all 50 states and for cities around the world.
- **Maps: Mapquest** (www.mapquest.com) is the best of the mapping sites; it lets you choose a specific address or destination and, in seconds, returns a map and detailed directions.
- **Time & Date** (www.timeanddate.com): See what time (and day) it is anywhere in the world.
- **Travel Warnings** (http://travel.state.gov, www.fco.gov.uk/travel, www.voyage.gc.ca, or www.dfat.gov.au/consular/advice): These sites report on places where health concerns or unrest might threaten American, British, Canadian, and Australian travelers. Generally, U.S. warnings are the most paranoid; Australian warnings are the most relaxed.
- **Universal Currency Converter** (www.xe.com/ucc): See what your dollar or pound is worth in more than 100 other countries.
- **ATM Locators: Visa ATM Locator** (www.visa.com) for locations of PLUS ATMs worldwide, or **MasterCard ATM Locator** (www.mastercard.com), for locations of Cirrus ATMs worldwide.

All have numerous outlets across the country, in most major cities and tourist destinations, including La Aurora International Airport. All of these companies sell prepaid GSM chips that can be used in any unlocked tri-band GSM cellphone. The main companies are **Claro** (© 147-100; www.claro.com.gt), which is a division of Telgua, the national telephone company; **Movistar** (© 502/2379-1960; www.movistar.com.gt), a division of the international firm Telefonica; and **Tigo** (© 502/2428-0000; www.tigo.com.gt), also marketed as Comcel. Prepaid chips come in denominations from Q10 to Q200 ($1.35–$26/70p–£14). Most companies charge around a Q50 ($6.65/ £3.50) activation fee.

That's why it's important to buy an "unlocked" world phone from the get-go. Many cellphone operators sell "locked" phones that restrict you from using any other removable computer memory phone chip (called a **SIM card**) than the ones they supply. Having an unlocked phone allows you to install a cheap, prepaid SIM card (found at a local retailer) in your destination country. (Show your phone to the salesperson; not all phones work on all networks.) You'll get a local phone number—and much, much lower calling rates. Unlocking an already locked phone can be complicated, but it can be done; just call your cellular operator and say you'll be going abroad for several months and want to use the phone with a local provider.

For many, **renting** a phone is a good idea. (Even worldphone owners will have to rent new phones if you're traveling to non-GSM regions such as Japan or Korea.) While you can rent a phone from any number of overseas sites, including kiosks at airports and at car rental agencies, we suggest renting the phone before you leave home. That way you can give loved ones and business associates your new number, make sure the phone works, and take the phone wherever you go—especially helpful for overseas trips through several countries, where local phone-rental agencies often bill in local currency and may not let you take the phone to another country.

Phone rental isn't cheap. You'll usually pay $40 to $50 per week, plus airtime fees of at least a dollar a minute. If you're traveling to Europe, though, local rental companies often offer free incoming calls within their home country, which can save you big bucks. The bottom line: Shop around.

Two good wireless rental companies are **InTouch USA** (② 800/872-7626; www.intouchglobal.com) and **RoadPost** (② 888/290-1606 or 905/272-5665; www.roadpost.com). Give them your itinerary, and they'll tell you what wireless products you need. InTouch will also, for free, advise you on whether your existing phone will work overseas; simply call ② 703/222-7161 between 9am and 4pm EST, or go to http://intouchglobal.com/travel.htm.

For trips of more than a few weeks spent in one country, **buying a phone** becomes economically attractive, as many nations have cheap, no-questions-asked prepaid phone systems. Once you arrive at your destination, stop by a local cellphone shop and get the cheapest package; you'll probably pay less than $100 for a phone and a starter calling card. Local calls may be as low as 10¢ per minute, and in many countries incoming calls are free.

Wilderness adventurers, or those heading to less-developed countries, might consider renting a **satellite phone ("satphone"),** which is different from a cellphone in that it connects to satellites and works where there's no cellular signal or ground-based tower. You can rent satellite phones from **RoadPost** (② 888/290-1606 or 905/272-5665; www.roadpost.com). InTouch USA (see above) offers a wider range of satphones but at higher rates. Per-minute call charges can be even cheaper than roaming charges with a regular cellphone, but the phone itself is more expensive (up to $150 a week), and depending on the service you choose, people calling you may incur high long-distance charges. As of this writing, satphones were outrageously expensive to buy, so consider your options before investing.

11 Getting There

BY PLANE

It takes between 3 and 8 hours to fly to Guatemala from most U.S. cities. Most international flights land at **La Aurora International Airport** (② 502/2332-6086; airport code GUA). A few international and regional airlines fly directly into **Flores Airport** (FRS) near Tikal. If you're only interested in visiting the Maya ruins at Tikal and touring the Petén, this is a good option. However, most visitors will want to fly in and out of Guatemala City.

The following airlines currently serve Guatemala from the United States, using the gateway cities listed. **American Airlines**

(© **800/433-7300** in the U.S. and Canada, or 502/2337-1177 in Guatemala; www.aa.com) has daily flights from Dallas, Denver, Miami, and Washington, D.C. **Continental** (© **800/231-0856** in the U.S. and Canada, or 502/2385-9610 in Guatemala; www.continental.com) offers direct flights daily from Houston, and once weekly from Newark. Continental also has a twice-weekly direct flight between Houston and Flores (FRS). **Delta** (© **800/241-4141** in the U.S. and Canada, or 800/300-0005 inside Guatemala; www.delta.com) has daily direct flights from Atlanta. **Mexicana** (© **800/531-7921** in the U.S. and Canada, or 502/2333-6001 in Guatemala; www.mexicana.com) offers several daily flights from their hub in Mexico City, with connections to and from numerous North American and European cities. **United Airlines** (© **800/538-2929** in the U.S. and Canada, or 502/2336-9923 in Guatemala; www.united.com) has direct daily flights from Los Angeles, and less frequent direct service from San Francisco, Chicago, New York (JFK), Washington (Dulles), and Miami. **US Airways** (© **800/622-1015** in the U.S. and Canada, or 502/2361-7803 in Guatemala; www.usairways.com) has direct flights daily from Charlotte. **Grupo Taca** (© **800/400-8222** in the U.S. and Canada, or 299-8222 in Costa Rica; www.grupotaca.com) is a conglomeration of the Central American airlines, with direct flights or connections to and from Boston, Chicago, Los Angeles, San Francisco, Houston, New Orleans, New York, Miami, and Washington. These flights often make connections through El Salvador.

From Europe, you can take any major carrier to a hub city such as Miami or New York and then make connections to Guatemala.

GETTING INTO TOWN FROM THE AIRPORT

You'll find various shuttle companies occupying makeshift booths—due to the airport construction—as you exit either the national or international terminal. These companies charge between Q30 and Q60 ($4–$8/£2.10–£4.20) to any hotel in Guatemala City; and between Q75 and Q90 ($10–$12/£5.25–£6.30) to Antigua. Many of the larger hotels also have regular complimentary airport shuttle buses, so be sure to check in advance if your hotel provides this service.

If you don't want to wait for the shuttle to fill or sit through various stops before arriving at your hotel, there are always taxis lined up at the airport terminal exits. A taxi downtown will cost around Q45 to Q75 ($6–$10/£3.15–£5.25).

If you're on a tight budget and need to take a bus to the city center, bus no. 32 runs downtown every 30 minutes between 6am and 8pm, with less frequent service before and after those hours. However, because of an increasing number of armed assaults on metropolitan buses, I recommend you avoid this option.

Avis, Budget, Hertz, National, Tabarini, and **Thrifty** all have car rental desks at the airport. See "Getting Around: By Car," later in this chapter, for more information.

GETTING THROUGH THE AIRPORT

With the federalization of airport security, screening procedures at U.S. airports are more stable and consistent than ever. Generally, you'll be fine if you arrive at the airport **1 hour** before a domestic flight and **2 hours** before an international flight; if you show up late, tell an airline employee, and he or she will probably whisk you to the front of the line.

Bring a **current, government-issued photo ID** such as a driver's license or passport. Keep your ID at the ready to present at check-in, the security checkpoint, and sometimes even the gate. (Children under 18 do not need government-issued photo IDs for domestic flights, but they do for international flights to most countries.)

In 2003, the TSA phased out **gate check-in** at all U.S. airports. Passengers with e-tickets, which have made paper tickets nearly obsolete, can beat the ticket-counter lines by using airport **electronic kiosks** or even **online check-in** from their home computers. Online check-in involves logging on to your airline's website, accessing your reservation, and printing out your boarding pass—and the airline may even offer you bonus miles to do so! If you're using a kiosk at the airport, bring the credit card you used to book the ticket or your frequent-flier card. Print out your boarding pass from the kiosk and simply proceed to the security checkpoint with your pass and a photo ID. If you're checking bags or looking to snag an exit-row seat, you'll be able to do so using most airline kiosks. Even the smaller airlines are employing the kiosk system, but always call your airline to make sure these alternatives are available. **Curbside check-in** is also a good way to avoid lines, although a few airlines still don't allow it; call for your airline's policy before you go.

Security checkpoint lines are getting shorter than they were during 2001 and 2002, but an orange alert, suspicious passenger, or high passenger volume can still make for a long wait. If you have trouble standing for long periods of time, tell an airline employee; the airline will provide a wheelchair. Speed up security by **not wearing metal objects** such as big belt buckles. If you've got metallic body parts, a note from your doctor can prevent a long chat with the security screeners. Keep in mind that only **ticketed passengers** are allowed past security, except for people escorting disabled passengers or children.

Federalization has stabilized **what you can carry on** and **what you can't**. The general rule is that sharp things are out, nail clippers are okay, and food and beverages must pass through the X-ray machine—but security screeners can't make you drink from your coffee cup. Bring food in your carry-on rather than checking it, as explosive-detection machines used on checked luggage have been known to mistake food (especially chocolate, for some reason) for bombs. Travelers in the U.S. are allowed one carry-on bag, plus a "personal item" such as a purse, briefcase, or laptop bag. Carry-on hoarders can stuff all sorts of things into a laptop bag; as long

---

Tips **Don't Stow It—Ship It**

If ease of travel is your main concern, and money is no object, consider shipping your luggage and sports equipment with one of the growing number of luggage-service companies that pick up, track, and deliver travel bags (often through couriers such as Federal Express). Traveling luggage-free, however convenient, isn't cheap: One-way overnight shipping can cost from $100 to $200, depending on what you're sending. Still, for some people, especially the elderly or the infirm, it's a sensible option. Specialists in door-to-door luggage delivery include **Virtual Bellhop** (www.virtualbellhop.com), **SkyCap International** (wwww.skycapinternational.com), **Luggage Express** (www.usxpluggage express.com), and **Sports Express** (www.sportsexpress.com).

as it has a laptop in it, it's still considered a personal item. The Transportation Security Administration (TSA) has issued a list of restricted items; check its website (www. tsa.gov/public/index.jsp) for details. Airport screeners may decide that your checked luggage warrants a hand search. You can now purchase luggage locks that allow screeners to open and relock a checked bag if hand searching is necessary. Look for Travel Sentry certified locks at luggage or travel shops and Brookstone stores (or online at www.brookstone.com). Luggage inspectors can open these TSA-approved locks with a special code or key—rather than having to cut them off the suitcase, as they normally do to conduct a hand search. For more information on the locks, visit www.travelsentry.org.

FLYING FOR LESS: TIPS FOR GETTING THE BEST AIRFARE

Passengers sharing the same airplane cabin rarely pay the same fare. Travelers who need to purchase tickets at the last minute, change your itinerary at a moment's notice, or fly one-way often get stuck paying the premium rate. Here are some ways to keep your airfare costs down.

- Passengers who can book your ticket either **long in advance** or at **the last minute,** or who fly **midweek** or at **less-trafficked hours,** may ·pay a fraction of the full fare. If your schedule is flexible, say so, and ask if you can secure a cheaper fare by changing your flight plans.
- Search **the Internet** for cheap fares (see "Planning Your Trip Online," earlier in this chapter).
- Keep an eye on local newspapers for **promotional specials** or **fare wars,** when airlines lower prices on their most popular routes. You rarely see fare wars offered for peak travel times, but if you can travel in the off-months, you may snag a bargain.

- **Consolidators,** also known as bucket shops, are great sources for international tickets, although they usually can't beat Internet fares within North America. Start by looking in the Sunday newspaper travel sections; U.S. travelers should focus on the *New York Times, Los Angeles Times,* and *Miami Herald.* For less-developed destinations, small travel agents who cater to immigrant communities in large cities often have the best deals. New York, Los Angeles, and Miami all have large Guatemalan immigrant populations. *Beware:* Bucket shop tickets are usually nonrefundable or rigged with stiff cancellation penalties, often as high as 50% to 75% of the ticket price, and some put you on charter airlines, which may leave at inconvenient times and experience delays. Several reliable consolidators are worldwide and available online. **STA Travel** has been the world's lead consolidator for students since purchasing Council Travel, but their fares are competitive for travelers of all ages. **ELTExpress (Flights.com;** ℰ **800/TRAV-800;** www.eltexpress. com) has excellent fares worldwide, particularly to Europe. They also have "local" websites in 12 countries. **FlyCheap** (ℰ **800/FLY-CHEAP;** www.1800flycheap.com) is owned by package-holiday megalith MyTravel, and has especially good fares to sunny destinations. **Air Tickets Direct** (ℰ **800/778-3447;** www.airtickets direct.com) is based in Montreal and leverages the currently weak Canadian dollar for low fares; they also book trips to places that U.S. travel agents won't touch, such as Cuba.
- Join **frequent-flier clubs.** Frequent-flier membership doesn't cost a cent, but it does entitle you to better seats, faster response to phone inquiries, and prompter service if your luggage

Travel in the Age of Bankruptcy

Airlines go bankrupt, so protect yourself by **buying your tickets with a credit card**, as the Fair Credit Billing Act guarantees that you can get your money back from the credit card company if a travel supplier goes under (and if you request the refund within 60 days of the bankruptcy). **Travel insurance** can also help, but make sure it covers "carrier default" for your specific travel provider. And be aware that if a U.S. airline goes bust mid-trip, a 2001 federal law requires other carriers to take you to your destination (albeit on a space-available basis) for a fee of no more than $25, provided you rebook within 60 days of the cancellation.

is stolen or your flight is canceled or delayed, or if you want to change your seat. And you don't have to fly to earn points; **frequent-flier credit cards** can earn you thousands of miles for doing your everyday shopping. With more than 70 mileage awards programs on the market, consumers have never had more options, but the system has never been more complicated—what with major airlines folding, new budget carriers emerging, and alliances forming (allowing you to earn points on partner airlines). Investigate the program details of your favorite airlines before you sink points into any one. Consider which airlines have hubs in the airport nearest you and, of those carriers, which have the most advantageous alliances, given your most common routes. To play the frequent-flier game to your advantage, consult Randy Petersen's **Inside Flyer** (www.insideflyer.com). Petersen and friends review all the programs in detail and post regular updates on changes in policies and trends. Petersen will also field direct questions (via e-mail) if a partner airline refuses to redeem points, for instance, or if you're still not sure after researching the various programs which one is right for you. It's well worth the $12 online subscription fee, good for 1 year.

LONG-HAUL FLIGHTS: HOW TO STAY COMFORTABLE

Long flights can be trying; stuffy air and cramped seats can make you feel as if you're being sent parcel post in a small box. But with a little advance planning, you can make an otherwise unpleasant experience almost bearable.

- Your choice of airline and airplane will definitely affect your leg room. Find more details at **www.seatguru. com**, which has extensive details about almost every seat on six major U.S. airlines. For international airlines, research firm Skytrax has posted a list of average seat pitches at **www.airlinequality.com**.
- Emergency exit seats and bulkhead seats typically have the most legroom. Emergency exit seats are usually left unassigned until the day of a flight (to ensure that someone able-bodied fills the seats); it's worth getting to the ticket counter early to snag one of these spots for a long flight. Many passengers find that bulkhead seating (the row facing the wall at the front of the cabin) offers more legroom, but keep in mind that bulkheads are where airlines often put baby bassinets, so you may be sitting next to an infant
- To have two seats for yourself in a three-seat row, try for an aisle seat in a center section toward the back of coach. If you're traveling with a

companion, book an aisle and a window seat. Middle seats are usually booked last, so chances are good you'll end up with three seats to yourselves. And in the event that a third passenger is assigned the middle seat, he or she will probably be more than happy to trade for a window or an aisle.

- Ask about entertainment options. Many airlines offer seatback video systems where you get to choose your movies or play video games—but only on some of their planes. (Boeing 777s are your best bet.)
- To sleep, avoid the last row of any section or the row in front of an emergency exit, as these seats are the least likely to recline. Avoid seats near highly trafficked toilet areas. Avoid seats in the back of many jets—these can be narrower than those in the rest of coach. You also may want to reserve a window seat so you can rest your head and avoid being bumped in the aisle.
- Get up, walk around, and stretch every 60 to 90 minutes to keep your blood flowing. This helps you avoid **deep vein thrombosis,** or "economy-class syndrome," a potentially deadly condition caused by sitting in cramped conditions for too long. Other preventive measures include drinking lots of water and avoiding alcohol (see next bullet). See "Avoiding 'Economy Class Syndrome'" on p. 33.
- Drink water before, during, and after your flight to combat the lack of humidity in airplane cabins—which can be drier than the Sahara. Avoid alcohol, which will dehydrate you.

Tips Coping with Jet Lag

Jetlag is a pitfall of traveling across time zones. If you're flying north-south and you feel sluggish when you touch down, your symptoms will be the result of dehydration and the general stress of air travel. When you travel east-west or vice versa, however, your body becomes thoroughly confused about what time it is, and everything from your digestion to your brain is knocked for a loop. Traveling east, say from Chicago to Paris, is more difficult on your internal clock than traveling west, say from Atlanta to Hawaii, because most peoples' bodies are more inclined to stay up late than fall asleep early.

Here are some tips for combating jet lag:

- **Reset your watch** to your destination time before you board the plane.
- **Drink lots of water** before, during, and after your flight. Avoid alcohol.
- **Exercise and sleep well** for a few days before your trip.
- If you have trouble sleeping on planes, **fly eastward on morning flights.**
- **Daylight** is the key to resetting your body clock. At the website for **Outside In** (www.bodyclock.com), you can get a customized plan of when to seek and avoid light.
- If you need help getting to sleep earlier than you usually would, some doctors recommend taking either the hormone **melatonin** or the sleeping pill **Ambien**—but not together. Some recommend that you take 2 to 5 milligrams of melatonin about 2 hours before your planned bedtime—but again, always check with your doctor on the best course of action for you.

Flying with Film & Video

Never pack film—exposed or unexposed—in checked bags, because the new, more powerful scanners in U.S. airports can fog film. The film you carry with you can be damaged by scanners as well. X-ray damage is cumulative; the faster the film and the more times you put it through a scanner, the more likely the damage. Film under 800 ASA is usually safe for up to five scans. If you're taking your film through additional scans, U.S. regulations permit you to demand hand inspections. In international airports, you're at the mercy of airport officials. On international flights, store your film in transparent baggies so you can remove it easily before you go through scanners. Keep in mind that airports are not the only places where your camera may be scanned: Highly trafficked attractions are X-raying visitors' bags with increasing frequency.

Most photo supply stores sell protective pouches designed to block damaging X-rays. The pouches fit both film and loaded cameras. They should protect your film in checked baggage, but they also may raise alarms and result in a hand inspection.

You'll have little to worry about if you are traveling with **digital cameras.** Unlike film, which is sensitive to light, the digital camera and storage cards are not affected by airport X-rays, according to Nikon. Still, if you plan to travel extensively, you may want to play it safe and hand-carry your digital equipment or ask that it be inspected by hand. See "Digital Photography on the Road," p. 43.

Carry-on scanners will not damage **videotape** in video cameras, but the magnetic fields emitted by the walk-through security gateways and hand-held inspection wands will. Always place your loaded camcorder on the screening conveyor belt or have it hand-inspected. Be sure your batteries are charged, as you may be required to turn the device on to ensure that it's what it appears to be.

• If you're flying with kids, don't forget to carry on toys, books, pacifiers, and chewing gum to help them relieve ear pressure buildup during ascent and descent. Let each child pack his or her own backpack with favorite toys.

BY CAR

It's possible to travel to Guatemala by car, but it can be difficult. The drive from the United States involves crossing the entire country of Mexico from north to south. Driving can be problematic for a variety of reasons, including bad roads, limited services, crime, corrupt border crossings, and visa formalities. If you do decide to undertake this adventure, take the **Gulf Coast route** from the border crossing at Brownsville, Texas, because it involves traveling the fewest miles through Mexico.

Those planning to travel this route should try to find a copy of *Driving the Pan-Am Highway to Mexico and Central America,* by Audrey and Raymond Pritchard (Costa Rica Books, 1997), which is out of print, but sometimes available online. There is also a wealth of information online at www.sanborns insurance.com and www.drivemeloco.com.

CAR DOCUMENTS   You will need a current driver's license, as well as your vehicle's registration and the original title (no photocopies), to enter Guatemala.

CENTRAL AMERICAN AUTO INSUR-ANCE   Contact **Sanborn's Insurance Company** (© 800/222-0158 or 956/686-0711; www.sanbornsinsurance.com), which has agents at various border towns in the U.S. These folks have been servicing this niche for more than 50 years. They can supply you with trip insurance for Mexico and Guatemala (you won't be able to buy insurance after you've left the U.S.), driving tips, and an itinerary.

CAR SAFETY   Be sure your car is in excellent working order. It's advisable not to drive at night because of the danger of being robbed by bandits. Also, drink only bottled beverages along the way to avoid any unpleasant microbes that might be lurking in the local tap water.

12 Packages for the Independent Traveler

Before you start your search for the lowest airfare, you may want to consider booking your flight as part of a travel package. Package tours are not the same thing as escorted tours. Package tours are simply a way to buy the airfare, accommodations, and other elements of your trip (such as car rentals, airport transfers, and sometimes even activities) at the same time and often at discounted prices—kind of like one-stop shopping. Packages are sold in bulk to tour operators—who resell them to the public at a cost that usually undercuts standard rates.

One good source of package deals is the airlines themselves. Most major airlines offer air/land packages, including **American Airlines Vacations** (© 800/321-2121; www.aavacations.com), **Delta Vacations** (© 800/221-6666; www.deltavacations.com), **Continental Airlines Vacations** (© 800/301-3800; www.covacations.com), and **United Vacations** (© 888/854-3899; www.unitedvacations.com). Several big **online travel agencies**—Expedia, Travelocity, Orbitz, Site59, and Lastminute.com—also do a brisk business in packages. If you're unsure about the pedigree of a smaller packager, check with the Better Business Bureau in the city where the company is based, or go online at www.bbb.org. If a packager won't tell you where they're based, don't fly with them.

Before you book your package through a tour company, remember that with a few phone calls and e-mails, you can often organize the same thing on your own without having to pay the sometimes hefty service fee. This book contains all the information and resources you need to design and book a wonderful trip, tailored to your particular interests and budget. Moreover, package vacations are still a nascent industry in Guatemala and do not offer the kinds of amazing bargains as those to Cancún or the Caribbean. In fact, many come with hidden charges and costs, so shop carefully.

Your best bet is often to do it yourself or to go with a Guatemalan-based specialist; many of these companies emphasize adventure travel or ecotourism and can put together a complete custom itinerary for you. For a complete listing of tour companies servicing Guatemala, see "Recommended Package & Escorted Tour Operators" and "Special-Interest & Adventure Tours," below.

Travel packages are also listed in the travel section of your local Sunday newspaper. Or check ads in the national travel magazines such as *Arthur Frommer's Budget Travel Magazine, Travel + Leisure,*

National Geographic Traveler, and *Condé Nast Traveler.*

Package tours can vary by leaps and bounds. Some offer a better class of hotels than others. Some offer the same hotels for lower prices. Some offer flights on scheduled airlines, while others book charters. Some limit your choice of accommodations and travel days. You are often required to make a large payment upfront. On the plus side, packages can save you money, offering group prices but allowing for independent travel. Some even let you add on a few guided excursions or escorted day trips (also at prices lower than if you booked them yourself) without booking an entirely escorted tour.

Before you invest in a package tour, get some answers. Ask about the **accommodations choices** and prices for each. Then look up the hotels' reviews in a Frommer's guide and check their rates online for your specific dates of travel. You'll also want to find out what **type of room** you get. If you need a certain type of room, ask for it; don't take whatever is thrown your way. Request a nonsmoking room, a quiet room, a room with a view, or whatever you fancy.

Finally, look for **hidden expenses.** Ask whether airport departure fees and taxes, for example, are included in the total cost.

13 Escorted General-Interest Tours

Escorted tours are structured group tours with a group leader. The price usually includes everything from airfare, hotels, and meals to tours, admission costs, and local transportation.

Despite the fact that escorted tours require big deposits and predetermine hotels, restaurants, and itineraries, many people derive security and peace of mind from the structure they offer. Escorted tours—whether they're navigated by bus, motor coach, train, or boat—let travelers sit back and enjoy the trip without having to drive or worry about details. They take you to the maximum number of sights in the minimum amount of time with the least amount of hassle. They're particularly convenient for people with limited mobility and can be a great way to make new friends.

On the downside, you'll have little opportunity for serendipitous interactions with locals. The tours can be jam packed with activities, leaving little room for individual sightseeing, whim, or adventure—plus they also often focus on the heavily visited sites, so you miss out on many a lesser-known gem.

Before you invest in an escorted tour, request a complete **schedule** of the trip to find out how much sightseeing is planned and whether you'll have enough time to relax or have an adventure of your own. Also ask about the **cancellation policy:** Is a deposit required? Can they cancel the trip if enough people don't sign up? Do you get a refund if they cancel? If *you* cancel? How late can you cancel if you are unable to go? When must you pay in full? If you choose an escorted tour, think strongly about purchasing trip-cancellation insurance, especially if the tour operator asks you to pay in advance. See the section on "Travel Insurance," p. 29. If you plan to travel alone, find out if they'll charge a **single supplement** or whether they can pair you with a roommate.

The **size** of the group is also important to know upfront. Generally, the smaller the group, the more flexible the itinerary, and the less time you'll spend waiting for people to get on and off the bus. Find out the **demographics** of the group as well. What is the age range? What is the gender breakdown? Is this mostly a trip for couples or singles?

Discuss what is included in the **price**. You may have to pay for transportation to and from the airport. A box lunch may be included in an excursion, but drinks might cost extra. Tips may not be included. Find out if you will be charged if you decide to opt out of certain activities or meals.

Before you invest in a package tour, get some answers. Ask about the **accommodations choices** and prices for each. You'll also want to find out what **type of room** you get. If you need a certain type of room, ask for it.

RECOMMENDED PACKAGE & ESCORTED TOUR OPERATORS

NORTH AMERICAN–BASED TOUR OPERATORS

These agencies and operators specialize in well-organized and coordinated tours that cover your entire stay. Many travelers prefer to have everything arranged and confirmed before arriving in Guatemala, and this is a good idea for first-timers.

- **Abercrombie & Kent** ✦✦ (✆ **800/554-7016;** www.abercrombiekent. com) is a luxury tour company that offers upscale trips around the globe. Their 12-day "Legacy of the Maya" includes 2 days at the Copán ruins in Honduras. Around $5,300 per person, airfare not included.
- **Caravan Tours** (✆ **800/227-2826;** www.caravantours.com). If you don't mind sharing your vacation with up to 45 fellow travelers, this is a great value. See six places (Guatemala City, Antigua, Lake Atitlán) in 11 days for around $1,000 per person. Airfare not included.
- **Overseas Adventure Travel** ✦✦ (✆ **800/493-6824;** www.oattravel. com) offers good-value natural history and "soft adventure" itineraries, with optional add-on excursions. Tours are limited to 16 people. The "Route of the Maya" 14-day package includes 8 days in Guatemala, and

also visits Copán in Honduras and ruins in Belize. Around $2,200 per person including round-trip airfare from Miami or Houston.

U.K.-BASED TOUR OPERATORS

- **Imaginative Traveller** (✆ **0800/316-2717** or 44/147-366-7337; www. imaginative-traveller.com) is a good value operator specializing in budget student, group, and family travel. Their offerings focus on the larger Maya world, and spend time in parts of southern Mexico and Belize. They do two different 14-day trips and a 28-day trip, which combines the two. Around $950 (£508) to $1,700 (£908) per person. Airfare not included.
- **Journey Latin America** ✦ (✆ **44/208-747-8315;** www.journeylatin america.co.uk) is a large British operator specializing in Latin American travel. They offer a range of escorted tours around Latin America, with some that spend much of the time in Guatemala. They also design custom itineraries, and often have excellent deals on airfare.

GUATEMALAN TOUR OPERATORS

Because many U.S.-based companies subcontract portions of their tours to established Guatemalan companies, some travelers like to set up their tours directly with these companies, thereby cutting out the middleman. While that means these packages are often less expensive than those offered by U.S. companies, it doesn't mean they're cheap. You still pay for the convenience of having all your arrangements handled for you.

Scores of tour agencies in Guatemala City, Antigua, and the other major tourist destinations offer a plethora of sightseeing and adventure options. These agencies, and the tour desks at most hotels, can arrange everything from tours of the

Maya ruins to village market shopping sprees. While it's generally quite easy to arrange most of these popular tours and adventures at the spur of the moment during your vacation, some are offered only when there are enough interested people or on set dates. If you have a specialized tour or activity in mind, it pays to contact the hotel you will be staying at or a few of the companies listed here before you leave home to find out what they might be doing when you arrive.

- **Clark Tours** (© 502/2412-4700; www.clarktours.com.gt) has been operating for more than 70 years in Guatemala, making it the oldest tour company in the country. They have several offices and are the official representatives of American Express in Guatemala. They offer many tours, including an afternoon in Antigua for around Q150 ($20/£11) per person; 2- to 4-day archaeology trips starting at around Q3,000 ($400/£210) per person; and the 14-day Antigua, Lake Atitlán, Chichicastenango, and Tikal trip for around Q12,750 ($1,700/£893) per person.

- **Maya Vacations** ☆ (© 502/233-4638; www.mayavacations.com) is a relatively new company run by very knowledgeable local operators. Their standard itineraries run the gamut from a 4-day/3-night circuit of Guatemala City, Antigua, and Chichicastenango for Q4,598 ($613/£322) per person to an 8-day/7-night highlight tour for around Q7,350 ($980/£515) per person. They also offer a wide range of active and adventure tours.

- **Via Venture** ☆☆ (© 502/7832-2509; www.viaventure.com). This well-run operation specializes in custom-designed itineraries using the finest high-end hotels in the country, as well as an excellent team of guides and ground transport services. They are also particularly strong in the area of adventure tourism and theme vacations. In addition to Guatemala, these folks run trips and combined itineraries into Belize and Honduras.

14 Special-Interest & Adventure Tours

There are plenty of options for active, adventure, special-interest, or theme vacations to Guatemala. Popular themes and activities include bird-watching, Maya archaeology, cave explorations, and mountain biking. In many cases, you may want to add on a specific theme tour or partake in some adventure activity as an a la carte option within the broader scope of your trip to Guatemala. However, some of you may want to build your entire itinerary around a specific theme or activity. The agencies listed below specialize in adventure tourism or specialized activities, as indicated. In addition to the agencies and operators listed below, most of the package and escort tour operators listed above offer a selection of themed specialty tours or adventure options.

GENERAL ADVENTURE TOUR & SPECIAL-INTEREST TOUR OPERATORS

- **Adrenalina Tours** ☆ (© 502/7832-1108 or 502/5535-6831; www.adrenalinatours.com). Not for pregnant women or those with heart conditions. This Guatemalan-based company specializes in strenuous hikes and volcano climbs—one is rated "dangerous due to toxic gases." They also offer 4WD off-road tours, with a vehicle, driver, and multilingual guide, for Q1,125 ($150/£79) per day, among their many options.

- **Adventure Life** (✆ **800/3440-6118** in the U.S. and Canada; www.adventurelife.com) has several different trips, including biking, kayaking and trekking, visiting villages and ruins, or Easter Week in Antigua. Prices range from 6 days for around Q6,375 ($850/£446) to 11 days for around Q16,500 ($2,200/£1,155) per person. Airfare not included.

- **AdventureSmith Explorations** (✆ **800/728-2875** in the U.S. and Canada; www.adventuresmith explorations.com) offers several different trips, with experiences running the gamut from rafting and cave exploration to Maya ruins and markets. Some include Belize, southern Mexico, or the Copán ruins in Honduras. Five days cost around Q6,000 ($800/£420); 9 days around Q15,000 ($2,000/£1,050) per person, not including airfare.

- **Art Workshops in Guatemala** (✆ **612/825-0747** in the U.S. and Canada; www.artguat.org). This group offers many creative opportunities, including nearly every genre of writing, plastic arts, and even yoga. While there are opportunities to try your hand at Maya weaving, that class watches the real experts at work and visits the markets where their works are sold. Ten-day tours run around Q12,000 to 13,500 ($1,600–$1,800/ £840–£945) per person, plus airfare, depending on workshop.

- **Bike Hike Adventures** (✆ **888/805-0061** in the U.S. and Canada, or 604/731-2442; www.bikehike.com) is a Vancouver-based company specializing in multiday, multi-adventure tours for small groups. Their 9-day tour will have you hiking, mountain biking, sea kayaking, and tree canopy exploring. You'll visit Guatemala City, Antigua, Chichicastenango, the Volcán Pacaya, Lake Atitlán, and Tikal.

They'll let you design your own trip, too. The cost for their 9-day adventure is around Q13,500 ($1,800/ £945) per person, not including airfare.

- **CA Tours** ✵ (✆ **44/132-983-6309** in the U.K., or 502/7832-9638 in Guatemala; www.catours.co.uk). If motorcycles are your thing, this is your trip. They offer two tours: 10 days with 1,207km (750 miles) of riding for Q14,250 ($1,900/£998); and 14 days with 1,770km (1,100 miles) for Q21,000 ($2,800/£1,470) per person; airfare not included. You can use the motorcycle they supply, or pick from several other models and pay extra for rental. They will also customize a tour for you.

- **Habitat for Humanity International** (✆ **502/7763-5308** in Guatemala; www.habitat.org) has several chapters in Guatemala and sometimes runs organized Global Village programs here. Their Global Village trips are large, group-escorted trips that include work on a Habitat for Humanity building project, as well as other cultural and educational experiences. The costs range from Q7,500 to Q11,250 ($1,000–$1,500/£525– £788), not including airfare, for a 9- to 14-day program.

- **GAP Adventures** ✵ (✆ **800/708-7761** in the U.S. and Canada, or 44/870-999-0144 in the U.K.; www. gapadventures.com) is a major international adventure and educational tour operator with a full plate of theme tours to Guatemala. Options include hard-core adventure activities, language-learning trips, and stints doing volunteer work. Their prices vary according to the trip and activity, but are very competitive.

- **Jim Cline Photo Tours** (✆ **877/ 350-1314** in the U.S. and Canada; www.jimcline.com) is guided by a professional photographer who teaches participants to see Guatemala through the camera lens. The 10-day "Living Maya" tour, limited to nine people, focuses on colonial architecture, colorful markets, small villages, the natural beauty of Lake Atitlán, and the Maya people. Cost is around Q16,500 ($2,200/£1,155) per person, plus airfare.

- **Maya Expeditions** (© 502/2363-4955; www.mayaexpeditions.com) are pioneers in adventure and ecotourism in Guatemala. They offer dozens of tour, activity, and theme options, including Maya archaeology, river rafting, and weaving. They also offer relaxing day tours. They use knowledgeable local guides and bring in academic experts. Contact them for prices.

- **The Sierra Club** ✯ (© 415/977-5588 in the U.S. and Canada; www.sierraclub.org) is an environmental organization that offers a 10-day trip that highlights Maya ruins and the jungle. In their own words, "If you are looking for five-star hotels, copious hot water, and gourmet food, this trip is not for you." This trip runs around Q15,000 ($2,000/£1,050) per person, part of which goes to support the land preservation organization. Airfare is not included.

15 Spanish-Language Programs

Guatemala is a major destination for folks looking to learn or brush up on some Spanish. You can find courses of varying lengths and degrees of intensiveness, and many that include cultural activities and day excursions. Some of the schools have reciprocal relationships with U.S. universities so, in some cases, you can even arrange for college credit. Most Spanish schools can arrange for homestays with a local Guatemalan family for a total-immersion experience. These homestays include a private room and either two or three meals daily taken with the family. Most of the schools integrate excursions and cultural programs into their curriculum. Classes are often small, or even one-on-one, and can last anywhere from 2 to 8 hours a day. Listed below are some of the larger and more established Spanish-language schools, with approximate costs. The majority are located either in Antigua or Quetzaltenango, but there are Spanish-language schools in such far-flung corners of the country as Monterrico and the Petén. Contact the schools for the most current price information.

Guatemalan Spanish is considered one of the most pure, in terms of clarity and pronunciation, in the Americas. Compared to the Spanish spoken in other Latin American countries, Guatemalan Spanish tends to be more clearly enunciated and slightly slower. This is one of the reasons language schools are so popular throughout Guatemala.

Quetzaltenango has the greatest concentration of language schools, followed in short order by Antigua. In broad strokes, the programs in Quetzaltenango are less expensive. In Antigua, you'll pay a slight premium for living and learning in arguably the hippest and most desirable city in the country. That said, in reality, the price difference is negligible for many, and is around Q375 to Q750 ($50–$100/£26–£53) per week. I personally recommend you decide where you want to spend your time and what kind of side trips and extracurricular adventures you might want to enjoy, and choose by location.

- **Academia de Español Guatemala** ✯, 7a Calle Oriente #15, Antigua (©502/7832-5057; www.acad.conexion.com), offers group and one-on-one classes. Their main facility features a lovely garden, with its own swimming pool, as well as free Internet and Wi-Fi connections. A 1-week program including 4 hours of private instruction per day, a homestay, and airport transfers costs Q1,725 ($230/£121).

• **Celas Maya Spanish School,** 6a Calle 14-55, Zona 1, Quetzaltenango (© **502/7761-4342;** www.celasmaya. edu.gt), offers intensive Spanish and Ki'che Mayan language classes. One of the larger and more popular schools in Xela, these folks charge between Q1,125 and Q1,350 ($150–$180/£79–£95) per week, for 5 hours daily of one-on-one instruction, including a homestay with a local family.

• **Centro Lingüístico Maya** ⭐, 5a Calle Poniente, #20, Antigua (© **502/ 7832-0656;** www.clmmaya.com), offers weeklong programs with 4 to 7 hours of private instruction per day. The 4-hour-per-day week runs Q863 ($115/£60), with the homestay costing an extra Q488 ($65/£34) per week.

• **Eco Escuela de Español** ⭐, San Andrés, El Petén (© **502/5940-1235;** www.ecoescuelaespanol.org), is a community-based language school program in a small village on the shore of Lake Petén Itzá. The program costs just Q1,125 ($150/£79) per week, including lodging and three meals daily with a local family, as well as 4 hours of daily class time, usually one-on-one.

• **Escuela de Español San José el Viejo** ⭐⭐, 5a Av. Sur, #34, Antigua (© **502/7832-3028;** www.sanjose elviejo.com), only offers private instruction. Their 32½-hour Monday-through-Friday program costs Q900 ($120/£63), not including room and board. These folks can arrange a local homestay for around Q750 ($100/£53) per week. They also have several very comfortable houses and apartments right on or near their campus.

• **Jardín de América Spanish School** ⭐, Calle 14 de Febrero, Panajachel (© **502/7762-2637;** www.jardinde america.com), is located in downtown Panajachel, just a few blocks from the shores of Lake Atitlán. Their homestay program places students with predominantly local Maya families for an interesting cultural experience. A weeklong program with 4 hours of instruction daily and homestay costs Q1,050 ($140/£74).

• **Proyecto Lingüístico Quezalteco** ⭐, 5a Calle 2-40, Zona 1, Quetzaltenango (© **502/7763-1061;** www. hermandad.com), is a very well-run school that integrates an understanding of Guatemala's social and political context into their learning experience. They actually have two campuses, one in downtown Xela and another in a more rural, mountain setting. A weeklong program, including 5 hours of daily private instruction and a homestay, costs Q1,350 ($180/£95).

• **San Pedro Spanish School,** San Pedro La Laguna, Lake Atitlán (© **502/ 5715-4604;** www.sanpedrospanish school.com), is an excellent little school that even offers classes in the Tz'utujil Mayan dialect. Rates run around Q750–Q1,125 ($100–$150/ £53–£79) per week for 4 hours of classes per day and a homestay with a local family.

• **Ulew Tinimit Spanish School** ⭐, 7a Av. 3-18, Zona 1, Quetzaltenango (© **502/7761-6242;** www.spanish guatemala.org), is one of the better Xela language schools. These folks also offer classes in Ki'che and Mam Mayan dialects. A 1-week program with 5 hours of class instruction daily and a homestay costs Q975 ($130/ £68).

16 Getting Around

SHUTTLE

For most of the major destinations, tourist shuttles or a private car and driver are your best means for getting around. There are a couple of major tourist shuttle services in Guatemala, and almost every hotel tour desk and local tour agency can book you a ride to just about any major tourist destination in the country either on a regularly scheduled shuttle or with a private car and driver.

The main tourist shuttle companies are **Atitrans** ✵ (© **502/7832-3371** 24-hr. reservation number; www.atitrans.com) and **Grayline Guatemala** (© **502/2383-8600;** www.graylineguatemala.com). Both of these companies offer private cars or vans with drivers; or you can contact **Clark Tours** (© **502/2412-4700;** www.clarktours.com.gt), **Maya Vacations** (© **502/233-4638;** www.mayavacations.com), or **Via Venture** ✵✵ (© **502/7832-2509;** www.viaventure.com).

Regularly scheduled shuttle rates from Guatemala City or Antigua to or from other major destinations run around Q90 to Q113 ($12–$15/£6.30–£7.90) for Panajachel; Q135 ($18/£9.45) for Chichicastenango; and Q300 to Q375 ($40–$50/£21–£26) for Flores/Tikal. A private car or van with driver should cost between Q600 and Q1,500 ($80–$200/£42–£105) per day, depending on the size and style of the vehicle and how many passengers are traveling.

BY BUS

This is by far the most economical way to get around Guatemala. Buses are inexpensive and go nearly everywhere in the country. There are two types: **Local buses** are the cheapest and slowest; they stop frequently and are generally very dilapidated. They also tend to be overcrowded, and you are much more likely to be the victim of a robbery on one of these. These buses are commonly referred to as "chicken buses" because the rural residents who depend on these buses often have chickens and other livestock as luggage. For all but the most adventurous types, I recommend you avoid these buses.

Express or **deluxe buses** run between Guatemala City and most beach towns and major cities; these tend to be newer units and much more comfortable. They also tend to be direct buses, thus much quicker. Most have working bathrooms, and some have televisions equipped with DVD players showing late-run movies.

Throughout the book, I've listed schedules and contact information for all the appropriate bus lines in the corresponding destination chapters.

BY CAR

Renting a car in Guatemala is no idle proposition. The roads are often dangerous. Guatemalan drivers, particularly bus and truck drivers, have apparently no concern for human life, their own or anybody else's. A brutal Darwinian survival of the fittest reigns on Guatemala's roads. Passing on blind curves seems to be the national sport. Pedestrians, horses, dogs, and other obstacles seem to appear out of nowhere.

I highly recommend you avoid driving at night at all costs. While rare, there have been armed robberies of tourists and Guatemalans along the highways and back roads of Guatemala, particularly at night. Moreover, the inherent dangers of oncoming traffic and unseen obstacles are heightened at night.

Never leave anything of value in a car. Always try to park in a secure parking lot. If that's not possible, try to find a spot where some local kid or industrious worker will guard your car for a tip.

These caveats aren't meant to entirely scare you off from driving in Guatemala. Thousands of tourists rent cars here every year, and the large majority of them encounter no problems. Renting a car is a good option for independent exploring, and it does provide a lot more freedom and save a lot of time over bus travel. Just keep your wits about you.

Note: It's sometimes cheaper to reserve a car in your home country rather than book when you arrive in Guatemala. If you know you'll be renting a car, it's always wise to reserve it well in advance for the high season because the rental fleet still can't match demand.

Among the agencies operating in Guatemala are: **Avis** (© **800/230-4898** in the U.S. or 502/2231-0017 in Guatemala; www.avis.com), **Budget** (© **800/ 527-0700** in the U.S. or 502/2232-7744 in Guatemala; www.budgetguatemala. com.gt), **Hertz** (© **800/654-3131** in the U.S. or 502/2470-3737 in Guatemala; www.hertz.com), **National** (© **800/227- 7368** in the U.S. or 502/2362-3000 in Guatemala; www.natcar.com), and **Thrifty** (© **800/847-4389** or 502/2379-8747 in Guatemala; www.thrifty.com). **Tabarini** (© **502/2331-2643;** www. tabarini.com) is a good Guatemalan company with offices in Guatemala City, Antigua, and Tikal.

Rates run between Q263 and Q600 ($35–$80/£18–£42) per day, depending upon the size and style of automobile, including unlimited mileage and full insurance.

GASOLINE Gasoline, or *gasolina* in Spanish, is sold as *normal* and *premium;* both are unleaded. Premium is just higher octane. Diesel is available at almost every gas station as well. Most rental cars run on premium, but always ask your rental agent what type of gas your car takes. Gas stations are widely available along the highways, and in all major cities, towns, and tourist destinations. When going off to remote places, try to leave with a full tank of gas because gas stations can be harder to find. At press time, premium cost Q26 ($3.45/£1.80) per gallon.

ROAD CONDITIONS Most of the major highways in Guatemala are in pretty good shape. However, once you venture off the major highways, the situation deteriorates quickly and dramatically.

Again, the major highways and tourist destinations are generally well-marked. Once you get off the beaten path, though, things change, and you may not

Car-Rental Tips

Although it's preferable to use the coverage provided by your home auto-insurance policy or credit card, check carefully to see if the coverage really holds in Guatemala. Many policies exclude 4WD vehicles and off-road driving—some of Guatemala can, in fact, be considered off-road. It's possible at some car-rental agencies to waive the insurance charges, but you'll have to pay all damages before leaving the country if you're in an accident. If you do take the insurance, you can expect a deductible of between $750 and $1,500. At some agencies, you can buy additional insurance to lower the deductible. To rent a car in Guatemala, you must be at least 21 years old and have a valid driver's license and a major credit card in your name. See "Getting Around" in chapter 4 for details on renting a car in Guatemala City. You can also rent cars in Antigua, and in Santa Elena and Flores, near Tikal.

encounter any signs or indications as you pass intersection after intersection.

RENTER'S INSURANCE   Even if you already hold your own **car-insurance policy** at home, coverage doesn't always extend abroad. Be sure to find out whether you'll be covered in Guatemala, whether your policy extends to all persons who will be driving the rental car, how much liability is covered in case an outside party is injured in an accident, and whether the *type* of vehicle you are renting is included under your contract.

Most **major credit cards** provide some degree of coverage as well—provided that they were used to pay for the rental. Again, terms vary widely, so be sure to call your credit card company directly before you rent. Usually, if you are **uninsured** or are **driving abroad,** your credit card provides primary coverage as long as you decline the rental agency's insurance. This means that the credit card will cover damage or theft of a rental car for the full cost of the vehicle. If you already have insurance, your credit card will provide secondary coverage, which basically covers your deductible. *Credit cards will not cover liability* or the cost of injury to an outside party and/or damage to an outside party's vehicle. If you don't hold an insurance policy, you might seriously want to consider purchasing additional liability insurance from your rental company. Be sure to check the terms, however. Some rental agencies cover liability only if the renter is not at fault; even then, the rental company's obligation varies from state to state.

The basic insurance coverage offered by most car rental companies, known as the **Loss/Damage Waiver (LDW)** or **Collision Damage Waiver (CDW),** can cost as much as $20 per day. It usually covers the full value of the vehicle, with no deductible if an outside party causes an accident or other damage to the rental car. Liability coverage varies according to

the company policy. If you're at fault in an accident, however, you will be covered for the full replacement value of the car, but not for liability. Most rental companies require a police report to process any claims you file, but your private insurer will not be notified of the accident.

Before driving off with a rental car, be sure that you inspect the exterior and point out to the rental company representative every tiny scratch, dent, tear, or any other damage. It's a common practice with many Guatemalan car rental companies to claim that you owe payment for minor dings and dents that the company finds when you return the car. Also, if you get into an accident, be sure that the rental company doesn't try to bill you for a higher amount than the deductible on your rental contract.

MAPS   Car rental agencies and the INGUAT information centers (see "Visitor Information," earlier in this chapter) at the airport and in downtown Guatemala City have adequate road maps. The most detailed map available is produced by **International Travel Maps** (www. itmb.com), which was updated in 2005 and is available online from the website listed.

DRIVING RULES   A current foreign driver's license is valid for the length of your 90-day tourist visa. Seat belts are required for the driver and front-seat passengers.

Official driving rules are often ignored. Drivers seldom use turn signals or obey posted speed limits. Transit police are a rarity, but they will bust you for speeding, so keep to the speed limit (usually 60–90kmph/37–56 mph) if you don't want to get pulled over. Never pay money directly to a police officer who stops you for any traffic violation. Speeding tickets can be charged to your credit card for up to a year after you leave the country if they are not paid before departure.

BREAKDOWNS Be warned that emergency services, both vehicular and medical, are extremely limited once you leave Guatemala City, Antigua, or any of the major tourist destinations, and their availability is directly related to the remoteness of your location at the time of breakdown.

If you're involved in a breakdown or accident, you should contact Guatemala's roadside assistance force (PROVIAL; © **502/2422-7878**), which patrols most of the major highways in the country. Alternately, you can call the police at © **110**. Finally, you can also call © **1500**, and they should be able to provide an English-speaking operator and redirect your call to the appropriate agency.

If the police do show up, you've got a fifty-fifty chance of finding them helpful or downright antagonistic. Many officers are unsympathetic to the problems of what they perceive to be rich tourists running around in fancy cars with lots of expensive toys and trinkets. Many are looking for an easy bribe. Success and happy endings run about equal with horror stories.

If you don't speak Spanish, expect added difficulty in any emergency or stressful situation. Don't expect that rural (or urban) police officers, hospital personnel, service-station personnel, or mechanics will speak English.

If your car breaks down and you're unable to get well off the road, check to see whether there are reflecting triangles in the trunk. If there are, place them as a warning for approaching traffic, arranged in a wedge that starts at the shoulder about 30m (98 ft.) back and nudges gradually toward your car. If your car has no triangles, try to create a similar warning marker using a pile of leaves or branches. Finally, there have been some reports of folks being robbed by seemingly friendly good Samaritans who stop to give assistance. To add insult to injury, there have even been reports of organized gangs who puncture tires of rental cars at rest stops or busy intersections, only to follow them, offer assistance, and make off with belongings and valuables.

BY PLANE
Guatemala still doesn't have a very extensive network of commuter airlines. The one major destination regularly serviced by commuter traffic is Tikal. **TACA Regional Airline** (© **502/2279-5821** or 502/2470-8222; www.taca.com) and **TAG Airlines** (© **502/2360-3038**; tag ventas@turbonett.com) both have regular service to Tikal. See chapter 8 for more information.

Charter aircraft can sometimes be hired to travel to some of the more outlying destinations like Quetzaltenango and Puerto Barrios. If you have a big enough group, or big enough budget, and want to charter a plane, contact **Aero Ruta Maya** (© **502/ 2360-4917**) or **TAG Airlines** (© **502/ 2360-3038**; tagventas@turbonett.com).

17 Tips on Accommodations

With the exception of a few large business-class hotels clustered in Guatemala City's Zona Viva, Guatemala has no truly large-scale resorts or hotels. What the country does have is a wealth of intimate and interesting **small to midsize hotels and resorts.** Most of these are quite comfortable and very reasonably priced by most international standards. A few very classy luxury boutique hotels are scattered around the country, and are found with relative abundance in Antigua and around Lake Atitlán. Real budget travelers will find a glut of very acceptable and very inexpensive options all across the country. *Warning:* Budget-oriented lodgings often feature shared bathrooms and either cold-water showers or showers heated by electrical heat-coil units mounted at the showerhead. These are

Autohotels

One type of hotel you may run across, especially in Guatemala City, is an *auto-hotel*. *Autohotels* are not self-service affairs—except for the most desperate. They are, however, semi-discreet operations used mainly for romantic liaisons. Most *autohotels* feature rooms with two-car garages with doors or curtains so that nosy spouses or private-eyes cannot see the license plates. *Autohotels* rent out by the hour, and are usually not of very much interest to the average tourist.

---

affectionately known as "suicide showers." If your hotel has one, do not try to adjust it while the water is running. Unless specifically noted, all the rooms I've listed in this guide have private bathrooms.

Note: Air-conditioning is not necessarily a given in many midscale hotels and even some upscale joints. In general, this is not a problem. Cooler nights and a well-placed ceiling fan are often more than enough to keep things pleasant, unless I mention otherwise in the hotel reviews.

A hotel is sometimes called a *posada* in Guatemala. As a general rule, a *posada* is a smaller, more humble and less luxurious option than a hotel. However, there are some very serious exceptions to this rule, particularly in Antigua, where some of the finest accommodations are called *posadas.*

In general, prices drop dramatically outside of Guatemala City, and the more popular destinations like Antigua, Lake Atitlán, and Tikal. In fact, outside of these destinations, you'll find very few hotel options charging more than Q600 ($80/£42) per night for a double, even for the swankiest room in town.

If you're traveling on a budget and staying in some of the less expensive hotels, one item you're likely to want to bring with you is a towel. Your hotel might not provide one at all, and even if it does, it might be awfully thin.

Throughout this book, I've separated hotel listings into several broad categories: **Very Expensive,** $120 (£63) and up; **Expensive,** $80 to $120 (£42–£63); **Moderate,** $45 to $80 (£24–£42); and

Inexpensive, under $45 (£24) double. *Unless otherwise noted, rates given in this book do not include the 12% IVA and 10% hotel tax.* These taxes will add considerably to the cost of your room, so do factor it in.

Frommer's uses a zero- to three-star rating system. This star system is a relative system, and not necessarily on a par with standard industry star-rating systems. A truly special bed-and-breakfast, run with style and aplomb, may get two or three stars, even though the rooms do not have televisions or air-conditioning. Meanwhile, a large resort with a host of modern amenities may receive one or no stars. Every hotel listed is in some way recommended. This book is selective, and I've done my best to list the best options in each price range and each region, while weeding out the hotels you should not even bother with.

SAVING ON YOUR HOTEL ROOM

The **rack rate** is the maximum rate that a hotel charges for a room. Hardly anybody pays this price, however, except in high season or on holidays. To lower the cost of your room:

- **Ask about special rates or other discounts.** Always ask whether a less expensive room than the first one quoted is available, or whether any special rates apply to you. You may qualify for corporate, student, military, senior, or other discounts. Mention membership in AAA, AARP, frequent-flier programs, or trade unions, which may entitle you to special deals as well. Find out the hotel policy on children—do kids stay free in the room or qualify for a special rate?

- **Dial direct.** When booking a room in a chain hotel, you'll often get a better deal by calling the individual hotel's reservation desk rather than the chain's main number.

- **Book online.** Many hotels offer Internet-only discounts, or supply rooms to Priceline, Hotwire, or Expedia at rates much lower than the ones you can get through the hotel itself. Shop around. And if you have special needs—a quiet room, a room with a view—call the hotel directly and make your needs known after you've booked online.

- **Remember the law of supply and demand.** Resort hotels are most crowded and therefore most expensive on weekends, so discounts are usually available for midweek stays. Business hotels in downtown locations are busiest during the week, so you can expect big discounts over the weekend. Many hotels have high-season and low-season prices, and booking the day after "high season" ends can mean big discounts.

- **Look into group or long-stay discounts.** If you come as part of a large group, you should be able to negotiate a bargain rate, since the hotel can then guarantee occupancy in a number of rooms. Likewise, if you're planning a long stay (at least 5 days), you might qualify for a discount. As a general rule, expect 1 night free after a 7-night stay.

- **Avoid excess charges and hidden costs.** When you book a room, ask whether the hotel charges for parking. Use your own cellphone, pay phones, or prepaid phone cards instead of dialing direct from hotel phones, which usually have exorbitant rates. And don't be tempted by the room's minibar offerings: Most hotels charge through the nose for water, soda, and snacks. Finally, ask about local taxes and service charges, which can increase the cost of a room by 15% or more. If a hotel insists upon tacking on a surprise "energy surcharge" that wasn't mentioned at check-in or a "resort fee" for amenities you didn't use, you can often make a case for getting it removed.

- **Carefully consider your hotel's meal plan.** If you enjoy eating out and sampling the local cuisine, it makes sense to choose a **Continental Plan (CP),** which includes breakfast only, or a **European Plan (EP),** which doesn't include any meals and allows you maximum flexibility. If you're more interested in saving money, opt for a **Modified American Plan (MAP),** which includes breakfast and one meal, or the **American Plan (AP),** which includes three meals. If you must choose a MAP, see if you can get a free lunch at your hotel if you decide to do dinner out.

- **Book an efficiency.** A room with a kitchenette allows you to shop for groceries and cook your own meals. This is a big money saver, especially for families on long stays.

- **Consider enrolling in hotel "frequent-stay" programs,** which are

---

Tips **Dial "E" for Easy**

For quick directions on how to call Guatemala, see the "Telephones" listing in the "Fast Facts: Guatemala" section at the end of this chapter.

upping the ante lately to win the loyalty of repeat customers. Frequent guests can now accumulate points or credits to earn free hotel nights, airline miles, in-room amenities, merchandise, tickets to concerts and events, discounts on sporting facilities—and even credit toward stock in the participating hotel, in the case of the Jameson Inn hotel group. Perks are awarded not only by many chain hotels and motels (Hilton HHonors, Marriott Rewards, Wyndham ByRequest, to name a few), but individual inns and B&Bs. Many chain hotels partner with other hotel chains, car rental firms, airlines, and credit card companies to give consumers additional incentive to do repeat business.

LANDING THE BEST ROOM

Somebody has to get the best room in the house. It might as well be you. You can start by joining the hotel's frequent-guest program, which may make you eligible for upgrades. A hotel-branded credit card usually gives its owner "silver" or "gold" status in frequent-guest programs for free. Always ask about a corner room. They're often larger and quieter, with more windows and light, and they often cost the same as standard rooms. When you make your reservation, ask if the hotel is renovating; if it is, request a room away from the construction. Ask about nonsmoking rooms; rooms with views; rooms with twin, queen- or king-size beds. If you're a light sleeper, request a quiet room away from vending machines, elevators, restaurants, bars, and discos. Ask for a room that has been most recently renovated or redecorated.

If you aren't happy with your room when you arrive, ask for another one. Most lodgings will be willing to accommodate you.

18 Tips on Dining

With the exception of some regional specialties, the most common and prevalent aspects of Guatemalan cuisine are rather unimpressive. Handmade fresh corn tortillas are the most basic staple of Guatemalan cooking. Tortillas, along with refried black beans, are usually served as an accompaniment to some simply grilled meat or chicken. Very few vegetables are typically served at Guatemalan meals.

You will find excellent restaurants serving a wide range of international cuisines in Guatemala City, Antigua, and Panajachel. However, outside the capital and these major tourist destinations, your options get very limited very fast. In fact, many destinations are so small or remote that you have no choice but to eat in the hotel's dining room. Even at the more popular destinations, the only choices aside from the hotel dining rooms are often cheap local places or overpriced tourist traps serving indifferent meals.

If you're looking for cheap eats, you'll find them in little restaurants known as *comedores,* which are the equivalent of diners in the United States. At a *comedor,* you'll find a limited and very inexpensive menu featuring some simple steak and chicken dishes, accompanied by rice, refried beans, and fresh tortillas.

Guatemalans tend to eat three meals a day, in similar fashion and hours to North Americans. Breakfast is usually served between 6:30am and 9am; lunch between noon and 2pm; and dinner between 6 and 10pm. Most meals and dining experiences are quite informal. In fact, there are only a few restaurants in the entire country that could be considered semi-formal, and none require a jacket or tie, although you could certainly wear them.

I have separated restaurant listings throughout this book into three price categories based on the average cost per person of a meal, including tax and service charge. The categories are **Expensive,** more than Q150 ($20/£11); **Moderate,** Q75 to Q150 ($10–$20/£5.25–£11); and **Inexpensive,** less than Q75 ($10/£5.25). Keep in mind that the 12% IVA tax added onto all bills is not a service charge. A tip of at least 10% is expected. If the service was particularly good and attentive, you should probably leave a little extra.

For a more detailed discussion of Guatemalan cuisine and dining, see "Guatemalan Food & Drink" in appendix A.

19 Recommended Books, Films & Music

I find reading books about specific periods of Guatemalan history more enriching than a broad overview, but if you're looking for a sweeping narrative, try Greg Grandin's *The Blood of Guatemala: A History of Race and Nation* (Duke University Press, 2000).

Any foray into Guatemalan literature should begin with *Men of Maize* (*Hombres de Maíz;* University of Pittsburgh Press, 1995) by the country's Nobel prize–winning author Miguel Angel Asturias. Asturias manages to integrate Guatemalan history, Maya mythology, and everyday life into a challenging and riveting prose style. Asturias's *The President* (*El Presidente;* Waveland Press, 1997) is also a very worthwhile read.

Probably the most internationally famous book to come out of Guatemala is *I, Rigoberta Menchú: An Indian Woman in Guatemala* (Verso, 1987), originally published in Spanish as *Me llamo Rigoberta Menchú y así me nació la conciencia,* an oral history of Menchú's revolutionary activities transcribed by t he French anthropologist Elisabeth Burgos-Debray. This book and Menchú's subsequent efforts to draw international attention to the atrocities of the Guatemalan military regime won her the Nobel Peace Prize in 1992, a fitting honor on the 500th anniversary of Columbus's first transatlantic voyage.

Years later, Middlebury College anthropologist David Stoll stirred international controversy when he published *Rigoberta Menchú and the Story of All Poor Guatemalans* (HarperCollins, 2000), which supposedly exposed inconsistencies in Menchú's story. Most pointedly, Stoll considers it unlikely that Menchú could have played a substantial leadership role in a peasant movement given the rigid patriarchy of that society. Menchú has since asserted that some events in the story were invented or embellished by the transcriber, Burgos-Debray. While the Nobel Committee and the international community as a whole have maintained their support for Menchú, you might want to pick up a copy of Stoll's book if only to get a murkier moral picture of that time of war.

For the strong of stomach, the Archdiocese of Guatemala's official report on the human rights abuses of the civil war, abridged and translated into English as *Guatemala: Never Again!* (Orbis Books, 1999), is a powerful history. The report was explosive: Days after delivering it, Bishop Juan Gerardi was bludgeoned to death in his own garage in Guatemala City. It's filled with vivid analysis and testimonials from victims, blaming 80% of the atrocities on the Guatemalan military.

While guided tours and pamphlets available at Maya ruins provide a fair amount of information, those truly seeking an in-depth look at the ancient civilization will want to have some more detailed reference material handy when visiting the many ruins in Guatemala. Recently updated, *The Maya* (Thames and Hudson, 2005), by Michael D. Coe, is a good primer on the history of this advanced and enigmatic culture. However, I find *A Forest of Kings: The Untold Story of the Ancient Maya* (Harper Perennial, 1992) by David Freidel and Linda Schele to be a better read, which gives a better feel for what life was like in the Maya world. To delve into the intricacy and reasoning behind the Maya aesthetic legacy, check out Mary Ellen Miller's book, *Maya Art and Architecture* (Thames and Hudson, 1999).

There is a host of excellent books specifically about Tikal. *Tikal: An Illustrated History of the Ancient Maya Capital,* by John Montgomery (Hippocrene Books, 2001), is a good place to start. *The Lords of Tikal: Rulers of an Ancient Maya City,* by Peter D. Harrison, et al. (Thames & Hudson, 2000), is a similar option. Although out of print, you might want to try to find a copy of *Tikal: Handbook of the Ancient Maya Ruins,* by William R. Coe, written under the auspices of the University Museum of the University of Pennsylvania. Archaeologists from the university, working in conjunction with Guatemalan officials, did most of the excellent excavation work at Tikal from 1956 to 1969. Birders will want to have a copy of *The Birds of Tikal: An Annotated Checklist* by Randall A. Beavers (Texas A&M University Press, 1992), or *The Birds of Tikal* by Frank B. Smithe (Natural History Press, 1966). The latter three books are hard to find, but you should be able to order used copies in the United States, and you can usually find copies of all of these in Flores or at Tikal.

The Popol Vuh, the Quiché Maya holy book, is a must-read for a window into traditional religious life and ancient culture. "This is the beginning of the ancient word," the mystical book begins, going on to detail the origins of human flesh in corn and the interventions of water-dwelling feathered serpents. In 1972, the Popul Vuh was declared Guatemala's National Book. Several good translations into English exist, including Dennis Tedlock's *Popol Vuh: The Definitive Edition Of The Mayan Book Of The Dawn Of Life And The Glories Of Gods and Kings* (Touchstone Press, 1996) and Allen J. Christenson's *Popol Vuh: The Sacred Book of the Mayas* (O Books, 2004).

Immensely popular in its day was *Incidents of Travel in Central America, Chiapas and Yucatan* (Volumes 1 and 2, originally published in 1841), a collection of descriptions of Maya sites by the American explorer and diplomat John Lloyd Stephens, featuring the illustrations of artist Frederick Catherwood. If you're looking for more contemporary works on the more contemporary Maya, *Scandals in the House of Birds* (Marsillo, 1997) by Nathaniel Tarn is a highly regarded, highly poetic ethnography of the Tz'utujil in Santiago de Atitlán.

If you're bringing along the little ones, or even if you're leaving them behind but want to share a bit of Maya culture with them, look for Pat Mora's beautifully illustrated book *The Night the Moon Fell: a Maya Myth* (Groundwood Books, 2000). Or, for a handy little picture book filled with photographs of Maya daily life, check out *Hands of the Maya: Villagers at Work and Play* by Rachel Crandell (Henry Holt & Company, 2002).

If you're taken by the marimba and the sounds of traditional Guatemalan music, you can find a good selection of compilation discs at www.cduniverse.com or www.towerrecords.com. I'd avoid the various vendors selling bootleg cassettes and CDs on the side of the road in Guatemala, since the quality can be sketchy, and the artists don't receive a dime. If you see a group you like while touring Guatemala, it is increasingly likely, though far from certain, that they will have a recording for sale. On the Caribbean coast you might hear a style called *punta* rock, a kind of Afro-rock and reggae fusion based on Garífuna rhythms. The Belize-based www. stonetreerecords.com or www.calabash music.com offer a good selection of *punta* records.

My favorite contemporary Guatemalan musician is Ricardo Arjona, a rocking songster and lyricist of the first order. Songs such as "Ella y El" ("She and He") and "Si el Norte Fuera el Sur" ("If North Were South") are smart works of social and political satire with very catchy melodies. Check out Arjona's *12 Grandes Exitos* (12 Greatest Hits, 2003) album. For a taste of quintessential '80s Guatemalan rock, look no further than the group Alux Nahual (www.aluxnahual. com) and their self-titled 1981 debut. Subsequent albums, including *Conquista*

(1982) and *Alto al fuego* (1987) helped establish the band as one of Guatemala's most famous and musically talented (though if you want to buy a disc, get the 1994 compilation *Leyenda I* or the 2001 *Antología I*). The group officially broke up in 1999, but you might be lucky enough to catch a reunion tour.

The Guatemalan film industry is still in its infancy. However, the country has had subtle appearances in mainstream American productions. If you need an excuse to watch *Star Wars* (Episode IV) again, look for Tikal in a cameo role as the Rebel Base (the "Massassi Outpost on the fourth moon of Yavin," for die-hard fans) toward the end of the movie. The 11th season of *Survivor* was also filmed at the Maya ruins of Yaxhá, and the tribes were named after ancient ceremonial cities.

FAST FACTS: Guatemala

American Express Clark Tours (© 502/2412-4700; www.clarktours.com.gt) is the official representative of American Express Travel Services in Guatemala. Their main offices are in Guatemala City at Clark Plaza, 7a Av. 14-76, Zona 9. They also have desks at the downtown Westin and Marriott hotels. To report lost or stolen Amex traveler's checks within Guatemala, call the local number above, or call © 801/964-6665 collect in the U.S.

Area Codes There are no regional area codes in Guatemala. Most phone numbers are eight digits. However, there are some anomalies. Some toll-free or public service numbers may be three-, four-, or six-digit numbers.

ATM Networks Guatemala has a well-developed network of ATMs. Just about every bank branch in the country, particularly in the major cities, towns, and tourist destinations, has an ATM or two. While many of Guatemala's ATMs will work fine with five- and six-digit PINs, some will only accept four-digit PINs. Before traveling, it's wise to change your PIN to avoid any unexpected hassles in getting access to quick cash.

Business Hours Banks are usually open Monday through Friday from 9am to 4pm, although many have begun to offer extended hours. Offices are open Monday through Friday from 8am to 5pm (many close for 1 hr. at lunch). Stores are generally open Monday through Saturday from 9am to 6pm (many close for 1 hr. at lunch). Stores in modern malls generally stay open until 8 or 9pm and don't close for lunch. Most bars are open until 1 or 2am.

Cameras & Film While I recommend bringing as much film as you foresee needing, and then waiting until you return home to develop it, if you'd rather not wait, your best bet is to head to one of the many branches of **Quick Photo** (© 502/2368-0600) or **Fuji Film** (© 502/2420-3900), both of which offer 1-hour developing service, as well as digital printing services, and carry a wide range of films, camera accessories, and replacement parts. Although your chances of having any serious repair work done are slim, you can head to one of the many branches of the chains mentioned above. Some of these have technicians on hand and carry a limited range of replacement and repair parts.

Car Rentals See "Getting Around" on p. 59.

Currency See "Money" on p. 22.

Driving Rules See "Getting Around" on p. 59.

Drugstores A drugstore or pharmacy is called a *farmacia* in Spanish. In Guatemala, they are also sometimes called *droguería*. Drugstores are relatively common throughout the country, although not necessarily well stocked. Those at hospitals and major clinics are often open 24 hours.

Electricity Guatemala uses standard U.S.-style two- and three-prong electric outlets with 110-volt AC current.

Embassies & Consulates All major consulates and embassies, where present, are in Guatemala City. **Canada,** 13a Calle 8-44, Zona 10 (© 502/2363-4348; www.guatemala.gc.ca); **United Kingdom,** Avenida de la Reforma and 16a Calle, Torre Internacional, Zona 10 (© 502/2367-5425; embassy@intelnett.com); and the **United States,** Av. de la Reforma 7-01, Zona 10 (© 502/2326-4000; www.usembassy.state.gov/guatemala).

Emergencies In case of any emergency, dial © **1500** from anywhere in Guatemala. This will connect you to **Asistur,** which will have a bilingual operator, who in turn can put you in contact with the police, fire department, or ambulance service, as necessary. Alternately, you can dial © **110** for the National Police; and © **125** for the Red Cross (Cruz Roja, in Spanish). Moreover, © **911** works as an emergency number from most phones in Guatemala.

Etiquette & Customs There are no overarching etiquette or customs concerns for visitors to Guatemala, though it is very important to respect the predominant Maya culture.

APPROPRIATE ATTIRE: In business situations, a suit or dressy women's clothing is appropriate. In all other situations, casual clothing is the norm. Tourists should be very careful about wearing traditional Maya garb. Many pieces of Maya dress carry specific gender, social, and cultural significance. If not a downright offense, it is seen as somewhat ridiculous when foreign men don an exclusively female piece of clothing. Women travelers run a similar risk.

AVOIDING OFFENSE: Guatemala's Maya population is relatively reserved and private. Most Maya are very wary of having their photographs taken, and it is considered impolite and even aggressive to do so without asking permission first. In many tourist destinations, local Maya will readily allow themselves to be photographed for a fee of a few *quetzales. The Global Etiquette Guide To Mexico and Latin America* (Wiley Publishing, Inc.) has a short chapter on Guatemala.

Holidays See "Guatemala Calendar of Events," earlier in this chapter.

Information See "Visitor Information," earlier in this chapter.

Internet Access Internet cafes are very common in all the major cities and tourist destinations around Guatemala. Rates run between Q3 and Q15 (40¢–$2/20p–£1.05) per hour.

Language Spanish is the official language of Guatemala. English is spoken at most tourist hotels, restaurants, and attractions. Outside of the tourist orbit, English is not widely spoken, and some rudimentary Spanish will go a long way. Some 23 Mayan dialects are also widely spoken around the country. In many rural areas, many residents speak their local dialect as their primary language, and a certain segment of the population may speak little or no Spanish.

Laundry Most folks rely on their hotel's laundry and dry cleaning services, although these can be expensive. The more popular tourist destinations have self-service and full-service laundromats as an alternative.

Liquor Laws The legal drinking age is 18, although it's almost never enforced. Liquor, everything from beer to hard spirits, is sold in specific liquor stores, as well as at most supermarkets and even convenience stores.

Lost & Found Be sure to tell all of your credit card companies the minute you discover your wallet has been lost or stolen, and file a report at the nearest police precinct. Your credit card company or insurer may require a police report number or record of the loss. Most credit card companies have an emergency toll-free number to call if your card is lost or stolen; they may be able to wire you a cash advance immediately or deliver an emergency credit card in a day or two. To report a lost or stolen **American Express** card from inside Guatemala, you can call ✆ **0800/012-3211**, or call collect to ✆ **336/393-1111** in the U.S.; for **MasterCard,** ✆ **800/999-1480**, or call collect to ✆ **636/722-7111** in the U.S.; for **Visa,** ✆ **800/999-0115**, or call collect to ✆ **410/581-9994** in the U.S.; and for **Diners Club,** call ✆ **502/2338-6801**, or call collect to ✆ **303/799-1504**.

If you need emergency cash over the weekend when all banks and American Express offices are closed, you can have money wired to you via **Western Union** (✆ **800/325-6000**; www.westernunion.com).

Identity theft and fraud are potential complications of losing your wallet, especially if you've lost your driver's license along with your cash and credit cards. Notify the major credit-reporting bureaus immediately; placing a fraud alert on your records may protect you against liability for criminal activity. The three major U.S. credit-reporting agencies are **Equifax** (✆ **800/766-0008**; www.equifax.com), **Experian** (✆ **888/397-3742**; www.experian.com), and **TransUnion** (✆ **800/680-7289**; www.transunion.com). Finally, if you've lost all forms of photo ID, call your airline and explain the situation; they might allow you to board the plane if you have a copy of your passport or birth certificate and a copy of the police report you've filed.

Mail A post office is called *correo* in Spanish. Most towns have a main *correo*, usually right near the central square. In addition, most hotels will post letters and post cards for you. It costs around Q5 (65¢/35p) to send a letter to the U.S. or Europe. Postcards to the same destinations cost Q3 (40¢/20p). However, it's best to send anything of any value via an established international courier service. **DHL,** 12a Calle 5-12, Zona 10 (✆ **502/2234-1704**; www.dhl.com) and **UPS,**

12a Calle 5-53, Zona 10 (℃ 502/2231-2421; www.ups.com), both have offices in Guatemala City, with nationwide coverage for pickup and delivery. DHL also has offices in Antigua and Panajachel. *Beware:* Despite what you may be told, packages sent overnight to U.S. addresses tend to take 3 to 4 days to reach their destination.

Maps **INGUAT (Guatemalan Tourism Commission;** ℃ 502/2421-2854; www.visit guatemala.com) will provide you with a pretty acceptable map that has the entire country on one side, and Guatemala City and Antigua on the other. The map is free, and you can pick one up at their booth at the airport, or by visiting their downtown office at 7a Av. 1-17, Zona 4.

Newspapers & Magazines La Prensa Libre is the country's most highly regarded daily newspaper, with an outstanding investigative reporting staff. The lower-brow *Nuestro Diario* has the highest circulation. There are several other daily papers, including *Siglo XXI*. There are currently no English-language newspapers. The free, monthly **Revue Magazine** (www.revuemag.com) is the most valuable locally produced information source, with museum, art gallery, and theater listings. It is widely available at hotels and other tourist haunts around the country.

Passports **For Residents of the United States:** Whether you're applying in person or by mail, you can download passport applications from the U.S. State Department website at **http://travel.state.gov**. To find your regional passport office, either check the U.S. State Department website, or call the **National Passport Information Center** toll-free number (℃ **877/487-2778**) for automated information.

For Residents of Canada: Passport applications are available at travel agencies throughout Canada or from the central **Passport Office,** Department of Foreign Affairs and International Trade, Ottawa, ON K1A 0G3 (℃ **800/567-6868;** www.ppt.gc.ca).

For Residents of the United Kingdom: To pick up an application for a standard 10-year passport (5-year passport for children under 16), visit your nearest passport office, major post office, or travel agency, contact the **United Kingdom Passport Service** at ℃ **0870/521-0410**, or search its website at www.ukpa.gov.uk.

For Residents of Ireland: You can apply for a 10-year passport at the **Passport Office,** Setanta Centre, Molesworth Street, Dublin 2 (℃ **01/671-1633**; www.irl gov.ie/iveagh). Those under age 18 and over 65 must apply for a €12 3-year passport. You can also apply at 1A South Mall, Cork (℃ **021/272-525**), or at most main post offices.

For Residents of Australia: You can pick up an application from your local post office or any branch of Passports Australia, but you must schedule an interview at the passport office to present your application materials. Call the **Australian Passport Information Service** at ℃ **131-232**, or visit the government website at www.passports.gov.au.

For Residents of New Zealand: You can pick up a passport application at any New Zealand Passports Office or download it from their website. Contact the **Passports Office** at ℃ **0800/225-050** in New Zealand or 04/474-8100, or log on to www.passports.govt.nz.

Pets If you want to bring your pet to Guatemala, you should first consult the Guatemalan embassy or consulate in your country. You will need to have a certified proof from a recognized veterinarian that your pet is free from all communicable diseases and current with all required vaccines. This proof must then be verified and approved by the Guatemalan authorities.

Police You can contact the **Policía Nacional (National Police)** by dialing ℂ **110** from any telephone in the country. The **tourist police (POLITUR)** is a small, specialized division of the larger police force, created to patrol specific tourist areas and specially trained to deal with tourists. Dial ℂ **502/5561-2073** to contact the tourism police. In the case of emergency, ℂ **911** will work from most phones. You can also call ℂ **1500**. This will connect you to Asistur, which will have a bilingual operator who in turn can put you in contact with the police, fire department, or ambulance service, as necessary.

Restrooms Public restrooms are hard to come by in Guatemala. You must usually count on the generosity of some hotel or restaurant, or duck into a museum or other attraction. Although it's rare that a tourist would be denied the use of the facilities, you should always ask first.

Safety See "Health & Safety," earlier in this chapter.

Smoking While not as bad as most of Europe, a large number of Guatemalans smoke, and public smoking regulations and smoke-free zones have yet to take hold. Restaurants are required by law to have nonsmoking areas, but enforcement is often lax, air circulation poor, and the separation almost nonexistent. Bars, discos, and clubs, on the whole, are often very smoke-filled in Guatemala.

Taxes There is a Q225 ($30/£16) tax that must be paid upon departure. Sometimes this is included in your airline ticket price. Be sure to check in advance. If not, you will have to pay the fee in cash at the airport. There is an additional airport security fee of Q20 ($2.65/£1.40). A 12% IVA (value added) tax is tacked on to the purchase of all goods and services. An additional 10% tax, on top of the 12% IVA, is added to all hotel rooms and lodgings.

Telephones **To call Guatemala:** If you're calling Guatemala from the United States:

1. Dial the international access code: 011.
2. Dial the country code 502.
3. Dial the number. The whole number you'd dial for a number in Guatemala would be 011-502-XXXX-XXXX.

To make international calls: To make international calls from Guatemala, first dial 00 and then the country code (U.S. or Canada 1, U.K. 44, Ireland 353, Australia 61, New Zealand 64). Next, dial the area code and number. For example, if you want to call the British Embassy in Washington, D.C., dial 00-1-202-588-7800.

For directory assistance: Dial ℂ **2333-1524** if you're looking for a number inside Guatemala, and dial ℂ **147-120** for numbers to all other countries.

For operator assistance: If you need operator assistance in making a call, dial ℂ **147-120** if you're trying to make an international call, and ℂ **147-110** if you want to call a number in Guatemala.

Toll-free numbers: There's no hard and fast rule about toll-free numbers in Guatemala. Numbers beginning with 0800 and 800 are almost always toll-free. However, some toll-free numbers are anomalies. Three-, four- and six-digit phone numbers are also often toll-free. Calling a 1-800 number in the U.S. from Guatemala is not toll-free. In fact, it costs the same as an overseas call.

Time Zone Guatemala is 6 hours behind Greenwich Mean Time, which is equivalent to Central Standard Time in the United States. It observed daylight saving time for the first time in 2006. It remains to be seen whether the country will continue to observe it. Daylight saving time is observed by setting clocks ahead 1 hour from the last Sunday in March to the last Sunday in October.

Tipping While there is a 12% IVA tax on all goods and services, none of this counts as a tip. In restaurants, a minimum tip of 10% is common and expected. Tip more if the service was exemplary. Taxi drivers do not expect, and are rarely given, a tip. Porters and bellmen should receive a Q3.75 to Q7.5 (50¢–$1/25p–50p) tip per bag.

Useful Phone Numbers **U.S. Dept. of State Travel Advisory** (② 202/647-5225; manned 24 hr.), **U.S. Passport Agency** (② 202/647-0518), **U.S. Centers for Disease Control International Traveler's Hot Line** (② 404/332-4559).

For directory assistance, call ② **2333-1524;** for an international operator and directory assistance, call ② **147-120.** To dial a direct international call, dial ② 00 + the country code + the area code + the phone number. To get the current time, dial ② **2333-1526.**

Water Drink only bottled water within Guatemala City and be especially careful to do so when traveling outside the capital, as water-borne diseases are very common in this country.

3

Suggested Guatemala Itineraries

From the natural beauty of Lake Atitlán and the country's colorful markets to the perfectly preserved architecture of Tikal and the thundering drums and dances of the Garífuna people, there's something for everyone in Guatemala.

By far the safest and easiest way to get around Guatemala is by small tourist shuttles and minivans. Several major shuttle companies and local tour agencies offer daily transfers between the country's major destinations. **Atitrans** (© **502/7832-3371** for 24-hr. reservation number; www.atitrans.com) and **Grayline Guatemala** (© **502/2383-8600;** www.grayline guatemala.com) are the best and most extensive shuttle services. Most fares run between Q90 and Q150 ($12–$20/ £6.30–£11). Alternatively, you can take the local bus lines, particularly those that offer deluxe or luxury class service. Despite the deluxe and luxury designations, this is a very economical means of travel, with fares averaging between Q30 and Q75 ($4–$10/£2.10–£5.25). The only major destination in Guatemala served by regular commuter airline service is Tikal. Those in a time crunch should fly, but if you can, I suggest traveling to Tikal by land, stopping in Cobán, Copán, and Lago Izabal along the way.

The following itineraries are designed to show you the best the country has to offer, with specific routes depending on your interests and travel companions. You can follow them to the letter or use them as basic guidelines, mixing and matching destinations, activities, and attractions from the rest of this book.

1 Guatemala in 1 Week

One week will allow you enough time to visit (and actually enjoy) four of Guatemala's prime destinations. This itinerary takes you to the best of Guatemala, and includes a colonial city, a breathtaking natural wonder, an extensive traditional market, and spectacular ancient Maya ruins. Not bad for 1 week.

Day ❶: Antigua
Once you arrive in Guatemala, head straight to Antigua, check into your hotel, and hit the streets. Get familiar with the city by starting out at **Plaza Mayor** ✺✺ (p. 127) in the center of town. Have a sunset cocktail at the **Sky Bar** at **Café Sky** ✺ (p. 138), and end the night with dinner at **Welten** ✺✺ (p. 136). If the weather's nice, be sure to grab a table near the pool.

Day ❷: The Colonial Core
Start your morning by visiting the major attractions around the city's colonial core. There are almost too many sights to see,

Guatemala in 1 Week

Ancient Ruins

0 40 mi
0 40 km

El Mirador
Carmelita
Río Azul
Belize City

Piedras Negras
Lacandón
Tikal
4 Tikal
Belize
Belmopan

Yaxhá
Flores
Melchor de Mencos

BELIZE

Sayaxché
Ixkun
El Ceibal
Poptún
San Luis

Cancuén

MEXICO

CARIBBEAN SEA

Barillas
Chisec
Livingston

Soloma
El Golfete
Río Dulce
Puerto Barrios

Huehuetenango
Cobán
El Estor
Lago Izabal

Santa Cruz Verapaz
Los Amates

Quiriguá

Santa Cruz del Quiché
Chichicastenango
Salamá
Zacapa
Copán

Totonicapán
3 Sololá
Guastatoya

Quetzaltenango
Lake Atitlán
Chimaltenango
Jalapa
Chiquimula

Takalik Abaj
2
Antigua
1 Guatemala City

Retalhuleu
Ocós
Mazatenango

HONDURAS

Champerico
Escuintla
Cuilapa
Jutiapa

Tulate
Semillero
Puerto San José
Iztapa

PACIFIC OCEAN
Tecojate
Sipacate
Monterrico

EL SALVADOR

1 Antigua
2 Lake Atitlán
3 Chichicastenango
4 Tikal

---

and it may be hard to choose. Your best bet is to sign up for a walking tour with **Antigua Tours** (p. 126). Many of their tours are led by longtime resident and well-known author Elizabeth Bell.

Spend the afternoon shopping at Antigua's fabulous shops, galleries, and local markets.

Don't miss the opportunity to have dinner, and perhaps a little jazz, at **Mesón Panza Verde** (p. 132). Toast your second night in the city with high-end tequila and mescal at **Tequila Bar** (p. 143).

Day **3**: Lake Atitlán

Since this is a relatively tight itinerary, I recommend you stay in or around **Panajachel** (p. 146). Spend the day walking around town, and be sure to visit the **Museo Lacustre Atitlán** (p. 151). For a good hike through some beautiful foliage, head to the **Reserva Natural Atitlán** (p. 151). Splurge for dinner with a meal at **Hotel Atitlán** (p. 153).

Day **4**: Around the Lake

Set aside the whole day to visit some of the other cities and towns around Lake Atitlán. Sign up for an organized tour, or head down to the docks and climb aboard one of the public boat taxis. You won't have time to visit the more than half-dozen towns and villages around the lake, but you must visit **Santiago de Atitlán** (p. 162). After that, and as time allows, I recommend **Santa Catarina Palopó** (p. 167) and **San Pedro La Laguna** (p. 157).

Day ⑤: Chichicastenango

Take a day trip to the **market in Chichicastenango** ✪✪✪ (p. 173). Chichicastenango, or Chichi, is a little more than an hour's drive from Panajachel, and all of the local tour agencies and hotel tour desks in Panajachel can arrange a guided tour or simple transfer. Even if you come here just to shop, be sure to take some time to visit the **Iglesia de Santo Tomás** ✪✪ (p. 174) and the **Museo de las Máscaras Ceremoniales** ✪ (p. 175).

You'll get back to Panajachel with plenty of time to enjoy the evening. Head to the **Sunset Café** (p. 156) for a namesake cocktail, and then head over to **El Bistro** ✪ (p. 156) for dinner. End your evening with a drink at the **Circus Bar** ✪✪ (p. 157).

Note: Chichicastenango's market is only open on Thursday and Sunday. Feel free to swap this day of the itinerary with any of the other 2 days around Lake Atitlán to match the market day schedule.

Days ⑥ & ⑦: Tikal ✪✪✪

In my opinion, **Tikal** (p. 195) is the most impressive ancient Maya city in all of Mesoamerica. You'll probably have to leave Panajachel at an ungodly hour to catch your flight to Tikal, but it'll be worth it. I suggest spending 1 night in the Tikal area, and true Maya buffs will want to stay at one of the hotels right at the archaeological site, which will allow you extra hours to explore. Those with a more passing interest will be better off staying in Flores or at one of the hotels on the lake.

Early international flights from Aurora International Airport in Guatemala City are hard to catch if you're flying from Tikal the same date, so you may have to adjust your itinerary to allow an overnight in either Antigua or Guatemala City before your flight home.

2 Guatemala in 2 Weeks

If you've got 2 weeks, you'll be able to hit all the highlights mentioned above, as well as some others, including the Caribbean coast and Lago Izabal. You'll also have time in Guatemala City, which has wonderful museums, restaurants, and nightlife.

Days ① & ②: Guatemala City

For this itinerary, I recommend booking a hotel in Zona 10, also known as **Zona Viva.** Once you've set your bags down, spend the afternoon at the side-by-side museums **Museo Ixchel del Traje Indígena** ✪✪ (p. 111) and **Museo Popol Vuh** ✪ (p. 111). The first deals almost entirely with the history, manufacturing, and artistry of traditional Guatemalan Maya textiles, while the latter provides a concise yet broad overview of Maya history.

Make dinner reservations at **Jake's** ✪✪ (p. 104), and spend the rest of the evening walking around Zona Viva, one of the city's few safe neighborhoods,

ducking into any bar or nightclub that strikes your fancy.

Begin Day 2 in Guatemala City's colonial center, or Zona 1. Start at **Plaza Mayor** ✪ (p. 109), referred to by some locals as "the center of all Guatemala," and make your way to the **Catedral Metropolitana** ✪✪ (p. 108) and the **Palacio Nacional** ✪ (p. 109). Take a break on a bench in one of the open-air plazas, and do some people-watching.

For dinner, reserve a table at **Tamarindos** ✪✪✪ (p. 104), my favorite restaurant in the city. After dinner, you'll want to explore the cafes, pubs, bars, and discos in **Cuatro Grados Norte** (p. 103), a hip section of Zona 4.

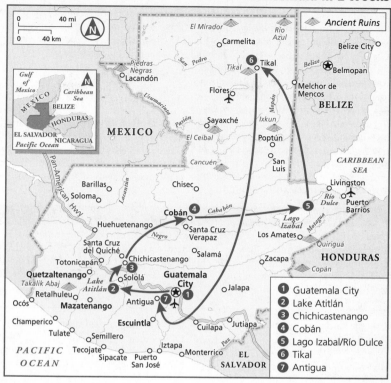

Guatemala in 2 Weeks

Ancient Ruins

Legend:
1. Guatemala City
2. Lake Atitlán
3. Chichicastenango
4. Cobán
5. Lago Izabal/Río Dulce
6. Tikal
7. Antigua

Days ❸, ❹ & ❺

For these days, follow the itinerary for the same 3 days in "Guatemala in 1 Week," above, beginning at Lake Atitlán and visiting Chichicastenango on market day.

Days ❻ & ❼: Cobán & Alta Verapaz

On your way to Cobán and the Alta Verapaz, be sure to stop at the **Biotopo del Quetzal** ⊛ (p. 232). Spend a couple hours hiking there and marveling at the richness of the tropical cloud forest. If you're very lucky, you may even spot a resplendent quetzal, the national bird of Guatemala.

Spend the afternoon in the small mountain city of Cobán. Visit the **Príncipe Maya Museum** ⊛⊛ (p. 226), and stop at the **Hotel La Posada** ⊛

(p. 230) for a break, some coffee, and a view of the town's main plaza.

Wake up early the next morning, and head for **Semuc Champey** ⊛⊛⊛ (p. 228), a stunning series of pools and waterfalls located about 2 hours out of town. Stop at the small town of **Lanquin**, but bypass the caves until later in the day. After you're done with Semuc Champey, try the new cave tour at **Kan' Ba** ⊛⊛ (p. 228). If you've still got the energy, head back to the **caves at Lanquin** (p. 228) around sunset, and watch the amazing spectacle of thousands of bats exiting the cave in search of food.

Days ❽ & ❾: Lago Izabal

From Cobán, head to **Lago Izabal** ⊛⊛ (p. 255) and the rough-and-tumble town of Fronteras. Get a cabin over the water at the **Catamaran Island Hotel** ✿ (p. 257). In the afternoon, take a boat tour to **El Castillo de San Felipe** ✿ (p. 251), and then go for dinner at the **Restaurante Río Bravo** ✿, which is also built out over the water. On the following day, take a **day tour down the Río Dulce to Livingston** ✿✿ (p. 251). The boat ride in each direction is stunning. In Livingston, you'll want to wander the few streets of this small Garífuna town. For lunch, order a plate of the local specialty, *tapado*, a seafood soup made with coconut milk.

Though time is short, I also recommend hiring a boat in Livingston for a trip to **Los Siete Altares** ✿✿ (p. 249), a beautiful series of jungle waterfalls.

Days ⑩ & ⑪: Tikal ✿✿✿
Follow the outline for days 6 and 7 in "Guatemala in 1 Week," above.

Days ⑫, ⑬ & ⑭: Antigua ✿✿✿
You'll finish up in **Antigua** (p. 120), Guatemala's most picturesque and enjoyable city. Follow the outline for "Antigua in 3 Days," below.

3 Guatemala for Families

Guatemala's not the typical family destination, but if your kids are inquisitive and adventurous, there's plenty here to keep them occupied and interested. Locals are quite friendly and accommodating to children, and you'll find a few hotels or attractions specifically geared toward families. This 10-day itinerary is designed for families with athletic and adventurous kids.

Day ❶: Antigua ✿✿✿
Arrive and head straight to **Antigua** (p. 120). Check into your hotel, and spend the afternoon walking the rugged cobblestone streets and getting to know this colonial-era city. Teenage boys will get a kick out of the central fountain on the **Plaza Mayor** ✿✿ (p. 127). In the afternoon, head up to the **Cerro de la Cruz** ✿ (p. 128) for a beautiful panoramic view of Antigua and the volcanoes that surround it. Parents might want to steal some time for shopping or a romantic dinner. Many hotels in Antigua have, or can arrange for, babysitters.

Day ❷: Volcán Pacaya
Venture 1½ hours outside of Antigua to the active **Volcán Pacaya** ✿✿ (p. 144). The climb is strenuous, but in the end you'll be treated to an otherworldly scene of volcanic smoke, ash, and recently molten lava. The descent can include some "ash skiing," which will appeal to any skateboarders or snowboarders in your group.

Day ❸: Quetzaltenango
Drive north to the bustling city of **Quetzaltenango** (p. 180). After settling into your hotel, use the afternoon to visit the small town of **San Andrés Xecul** (p. 185) and its church. The church is painted in a dizzying mass of bold primary colors, and the intricate facade is not to be missed. After marveling at the main church, head uphill to the town's smaller church, where you're likely to see locals praying in a vacant lot and cemetery just next to the church.

Day ❹: Around Quetzaltenango
Active families will want to spend this day climbing **Volcán Santa María** ✿✿ (p. 184). At 3,677m (12,256 ft.), this is a long and challenging climb, but the view from the top is impressive. I especially like staring down into the crater of Santa María's very active sister volcano **Santiaguito.** Less athletic families might opt to visit the **Laguna de Chicabal** ✿ (p. 186), a pretty lake formed inside the crater of

Guatemala for Families

1. Antigua
2. Volcán Pacaya
3. Quetzaltenango
4. Xocomil and Xetulul
5. Cobán
6. Lago Izabal/ Río Dulce
7. Livingston
8. Guatemala City

Ancient Ruins

MEXICO

BELIZE

HONDURAS

EL SALVADOR

CARIBBEAN SEA

PACIFIC OCEAN

an extinct volcano. Real laid-back families can opt to soak in the sulfur hot springs at **Las Fuentes Georginas** ✿ (p. 184).

Day ⑤: Time for a Theme Park

Take a day trip from Quetzaltenango to the side-by-side water and theme park attractions of **Xocomil** ✿✿ (p. 275) and **Xetulul** ✿ (p. 275). Make sure your kids don't focus on comparing this to Disney World or Six Flags. Instead, have them relish in the fact that they're in Guatemala and have a chance to interact with local kids. If I had to pick, I would choose the Xocomil water park, though you can easily visit both in 1 day. Both feature plenty of modern rides and attractions, including those with an ancient Maya theme and design.

Day ⑥: Cobán

Guatemala's Alta Verapaz region is a beautiful area of wild forests, raging rivers, and extensive cave networks. The drive here will take up much of your day, but be sure to stop at the **Biotopo del Quetzal** ✿ (p. 232) on the way. Spend a couple hours hiking and see if your kids can spot a resplendent quetzal, the national bird of Guatemala.

Day ⑦: Semuc Champey ✿✿✿

Semuc Champey (p. 228) is often described as the most beautiful spot in Guatemala, and I agree. To get here, sign up for a tour from Cobán. After you're done with Semuc Champey, try the cave tour at **Kan' Ba** ✿✿ (p. 228). At the end of the cave tour, ask for an inner tube, and float down the Cahabón River to Hostal Las Marias, where you can have lunch. Time your day so that you can visit the **caves at Lanquin** (p. 228) in the late afternoon, when thousands of bats exit the cave mouth to feed.

Day ❽: Río Dulce

From Cobán, head to the town of Fronteras on the Río Dulce. Kids will love staying in an over-water cabin at the **Catamaran Island Hotel** ✿ (p. 257). If you can drag the kids away from the pool, take an afternoon boat tour to **El Castillo de San Felipe** ✿ (p. 251), where they can imagine themselves pirates storming the castle.

Day ❾: Livingston

In the early morning take a boat down the Río Dulce to Livingston. The boat ride is beautiful. In Livingston, check into the **Hotel Villa Caribe** ✿✿ (p. 252),

which has a lovely setting overlooking the ocean and the best pool on Guatemala's Caribbean coast. Spend the day on a guided hike to **Los Siete Altares** ✿✿ (p. 249) with a local Garífuna guide. The tour should take you through town and then on a brief dugout canoe ride through some mangroves, leaving you on the beach a few miles from the waterfalls. (You can hike here.) Active kids will enjoy jumping off the top of the tallest waterfall here, but parents should use discretion in deciding if you think it's safe for their child. For dinner, reserve a table at the Hotel Villa Caribe, which features a nightly presentation of Garífuna drumming and dancing.

Day ❿: Fly Home

You'll have to take a very early boat out of Livingston, but you should have plenty of time to get from Livingston to Guatemala City in time for your return flight home.

4 Maya Ruins Highlights Tour

Guatemala occupies the heart of the ancient Maya world, which spreads into southern Mexico, present-day Belize, and parts of Honduras and El Salvador. This 12-day itinerary will take you to most of the major Maya sites covered in this book, including Copán in Honduras. The best way to undertake this trip is to hire a private car and driver. See "Getting Around" in chapter 2 for further information.

Day ❶: Guatemala City

Once you've settled in, head to the **Museo Popol Vuh** ✿ (p. 111), followed by the **Museo Nacional de Etnología y Arqueología** ✿✿ (p. 112). These two downtown museums will give you a good introduction to the overall history and extant findings of Guatemala's ancient Maya. In the afternoon, visit **Parque Arqueológico Kaminaljuyú** (p. 110), the ruins of a pre-Classic city located on the outskirts of current-day Guatemala City.

Days ❷ & ❸: Takalik Abaj ✿✿

From Guatemala City, journey to another pre-Classic site, **Takalik Abaj** ✿✿ (p. 274).

A great part of the charm of visiting these ruins is the chance to stay on-site at the lovely **Takalik Maya Lodge** ✿✿ (p. 274). Takalik Abaj has some interesting features you won't find at other ruins on this route, including a T-shaped ball court and *barrigón,* or "fat-bellied," sculptures.

Days ❹ & ❺: Copán ✿✿✿

From Takalik Abaj, a long drive and border crossing stand between you and the fabulous Classic-era ruins of **Copán** ✿✿✿ (p. 237). Next to Tikal, Copán is my favorite Maya archaeological site. It's somewhat less extensive, and fewer plazas and pyramids have been excavated, but Copán features some of the most ornate

Maya Highlights

Ancient Ruins

1. Guatemala City
2. Takalik Abaj
3. Copán
4. Chiminos Island Lodge
5. Tikal
6. Yaxhá

and best preserved examples of Maya architectural and historical sculpture to be found. The **Museum of Maya Sculpture** (p. 240) is worth a visit in and of itself. You'll also want to be sure to tour the recently opened **Rosalia and Jaguar Tunnels** (p. 242).

Day 6: En Route to Chiminos Island Lodge

From Copán you'll be driving to **Chiminos Island Lodge** ✹✹ (p. 213). You'll have to leave your car and driver in the town of **Sayaxché,** where you'll pick up a boat to this lovely isolated lodge. On your way from Copán, take a minor detour to the small Maya ruins at **Quiriguá** (p. 261). Quiriguá features several massive carved stelae. The tallest (here and in the Maya

world) is more than 10m (35 ft.) tall, and weighs more than 65 tons. Quiriguá also has several massive stones, which have been carved into the zoomorphic shapes of frogs, serpents, turtles, and mythical beasts, and covered with hieroglyphs.

Days 7 & 8: Lesser-Known Ruins

Chiminos Island Lodge makes a great base for exploring several lesser-known Maya ruins, including **El Ceibal** ✹ (p. 213), **Aguateca** (p. 213), and **Petexbatún** (p. 213). All of these can be visited on organized tours available through the lodge.

Days 9 & 10: Tikal

By now you're ready to visit **Tikal** ✹✹✹ (p. 195), which I consider the most impressive of all the Maya archaeological sites in Mesoamerica. If you're using this itinerary, you'll want to stay at the **Jungle Lodge** ⭐ (p. 205), which is located just outside the entrance to the archaeological site, and is as close as you can get without pitching a tent inside the ancient city. See chapter 8 for a detailed walking tour of the Tikal ruins.

Days ⓫ & ⓬: Ruins around Tikal
You can either stay at the Jungle Lodge or move to one of the hotels in Flores or on the shores of Lake Petén Itzá. Whichever you choose, you should still stick around this region and explore the other ruins around Tikal, including **Yaxhá** ⭐⭐ (p. 213), where one season of the reality series *Survivor* was shot. Other sites worth exploring include **Nakum** (p. 213), **Uaxactún** (p. 214), and **El Zotz** ⭐ (p. 211).

5 Antigua in 3 Days

Diminutive Antigua is one of the finest colonial cities in all of the Americas. Its rough cobblestone streets feature a dense mix of old colonial buildings, impressive Catholic churches, and various monasteries and convents. A good portion of these lie in ruins due to the many earthquakes and natural disasters that have plagued the area and led to Antigua's forced evacuation in 1777. If you're like me, you'll fall under the spell of this enchanting city, and 3 days will seem like too little time to fully enjoy its many charms. Still, the itinerary below will give you a good dose of some of the best Antigua has to offer.

Day ❶: Getting Acquainted
After arriving at your hotel, spend the rest of the day getting your bearings by starting out at the **Plaza Mayor** ⭐⭐ (p. 127), the center of the city and its principal reference point, and then strolling around Antigua's colonial core.

In the late afternoon, grab a taxi and head to the **Cerro de la Cruz** ⭐ (p. 128), where you'll get a great panoramic view of the city as the sun sets behind the outlying volcanoes.

For dinner, sample some traditional Guatemalan cuisine at **La Fonda de la Calle Real** ⭐ (p. 137), and then stroll around the Plaza Mayor, or head to **Reilly's** ⭐ (p. 142) for a nightcap.

Day ❷: Walking Around
Take a morning walking tour with **Antigua Tours** ⭐ (p. 126). These tours are highly informative and take you to most of the prime attractions in Antigua. The company has excellent guides, and many of their tours are led by longtime resident and well-known author Elizabeth Bell.

Use the afternoon to hit any of the major sites or attractions you feel you've missed or need more time to fully explore. If you find yourself around the Plaza Mayor and wanting a coffee break, duck into the **Café Condesa** (p. 137).

Have a sunset cocktail at the **Sky Bar** at **Café Sky** ⭐ (p. 138) and dinner at a poolside table at the **Welten** ⭐⭐ (p. 136) if the weather is nice.

Day ❸: Active Pursuits
It's time to get a little active, so sign up to climb **Volcán Pacaya** ⭐⭐ (p. 144). This is an exciting and energetic climb, but it's also accessible to most people in reasonably good shape. If you do the morning tour, you should be back in Antigua by 1pm.

Save the afternoon to do some shopping. Be sure to visit **Casa de Artes** ⭐

Map labels:

To Lake Atitlán, Chimaltenango & Quetzaltenango

Calle Ancha de los Herederos

Calle de Cajón

Calle de las Animas

To Cerro de la Cruz

Calle de los Nazareños — Callejón Lemus — Calle de los Carpinteros

Candelaria

0 — 200 meters
0 — 200 yards

N

MEXICO — Tikal — BELIZE — Livingston — L. Izabal — Lake Atitlán — Antigua — Guatemala City — HOND. — EL SAL.

Calle Camposeco — La Merced — Santa Rosa

La Recolección — Calle de Platerias — 1a Calle Poniente — 1a Calle Oriente — Calle de Platerias — Callejón de Rubia

Santa Catalina Arch — Capuchinas — Santo Domingo

San Jerónimo

San Lázaro Cemetery

2a Calle Poniente — 2a Calle Oriente

3a Calle Poniente — 3a Calle Oriente — Calle do los Carros

Market & Bus Station

4a Calle Poniente — Palacio del Noble Ayuntamiento — 4a Calle Oriente — To Guatemala City, Volcán Pacaya

Landivar Monument

Portal de Comercio — Cathedral San José — Concepción

5a Calle Poniente — 5a Calle Oriente

6a Calle Poniente — Palacio de Los Capitanes — Colonial Museum — 6a Calle Oriente

San Pedro — Santa Clara

7a Calle Poniente — 7a Calle Oriente — Calle de Chiplilapa

San José El Viejo — 8a Calle Oriente — San Francisco

Callejón de San José

Calle Belén — Plaza de la Paz — Belén

Escuela de Cristo — Guadalupe

Los Remedios — Calle de Santa Ana — Santa Ana

Río Pensativo

Alameda Santa Lucía

1. Mesón Panza Verde
2. Casa de Artes
3. Café Sky
4. Tequila Bar
5. Joyería del Angel
6. Plaza Mayor
7. Café Condesa
8. La Fonda de la Calle Real
9. Mercado de Artesanías y Campañia de Jesús
10. Reilly's
11. Nim Po't
12. Textura

(p. 140), **Joyería del Angel** ✸✸ (p. 140), and **Textura** ✸✸ (p. 141). If you're looking for bargains, try **Nim Po't** ✸✸✸ (p. 141) and the **Mercado de Artesanías y Compañía de Jesús** ✸ (p. 141).

For your final dinner, pull out all the stops and reserve a table (possibly accompanied by some jazz) at the **Mesón Panza Verde** ✸✸✸ (p. 132). Wind up your last night with some high-end tequila or mescal at **Tequila Bar** ✸✸ (p. 143).

4

Guatemala City

Guatemala City is the country's capital and largest city. In fact, with a population of nearly three million, it's the largest city in Central America.

Guatemala City was founded as the country's third capital in 1776, following the destruction of two earlier attempts by natural disasters—earthquakes and mudslides. Christened with the unwieldy name of La Nueva Guatemala de La Asunción de la Valle de la Ermita by Spain's King Charles III, it's most commonly known by its simple abbreviation, Guate. Long before the Spaniards moved their capital here, this was the site of the pre-Classic Maya city of Kaminaljuyú, whose ruins you can still visit. The city is set on a broad plateau at an elevation of 1,468m (4,897 ft.) above sea level, and is surrounded by mountains and volcanoes on all sides.

Despite its well-deserved reputation as a sometimes violent and dangerous place, Guatemala City has a lot to offer travelers. The principal commercial and tourist zones are full of fine hotels and excellent restaurants, and the nightlife found in Zona Viva and Cuatro Grados Norte is the best in the country. The city boasts theaters, art galleries, and several worthwhile museums.

1 Orientation

ARRIVING

BY PLANE

All flights into Guatemala City land at **La Aurora International Airport** (© 502/ **2332-6086;** airport code GUA), which is located in Zona 13 on the edge of the city center and about 25km (16 miles) from Antigua. The airport is currently in the midst of a major remodel and expansion. The new and improved airport is expected to be ready sometime late in 2007. See chapter 2 for details about airlines that service Guatemala City.

There is an **INGUAT** (Guatemalan Tourism Commission; www.visitguatemala. com) information booth inside the airport, open Monday through Friday from 6am until 9pm, and Saturday and Sunday from 8am until 8pm.

The **Banquetzal** (© 502/2347-5081; www.banquetzal.com.gt) in the airport exchanges dollars and some European currencies, and will cash traveler's checks. It's open Monday through Friday from 6am to 8pm, and Saturday through Sunday from 6am to 6pm.

You'll find various shuttle companies occupying makeshift booths—due to the airport construction—as you exit either the national or international terminal. These companies charge between Q30 and Q60 ($4–$8/£2.10–£4.20) to any hotel in Guatemala City, and between Q75 and Q90 ($10–$12/£5.25–£6.30) to Antigua. Many of the larger hotels also have regular complimentary airport shuttle buses, so be sure to check in advance if your hotel provides this service.

If you don't want to wait for the shuttle to fill or sit through various stops before arriving at your hotel, there are always taxis lined up at the airport terminal exits. A taxi downtown will cost around Q45 to Q75 ($6–$10/£3.15–£5.25).

If you're on a tight budget and need to take a bus to the city center, bus no. 32 runs downtown every 30 minutes between 6am and 8pm, with less frequent service before and after those hours. *Warning:* Because of an increasing number of armed assaults on metropolitan buses, I recommend you avoid this option.

Avis, Budget, Hertz, National, Tabarini, and **Thrifty** all have car rental desks at the airport. See "Getting Around: By Car" below, for more information.

BY BUS

Guatemala's bus system is a chaotic mess. Scores of independent companies provide service to just about every nook and cranny in the country. However, there is little rhyme or reason to their terminal locations. If you arrive in town by bus, you may end up at the large and hectic main bus terminal and market area in Zona 4, or at any number of private terminals around the city, often in Zona 1. It's always easy to find a taxi near any of the bus terminals, and I recommend taking one to your final destination in the city, which should cost Q45 to Q75 ($6–$10/£3.15–£5.25).

Warning: Do not arrive by bus at night if at all possible, as the bus terminal and surrounding area are very dangerous at night. If you do, hop in a cab immediately after you arrive.

BY CAR

Unless you're already familiar with the city, arriving by car can be a confusing and challenging endeavor. Prepare for gridlock and a general disregard for anything resembling common courtesy. The road in from Antigua and the Western Highlands turns into Calzada Roosevelt, which becomes the Bulevar Liberación as it heads toward Zona 10. If you're heading to Zona 1, take the Anillo Periférico to the northeast soon after entering the urban sprawl.

The road from the Pacific Coast (CA-9) enters Guatemala City from the southwest and turns into Calzada Raul Aguilar Batreó as it heads toward downtown. On the other side, CA-9 enters the city from the northeast, bringing in traffic from the Atlantic Coast, El Oriente, and Las Verapaces.

VISITOR INFORMATION

The **Guatemalan Tourism Commission (INGUAT;** © **502/2421-2854;** www.visit guatemala.com) has an airport booth for arriving tourists, as well as a main office at 7a Av. 1-17, Zona 4. This office is open Monday through Friday from 8am until 4pm, and can provide maps and brochures. They can also make a call for you if you need a hotel or car-rental reservation. To get tourist assistance and information from anywhere within Guatemala, dial © **1500.**

Hotel concierges, tour desks, and local travel agencies are another good source of information. There are scores of tour agencies around Guatemala City. I recommend **Clark Tours,** 7a Av. 14-76, Zona 9, inside Clark Plaza (© **502/2412-4700;** www. clarktours.com.gt); **Grayline Guatemala,** 1a Av. 13-22, Zona 10, inside the Holiday Inn (© **502/2383-8600;** www.graylineguatemala.com); and **Maya Vacations,** 12a Calle 2-04, Zona 9 (© **502/233-4638;** www.mayavacations.com).

CITY LAYOUT

Guatemala City is divided into 21 zones or *"zonas."* The *zonas* are numbered sequentially in a spiral pattern beginning with Zona 1, the most central and oldest zone in the city. In general, the city is laid out on a standard grid, with *avenidas* (avenues) running roughly north-south, and *calles* (streets) running east-west. Of the 21 zones, below are those that you're likely to visit, as they hold the majority of the city's hotels, restaurants, and major attractions.

THE NEIGHBORHOODS IN BRIEF

Zona 1 This is the most central and oldest section of the city, home to the Plaza Mayor, Metropolitan Cathedral, and National Theater, as well as many budget hotels, stores, and restaurants. Several buildings date back to the capital's founding in 1775, when a *mudéjar* (Moorish) architectural style was so fashionable and uniform that the only thing that distinguished one private home from another was the size. Unfortunately, other aspects of the urban environment can overshadow the neighborhood's charms. Traffic noise and exhaust fumes flood the crowded streets and avenues. Be very cautious when exploring this area and avoid going out at night, as petty theft and even gun violence are common. The U.S. State Department prohibits government employees from staying in hotels in this area.

Zona 4 Just south of Zona 1, this area was once known as the Cantón de Exposición, as its center was the Guatemala Pavilion from the 1890 Paris World's Fair. A touch of Paris still remains: the Torre del Reformador, a smaller version of the Eiffel Tower built in 1935 to commemorate the progressive administration of President Justo Rufino Barrios (1873–85). Travelers will want to be aware of the central INGUAT office here, housed in the Civic Center along with the Bank of Guatemala, the Supreme Court of Justice, and other government buildings. Nearby, the compact Cuatro Grados Norte is a pedestrian-friendly and safe section of bars, restaurants, shops, and discos. The sprawling, chaotic second-class bus terminal and market are in this zone as well.

Zonas 9 & 10 These ritzy zones straddle the Avenida La Reforma in the southern part of the city center, with Zona 9 to the west and Zona 10 to the east. The streets are lined with trees

---

Fun Fact Breaking the Code

Guatemalan addresses may look confusing, but they're actually easy to understand. All addresses are written beginning with the *avenida* or *calle* that the building, business, or house is on, followed by the nearest cross street and actual building number, written out as a two-number hyphen combination. This is then followed by the zone. For example, the INGUAT Office on 7a Av. 1-17, Zona 4 is located at no. 17, on Avenida 7, near the cross street of 1a Calle in Zona 4. Be very careful, first and foremost, that you're in the correct zone. 7a Av. 1-17, Zona 4; and 7a Av. 1-17, Zona 10, are two radically different addresses.

(*Fun Fact* **He's Gone to Zona 20**

Though there is no actual Zona 20, you may hear locals refer to it. In a bit of local gallows humor, when someone dies in Guatemala City, they say, *"Se fue para la zona 20,"* which translates to "He's gone to Zona 20."

and gardens, embassies and eateries, luxury hotels and shops. Zona 10 is also known as the "Zona Viva" because of its abundance of hotels, restaurants, and bars. The streets in Zona 10 are relatively safe, and the area has a hopping nightlife. More than just a playground for the well-healed, Zona 10 is also home to the Museo Ixchel del Traje Indígena, Botanical Garden, and Popol Vuh Museum, with its notable collection of pre-Columbian pottery.

Zona 13 The airport, several museums, and the Aurora Zoo are all in Zona 13, southwest of Zona 9. It's a pleasant place to spend an afternoon or a night if you have an early morning flight from La Aurora airport. The hotels in Zona 9 and Zona 10 are also quite close to the airport.

2 Getting Around

Note: Guatemala City has an extensive network of metropolitan buses, but a vast number of assaults take place on them at all times of day and night. I highly recommend you take a taxi instead.

BY TAXI

Taxis are plentiful and relatively inexpensive, and while they're supposed to use meters, many don't. It's always best to ask before taking off whether it will be a metered ride, and if not, to negotiate the price in advance. A ride anywhere in the city should cost between Q15 and Q75 ($2–$10/£1.05–£5.25).

If you need to call a cab, ask your hotel or try **Taxi Amarillo Express** (✆ 502/ 2470-1515), **Taxi Metro** (✆ 502/2439-7124), **Taxis 2000** (✆ 502/2433-9984), or **Taxis Plaza** (✆ 502/2331-8519). Taxi Amarillo Express cabs all use meters.

ON FOOT

Guatemala City is not very conducive to exploring by foot. The city is spread out, and many of the major attractions are far from one another. Plus street crime is a problem. It's relatively safe to walk around *zonas* 1, 4, 9, 10, and 13 by day. However, with few exceptions, you should never walk around Guatemala City at night. Those few exceptions include the most developed parts of Zona 10, or the Zona Viva; and the hip, new strip of bars and restaurants in Zona 4, known as Cuatro Grados Norte.

BY CAR

Driving in Guatemala City falls somewhere between a headache and a nightmare. There is little need to navigate Guatemala City in a car. I highly recommend you take taxis and leave the driving to others. If you do find yourself driving around Guatemala City, go slow, as pedestrians and vehicles can appear out of nowhere.

If you want to rent a car, the following all have airport locations, and some have locations in town: **Avis** (✆ 502/2231-0017; www.avis.com); **Budget,** 6a Av. 11-24, Zona 9 (✆ 502/2232-7744; www.budgetguatemala.com.gt); **Hertz,** Av. Hincapié

Guatemala City

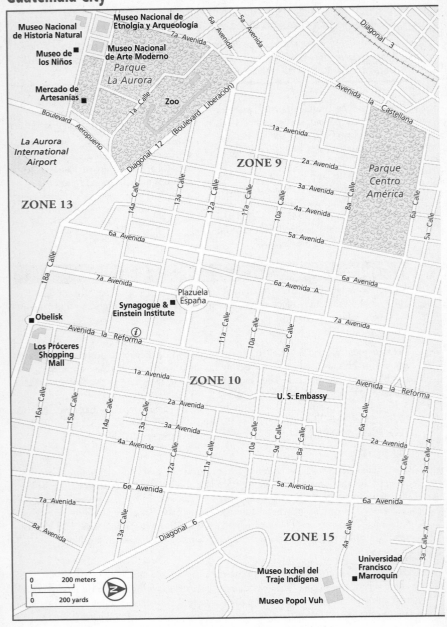

Museo Nacional
de Historia Natural

Museo de
los Niños

Mercado de
Artesanías

Museo Nacional de
Etnolgía y Arqueología

7a Avenida

Museo Nacional
de Arte Moderno

*Parque
La Aurora*

Zoo

6a Avenida

5a Avenida

Diagonal 3

Avenida la Castellana

La Aurora
International
Airport

ZONE 13

Boulevard Aeropuerto

1a Calle

Diagonal 12 (Boulevard Liberación)

1a Avenida

ZONE 9

2a Avenida

3a Avenida

4a Avenida

5a Avenida

Parque
Centro
América

8a Calle

6a Calle

5a Calle

14a Calle

13a Calle

12a Calle

11a Calle

10a Calle

6a Avenida

18a Calle

7a Avenida

6a Avenida A

6a Avenida

Plazuela
España

Synagogue &
Einstein Institute

7a Avenida

11a Calle

10a Calle

9a Calle

Obelisk

Avenida la Reforma

Los Próceres
Shopping
Mall

1a Avenida

ZONE 10

U. S. Embassy

Avenida la Reforma

16a Calle

15a Calle

14a Calle

13a Calle

2a Avenida

3a Avenida

4a Avenida

12a Calle

11a Calle

10a Calle

9a Calle

8a Calle

6a Calle

2a Avenida

4a Calle

3a Calle A

7a Avenida

6e Avenida

5a Avenida

6a Avenida

8a Avenida

13a Calle

Diagonal 6

ZONE 15

4a Calle

3a Calle A

Museo Ixchel del
Traje Indígena

Museo Popol Vuh

Universidad
Francisco
Marroquín

0   200 meters

0   200 yards

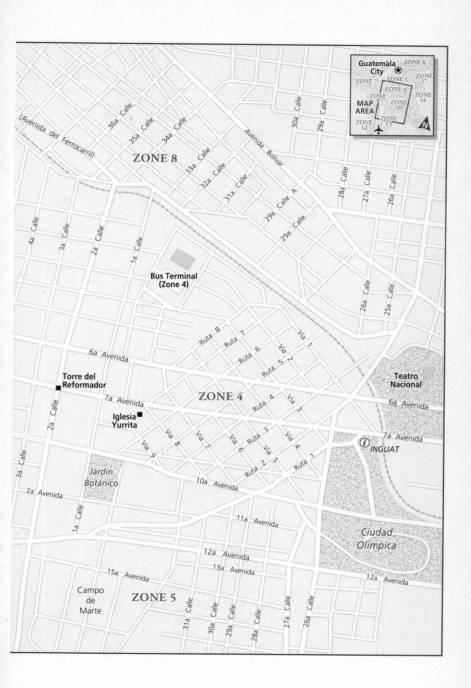

Fun Fact **Killer Tomatoes**

Guatemala's urban buses are the popular stamping ground for armed robbers and muggers. They are also largely driven by aggressive and carefree drivers whose homicidal tendencies might be better served in the armed forces. These factors, along with the fact that they are painted a deep red, have led local residents to dub them *"los tomates asesinos,"* or "the killer tomatoes."

11-01, Zona 13, and at several hotels in Zona 10 (© 502/2470-3737; www.rentautos. com.gt); **National,** 14a Calle 7-57, Zona 9 (© 502/2362-3000; www.nationalcar. com); and **Thrifty** (© 502/2379-8747; www.thrifty.com). **Tabarini** (© 502/2331-2643; www.tabarini.com) is a good local company with offices at 2a Calle A 7-30, Zona 10, as well as at the airport.

Rates run from Q263 to Q600 ($35–$80/£18–£42) per day, depending upon the size and style of automobile, and include unlimited mileage and full insurance.

Guatemala also has an extensive network of buses servicing almost every little town and village in the country, including all the major tourist destinations. Unfortunately, the system is very complex and entirely decentralized. Specific bus information is listed in the individual destination chapters throughout the book.

FAST FACTS: Guatemala City

Airport See "Arriving," above.

American Express In Guatemala, **Clark Tours,** Clark Plaza, 7a Av. 14-76, Zona 9 (© **502/2412-4700;** www.clarktours.com.gt), is the official representative of American Express Travel Services. They also have desks at the downtown Westin and Marriott hotels. To report lost or stolen Amex traveler's checks within Guatemala, call the local number above, or call © **801/964-6665** collect in the U.S.

Babysitters Hotels offering regular, dependable babysitting service are few and far between. If you need a babysitter, make sure that your hotel offers this service, and be sure to ask whether the babysitters are bilingual. In many cases, they are not. This is usually not a problem with infants and toddlers, but it can cause problems with older children. Babysitters charge between Q15 and Q45 ($2–$6/£1.05–£3.15) per hour.

Banks You'll have no trouble finding a bank in Guatemala City. Numerous bank branches can be found all over *zonas* 1, 4, 9, 10, and 13. Banks are usually open Monday through Friday from 9am to 4pm, although many have begun to offer extended hours. The most widespread banks include **Banquetzal** (www.banquetzal. com.gt), **Banrural** (www.banrural.com), **Banco G&T** (www.gytcontinental.com.gt), **Banco de Guatemala** (www.banguat.gob.gt), and **Banco Industrial** (www.bi.com.gt).

Bookstores Bibliophiles will be disappointed in Guatemala City. You'd be better off purchasing any specific reading material, for pleasure or research, before your trip. The best bookstore in the city for tourists is **Sophos,** Av. La Reforma 13-89, Zona 10 (© **502/2334-6797;** www.sophosenlinea.com), which also has a lovely coffee shop attached. **L'Areté,** Avenida La Reforma and 16a Calle, Zona 9 (© **502/2360-2233**); **Gémenis Bookstore,** 3a Av. 17-05, Zona 14 (© **502/2366-1031**); and **Vista Hermosa Book Shop,** 2a Calle 18-50, Zona 15 (© **502/2369-1003**), also carry books in English.

Camera Repair **Quick Photo** (© **502/2368-0600**) and **Fuji Film** (© **502/2420-3900**) both have technicians on hand, and carry a limited range of replacement and repair parts.

Car Rentals See "Getting Around: By Car," above.

Cellphones There are several competing cellphone companies in Guatemala that have numerous outlets across the city, including at the airport. All sell prepaid GSM chips that can be used in any unlocked tri-band GSM cellphone. Storefronts at the airport, and at many hotels around the city, will also rent out cellphones. The main companies are **Claro** (© **147-100**; www.claro.com.gt), which is a division of Telgua, the national telephone company; **Movistar** (© **502/2379-1960**; www.movistar.com.gt), which is a division of the international firm Telefonica; and **Tigo** (© **502/2428-0000**; www.tigo.com.gt), which is also marketed as Comcel. Prepaid chips come in denominations from Q10 to Q200 ($1.35–$27/70p–£14). Most companies charge an activation fee of around Q50 ($6.65/£3.50). Rentals run between Q15 and Q45 ($2–$6/£1.05–£3.15) per day.

Currency Exchange All banks will exchange money for a small service charge. Many of the hotels, restaurants, and shops in Guatemala City will also accept U.S. dollars and euros, though many give less than advantageous exchange rates. A branch of **Banquetzal** (© **502/2347-5081**; www.banquetzal.com.gt) is located at the international airport, open Monday through Friday 6am to 8pm, Saturday through Sunday 6am to 6pm.

Dentists Call your embassy, which will have a list of recommended dentists, or ask your hotel. Alternately, you can try **Clínica Dental de Especialistas,** 7a Av. 9-71, Zona 9 (© **502/2362-9983**).

Doctors Contact your embassy for information on doctors in Guatemala City, or see "Hospitals," below.

Drugstores A drugstore or pharmacy is called a *farmacia* in Spanish. In Guatemala, they are also sometimes called *droguería*. There are scores of pharmacies around Guatemala City, and most major hotels have one attached or nearby. Ask your hotel, or call **Farmacias Klee** (© **502/2360-8383**), which offers 24-hour delivery service for a small fee. In Zona 10, try **Osco,** 16a Calle and 4a Avenida (© **502/2337-1566**).

Embassies & Consulates See "Fast Facts: Guatemala" in chapter 2.

Emergencies In case of an emergency, dial © **1500** from anywhere in Guatemala. This will connect you to a bilingual operator at Asistur who can put you in contact with the police, fire department, or ambulance service. Dial © **110** for the **National Police,** and © **125** for the **Red Cross (Cruz Roja,** in Spanish). As in the U.S., © **911** works as an emergency number from most phones in Guatemala.

Express Mail Services Most hotels can arrange for express mail pickup, or you can contact **DHL,** 12a Calle 5-12, Zona 10 (© **502/2234-1704;** www.dhl.com); or **UPS,** 12a Calle 5-53, Zona 10 (© **502/2231-2421;** www.ups.com).

Eyeglasses An eyeglass store is called *óptica* in Spanish. There are many around Guatemala City, but your best bet is to ask your hotel. If you need to see an optometrist, contact **Visión Ingetral,** 2a Av. 9-03, Zona 9 (℃ **502/2334-2301**).

Hospitals **Hospital Centro Médico,** 6a Av. 3-47, Zona 10 (℃ **502/2279-4973**), is an excellent private hospital, with English-speaking doctors on staff. Alternately, the **Hospital General San Juan de Dios,** 1a Avenida and 10a Calle, Zona 1 (℃ **502/ 2220-8396**), is the biggest and best equipped public hospital in the city.

Internet Access A fair number of hotels and restaurants around town provide free wireless access. Internet cafes are very common in Guatemala City. Rates run between Q3 and Q8 (40¢–$1.05/20p–60p) per hour. In Zona 1, I like **Uranus Café Net,** 14a Calle 10-32, Zona 1 (℃ **502/2232-9368**), while in Zona 10, I recommend **Café Internet,** 5a Avenida and 16a Calle, Zona 10 (℃ **502/2337-4060**). For a good, free Wi-Fi hot spot, head to **Caffe di Fiore,** 15a Av. 16-66, Zona 10 (℃ **502/2366-9877**).

Laundry & Dry Cleaning Most folks rely on their hotel's laundry and dry cleaning services, although these can be expensive. You can also try the **Lavandería Interdry,** 18a Calle 11-12, Zona 1 (℃ **502/2251-4063**), or **Lavanderías Max de Guatemala,** Bulevar Los Próceres 19-42, Zona 10 (℃ **502/2367-3678**).

Maps **INGUAT** (℃ **502/2421-2854;** www.visitguatemala.com) will provide you with a pretty acceptable map that has the entire country on one side and Guatemala City and Antigua on the other. The map is free, and you can pick one up at their booth at the airport or by visiting their downtown office at 7a Av. 1-17, Zona 4. You can also buy good detailed maps in most gift shops and at **Sophos,** Av. La Reforma 13-89, Zona 10 (℃ **502/2334-6797;** www.sophosenlinea.com).

Newspapers & Magazines *La Prensa Libre* is the country's most highly regarded daily newspaper, with an outstanding investigative reporting staff. The lower-brow *Nuestro Diario* has the highest circulation. There are several other daily papers, including *Siglo XXI.* There are currently no English-language newspapers. The free, monthly **Revue Magazine** (www.revuemag.com) is the most valuable locally produced information source, with museum, art gallery, and theater listings. It's widely available at hotels and other tourist haunts around the country.

Photographic Needs While I recommend bringing as much film as you foresee needing, and then waiting until you return home to develop it, those who can't wait can head to **Quick Photo** (℃ **502/2368-0600**) and **Fuji Film** (℃ **502/ 2420-3900**), both of which offer 1-hour developing service, as well as digital printing services, and carry a wide range of film, camera accessories, and replacement parts.

Police You can contact the National Police by dialing ℃ **110** from any telephone in the country. The **tourist police (POLITUR)** is a small, specialized division of the larger police force, created to patrol specific tourist areas and trained to deal with tourists. Dial ℃ **502/5561-2073** to contact them. In an emergency, ℃ **911** will work from most phones. You can also call ℃ **1500,** which will connect you to a bilingual operator at Asistur.

Post Office A post office is called *correo* in Spanish. The main **post office**, 7a Av. 12-11, Zona 1 (℡ **502/2232-6101**), is a beautiful building. It costs around Q5 (65¢/35p) to send a letter to the U.S. or Europe. Postcards to the same destinations cost Q3 (40¢/20p).

Restrooms There are few public restrooms available around town. Most hotels and restaurants will let travelers use their facilities, although they are happiest if you are a paying client.

Safety Safety is an issue in Guatemala City. I highly recommend that you stick to the most affluent and touristy sections of town highlighted in this book. Also, it's unwise to walk anywhere in Guatemala City after dark. Basic common sense and street-smarts are to be employed. Don't wear flashy jewelry or wave wads of cash around. Be aware of your surroundings, and avoid any people and places that make you feel uncomfortable. Rental cars generally stick out and are easily spotted by thieves, who know that such cars are likely to be full of expensive camera equipment, money, and other valuables. Don't ever leave anything of value in an unattended parked car.

Taxes A Q225 ($30/£16) departure tax must be paid upon departure. Sometimes this is included in your airline ticket price. Be sure to check in advance. If not, you'll have to pay the fee in cash at the airport. There is an additional airport security fee of Q20 ($2.65/£1.40). A 12% IVA (value added) tax is tacked on to the purchase of all goods and services. An additional 10% tax, on top of the 12% IVA, is added to all hotel rooms and lodgings.

Taxis See "Getting Around," above.

Time Zone Guatemala City is on Central Standard Time, 6 hours behind Greenwich Mean Time. It observed daylight saving time for the first time in 2006, but it remains to be seen whether the country will continue to observe it.

Useful Telephone Numbers For directory assistance, call ℡ **124**; for an international operator and directory assistance, call ℡ **147-110**. To make a direct international call, dial ℡ **00** + the country code + the area code + the phone number. To get the current time, dial ℡ **333-1526**.

Water Drink only bottled water within Guatemala City and be especially careful to do so when traveling outside the capital, as water-borne diseases are very common in this country.

Weather The weather in Guatemala City is mild year-round, with an average daytime temperature of around 70°F (21°C), and a rainy season May through October. For more details, see "When to Go" in chapter 2.

3 Where to Stay

There are tons of good hotel options in Guatemala City, with something to fit any budget. Most visitors choose to stay in the ritzier and safer side-by-side neighborhoods of *zonas* 9 and 10, which I highly recommend. Budget travelers and those seeking a heavy dose of the city's colonial center gravitate to Zona 1, but keep in mind that you need to be very careful about walking around this neighborhood at night.

Adoptions

Adoptions of Guatemalan-born children by foreign couples, particularly Americans, is a booming phenomenon. Many of the high-end hotels in Guatemala City have whole floors dedicated to serving adoptive parents as they go through the process.

Guatemala is an attractive choice for international adoption for a number of reasons. There are few restrictions on who can adopt in Guatemala. The government of Guatemala requires only a short visit, and Guatemala is a lot closer to the U.S. than countries in Asia or Africa, where adoptions by foreign nationals are also encouraged.

The number of adoptions in Guatemala continues to grow. In 2005, there were 3,783 adoptions—a 50% increase from 2003. Recent adoptions have been evenly split between girls and boys, and most of the children are infants under 1 year of age.

As with any important interaction, it goes without saying that you should beware of shady dealers. Tragically, child trafficking in Guatemala is a reality. There are many legitimate organizations (secular and religious) that will coordinate the process for you. Ask to speak to some adoptive parents to get a feel for an agency before making a decision.

The adoption process can be completed in as little as 6 months, but can be expensive. In 1995, country fees were $19,000. This goes toward bureaucratic costs and attorney fees, but also pays for foster care and medical care of your child from acceptance of referral until the adoption is finalized.

Prospective parents are required to complete a dossier outlining their qualifications. After the documents are translated, the couple is paired with a child, or "referral." When the prospective parents accept a referral, the power of attorney is given to a lawyer in Guatemala, who acts on their behalf throughout the process. The child and the birth mother are then DNA tested in an effort to guard the child and the birth mother against baby trafficking. The attorney will meet with the birth mother four times during the adoption process. The attorney then petitions the official governmental adoption office for approval.

Upon approval, a decree is written, the infant becomes the child of the adoptive parents, and the parents travel to Guatemala to meet their child. The adoption is then complete. Some parents make several trips in advance to meet the child and lay some groundwork.

Not surprisingly, there are U.S. Department of Immigration requirements as well. The main document is the I-600A. However, the U.S. Embassy in Guatemala is accustomed to working with prospective adoptive parents, and they are quite helpful throughout the process.

ZONAS 9 & 10

These side-by-side zones contain the greatest concentration of hotels, restaurants, bars, and shops in the city, and heavy police presence makes them relatively safe for strolling and exploring on foot. Most of the hotels here are high-end business-class affairs, but there are actually options to fit most budgets. This area, particularly Zona 10, is often referred to as Zona Viva, or the "Alive Zone," because of all the dining and nightlife options.

VERY EXPENSIVE

In addition to the places listed below, the **Guatemala City Marriott,** 7a Av. 15-45, Zona 9 (© **800/228-9290** in the U.S. and Canada, or 502/2410-1777; www.marriott. com), is another excellent high-end hotel, though I think the similar-class hotels listed below are better located.

Real InterContinental ✸✸✸   This is my favorite of the high-end, business-class hotels in this area. The rooms, facilities, and service are a notch above the competition, though most of the hotels in this class do a very good job. Rooms are spacious and in great condition, and all are carpeted and feature firm beds and 25-inch flatscreen televisions. Business rooms come with a fully equipped workstation that features a combination fax machine, scanner, and copier, as well as an ergonomic chair and an in-room coffeemaker. Rooms on the InterClub floors have separate check-in desks, butler services, and a private lounge with regularly replenished snacks, free continental breakfast, and daily complimentary cocktail hour. Add Q113 ($15/£7.90) for a business room and Q225 ($30/£16) for an InterClub room. There's an attractive pool area with a large Jacuzzi nearby. The hotel is situated on a busy corner in the Zona Viva, with scores of good restaurants, bars, and shops just steps away.

14a Calle 2-51, Zona 10. © **502/2379-4446.** Fax 502/2379-4447. www.interconti.com. 239 units. Q1,088–Q1,425 ($145–$190/£76–£100) double; Q1,875 ($250/£131) junior suite; Q4,125 ($550/£289) Governor suite. AE, DISC, MC, V. Free valet parking. **Amenities:** 2 restaurants; 2 bars; pool; Jacuzzi; well-equipped gym and spa; tour desk; car rental desk; salon; 24-hr. room service; babysitting; laundry service; nonsmoking rooms. *In room:* A/C, TV, dataport, minibar, hair dryer, safe.

Westin Camino Real ✸✸ *Kids*   This long-standing and popular Zona 10 hotel has aged well. The Grand Lobby, while not huge, features stately marble floors and a beautiful domed ceiling with intricate stained-glass work. The rooms have all been regularly updated to Westin's corporate standards, with their trademark "Heavenly Sleep & Shower" beds and fancy shower heads. Standard rooms come with either one king or two queen-size beds. Because the hotel is built in an arc, rooms on the east side are slightly larger. The junior suites have separate sitting rooms and 29-inch flatscreen televisions. The sixth floor is dedicated to families, particularly those with small children or those visiting Guatemala to finalize adoptions. The executive floors have a few more business perks, including in-room fax machines and a small TV in the bathroom. The large pool is the best hotel pool in the city. The hotel has a free airport shuttle, and high-speed Internet connections are available in every room for a fee.

14a Calle and Av. La Reforma, Zona 10. © **800/228-3000** in the U.S. and Canada, or 502/2333-3000 in Guatemala. Fax 502/2337-4313. www.westin.com. 271 units. Q1,050–Q1,650 ($140–$220/£735–£116) double; Q1,800–Q2,100 ($240–$280/£126–£147) executive level and suites. AE, DC, MC, V. Free parking. **Amenities:** 2 restaurants; 2 bars; lounge; 3 pools; lit outdoor tennis court; well-equipped gym and spa services; concierge; shopping arcade; salon; 24-hr. room service; babysitting; laundry service; nonsmoking rooms; 24-hr. casino; indoor squash court. *In room:* A/C, TV, minibar, coffeemaker, hair dryer, safe.

EXPENSIVE

In addition to the hotels listed below, the **Holiday Inn,** 1a Av. 13-22, Zona 10 (© **502/2421-0000;** www.holidayinn.com), is a good option. This hotel was previously run

Zonas 9, 10, 13 & Environs

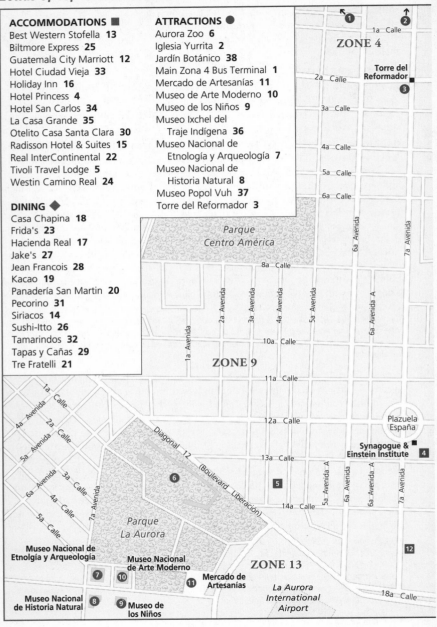

ACCOMMODATIONS ■
Best Western Stofella **13**
Biltmore Express **25**
Guatemala City Marriott **12**
Hotel Ciudad Vieja **33**
Holiday Inn **16**
Hotel Princess **4**
Hotel San Carlos **34**
La Casa Grande **35**
Otelito Casa Santa Clara **30**
Radisson Hotel & Suites **15**
Real InterContinental **22**
Tivoli Travel Lodge **5**
Westin Camino Real **24**

DINING ◆
Casa Chapina **18**
Frida's **23**
Hacienda Real **17**
Jake's **27**
Jean Francois **28**
Kacao **19**
Panadería San Martin **20**
Pecorino **31**
Siriacos **14**
Sushi-Itto **26**
Tamarindos **32**
Tapas y Cañas **29**
Tre Fratelli **21**

ATTRACTIONS ●
Aurora Zoo **6**
Iglesia Yurrita **2**
Jardín Botánico **38**
Main Zona 4 Bus Terminal **1**
Mercado de Artesanías **11**
Museo de Arte Moderno **10**
Museo de los Niños **9**
Museo Ixchel del
   Traje Indígena **36**
Museo Nacional de
   Etnología y Arqueología **7**
Museo Nacional de
   Historia Natural **8**
Museo Popol Vuh **37**
Torre del Reformador **3**

ZONE 4

1a Calle

Torre del
Reformador

2a Calle

3a Calle

4a Calle

5a Calle

6a Calle

6a Avenida

7a Avenida

Parque
Centro América

8a Calle

ZONE 9

1a Avenida

2a Avenida

3a Avenida

4a Avenida

5a Avenida

6a Avenida A

10a Calle

11a Calle

12a Calle

13a Calle

14a Calle

Plazuela
España

Synagogue &
Einstein Institute

Diagonal 12

(Boulevard Liberación)

1a Calle

4a Avenida

2a Calle

5a Avenida

3a Calle

6a Avenida

4a Calle

7a Avenida

5a Calle

Parque
La Aurora

Museo Nacional de
Etnolgía y Arqueología

Museo Nacional
de Arte Moderno

Mercado de
Artesanías

ZONE 13

La Aurora
International
Airport

5a Avenida A

6a Avenida A

7a Avenida

18a Calle

Museo Nacional
de Historia Natural

Museo de
los Niños

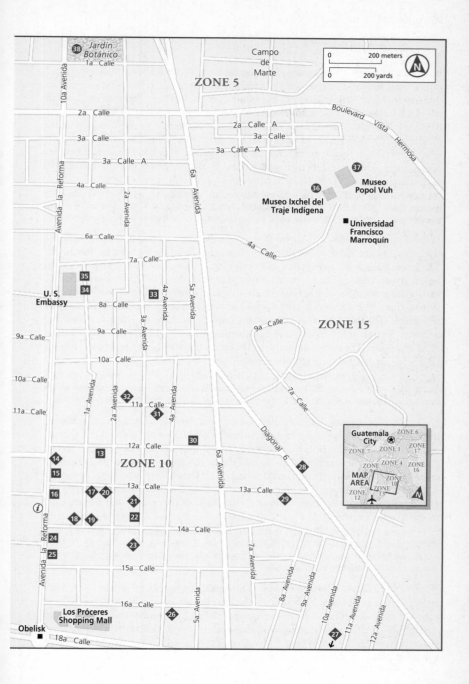

Jardín Botánico
1a Calle

Campo de Marte

ZONE 5

0   200 meters
0   200 yards

10a Avenida

2a Calle
3a Calle
3a Calle A
4a Calle
6a Calle

Avenida la Reforma

2a Avenida

6a Avenida

2a Calle A
3a Calle
3a Calle A

Boulevard Vista Hermosa

Museo Popol Vuh
Museo Ixchel del Traje Indígena

4a Calle

Universidad Francisco Marroquín

7a Calle

U. S. Embassy
8a Calle

9a Calle
9a Calle
10a Calle

10a Calle

11a Calle

3a Avenida
4a Avenida
5a Avenida

ZONE 15

9a Calle

7a Calle

Diagonal 6

1a Avenida
2a Avenida
4a Avenida

11a Calle

12a Calle

ZONE 10

13a Calle

14a Calle

15a Calle

16a Calle

Avenida la Reforma

6a Avenida

13a Calle

7a Avenida

5a Avenida

8a Avenida
9a Avenida

10a Avenida
11a Avenida
12a Avenida

Guatemala City
ZONE 6
ZONE 7 ZONE 1 ZONE 17
ZONE 4
ZONE 2 ZONE 16
MAP AREA ZONE 10
ZONE 12 ZONE 13

Los Próceres Shopping Mall

Obelisk
18a Calle

97

by the Sol Meliá chain, but has been under the management of Holiday Inn for the past couple of years.

Biltmore Express   This cookie-cutter business-class hotel has acceptable rooms and professional service. The rooms are all carpeted and come with either one king-size or two double beds. I think it's worth the splurge for one of their "Parlor Suites," which are much larger and come with a kitchenette and larger bathroom. The best features here are the location and the fact that this hotel is connected to the Westin Camino Real. For Q75 ($10/£5.25) per day, guests at the Biltmore Express can use the pool, gym, tennis court, squash court, and spa at the Westin. This hotel also has a free airport shuttle. There are Ethernet connections in all the rooms offering broadband access for another Q75 ($10/£5.25) per day.

15a Calle 0-31, Zona 10. ℂ 502/2338-5000. Fax 502/2338-5005. www.biltmoreexpress.com.gt. 116 units. Q713 ($95/£50) double; Q863 ($115/£60) parlor suite. Rates include continental breakfast. AE, DC, MC, V. Free parking. Amenities: Restaurant; bar; tour desk; 24-hr. room service; laundry; nonsmoking rooms. *In room:* A/C, TV, dataport, safe.

Hotel Princess *Value*   This comfortable hotel is well located and offers many of the perks and amenities of the fancier business-class hotels in the area for much less. The lobby features flowering vines and open interior space that soars up five stories to a glass atrium ceiling. The rooms are outfitted in what they call "English-style decor," with a dark stained-wood headboard above the bed and an elegant wood armoire. Rooms come with either one king-size bed or two doubles. Most have large, 27-inch televisions. The bathrooms are somewhat compact, but have nice marble floors and counters. Twelve of the rooms have balconies, and I recommend you request one of these if possible. The corner units are the largest rooms, with bigger bedrooms, though I'd opt for the balcony over the extra space if given the choice.

13a Calle 7-65, Zona 9. ℂ 502/2423-0909. Fax 502/2334-4546. www.hotelesprincess.com. 108 units. Q600–Q825 ($80–$110/£42–£58) double. AE, DC, MC, V. Free parking. Amenities: Restaurant; bar; small pool; small exercise room; sauna; 24-hr. room service; free Wi-Fi; laundry service; nonsmoking rooms. *In room:* A/C, TV, hair dryer, safe.

Hotel San Carlos *Finds*   Located right on the busy Avenida La Reforma, this charming three-story hotel features a Tudor exterior that's a little out of place in this Central American country. The British influence is carried over to the rooms, which feature antique furniture or knockoffs. My favorite rooms have plenty of space and varnished wood floors. This place is very similar in feel to La Casa Grande (below), but trumps it in terms of amenities and comfort. As with La Casa Grande, these folks often cater to prospective adoptive parents or those in the middle of the process, and are very close to the American embassy. The San Carlos has a small lap pool in a pretty garden area.

Av. La Reforma 7-89, Zona 10. ℂ 502/2332-6055. Fax 502/2331-6056. www.hsancarlos.com. 17 units. Q675 ($90/£47) double; Q938–Q1,313 ($125–$175/£66–£92) suites. Rates include continental breakfast. AE, DC, MC, V. Free parking. Amenities: Restaurant; bar; lounge; pool; tour desk; room service 6am–10pm; salon; laundry service. *In room:* TV, dataport, coffeemaker, hair dryer, safe.

Otelito Casa Santa Clara *Finds*   This small, boutique hotel is the most hip and stylish option in the area. Each room is distinct, but all feature minimalist decor and subdued tones. Most have one or two queen-size beds, and either wood or tile floors. The bathrooms all feature marble floors and showers with thick seamless glass walls and doors. I like the "Pistachio" and "Mandarina" rooms, which are second-floor units toward the back of the building. The suite here comes with a Jacuzzi tub and separate sitting room. The hotel's very elegant restaurant sits in a high-roofed atrium area just off the reception, and serves an excellent breakfast and changing seasonal dinner menu.

12a Calle 4-51, Zona 10. (C)/fax **502/2339-1811**. www.otelito.com. 12 units. Q638–Q900 ($85–$120/£45–£63) double; Q1,200 ($160/£84) suite. AE, DC, MC, V. Free valet parking. **Amenities:** Restaurant; bar; room service; free Wi-Fi. *In room:* A/C, TV, minibar, hair dryer, safe.

Radisson Hotel & Suites 𝒜𝒜 This is another excellent and well-located business-class hotel in Zona 10. The rooms are all quite large and well appointed, with modern decor and all the amenities you might expect. In fact, all rooms could really be classified as suites, or at the very least junior suites. Each has a large sitting area, dry bar, and kitchenette. The rooms also come with DVD players, and the hotel has an extensive library of titles available for rental. Wi-Fi is available in public areas and in most of the rooms, and Ethernet connections are available in all rooms. The service here is excellent. Separate floors are reserved for single women travelers, families, or those involved in the adoption process. There's a small sushi bar and restaurant just off the lobby, in addition to their more typical restaurant serving international fare.

1a Av. 12-46, Zona 10. (C) **800/333-3333** in the U.S. and Canada, or 502/2421-5151 in Guatemala. Fax 502/2332-9772. www.radisson.com. 115 units. Q675–Q900 ($90–$120/£47–£63) double. AE, DC, MC, V. Free parking. **Amenities:** 2 restaurants; bar; small gym; sauna; Jacuzzi; tour desk; room service 6am–11pm; in-room massage; babysitting; laundry service; nonsmoking rooms. *In room:* A/C, TV, minibar, coffeemaker, kitchenette, hair dryer, safe.

MODERATE

Best Western Stofella 𝒜 *Value* This well-located modern hotel is everything you might expect from a popular chain, but not much more. The rooms are well-appointed and well-equipped, but lack anything in the way of style or personality. The gaudy floral bedspreads could really use some updating. Still, it's located on an excellent street in the heart of the Zona Viva, and the price is right. In fact, if you book on the Internet, you can often get a better deal. Service is attentive and accommodating, and a host of restaurants, bars, and shops are within easy walking distance.

2a Av. 12-28, Zona 10. (C) **502/2338-5600**. Fax 502/2331-0823. www.stofella.com. 70 units. Q450–Q675 ($60–$90/£32–£47) double. AE, DISC, MC, V. Free parking. **Amenities:** Restaurant; bar; small gym; Jacuzzi; 24-hr. room service; laundry service. *In room:* A/C, TV, dataport, hair dryer, safe.

La Casa Grande *Kids* This small boutique hotel harkens back to an earlier time. With whitewashed walls and a red-clay tile roof, this two-story building is an anomaly in an area of high-rise glass and steel buildings. Rooms feature antique tile floors and Victorian-style furnishings and decor. Even though the main building is set back from the street, the rooms closest to the street can be noisy. This hotel has earned its current popularity by catering mostly to families in the country to meet, bond with, and adopt Guatemalan infants. The hotel is next door to the United States embassy, and provides many services and facilities for these new families. La Casa Grande has several pleasant courtyard and interior sitting areas.

Av. La Reforma 7-57, Zona 10. (C)/fax **502/2332-0914**. www.casagrande-gua.com. 28 units. Q413–Q563 ($55–$75/£29–£39) double. AE, DISC, MC, V. Free parking. **Amenities:** Restaurant; bar; room service 6am–10pm; laundry service. *In room:* TV, minibar, coffeemaker, hair dryer.

INEXPENSIVE

Hotel Ciudad Vieja This is probably the best budget option in a section of town dominated by high-end, high-rise hotels. This place is a definite step up in quality and price from the backpacker options you'll find in Zona 1, but still inexpensive enough to qualify as a bargain here. The rooms are of good size, with comfortable beds and tasteful decorations. Perhaps the best thing this hotel has going for it is its large garden area. The more informal restaurant here is located in a lovely courtyard, in a large glass atrium. The intimate bar, with its low vaulted ceiling, is a popular meeting place for guests.

8a Calle 3-67, Zona 10. Ⓒ **502/2331-9104.** www.hotelciudadvieja.com. 26 units. Q375 ($50/£26) double. Rates include full breakfast. AE, DC, MC, V. Free parking. **Amenities:** 2 restaurants; bar; laundry service; nonsmoking rooms. *In room:* TV, free Wi-Fi.

Tivoli Travel Lodge *Value*   This small bed-and-breakfast offers good value in a safe and homelike environment. The rooms and public facilities are modest, but the rooms are quite attractive, with firm beds with heavy wooden headboards and attractive decor. The owners here are very helpful and have a good in-house tour operation.

5a Av. A 13-42, Zona 9. Ⓒ **502/5510-0032.** Fax 502/5506-7695. www.tivolitravellodge.com. 5 units. Q240 ($32/£17) double. Rates include breakfast. AE, MC, V. Free parking. **Amenities:** Restaurant; bar; tour desk; laundry service; non-smoking rooms. *In room:* TV, free Wi-Fi.

ZONA 1

This is the heart of the downtown colonial core of Guatemala City, and is often referred to as the "Old Town," or "Old City." The area is convenient for visiting many of the city's colonial-era attractions, and is full of hotels. You'll definitely get more bang for your buck down here as well. However, this is a busy part of town, and tourists are often targeted for pickpocketing and petty crime. Tourists need to be particularly careful after dark, when I recommend you take a taxi, even for short trips.

MODERATE

Hotel Royal Palace ✦ *Finds*   This is the most atmospheric option in the Old Town. From the crystal chandeliers in the grand lobby to the well-maintained rooms, this classic hotel maintains all the charm and ambience of a bygone era. The rooms are large and stylish, some with carpeting and others with antique tile floors. My favorite rooms are those with balconies overlooking the street, where you can watch the daily parade from the comfort of your own room. (The trade-off for this great people-watching is more street noise.) The sparsely equipped gym is a bit of an embarrassment, but the cedar sauna is quite inviting.

6a Av. 12-66, Zona 1. Ⓒ **502/2220-8970.** Fax 502/2238-3715. www.hotelroyalpalace.com. 74 units. Q413 ($55/£29) double; Q488 ($65/£34) junior suite. Rates include 22% tax. AE, DISC, MC, V. Free parking. **Amenities:** Restaurant; bar; gym; sauna; concierge; tour desk; 24-hr. room service; laundry service. *In room:* TV, hair dryer, safe.

INEXPENSIVE

In addition to the places listed below, **Hotel Spring,** 8a Av. 12-65, Zona 1 (Ⓒ **502/ 2230-2858**); and **Hotel Ajau** (Ⓒ **502/2232-0488;** hotelajau@hotmail.com), 8a Av. 15-62, Zona 1, are two other good budget options.

Chalet Suizo *Overrated*   This popular budget hotel is clean and safe, but lacks any charm or style. Rooms are spotless but very basic, with bare walls and nondescript decor. Each floor shares a broad interior veranda with various sitting areas, and the hotel has a nice central courtyard garden, which makes this a great place to meet fellow travelers.

7 Calle 14-34, Zona 1. Ⓒ **502/2251-3786.** Fax 502/2232-0429. 30 units (15 with private bathroom). Q150 ($20/ £14) double with shared bathroom; Q225 ($30/£16) double with private bathroom. MC, V. Free parking. **Amenities:** Restaurant; tour desk; laundry service. *In room:* No phone.

Hotel Colonial   The exterior and interior public areas of this downtown hotel are extremely charming. I especially like the interior central courtyard, with its fountain

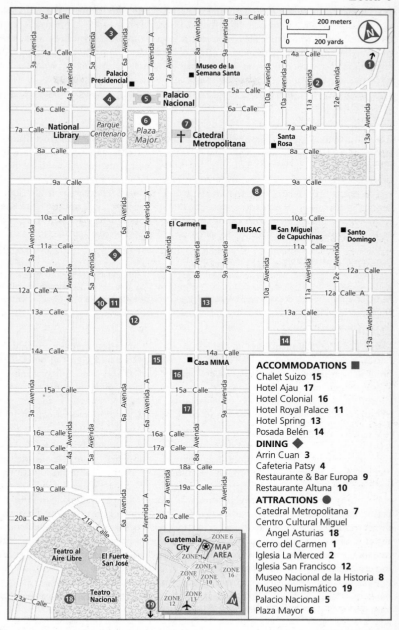

ACCOMMODATIONS ■
Chalet Suizo **15**
Hotel Ajau **17**
Hotel Colonial **16**
Hotel Royal Palace **11**
Hotel Spring **13**
Posada Belén **14**

DINING ◆
Arrin Cuan **3**
Cafeteria Patsy **4**
Restaurante & Bar Europa **9**
Restaurante Altuna **10**

ATTRACTIONS ●
Catedral Metropolitana **7**
Centro Cultural Miguel
 Ángel Asturias **18**
Cerro del Carmen **1**
Iglesia La Merced **2**
Iglesia San Francisco **12**
Museo Nacional de la Historia **8**
Museo Numismático **19**
Palacio Nacional **5**
Plaza Mayor **6**

and wrought-iron furniture. The rooms are fairly simple and plain, and some could use updating and maintenance. Still, for the price, this is a good, safe budget option in the heart of downtown. Most of the rooms have two or three twin beds, and either varnished wood or antique tile floors. The more expensive rooms have more space. My favorites are the second-floor units with small balconies overlooking 7a Avenida. The restaurant serves simple and acceptable Guatemalan and international fare.

7a Av. 14-19, Zona 1. Ⓒ **502/2232-6722** or 502/2232-2955. Fax 2232-8671. www.hotelcolonial.net. 42 units. Q113–Q180 ($15–$24/£7.90–£13) double. MC, V. Free parking. **Amenities:** Restaurant; laundry service; nonsmoking rooms. *In room:* TV, no phone.

Posada Belén ⚜ ⓥₐₗᵤₑ   If you're looking for a charming, family-run bed-and-breakfast at a very reasonable price, this should be your first choice in Zona 1. In fact, it's my top budget choice in the whole city. The converted colonial-era home that houses this hotel was built in 1873, and features a lush and beautiful interior garden. Rooms are decorated in a mixed style with rustic wood furniture, checkerboard tile floors, washed walls, and local arts and crafts. The hotel is set on a short transited street, so its rooms are quieter than many of the downtown options. This place advertises itself as a "museum," and they have a very extensive collection of Maya artifacts and colonial-era art and carvings. The owners and their in-house guides and drivers are very friendly, knowledgeable, and professional.

13a Calle A10-30, Zona 1. Ⓒ **866/864-8283** in the U.S. and Canada, or 502/2253-4530 or 502/2232-9226 in Guatemala. Fax 502/2251-3478. www.posadabelen.com. 11 units. Q334 ($45/£23) double. Rates include full breakfast. AE, DC, DISC, MC, V. Free parking. **Amenities:** Restaurant; lounge; tour desk; room service 7am–10pm; laundry service. *In room:* Safe, no phone.

ZONA 11

While not generally mentioned in the typical list of tourist-recommended neighborhoods, Zona 11 is home to the Tikal Futura, a major, modern high-rise hotel. This hotel is located right at the point where the highway to and from Antigua and the Western Highlands enters the downtown area. If you're planning on renting a car, it's convenient to stay here and have it delivered to the hotel. When you head out, simply turn right as you exit the hotel, and you'll be on Calzada Roosevelt, which soon turns into CA-1.

Grand Tikal Futura ⚜⚜   Originally built and run as a Grand Hyatt, this hotel features a soaring atrium lobby hung heavy with flowing vines. From the outside, the architecture is meant to suggest the shape of the pyramids at its namesake archaeological site, although I never quite get that impression. The rooms are all very comfortable and up to luxury standards, with lots of space, plenty of shiny marble in the bathroom, and all the modern amenities you could want. The rooms on the higher floors command fabulous views. The gym and spa are perhaps the best of any hotel in the city, with a lovely indoor pool and a large, well-equipped workout area with separate locker rooms. The hotel is connected to a large modern mall, with a food court, movie theaters, and scores of shops. The hotel features a good Thai restaurant and popular bar, and also provides a free airport shuttle.

Calzada Roosevelt 22-43, Zona 11 Ⓒ **502/2410-0800**. Fax 502/2440-4050. www.grandtikalfutura.com.gt. 205 units. Q750–Q975 ($100–$130/£53–£68) double; Q1,500 ($200/£105) executive suite; Q4,500–Q5,250 ($600–$700/£315–£368) diplomatic or presidential suite. AE, DISC, MC, V. Free parking. **Amenities:** 2 restaurants; bar; lounge; indoor pool; 2 outdoor lit tennis courts; Jacuzzi; well-equipped gym and spa; tour desk; salon; shopping arcade; 24-hr. room service; in-room massage; babysitting; laundry service; nonsmoking rooms; 2 squash courts. *In room:* A/C, TV, dataport, hair dryer, coffeemaker, safe, Wi-Fi.

ZONA 13 (NEAR THE AIRPORT)

There are a couple of hotel choices right near the airport. However, given the fact that hotels in zonas 9 and 10 are less than 10 minutes away from the airport by taxi, this is a very limited advantage and minor consideration. You'll enjoy much better access to restaurants, bars, and shopping if you stay at any of the hotels listed above. However, these are two good options if you really want to be close to the airport.

EXPENSIVE

Crowne Plaza ⓖ   If you have your heart set on finding a modern, business-class hotel right near the airport, look no further. In fact, this is your only option in this category. The Crowne Plaza is everything you might expect and could want, especially if you're only staying here before or just after a flight. Most of the rooms were renovated in 2005, so they're in good shape, and many have excellent views of the surrounding mountains and volcanoes. All of the rooms offer free Wi-Fi access. The gym and spa are modern and well-equipped, and for those looking for less health-conscious entertainment, there's a casino attached to the hotel.

Av. Las Ameritas 9-08, Zona 13. ⓒ **502/2422-5000.** Fax 502/2422-5001. www.crowneplaza.com. 183 units. Q788 ($105/£552) double; Q1,013 ($135/£71) executive level or junior suite; Q1,875 ($250/£131) suite. AE, DISC, MC, V. Free parking. **Amenities:** Restaurant; bar; lounge; midsize outdoor pool; Jacuzzi; well-equipped gym and spa; tour desk; car rental desk; salon; room service 6am–2am; babysitting, laundry service; nonsmoking rooms; casino. *In room:* A/C, TV, dataport, coffeemaker, safe, Wi-Fi.

INEXPENSIVE

Dos Lunas Guest House ⓥ𝘢𝘭𝘶𝘦   This basic hotel is somewhere between a hostel and a cozy bed-and-breakfast. Rooms are simple and very well-maintained, and the shared bathrooms are kept spotless. The one room with its own bathroom is very nice, and has a queen-size bed with a carved-wood headboard. There are a couple small interior gardens and a common lounge area with cable television. Free Internet access is available on the public computers, and the hotel will provide free airport pickup if you provide your flight information.

21a Calle 10-92, Zona 13. ⓒ/fax **502/2334-5264** or ⓒ 502/2332-5691. www.hoteldoslunas.com. 6 units (1 with private bathroom). Q75 ($10/£5.25) per person shared bathroom; Q225 ($30/£16) double. Rates include full breakfast. MC, V. Free parking. **Amenities:** Restaurant; tour desk; laundry service. *In room:* No phone.

4 Where to Dine

Guatemala City has some excellent restaurants. As with the hotels, the best and most varied selection of restaurants is to be found in *zonas* 9 and 10. Likewise, there are some good restaurants in Zona 1, particularly for lunch, as the area can be a little sketchy at night. One excellent exception is the 2-square-block pedestrian mall area of Zona 4 known as **Cuatro Grados Norte,** which is full of bars, restaurants, shops, and art galleries.

For those with problems adjusting to the local flavor, you'll find no shortage of fast-food chains, including **McDonald's, Burger King, Pizza Hut, Wendy's, Quiznos,** and **KFC.** If you want to sample a local version, try the fried chicken at **Pollo Campero.**

ZONAS 9 & 10

In addition to the places listed below, **Siriacos,** 1a Av. 12-16, Zona 10 (ⓒ **502/2334-6316**), and the restaurant at the boutique hotel **Otelito Casa Santa Clara,** 12a Calle 4-51, Zona 10 (ⓒ **502/2339-1811**), are two excellent, upscale fusion restaurants with many local fans. For French food, try **Jean François,** Diagonal 6 13-63, Zona 10

(© **502/2333-4786**), and for sushi try **Sushi-Itto,** 4a Av. 16-01, Zona 10 (© **502/ 2368-0181**). Refined Italian food can be found at **Pecorino,** 11a Calle 3-36, Zona 10 (© **502/2360-3035**).

VERY EXPENSIVE

Jake's ✸✸ INTERNATIONAL/FUSION   This long-standing and very popular restaurant is perennially—and still—one of the top spots in Guatemala City. Like Tamarindos (below), this place features a long menu with a wide range of dishes culled from various world cuisines, but the vibe and execution are a bit more conservative on many levels. You can get a straight Caesar or Caprese salad, as well as any number of pasta plates. Steaks are of excellent cut and perfectly prepared. Service is semi-formal and very attentive. The "tablecloths" are blank sheets of white paper, and there's a cup of crayons on every table. There's a cool bar off the front of the operation. Jake's also has an extensive and reasonably priced wine list.

17a Calle 10-40, Zona 10. © 502/2368-0351. Reservations recommended. Main courses Q75–Q215 ($10–$29/ £5.50–£15). AE, DC, MC, V. Mon–Sat noon–3pm and 7–10:30pm, Sun noon–4pm.

Tamarindos ✸✸✸ *(Finds)* INTERNATIONAL/FUSION   This is my favorite restaurant in town. It offers a perfect blend of creative and artful cooking, accompanied by attentive service and a very attractive ambience. The restaurant is also very popular with Guatemala City's upper crust, which is evident from all the oversize SUVs, chauffeurs, and bodyguards lined up out front. Once you run that gauntlet and are inside, there are several different dining rooms, each with its own decor. All feature subdued lighting combined with a minimalist modern aesthetic. White muslin is draped from ceiling beams, and glass doors and screens divide the spaces. The menu is long and eclectic, running the gamut from steak with a chile poblano sauce to moo shu duck. Italy and Asia are the dominant culinary influences, with everything from sushi to risotto, but there are some traditional Continental dishes on the menu as well. However, don't dismiss the specials. On a recent visit, I sampled an appetizer of homemade ravioli stuffed with pear and ricotta cheese, served over a bed of caramelized onions with a red cherry and balsamic vinegar sauce. It was one of the most memorable dishes I've had in my life. Save room for dessert; their molten *bomba de chocolate* (chocolate bomb) is superb.

11a Calle 2-19A, Zona 10. © 502/2360-2815. Reservations recommended. Main courses Q68–Q230 ($9–$30/ £4.80–£16). AE, DC, MC, V. Mon–Sat noon–4pm and 7:30–10:30pm.

EXPENSIVE

Kacao ✸✸ *(Finds)* GUATEMALAN   This elegant restaurant is *the* place to come for traditional Guatemalan cooking prepared and presented with style and flare. Various regional specialties include *pepian,* chicken in a pumpkin seed and tomato sauce from the Western Highlands, and *tapado,* spicy Caribbean seafood soup in coconut milk. The silky blackbean soup is finished off in a clay bowl and baked in the oven. There are a host of steak, poultry, and seafood options. For dessert, try the fried apple rings served with a vanilla-rum sauce. The restaurant decor is as traditional as the menu. Waiters wear traditional Maya garb, and the tablecloths are old *huipiles.* Service can be a tad slow, but it's worth the wait.

1a Av. 13-44, Zona 10. © 502/2237-4188 or 502/2377-4189. Reservations recommended. Main courses Q79–Q165 ($11–$22/£5.50–£12). AE, DC, MC, V. Daily noon–4pm and 6–11pm.

MODERATE

Casa Chapina ✸ GUATEMALAN   While nowhere near as formal or fancy as Kacao, this is another good option for traditional Guatemalan cooking. The first thing you'll notice is the open area where local women are hand-making fresh tortillas on steel *comales* over open flames. The rest of the space features high ceilings, wood furniture, and various wall hangings of traditional Guatemalan textiles. Unfortunately, there are also a couple of TVs showing sporting events or whatever the staff wants to watch when there's no game on. Wandering mariachi groups come through from time to time and will play you a song or two for a few *quetzales*. The menu is heavy on steak and grilled chicken dishes. Every meal is served with three different sauces, two of which are fairly spicy. Be sure to ask for some of those fresh tortillas, or you may be served some mediocre garlic bread.

1a Av. 13–42, Zona 10. *C* **502/2337-0143** or 502/2368-0663. Main courses Q50–Q80 ($6.65–$11/£3.50–£5.60). AE, DC, MC, V. Daily 7am–11pm.

Frida's *(Finds* MEXICAN   While I find the Mexican fare here average at best, I do enjoy the convivial atmosphere and lively crowd that fills this casual joint. I usually order nachos and other appetizers to accompany the delicious, but slightly sweet, margaritas. If hungrier, I opt for the *enchiladas de mole poblana,* corn tortillas stuffed with shredded chicken and topped with a spicy, chocolate-based sauce. The tortilla soup is also very good. The decor features reproductions of artwork by the joint's namesake, the late Mexican artist, Frida Kahlo.

3a Av. 14-60, Zona 10. *C* **502/2367-1611**. Reservations recommended. Main courses Q40–Q70 ($5.35–$9.35/£2.80–£4.90). AE, DC, MC, V. Daily noon–1am.

Hacienda Real *★★* STEAKHOUSE   This is one of the city's best steakhouses, and their success has allowed them to open several branches around town. This is the first and best location, and the only one truly close to the main tourist trail. The interior is quite atmospheric, with heavy wooden tables and chairs, several dining rooms, and an open courtyard area. Antique wood-cart wheels lean against the walls, and an abundance of ferns and potted plants are spread about. The plain grilled steaks are superb. If you want more flavor, order the *lomito pimienta,* which comes with a green pepper sauce.

13 Calle 1-10, Zona 10. Tel **502/2333-5408**. Reservations recommended. Main courses Q65–Q150 ($8.65–$20/ £4.55–£11). AE, DC, MC, V. Daily noon–10:30pm.

Tapas y Cañas *★* SPANISH   Head to Altuna (see below) if you want traditional Spanish fare and ambience, but come here if you're looking for a more modern interpretation of Spain's classic cooking. Sure you can get some pretty traditional tapas and main dishes, but they are served up on fancy white plates, with artistic arrangements and ornamental dustings of ground peppers and herbs. You'll also find dishes that take their cue from other cuisines, like the tangy barbecued lamb chops. The main dining room has a modern feel, with clean lines, dim lighting, and contemporary tables, chairs, and settings, while the exposed brick wall, red tile floors, and wood beam ceilings hark back to an earlier era.

13a Calle 7-78, Zona 10. *C* **502/2367-2166**. Reservations recommended. Tapas Q30–Q60 ($4–$8/£2.10–£4.20); main courses Q55–Q95 ($7.35–$13/£3.85–£6.65). AE, DC, MC, V. Daily noon–11pm.

Tre Fratelli ITALIAN   This popular chain, with branches across Central America and a couple in California and Texas, serves respectable northern Italian fare with a slight American flare. I love the sidewalk tables that are set off a busy section of the Zona Viva. I like to start things off with their Cinque Domande salad, which features mixed lettuce, Gorgonzola cheese, almonds, and a delicious balsamic vinegar dressing. For a main, I recommend the Bistecca Inferno, a thick cut of meat with a spicy brandy-cream sauce. There's also a wide selection of pastas, and several good pizzas cooked in a wood-fired oven. The portions here are pretty hefty, so come with an appetite.

2a Av. 13-25, Zona 10. ℂ **502/2366-3164.** Reservations recommended. Pizzas Q44–Q59 ($5.85–$7.85/ £3.10–£4.10); pastas Q59–Q84 ($7.85–$11/£4.15–£5.90); main courses Q74–Q89 ($9.85–$12/£5.20–£6.20). AE, DC, MC, V. Daily noon–11pm.

INEXPENSIVE

Panadería San Martin *Value* COFFEE SHOP/BAKERY   Set on a busy corner in the heart of the Zona Viva, this place is extremely popular and busy throughout the day. Folks come here for breakfast, lunch, or a coffee break, and the San Martin handles them all well. Breakfasts are excellent, and you can't beat the lunch special of soup alongside a half-sandwich and a half-salad for Q40 ($5.35/£2.80). These folks have a bakery on premises, and a wide selection of sweets and gourmet coffees. The indoor seating is a bit too sterile for me, with its high-backed booths and Formica tables. I prefer to grab a seat in the shady outdoor patio or on the front veranda.

13a Calle 1-62, Zona 10. ℂ **502/2385-4929.** Reservations not accepted. Main courses Q22–Q40 ($3–$5.35/ £1.55–£2.80). AE, DC, MC, V. Daily 6am–8:30pm.

ZONA 1
MODERATE

Restaurante Altuna ✿ SPANISH   The old-world charm of this Spanish restaurant fits perfectly with the architecture and Spanish colonial history of Zona 1. This place is light on tapas, but has a long list of main dishes. There's excellent paella, of course, but I also recommend squid in its own ink, as well as the *bacalao a la Vizcaina,* which uses imported cod in a tasty medley of tomatoes, peppers, and garlic. In addition, fish and shrimp come in a score of different preparations. Terrestrial fare includes a delicious rabbit stew and several steak options. Service is relatively formal and reserved, but very professional. This place has an extensive and fairly priced wine list. There's a second branch of Altuna in the trendy Zona Viva at 10a Calle 0-45, Zona 10 (ℂ **502/ 2332-6576**).

5a Av. 12-31, Zona 1. ℂ **502/2251-7185** or 502/2232-0669. www.restaurantealtuna.com. Reservations recommended. Main courses Q51–Q155 ($6.80–$21/£3.60–£11). AE, DC, MC, V. Daily noon–10pm.

INEXPENSIVE

For a quick coffee break or light bite, head to **Cafetería Patsy,** 6a Calle 5-13, Zona 1 (ℂ **502/2285-0331**), a simple and bright cafe on a busy corner of the Plaza Mayor.

Arrin Cuan ✿ *Kids* GUATEMALAN   This is my favorite restaurant in Zona 1. The rambling old building that houses the classic Guatemalan eatery is a quiet retreat in this busy area. The main dining room features wood tables crammed around the edges of a small interior garden. Hanging ferns and potted plants liven everything up. The menu is heavy on Guatemalan classics, with such regional dishes as *kac ik,* a filling turkey soup from the Alta Verapaz. If you want to sample something really exotic, order the *tepezquintle,* a large rodent served grilled over hot charcoal. This place has a children's play area, and plenty of free parking in a guarded lot across the street. They also have a branch in the Zona Viva at 16a Calle 4-32, Zona 10 (ℂ **502/2366-2660**), but I prefer this original site. A marimba band plays most days during lunch and dinner.

5a Av. 3-27, Zona 1. ℂ **502/2238-0242.** www.arrincuan.com. Main courses Q45–Q75 ($6–$10/£3.15–£5.25). AE, DC, MC, V. Daily 7am–10pm.

Restaurante & Bar Europa *(Finds* AMERICAN/INTERNATIONAL   For more than a decade this has been *the* hangout for American expatriates, Peace Corps workers, and assorted travelers. You can get excellent burgers and club sandwiches, as well as spicy, thick chili and a wide range of bar and comfort food. Breakfasts are huge, and this might be the only place in Guatemala to get good hash browns in the morning. The upstairs bar will always have a sports game on, and the place gets hopping during any playoff season.

11a Calle 5-16, Zona 1. ⓒ 502/2253-4929. Main courses Q30–Q75 ($4–$10/£2.10–£5.25). AE, DC, MC, V. Mon–Sat 8am–1am.

ZONA 4
INEXPENSIVE
L'Osteria *ⓡ (Kids* ITALIAN/PIZZA   This is my favorite restaurant in the Cuatro Grados Norte area. The menu is fairly limited, with not much more than a range of pasta dishes and thin-crust pizzas. Still, they do both of these well, and the setting is very enjoyable. The pizzas are cooked in a wood-burning brick oven, and the pasta portions are large. For a change, you could get the eggplant parmigiana or some hearty minestrone soup. The ambience is casual and homey. On sunny afternoons, I like to grab one of the outdoor tables underneath the hanging vines on the large front patio, which offers a great view of the pedestrian traffic outside the restaurant's iron fence. This is a great option for families, especially on Sundays, when a magician or a storyteller usually performs in the afternoon.

Ruta 2, 4-75, Zona 4. ⓒ 502/2379-8719. Main courses Q60–Q90 ($8–$12/£2.40–£6.30). AE, DC, MC, V. Tues–Thurs 11am–3pm and 6–10:30pm; Fri–Sat 11am–3pm and 6pm–midnight; Sun 11am–9pm.

ZONA 14
EXPENSIVE
Ambia *ⓡⓡⓡ (Finds* INTERNATIONAL/FUSION   This slightly hard-to-find restaurant is worth the effort. It's set on the grounds of a small complex of shops, most of which specialize in high-end kitchen design, wine, foodstuffs, and kitchen wares. The main dining area is outdoors on a large stone patio under a soaring roof, or out in the open under canvas umbrellas. A few additional tables are set on a covered veranda overlooking this patio, and there's another quiet room for more intimate occasions. The menu and wine list are both huge and inviting. They call what they do "New Age," though I liken it to the fusion cuisine you'll find most places. The menu features a fair number of vegetarian items, and there's a heavy Asian influence throughout.

10a Av. 5-49, Zona 14. ⓒ 502/2322-3232. Reservations recommended. Main courses Q75–Q195 ($10–$26/£5.25–£14). AE, MC, V. Mon–Sat noon–3:30pm and 7–10:30pm; Sun noon–3:30pm.

5 What to See & Do

While it's certainly easy to visit all of these attractions on your own by taxi, many travelers like the convenience and built-in guide offered by organized city tours. **Clark Tours,** 7a Av. 14-76, Zona 9, inside Clark Plaza (ⓒ **502/2412-4700;** www.clarktours. com.gt); **Grayline Guatemala,** 1a Av. 13-22, Zona 10, inside the Holiday Inn (ⓒ **502/ 2383-8600;** www.graylineguatemala.com); and **Maya Vacations,** 12a Calle 2-04, Zona 9 (ⓒ **502/233-4638;** www.mayavacations.com), all offer city tours. Most of these combine a tour around the principal attractions of Zona 1 and the colonial core, with stops at the **Museo Popul Vuh, Museo Ixchel del Traje Indígena,** and one of the city's large markets.

ZONA 1

Catedral Metropolitana (Metropolitan Cathedral) ✸✸ This stately, blue-domed, earthquake-resistant cathedral was completed in 1868 after 86 years of construction. The neoclassical structure inspires both austerity and awe, with its stone floors, colonial paintings, lofty arches, and bursts of gold at its altars. Perhaps the cathedral's most striking feature is the entrance, which is supported by 12 pillars, each of which is inscribed with the names of hundreds of Guatemalans who died or "disappeared" during the civil war. The interior is large and filled with religious icons, carvings, and artworks. You can tour the cathedral in about 20 minutes.

8a Calle and 7a Av., Zona 1. No phone. Free admission. Daily 8am–8pm.

Centro Cultural Miguel Angel Asturias (Miguel Angel Asturias Cultural Center) ✸ Set on a hill overlooking downtown and named for Guatemala's most renowned literary figure, this complex houses the National Theater, a chamber theater, and an open-air theater within a modernist structure that almost looks like an ocean liner. Built originally in 1827 among the ruins of the San José military fortress, the complex has grown and was officially inaugurated in 1978. Among the theaters and galleries, you can find a variety of reasonably priced shows and exhibitions, ranging from plays by Guatemalan authors and Shakespeare in Spanish to marimba concerts and ballet. The view from the top is beautiful. This complex also contains a military museum, a small art gallery, conference rooms, and three cafeterias.

24a Calle 3-81, Centro Cívico, Zona 1. ✆ 502/2232-4041. Free admission. Daily 8am–6pm. Various theater, dance, and concert performances take place at night. Ticket prices vary.

Cerro del Carmen The name of this spot translates to "Carmen Hill," and it's a beautiful perch from which to take in the view of Guatemala City below. Adorning the hilltop is a Carmelite hermitage, which was left close to ruins by the 1976 earthquake. However, this hermitage does possess a beautiful silver embossed image of the Virgin of Carmen that dates back to the early 1600s. Be careful when visiting this area, and definitely do not come here after dark.

1a Av. and 1a Calle A, Zona 1. No phone. Free admission. Daily 24 hr.

Iglesia La Merced (La Merced Church) ✸ Not to be confused with its more famous sister church of the same name in Antigua, this lovely baroque-style building has one of the most ornate facades of any Catholic church in Guatemala City. The interior is quite stunning as well, and features an extensive collection of religious art, sculpture, and relics. Originally built and administered by the order of La Merced, it was taken over by the Jesuits in the early 19th century.

5a Calle and 11a Av., Zona 1. ✆ 502/2232-0631. Free admission. Daily 6am–6pm.

Iglesia San Francisco (San Francisco Church) ✸✸ The namesake Franciscan order built this baroque church in the early 19th century. The main altar is an impressive piece of work, at almost 91m (300 ft.) tall and 12m (40 ft.) wide. The church is famous for its woodcarvings, which include its main altar and a couple of beautiful pieces donated by King Charles V of Spain.

13a Calle and 6a Av., Zona 1. ✆ 502/2232-6325. Free admission. Daily 6am–5pm.

Museo Nacional de la Historia (National History Museum) This modest history museum is located in a beautiful old building that once housed the National Property Registry. The museum contains a collection of paintings and historical artifacts, mostly from the 18th and 19th centuries and relating to past governments, presidents, and other important historical figures. One room is a re-creation of former President Jorge Ubico's living room. The museum is a bit unimaginative and provincial in my opinion, but it merits a half-hour visit as you walk around Zona 1.

9a Calle 9-70, Zona 1. (C) 502/2253-6149. Admission Q10 ($1.35/70p). Mon–Fri 9am–5:30pm.

Museo Numismático (Numismatic Museum)   Coin and bill collectors will want to stop by this new museum, which is largely the initiative of the Banco de Guatemala. In addition to a broad collection of the country's currency throughout the ages, which ranges from shells, obsidian, and cacao beans to more modern pieces of coinage and paper money, the museum also features a few early instruments for fashioning coins and a hefty ingot of gold dating back to the colonial era.

Plazoleta del Banco de Guatemala (Bank of Guatemala Plaza), Centro Cívico, Zona 1. (C) 502/2429-6000. www.banguat. gob.gt. Free admission. Mon–Fri 9am–3pm.

Palacio Nacional (National Palace) ⍟   The grand *palacio,* the Plaza Mayor's most ornate building, once housed the nation's executive branch. It was built by prison laborers under the order of President Jorge Ubico, and was completed in 1943. Many of the 350 rooms are off-limits to the public, but those that *are* open are definitely impressive. Above the Sala de Recepción hangs a sizeable Bohemian crystal chandelier, on which brass and golden *quetzales* perch. A second chandelier, this one of solid 18-karat gold, adorns the Sala de Banquetes. In 1980, a car bomb shattered the stained-glass windows on the second floor, which ironically had depicted the 10 Virtues of a Good Nation. Like the nation's virtues themselves, most of the windows have been reconstructed. There's a permanent collection of fine art, as well as several rotating gallery spaces. Free 45-minute tours are offered throughout the day. The highlight of the tour is often a stop at the Presidential Balcony, where you can imagine yourself addressing the nation.

6a Calle, between 6a Av. and 7a Av., Zona 1. (C) 502/2253-0748. Free admission. Daily 9am–noon and 2–5pm.

Plaza Mayor ⍟   Called the "center of all Guatemala," the Plaza Mayor brings together the great powers of Guatemalan society: the government, the church, the army, and the people. It consists of two large plazas, the Parque del Centenario with its central fountain, and the Plaza de las Armas, intended as a military parade ground. The Plaza Mayor was first laid out and designed in 1778, just 2 years after the city was founded. The impressive buildings surrounding the plaza include the Catedral Metropolitana, the Palacio Nacional, and the National Library. Next to the Guatemalan flag in front of the Palacio Nacional burns an Eternal Flame dedicated to the "anonymous heroes of peace." Crowds gather here to celebrate holidays, protest, and sell their goods. The makeshift market here is busiest on Sundays, when vendors offer a wide variety of crafts at reasonable prices, though you might be able to find better deals in the small towns along Lake Atitlán or in Quetzaltenango. While the Plaza Mayor and its surrounding buildings still exude a strong air of colonial charm, I find the placement of a Wendy's franchise right on the corner by the Catedral Metropolitana a little off-putting.

Between 6a Calle and 8a Calle, and between 5a Av. and 7a Av., Zona 1. No phone. Free admission. Daily 24 hr.

ZONA 2

Mapa en Relieve (Relief Map) *Kids*   While I find this attraction a bit cheesy, and the off-scale accentuation of the mountains a bit disconcerting, it's still a great way to get a feel for the lay of the land, and kids love it. What's more awe-inspiring is that this map, constructed in 1904, was done far before the existence of resources such as Google Earth and satellite imaging. Its designer, Francisco Vela, did an impressive job, even if the mountains and volcanoes do come across a bit too tall and pointy. The map shows the country's major roads, rivers, lakes, and railways. Despite its age, this attraction has weathered the years well. The map is massive, covering an area of some 40 by 80m (130 by 260 ft.), and an observation tower gives you a good view. The map isn't in a particularly safe neighborhood, so it's best to come and go by taxi. Allow about 30 minutes to take in this exhibit.

Parque Minerva, Av. Simeón Cañas, Zona 4. (℗ 502/2254-1114. Admission Q15 ($2/£1.05). Daily 9am–5pm.

ZONA 4

Iglesia Yurrita *(Finds* This is not your run-of-the-mill colonial *iglesia.* This captivating structure, with an ornate blood-red tower and stone masonry, was built in 1929 by the Yurrita family. The architecture shows a mix of styles from neo-Gothic to baroque. Many people think it could be the work of Antoni Gaudí, the famous Spanish architect. The interior colors and artwork are almost as spectacular as the exterior. Look for the painted glass window made to look like the daytime sky. This church is also known as La Capilla de Nuestra Señora de las Angustias (The Chapel of Our Lady of Anguish). You can tour the church in about 15 to 20 minutes, so come in a taxi and have the driver wait for you.

Ruta 6 and Vía 8, Calle Mariscal Cruz, Zona 4. (℗ 502/2312-5143. Free admission. Daily 8am–6pm.

ZONA 7

Parque Arqueológico Kaminaljuyú (Kaminaljuyú Archaeological Park) This was a major pre-Classic Maya city that seemed to have both ceremonial and trade functions. As early as A.D. 100, there were more than 200 structures here. The site was only discovered in the 1970s, when construction work unearthed it. The hieroglyphics discovered here predated those from other major Maya sites, and helped push back the first proven examples of Maya literacy. Most of the ruins remain buried, but the bases of a few pyramids and some tombs have been excavated. One of the more striking features of visiting this site is the fact that it exists in the midst of Guatemala City's major urban sprawl. Allow about an hour to visit this site.

12a Av. 11-65, Zona 7. (℗ 502/2322-5571. Admission Q15 ($2/£1.05). Mon–Sat 8am–4pm.

ZONA 10

Zona 10 is also commonly referred to as Zona Viva, though only the small section of Zona 10 with the greatest concentration of hotels, restaurants, and shops falls under this category. Its western boundary is defined by the broad, tree-lined Avenida La Reforma; to the west of the avenue lies Zona 9. Avenida La Reforma was modeled after the Champs Elysees in Paris. At the southern end of the avenue is the Plaza Obelisco, which is a broad rotunda at the center of which sits a tall obelisk and the eternal flame of Guatemala.

Jardín Botánico (Botanical Garden) Guatemala City's almost 18,000-sq.-m (200,000-sq.-ft.) Botanical Garden was the first in Central America and the only one in the country. It displays more than 700 varieties of local and exotic plants, including many endangered species. All exhibits are labeled with their common name in Spanish and their scientific name in Latin. Of late, the Botanical Garden has had some maintenance problems resulting from its precarious financial position. Various international institutions such as the Missouri Botanical Garden have offered to become involved, and hopefully the financial and overall situation will improve.

Calle Mariscal Cruz 1-56, Zona 10. (C) 502/2334-6064. Admission Q10 ($1.35/70p). Mon–Fri 8am–3pm; Sat 8am–noon.

Museo Ixchel del Traje Indígena (Ixchel Museum of Indigenous Dress) 𝕽𝕽

Ixchel was the Maya goddess of fertility and weaving, and she certainly inspired artistic talent in her people. A collection of textiles from approximately 120 indigenous communities is on display here, providing a good introduction to and history of the crafts travelers are likely to see on their journey across the country. The museum also has two permanent exhibitions of paintings: 61 watercolors of Maya traditional dress from the collection of Carmen de Pettersen, and 48 oil paintings of the Cakchiquel artist Andrés Curruchiche. Three 13-minute videos are shown by request on the second floor. I recommend you ask to see the one on traditional fabrics even before you tour the museum. Allow about 1 hour to visit the museum, a little more if you watch all the videos. It's located on the tranquil campus of a small university, making it a nice place to bring a picnic lunch.

Universidad Francisco Marroquín, end of 6a Calle, Zona 10. (C) 502/2231-3739. www.museoixchel.org. Admission Q30 ($4/£2.10). Mon–Fri 8am–5:30pm; Sat 9am–1pm.

Museo Popol Vuh 𝕽

Named for the most famous Maya holy text, this museum houses an impressive collection of pre-Columbian art, spread through some six or seven small rooms. It's adjacent to the Museo Ixchel (see above) on the campus of the Universidad Francisco Marroquín. The collection includes stone sculpture, multicolored pottery, incense holders, and even funeral pyres. Don't miss the huge "Lord Bat" sculpture. There's also an area featuring colonial art, along with other folklore such as traditional dance masks and clothing. The museum offers special events, public lectures, and courses on everything from Maya cuisine to Egyptology. It should take you about 1 hour to tour this museum.

Universidad Francisco Marroquín, end of 6a Calle, Zona 10. (C) 502/2361-2301. Admission Q25 ($3.35/£1.75), Q15 ($2/£1.05) students, Q10 ($1.35/70p) children under 12. Mon–Fri 9am–5pm; Sat 9am–1pm.

ZONA 13

This is a modern and well-maintained part of the city, which includes the airport, several prominent museums, and the city's zoo. Any trip to the attractions in this *zona* should also include a stop at the **Mercado de Artesanías (Artisans' Market;** see "Shopping" below).

Aurora Zoo 𝕽 𝙆𝙞𝙙𝙨

Small by world standards but surprisingly well-maintained and attended, the Aurora Zoo is a nice spot to pose for pictures with the wild Guatemalan animals you might not have seen on your journey through the country. Dating back to 1924, the zoo has one of the most impressive collections of animal life in Central America, and features giraffes, hippos, water buffalo, leopards, and lions. Education, conservation, and rehabilitation are the zoo's mission, and they carry it out well. The park is divided into four sections: the African savanna, the Tropics, Asia, and the petting zoo. Various lectures and programs for children are held daily.

Boulevard Juan Pablo II, Zona 13. (C) 502/2475-0894. www.laurorazoo.centroamerica.com. Admission Q18 ($2.40/£1.25) adults, Q8 ($1.05/55p) children under 16. Tues–Sun 9am–5pm.

Museo de Arte Moderno (Museum of Modern Art)

If you're looking for cutting-edge Guatemalan modern art (modern meaning 1800 to the present), a visit here is a must. Avant-garde paintings, caricatures, photographs, sculptures, and other objects fill the halls of this almost-colonial building. Exhibitions include works of national and international artists, mostly Latin Americans. The layout of the building is confusing, but getting lost can result in some interesting sightseeing.

5a Calle and 7a Av., Finca La Aurora, Local 6, Zona 13. © **502/2472-0467.** Admission Q10 ($1.35/70p). Tues–Fri 9am–4pm; Sat–Sun 9am–noon and 2–4pm.

Museo de los Niños (Children's Museum) 😴 *(Kids)*   The museum sets out to secure the future of Guatemala by educating its children—and if it were left up to the building's architects, it's clear that the future would take place on the moon. The lunar-colonial structure houses a wide variety of exhibits for the young and young at heart. If you have a few hours to spare in Guatemala City, let your inner child enjoy the gigantic game of Operation, or ride a bicycle with a skeleton attached to a neighboring bicycle to demonstrate bone movement. Other exhibits, such as the centrifugal force simulator and the static electricity generator, don't *appear* to be 100% harmless to children, inner or otherwise, but don't worry, they're safe. This place is very close to the zoo, making these two attractions a good combination outing for families with children.

5a Calle 10-00, Finca La Aurora, Zona 13. © **502/2475-5076.** Admission Q35 ($4.65/£2.45). Tues–Thurs 8am–noon and 1–5pm; Fri 8am–noon and 1–6pm; Sat–Sun 10am–1:30pm and 2:30–6pm.

Museo Nacional de Etnología y Arqueología (National Museum of Ethnology and Archaeology) 😴😴   The National Ethnology and Archaeology Museum houses the most important collection of Maya archaeological artifacts in the country. It traces indigenous history over the centuries and through the present day, using several hundred Maya artifacts to tell the story. (Unfortunately the only written descriptions are in Spanish.) Exhibits include a room dedicated to Maya technology (paper, and ceramic, shell, and bone tools), as well as a display of indigenous clothing. The highlight of the collection is the jade exhibit, with earrings, bracelets, masks, and an impressive scale model of Tikal. It should take you about an hour to 90 minutes to take everything in.

5a Calle and 7a Av., Finca La Aurora, Local 5, Zona 13. © **502/2472-0478.** Admission Q30 ($4/£2.10). Tues–Fri 9am–4pm; Sat 9am–noon and 2–4pm.

Museo Nacional de Historia Natural (National Museum of Natural History) The museum's founder, Professor Jorge Ibarra, ran the place from its inception in 1950 until 1996, and his name was recently added to the official name of the museum. It's divided into 20 areas, from the Origin of the Universe to an area dedicated to us mammals. While this incarnation of a popular museum is not as extensive as others in major cities around the world, you won't find a room honoring the "Poc" species of duck, an animal native only to Guatemala and close to extinction, anywhere else. Accompanying the museum is a library of books on ecology meant for children.

6a Calle 7-30, Finca La Aurora, Zona 13. © **502/2472-0468.** Admission Q15 ($2/£1.05). Tues–Fri 9am–4pm; Sat–Sun 9am–noon and 2–4pm.

6 Outdoor Activities

Guatemala City is a hectic, somewhat dangerous, congested urban center, and not a particularly inviting place to pursue most outdoor activities. If you want to exercise or get out into nature, you're best off leaving the city.

BIKING   Though you can forget about riding a bicycle in Guatemala City, several tour companies organize mountain biking trips in the hills, mountains, and volcanoes just outside the city. Your best bet is to contact **Old Town Outfitters** ✿✿ (© 502/ 5399-0440; www.bikeguatemala.com), which is based in Antigua and can arrange transportation for you to join any of their daily mountain bike rides. See chapter 5 for more information.

GOLF   Guatemala is not known for its golf, but there are actually several good golf courses close to the city. All of the courses are private or country clubs, but most will usually let outside guests play with advance notice. If you plan on going to Guatemala to play golf, contact the courses below in advance to arrange some playing time. Alternatively, many of the higher-end business hotels in Guatemala City have relationships with one or more of the courses, and can usually arrange tee-times. Greens fees are relatively inexpensive, running between Q335–Q670 ($45–$90/£23–£47).

The **Mayan Golf Club** (© 502/6631-0045; www.mayangolf.com) is one of the best, and is the oldest in Central American (it was founded in 1918, though their course has moved since then). The current course is located 10km (6 miles) from the airport. This regulation 18-hole course plays fairly easy, and offers excellent views of the Pacaya and Agua volcanoes, as well as Lake Amatitlán.

Another good option is the **Hacienda Nueva Country Club** (© 502/6628-1000; www.haciendanueva.com), a modern facility located about 20km (12 miles) outside of downtown at Km 25 of Ruta Nacional 18 on the road to Mataquescuintla.

The **Alta Vista Golf & Tennis Club** (© 502/6641-5057; www.altavistagolf.com) has the most challenging course in the country. This place is located just beyond the Hacienda Nueva Country Club at Km 26.5 of Ruta Nacional 18 on the road to Mataquescuintla.

JOGGING   As is the case with biking, Guatemala City is not very amenable to jogging. There are no public parks or outdoor spaces I can recommend as safe and secure for a foreigner to go jogging, and the busy streets of the secure Zona 10 district are not suitable. If you want to run, try the **Grand Tikal Futura** (© 502/2410-0800; www.grandtikalfutura.com.gt), which has a small outdoor jogging track.

SPAS & GYMS   You can certainly burn some calories or get a nice pampering massage while in Guatemala City. Most of the high-end business hotels in town have some sort of spa or exercise room, which vary widely in terms of quantity and quality. The best equipped hotel spas I've found include those at the **Real InterContinental** (© 502/2379-4446; www.interconti.com), the **Westin Camino Real** (© 502/2333-3000; www.westin.com), the **Crowne Plaza** (© 502/2422-5000; www.crowne plaza.com), and the **Grand Tikal Futura** (© 502/2410-0800; www.grandtikalfutura. com.gt).

SWIMMING   The tropical daytime heat makes a cooling dip quite inviting. Several of the higher-end hotels in Guatemala City have pools, but none of them will let outside guests use their facilities, even for a fee. If you really want to have access to a swimming pool, check the listing information under "Where To Stay," earlier in this chapter, and make sure you choose a hotel with a swimming pool.

TENNIS   The **Westin Camino Real** (© 502/2333-3000; www.westin.com) and the **Grand Tikal Futura** (© 502/2410-0800; www.grandtikalfutura.com.gt) are the only downtown hotels with tennis courts. If you're a die-hard tennis player and must play while in town, you should stay at one of these hotels. There are no other public facilities open to tourists downtown. Alternatively, you can contact any of the golf and country clubs listed above; all of these have multiple tennis courts, and will allow outside guests to play with advance reservations.

7 Shopping

In many respects, Guatemala City is a great place for shopping, particularly if you're interested in Guatemalan arts and crafts. While it's much more fun and culturally interesting to visit one of the traditional markets, like that in Chichicastenango or Santiago Atitlán, you can find just about anything made and sold throughout Guatemala on sale in the city. Moreover, you can find these arts and crafts in large, expansive markets, as well as in small, boutique shops. *Note:* It is illegal to export any pre-Columbian artifacts out of Guatemala.

THE SHOPPING SCENE

There are two main markets in Guatemala City, the **Mercado Central,** or Central Market, in Zona 1, and **Mercado de Artesanías (Artisans' Market),** in Zona 13. Both are massive and stocked with a wide range of arts, crafts, textiles, and souvenirs available throughout the country. Aside from these, the greatest concentration of shops can be found in the Zona Viva. These shops tend to be higher-end, and you'll often pay a premium price for the same goods available at the markets. However, the markets are often flooded with low-quality items, which are often weeded out from the offerings at the higher-end shops.

In addition to the Mercado Central, Guatemalans love to shop for bargains along 6a Avenida in Zona 1. This busy city street is crammed with makeshift stands and kiosks selling everything from bootleg CDs and DVDs to housewares and clothing. However, be careful; this is a busy and crowded area, and pickpockets feast on tourists.

Middle- and upper-class Guatemalans tend to shop in modern malls. Some of the malls in Guatemala City include **Centro Comercial Miraflores,** Calzada Roosevelt, Zona 11; **Centro Comercial Tikal Futura,** Calzada Roosevelt, Zona 11; and **Gran Cento Comercial Los Próceres,** 16a Calle, Zona 10, all of which could rival those in other parts of the world.

SHOPPING A TO Z
ANTIQUES

Antigüedades lo de Víctor *(finds)*   This downtown shop, which occupies a colonial-era home, has everything antique, from knickknacks to large pieces of furniture. If you can't find anything to your liking, check other shops on this street, as there are several antiques dealers here. 12a Calle 3-39, Zona 1. (*C*) **502/2232-7276.**

ART

Carlos Woods Arte Antiguo y Contemporáneo ✸✸   After several generations of focusing on antiques and classic artwork, this family-run gallery moved into a new space and began adding contemporary works to their repertoire. The lighting, architecture, and well-thought-out displays make this place feel as much like a museum as a gallery. 10a Av. 5-49, Zona 14. (*C*) **502/2366-6883.**

El Atico   This stylish gallery features paintings, sculptures, and installation art by contemporary Guatemalan artists. 4a Av. 15-45, Zona 14. (*C*) **502/2368-0853.**

Galería El Túnel ⌖   In my opinion, this is the best art gallery in the Old Town. The gallery has a permanent collection and rotating exhibits of Guatemalan art and sculpture. They also occasionally offer painting classes and other workshops. 16a Calle 5-30, Zona 1. © 502/2238-3021.

BOOKS

Sophos ⌖⌖   This hip and contemporary bookstore and cafe would fit right into the landscape in Seattle, New York, or Paris. They carry a wide selection of titles in Spanish and English, and feature rotating art exhibits and regular workshops, performances, readings, and book signings. Av. La Reforma 13-89, Zona 10. © 502/2334-6797. www.sophosenlinea.com.

HANDICRAFTS, SOUVENIRS & TEXTILES

Colección 21 ⌖   This is an excellent shop and gallery with a wide range of arts, crafts, textiles, and jewelry of generally high quality. They also have a collection of contemporary painting, as well as some antiques. 12a Calle 4-65, Zona 14. © 502/2363-0649.

Mercado de Artesanías (Artisans' Market) *Value*   This massive market area is geared toward tourists, but is the place to come in Guatemala City for the broadest range of crafts and souvenirs. Because of its convenient location near the airport and the Finca La Aurora, you can combine a visit to this market with several museums and attractions in the same zone. 6a Calle 10-95, Zona 13. © 502/2472-0208.

In Nola ⌖⌖ *Finds*   This place is the Zona Viva outgrowth of the long-standing Lin Canola (below). It has a broad and generally high-quality selection of Guatemalan goods. The emphasis is on textiles, and this is a great place to buy fabrics by the yard. They also stock clothing, bedroom linens and coverings, and table settings. In addition, you can find a wide range of woodcarvings, leather goods, and ceramic wares. 18a Calle 21-31, Zona 10. © 502/2367-2424. www.in-nola.com.

Lin Canola ⌖⌖   This popular store features a massive selection of Guatemalan cloth and textile products, as well as other arts and crafts items. This is a great place to buy local fabrics in bulk. Originally operated out of the Mercado Central, they now have this downtown outlet, as well as their even newer sister storefront, In Nola, in the upscale Zona 10 neighborhood. 5 Calle 9-60, Zona 1. © 502/2253-0138. www.lin-canola.com.

Mercado Central (Central Market) ⌖ *Value*   This massive indoor market takes up several floors, covering a square city block in a building just behind the Catedral Metropolitana. This is your best bet for getting good deals on native wares. Offerings range from clothing and textiles to housewares and handicrafts. This market is actually frequented by Guatemalans more than tourists. Be careful of pickpockets. 9a Av. between 6a Calle and 8a Calle. No phone.

JEWELRY

Albuhi ⌖   This pretty shop specializes in silver and pewter ware. In addition to handmade jewelry, you can also get picture frames and an assortment of religious items, from crosses to ornate saints. Bulevar Los Próceres 22-02, Zona 10. © 502/2368-2904.

Aparicio ⌖   These folks carry high-end, one-of-a-kind jewelry in gold and silver, either plain or set with a wide range of gemstones. They also carry a broad selection of fine watches, as well as Swarovski jewelry and crystals. In addition to the storefront listed here, they have another outlet at the Gran Centro Comercial in Zona 4. 12a Calle 1-25, Centro Comercial Gémenis 10, Zona 10. © 502/2335-3404.

Glam   If you're looking for some modern and eclectic jewelry, I find the designs here more creative than at most other local outlets, though you'll still find pieces using the traditional Guatemalan staples of the jewelry trade—jade, amber, and silver. 18a Calle 10-50, Plaza La Villa, Zona 10. ✆ 502/2363-3307.

LEATHER

Robert Fine Leather   This is the place to come for high-end leatherworks and clothing in Guatemala City. Offerings range from belts and wallets to fine leather jackets and pants for both men and women. Much of the work, however, is imported from Ecuador. 12a Calle 1-25, Centro Comercial Géminis 10, Zona 10. ✆ 502/2335-2795.

LIQUOR

The Guatemalan **Zacapa rum** ✸✸✸ is one of the finest rums in the world. The 23-year-old Zacapa Centenario dark rum is as rich and smooth as a fine cognac. This rum has won widespread acclaim in international tasting competitions, and the company claims that part of their success and secret lies in the fact that the rum is initially distilled at sea level, near where the sugar cane is grown, and brought to a separate facility high in the Guatemalan mountains to age. Zacapa rums also come in 15- and 25-year aged varieties. For decades, the Centenario came in a bottle entirely covered in a woven reed. Today, these bottles are increasingly rare, and while the newer packaging features only a thin band of the weaving, the rum is just as good. You can get Zacapa rum at liquor stores and supermarkets across the city (and country). However, you'll find the best prices, oddly, at the airport. It's convenient to know you can save that last bit of shopping until the last minute.

8 Guatemala City After Dark

Guatemala City is a large, metropolitan city. However, its after-dark pleasures are somewhat limited. Part of this is due to the famously dangerous nature of much of the city, especially after dark. Many of the late-night offerings are confined to a couple of very concentrated and centralized "safe" areas, which gives the scene a little bit of an apartheid feel. Still, if you're looking for a concert, theater performance, or night on the town, you should be able to find something here to fit the bill.

THE PERFORMING ARTS

Guatemala's performing arts scene is relatively thin, which could be due to the high levels of poverty and illiteracy.

The greatest number of high-quality performances take place at the **Centro Cultural Miguel Angel Asturias** ✸✸, 24a Calle 3-81, Centro Cívico, Zona 1 (✆ 502/2232-4041), which features the country's largest, most modern and most impressive theater. Offerings range from local and visiting ballet companies and symphonies to theater and modern dance. A couple of satellite theater and gallery spaces often host smaller events, which include conferences, poetry readings, and film cycles.

Another principal venue for the performing arts is the theater at the **Instituto Guatemalteco Americano** ✸ (IGA; ✆ 502/2422-5555; www.iga.edu), which is located at 9a Av. 0-51, Zona 4, on the outskirts of Cuatro Grados Norte. These folks maintain a steady schedule of events that range from children's and traditional theater to art film cycles and dance performances. Check out their website for current event schedules.

The **Centro Cultural de España,** Vía 5, 1-23, Zona 4 (© **502/2385-9066;** www.centroculturalespana.com.gt), is located right on the main drag of Cuatro Grados Norte, close to the IGA. In addition to their small gallery space, they have a regular schedule of artistic, literary, and cultural events.

Your best bet for finding out what might be playing is to ask your hotel concierge, check the websites listed above, or pick up a copy of the free monthly *Revue Magazine* (www.revuemag.com), which is widely available at hotels and other tourist haunts around the country. If you can read Spanish, *Recrearte* (www.revistarecrearte. com) is another good source of information, with local listings for theater, concerts, and art galleries.

Ticket prices can range from Q30 to as high as Q450 ($4–$60/£2.10–£32) depending on the event and the star clout of the main act.

THE BAR SCENE

For visitors and locals alike, there are two main after-dark destinations—the Zona Viva and Cuatro Grados Norte. Both offer a broad range of bars, restaurants, and clubs in a compact area that's safe and pedestrian-friendly. Most bars don't charge a cover unless there's a live act, in which case the cover is anywhere from Q15 to Q75 ($2–$10/£1.05–£5.25). Discos and dance clubs often have a cover of between Q15 and Q45 ($2–$6/£1.05–£3.15).

Cheers American tourists feeling homesick, or those looking for some classic rock, a pool table, or a sporting event on a big-screen television, should come here. The menu is classic American-style bar food, with spicy chicken wings, nachos, and big burgers. In addition to the three pool tables, they've got dart boards and a foosball table. Open Monday to Saturday 9am to 1am, Sunday noon to midnight. 13a Calle 0-40, Zona 10. © **502/2368-2089.**

Del Paseo This is a great spot in Cuatro Grados Norte for a few drinks, some conversation, and a light bite with friends. As much a cafe and bistro as a bar, this place has live music most Thursdays and some weekends. Open daily noon until around 2am. Cuatro Grados Norte, Zona 4. © **502/2385-9046.**

Kahlua ⚓ This is one of the better dance spots in town, with a loud and lively vibe. The sound system is excellent, the main dance floor is quite large, and there's an interesting light show. There are several side rooms here, as well as a restaurant if you want a break from the pounding rhythms. Open Wednesday to Saturday 8pm to 3am. 1a Av. 15-06, Zona 10. © **502/2333-7468.**

Kloster This German-style pub has its own selection of microbrew beers. Tap beer is served in a variety of sizes, including by the meter, which is a massively tall glass that rests with an air of precarious danger on the tables or long wooden bar. The bar menu features several fondue options. In addition to the bar listed here, these folks have another outlet on the main drag in Cuatro Grados Norte. Open daily noon to 1am. 13a Calle 2-75, Zona 10. © **502/2334-3882.**

La Bodeguita del Centro ⚓⚓ *Finds* The spirit of the beatnik culture is alive here. You can't miss the brightly contrasting primary colors that define the exterior of this popular spot. La Bodeguita often has live music, as well as the occasional theater piece or poetry reading. The programming here is nothing if not eclectic. The live music might be jazz, folk, or hard-core punk. Open Tuesday to Sunday noon to 2am. 12a Calle 3-55, Zona 1. © **502/2221-4904.** Cover ranges Q5–Q30 (65¢–$4/35p–£2.10).

Señor Tortuga, Fun, Food and Music   Everything you'll find here is in the name of the place, which is a takeoff on the popular Señor Frogs chain; the same loud, rowdy fun is offered. The crowd is a broad mix of locals and tourists, with locals outnumbering the tourists by a fair amount. Open daily noon to 1am. 8a Av. 18-56, Zona 10. © 502/2363-0992.

Shakespeare Pub ⚘   This simple English pub is popular with the local expatriate crowd and visitors. You'll find it just below the ground floor of a high-rise building and commercial center (though it's visible from the street). Open daily noon to 1am. 13a Calle and 1a Av., Torre Santa Clara II, Zona 10. © 502/2331-2641.

Trovajazz ⚘⚘   This hip bar in Cuatro Grados Norte is my favorite haunt for live music. There's a band or act playing here most nights, and as the name implies, the music can range from *trova* (Latin American folk songs) to jazz. Open nightly until 1 or 2am, depending on the crowd. Vía 6 3-55, Zona 4. © 502/2334-1241.

THE GAY & LESBIAN SCENE

Guatemala is a largely Catholic, socially conservative Central American nation, and in general terms the nation can be rather homophobic. Public displays of same-sex affection are rare, and violence against prominent gay and lesbian activists is not unheard of. For these reasons, the local gay and lesbian communities are pretty discreet. Many gay and lesbian organizations guard their privacy, and the club scene is changeable and not well publicized.

For good, comprehensive information on the current situation for gay men, check out **Gay Guatemala** (www.gayguatemala.com), which appears in both English and Spanish. Information on the lesbian scene, and specifically lesbian clubs and bars, is much harder to come by. In general, the clubs and bars mentioned below tend to be predominantly gay, but all are pretty lesbian-friendly.

The most established gay and lesbian bars are **Pandora's Box,** Ruta 3, 3-08, Zona 4 (© 502/2332-2823); **Metropole,** 6a Calle, between 3a Avenida and 4a Avenida, Zona 1; **Ephebus Bar,** 4a Calle 5-30, Zona 1 (© 502/2253-4119); **Genetic,** Ruta 3, 3-08, Zona 4; and **El Encuentro,** 6a Av. 12-51, Zona 1 (© 502/2230-4459).

CINEMAS

All of the modern malls have multiplex cinemas showing late-run American movies, usually subtitled, but sometimes dubbed. Your best bets are the **Cinépolis,** Centro Comercial Miraflores, Calzada Roosevelt, Zona 11 (© 502/2470-8367; www.cinepolis. com.gt); **Cines Tikal Futura,** Centro Comercial Tikal Futura; Calzada Roosevelt, Zona 11 (© 502/2440-3297); and **Cines Próceres,** Centro Comercial Los Próceres, 16a Calle, Zona 10 (© 502/2332-8508). Check any of the local, Spanish-language daily papers for current schedules.

9 Side Trips from Guatemala City

Several side trips out of Guatemala are possible, ranging from day trips and tours to multiday excursions. I highly recommend you take any of these trips as part of an organized tour. All of the major hotels have tour desks that can arrange these for you. Alternatively, you can contact **Clark Tours,** 7a Av. 14-76, Zona 9, inside Clark Plaza (© 502/2412-4700; www.clarktours.com.gt); **Grayline Guatemala,** 1a Av. 13-22 Zona 10, inside the Holiday Inn (© 502/2383-8600; www.graylineguatemala.com); and **Maya Vacations,** 12a Calle 2-04 Zona 9 (© 502/233-4638; www.mayavacations.com).

THE TRAVELOCITY GUARANTEE

...THAT SAYS EVERYTHING YOU BOOK WILL BE RIGHT, OR WE'LL WORK WITH OUR TRAVEL PARTNERS TO MAKE IT RIGHT, RIGHT AWAY.

To drive home the point, we're going to use the word "right" in every single sentence.

Let's get right to it. Right to the meat! Only Travelocity guarantees everything about your booking will be right, or we'll work with our travel partners to make it right, right away. Right on!

Here's a picture taken smack dab right in the middle of Antigua, where the Guarantee also covers you.

The Guarantee covers all but one of the items pictured to the right.

For example, what if the ocean view you booked actually looks out at a downright ugly parking lot? You'd be right to call – we're there for you. And no one in their right mind would be pleased to learn the rental car place has closed and left them stranded. Call Travelocity and we'll help get you back on the right track.

Now, you may be thinking, "Yeah, right, I'm so sure." That's OK; you have the right to remain skeptical. That is until we mention help is always right around the corner. Call us right off the bat, knowing our customer service reps are there for you 24/7. Righting wrongs. Left and right.

Now if you're guessing there are some things we can't control, like the weather, well you're right. But we can help you with most things – to get all the details in righting,* visit travelocity.com/guarantee.

*Sorry, spelling things right is one of the few things not covered under the Guarantee.

I'd give my right arm for a guarantee like this, although I'm glad I don't have to.

In addition to the tours listed below, day tours by land are available to the Maya sites of Quiriguá and Copán in Honduras. Multiday trips to any of the other regions in Guatemala mentioned below can also be arranged. ·

TOP TOURS & EXCURSIONS

ANTIGUA 🔅🔅🔅   The fabulous colonial city of Antigua is just 45 minutes away from Guatemala City by car or bus. All of the local tour companies offer half- and full-day tours to Antigua. I definitely recommend you sign up for a full-day tour if possible. Antigua is *that* beautiful, and there is *that* much to see. Half-day tours cost Q263 to Q338 ($35–$45/£18–£24), including lunch and entrance fees to all attractions. Full-day tours cost Q375 to Q450 ($50–$60/£26–£32), including lunch. For more information on Antigua, see chapter 5.

CHICHICASTENANGO ON MARKET DAY 🔅🔅🔅   If you're in Guatemala City with a free Thursday or Sunday, you'll want to take a day trip to the fabulous market in Chichicastenango. These tours also hit Panajachel and Lake Atitlán on the way back, so you get to kill two or more birds with one stone. This is a full-day tour, with a fair amount of travel time, but it's worth it. These tours cost between Q525 and Q675 ($70–$90/£37–£47), and include lunch. For more information on Chichicas-. tenango and its market, see chapter 7.

LAKE ATITLAN 🔅🔅   Even if there's no market happening in Chichicastenango, you might consider a day trip to Lake Atitlán, one of the most beautiful spots in all of Guatemala. All of the tour agencies in town can arrange this outing, which takes a full day, and includes visits to Sololá, Panajachel, and one or two of the villages around the shores of the lake. These tours cost between Q450 and Q480 ($60–$80/£32–£34), and include lunch. For more information on Lake Atitlán and its surrounding villages, see chapter 6.

TIKAL 🔅🔅🔅   Perhaps the most popular day tour out of Guatemala City is to the amazing Maya ruins of Tikal. These tours generally involve a very early morning flight and even earlier hotel pickup. The tours give you a good, full-day in Tikal. However, if you've got the time, I seriously recommend you add at least a 1-night extension to the tour. These tours run around Q1,650 to Q2,250 ($220–$300/£116–£158), including round-trip airfare, park entrance fee, and a guide. Budget an additional Q375 to Q1,125 ($50–$150/£26–£79) per person per day for multiday excursions, depending on the level of accommodations chosen. For more information on Tikal, see chapter 8.

MIXCO VIEJO   This interesting site was an ancient Maya city built during the 12th and 13th centuries. Like many other Maya cities of the era, it was built on a plateau with steep canyon walls to protect it from other Maya groups. It was also one of the last Maya cities to fall against the Spanish conquistadors. The site features several pyramids and a well-preserved ball court. Mixco Viejo is located about 64km (40 miles) from Guatemala City. Tours here usually stop at the large and abundant fruit and vegetable market just outside the ruins. Full-day tours cost between Q375 and Q450 ($50–$60/£26–£32), including lunch.

5

Antigua

Simply put, **Antigua** ✮✮✮ is a gem, an enchanting blend of restored colonial-era architecture and rugged cobblestone streets, peppered with ruins and brimming with all the amenities a traveler could want—beautiful boutique hotels, fine restaurants, and plenty of shopping and activity options. Antigua sits in a small valley surrounded by towering volcanoes, which are clearly visible over the red tile roofs and church bell towers that dominate the small city's skyline. The colonial core of Antigua is extremely compact and well-suited to exploring on foot.

Antigua was Guatemala's capital from 1543 until 1776. It was founded after mudslides and flooding destroyed the country's first capital, in what is today Ciudad Vieja, in 1541. Designed by Italian civil architect Juan Francisco Antonielli and originally christened La Muy Noble y Muy Leal Ciudad de Santiago de los Caballeros de Goathemala (The Very Noble and Very Loyal City of Santiago of the Knights of Guatemala), it was for centuries perhaps the New World's finest city. In fact, it was declared the Capitancy General, which in effect granted it status as the government seat for all of Mexico and Central America. Antigua flourished throughout the 17th and on into the 18th centuries, with the massive wealth generated by the Spanish conquest being poured into the construction of churches, government buildings, universities, convents and monasteries, private homes, and military garrisons.

Many of those impressive buildings were knocked down in a steady string of earthquakes, and after a massive earthquake in 1773 destroyed most of the city, the government seat was relocated to present-day Guatemala City. There was great resistance to the move, and in 1777, the government actually instituted a law making it illegal to live in Antigua. Eventually, the city was almost entirely abandoned and stayed that way until the 20th century. It wasn't until the capital was moved to Guatemala City that the former city of Santiago de Guatemala was renamed Antigua, or La Antigua, which was a short way of saying "the old capital." In 1944, Antigua was declared a National Monument by the Government of Guatemala, and in 1979, UNESCO named it a World Heritage Site.

Antigua has the most elaborate and stunning **Holy Week celebrations** ✮✮✮ in all of Guatemala, and perhaps even the Americas. During Holy Week, the streets are decorated with intricate and beautiful *alfombras* (rugs) made of colored sawdust and flower petals. A steady stream of religious processions parade through the streets and over these *alfombras,* which are quickly replaced with new ones. While the Holy Week celebrations here are the city's principal civic celebration, Antigua also goes all out each year on and around July 25, the feast day of the city's Patron Saint Santiago, or Saint James.

1 Orientation

40km (25 miles) SW of Guatemala City; 108km (67 miles) SE of Chichicastenango; 80km (50 miles) SE of Panajachel

ARRIVING

BY PLANE

The nearest airport to Antigua is **La Aurora International Airport** (© 502/2332-6086; airport code GUA) in Guatemala City. Since Antigua is so close to Guatemala City, many visitors book their first and last nights—and often a few more—in Antigua. Once you've made it through Customs, you can be settled into your hotel in Antigua in less than an hour.

Getting into Town from the Airport

BY TAXI   A taxi is the fastest, safest, and easiest way to get from the airport or Guatemala City to Antigua. A taxi should cost between Q200 and Q300 ($27–$40/£14–£21). If you speak good Spanish, you may be able to get them down to around Q150 ($20/£11). Expect to pay the higher rate, and maybe even a little more, after dark. If you're already in Guatemala City, these rates are good from most anywhere in the city.

BY SHUTTLE   The most common way to get to and from Antigua is on a minivan shuttle. Several companies operate regular minivan shuttles between Antigua and most major tourist destinations, including the airport, downtown Guatemala City, Lake Atitlán, and Chichicastenango.

If you're coming to Antigua directly from the airport, you'll find several kiosks for these shuttles after clearing Customs. All charge between Q75 and Q90 ($10–$12/£5.25–£6.30) per person, and will leave as soon as they are full, which shouldn't take more than a few minutes.

If you're already in Guatemala City, or arriving from any other destination, ask your hotel or any tour agency about booking a shuttle to Antigua. Alternately, you can book directly with **Atitrans** (© 502/7832-3371 for 24-hr. reservation number; www.atitrans.com) or **Grayline Guatemala** (© 502/2383-8600; www.graylineguatemala.com).

Rates between Antigua and other popular destinations run around Q90 to Q113 ($12–$15/£6.30–£7.90) for Panajachel; Q135 to Q150 ($18–$20/£9.45–£11) for Chichicastenango; and Q300 to Q375 ($40–$50/£21–£27) for Flores/Tikal.

BY CAR   The best route to Antigua from Guatemala City is to take the Calzada Roosevelt out of town. The Calzada Roosevelt heads northwest out of Guatemala City, through Zona 11 (passing right in front of the Tikal Futura Hotel), before turning into the Pan American Highway (CA-1). Take this and exit at San Lucas. From here you'll take the new, well-paved, windy highway (RN10) into Antigua. The ride takes about 40 to 45 minutes with no traffic.

BY BUS   The bus terminal for local buses from Guatemala City to Antigua is located at 18a Calle between avenidas 4a and 5a, Zona 1. Buses leave every 15 minutes or so, usually as they fill up, between 5am and 9pm, with more sporadic service from around 4am to about 11pm. The fare is Q5 (65¢/35p) for the 1-hour ride. The main bus terminal in Antigua is at the end of 4a Calle Poniente, next to the Municipal Market. Buses leaving Antigua for Guatemala City follow roughly the same schedule.

VISITOR INFORMATION

The Guatemala Tourism Commission, **INGUAT,** 5a Calle and 4a Avenida Sur (© 800/464-8281 toll free in the U.S. and Canada, or 502/7832-0763 in Antigua; www.visit

guatemala.com), is located on the southeast corner of the Plaza Mayor, cater-cornered from the cathedral, in the **Palacio de los Capitanes Generales** building. The bilingual staff offers regional brochures, basic maps, and a score of hotel and tour fliers. The office is open Monday through Friday 8am to 5pm, and Saturday through Sunday 9am to 5pm.

Local travel agencies and hotel tour desks are another good source of information. There are numerous travel agencies all over town. Some of the best include **Don Quijote Travel Agency,** 7a Av. Norte, #56 (© 502/5611-5670); **Lax Travel Antigua** ✮, 3a Calle Poniente, #12 (© 502/7832-1621); **Sin Fronteras** ✮, 5a Av. Norte, #15A (© 502/7832-1017); **Rainbow Travel Center** ✮, 7a Av. Sur, #8 (© 502/7832-4202; www.rainbowtravelcenter.com); and **Via Venture** ✮✮, 2a Calle Oriente, #22 (© 502/ 7832-2509; www.viaventure.com).

If you need assistance, dial **Asistur** (© **1500**) toll free from any phone in Guatemala. Asistur has bilingual operators who can answer questions or put you in direct contact with the appropriate authorities in the case of an emergency. You can also contact the **tourism police** (© **502/7832-0532** or 502/7832-0533), which has its 24-hour office on 4a Avenida Norte on the side of the Palacio del Ayuntamiento.

2 Getting Around

ON FOOT   Antigua is walkable, and cars and taxis are unnecessary to explore the colonial core of the city. The entire downtown section of Antigua, which is where most tourist attractions are, extends less than 10 blocks in any direction from the Plaza Mayor.

BY TAXI   Taxis and tuk tuks are plentiful in Antigua. A ride anywhere in the city should cost between Q10 and Q20 ($1.35–$2.65/70p–£1.40). Most of the taxis in Antigua use meters, but if the one you get into doesn't, be sure to negotiate a firm price beforehand. If you need to call a cab, ask your hotel, or try **Taxis Antigua** (© **502/7832-0479** or 502/5403-1889).

BY CAR   While you won't need a car to explore Antigua, you may want one for a trip to Chichicastenango, Lake Atitlán, or other nearby towns. In Antigua, try **Tabarini,** 6a Av. Sur, #22 (© **502/7832-8107;** www.tabarini.com); or **Ceiba Rent,** 6a Calle Poniente, #6D (© **502/7832-4168** or 502/5215-8269; www.ceibarent.com).

If you prefer to maneuver the narrow streets of Antigua in a motorcycle or scooter, contact **Ceiba Rent** (above) or **Planet Scooter,** 5a Avenida Sur and 9a Calle Poniente, #9 (© **5548-5335;** www.planet-scooter.gt.com).

Tips Watch Your Step

The passage of time and several serious earthquakes have turned Antigua's streets and sidewalks into rough and treacherous walkways. It's very easy to twist an ankle, trip, or fall if you're not careful. Bring comfortable, flat walking shoes or sneakers (ladies, leave your heels at the hotel). Most of Antigua's streets and avenues were built before the era of cars, so sidewalks tend to be very narrow, forcing you frequently to walk in the street. However, it's no longer the 16th or 17th century, so keep an eye out for cars and motorcycles.

Rates run between Q300 and Q800 ($40–$80/£21–£56) per day for a car or motorcycle, between Q263 and Q338 ($35–$45/£18–£24) per day for a scooter.

CITY LAYOUT

Antigua is laid out in a simple grid, with the **Plaza Mayor,** or Parque Central (Central Park), at its center. *Avenidas* (avenues) run north-south, and *calles* (streets) run east-west. North of Plaza Mayor, the *avenidas* carry the suffix *norte;* south of Plaza Mayor they are followed by the suffix *sur.* Directions on *calles* east of Plaza Mayor are indicated by the suffix *oriente;* while those to the west are *poniente.* Unlike most cities in Guatemala, Antigua doesn't use the Zona system; instead each individual building is numbered.

Three main volcanoes are visible from various points in Antigua and can help you stay oriented. The solitary **Volcán de Agua** is almost due south of the city. A bit more to the southwest are **Volcán Acatenango** and **Volcán Fuego.** The latter is quite active, and you can often see a long plume of smoke rising from its crater. To the north of the city is the **Cerro de la Cruz,** a high hilltop with a large Catholic cross atop it.

FAST FACTS: Antigua

American Express In Guatemala, **Clark Tours** (© 502/2412-4700; www.clark tours.com.gt) is the official representative of American Express Travel Services. Their main offices are in Guatemala City at Clark Plaza, 7a Av. 14-76, Zona 9. They also have desks at the downtown Westin and Marriott hotels.

Babysitters Hotels offering regular, dependable babysitting service are few and far between. If you'll need a babysitter, make sure that your hotel offers this service, and be sure to ask whether the babysitters are bilingual. In many cases, they are not. This is usually not a problem with infants and toddlers, but it can cause problems with older children. Babysitters charge between Q15 and Q45 ($2–$6/£1.05–£3.15) per hour.

Banks Many banks have branches right on the Plaza Mayor or within a 2-block radius, including **Banquetzal,** 4a Calle Poniente and 5a Avenida Norte (© 502/ 7832-1111); **Banco Industrial,** 5a Av. Sur, #4 (© 502/2420-3000); and **Bancafé,** 4a Calle Poniente, #1A (© 502/7832-4876). All of these have ATMs, will change money, and make cash advances against a credit card.

Bookstores There are several good bookstores in Antigua. The best one for tourists is **La Casa del Conde,** 5a Av. Norte, #4 (© 502/7832-3322), located in a small shopping complex on the west side of the Plaza Mayor. Also try **Librería del Pensativo** ✒, Calle del Arco, #29 (© 502/7832-0729) for literature; or **Rainbow Café and Bookstore,** 7a Av. Sur, #8 (© 502/7832-1919).

Currency Exchange All banks (see above) will exchange money for a nominal service charge. Almost all of the hotels, restaurants, and shops in Antigua will also accept U.S. dollars and euros, though many give less than advantageous exchange rates.

Dentists Try **Clínicas Ovalle,** 2a Av. Norte, #3 (© 502/7832-0275); call your embassy, which should have a list of recommended dentists; or ask at your hotel.

Doctors Contact your embassy for information on doctors in both Antigua and Guatemala City, or ask your hotel for a recommendation. Also, see "Hospitals," below.

Drugstores A drugstore or pharmacy is called a *farmacia* in Spanish. There are scores of *farmacias* around Antigua, and you can probably find one simply by walking around. **Farmacia Fénix,** 5a Calle Poniente, #11C (✆ **502/7832-0503**), offers free delivery and has several outlets.

Embassies & Consulates See "Fast Facts: Guatemala" in chapter 2.

Emergencies Dial ✆ **1500** from anywhere in Guatemala. This will connect you to Asistur, which will have a bilingual operator who can put you in contact with the police, fire department, or ambulance service.

Express Mail Services Many of the shops around Antigua offer courier shipping of your purchases. If you want to do it yourself, head to **DHL,** 6a Calle Poniente and 6a Avenida Sur (✆ **502/7832-3718**; www.dhl.co).

Eyeglasses There are several *ópticas* (eyeglass stores) around Antigua, including **Optica Santa Lucía,** 5a Calle Poniente, #28 (✆ **502/7832-7945**); and **Centro Visual G&G,** 5a Av. Sur, #20A (✆ **502/7832-9263**), both of which have resident ophthalmologists.

Hospitals For tourists, the best hospital is **Hospital Privado Hermano Pedro,** Av. La Recolección, #4 (✆ **502/7832-1190**), a modern 24-hour private hospital offering a wide range of services, including emergency and trauma units.

Internet Access There are a host of Internet cafes around Antigua, and a growing number of hotels are offering Wi-Fi. **Roy.com,** 4a Calle Oriente, #8 (✆ **502/7832-2990**), has a couple of branches around town; or try **Conexiones,** 4a Calle Oriente, #14 (✆ **502/7832-3768**; www.conexion.com); or **The Funkey Monkey,** 5a Av. Sur, #6 (✆ **502/7832-4195**). Rates run Q3 to Q8 (40¢–$1.05/20p–55p) per hour.

Laundry & Dry Cleaning Most folks use their hotel's laundry service, but if your hotel can't do it or is too expensive, try **Detalles Dry Cleaning & Lavandería,** 6a Av. Norte, #38 (✆ **502/7832-5973**), which has coin-operated machines as well as wash and fold options. **Rainbow Laundry,** 6a Av. Sur, #15 (✆ **502/7832-2745**), offers pickup and drop-off service.

Maps The city map in this book should be just fine, but you can also ask your hotel or go to the Guatemalan Tourism Commission, **INGUAT,** 5a Calle and 4a Avenida Sur (✆ **502/7832-0763**), to pick up a useful city map.

Photographic Needs There are a host of photo shops and 1-hour developing outfits in Antigua. If you have camera troubles, your chances of having any serious repair work are slim. Your best bet is **Foto Angel,** 5a Calle Poniente, #3B (✆ **502/7832-2919**).

Police The main Antigua station is at the Palacio de los Capitanes Generales (✆ **502/7832-2266**), right on Plaza Mayor. The **tourism police** (✆ **502/7832-0532** or 502/7832-0533) is a division of the larger police force with bilingual officers trained specifically to deal with tourists. Their office is just around the corner on 4a Avenida Norte, and is open 24 hours.

Post Office The main post office (℃ **502/7832-2164**) is located at 4a Calle Poniente and Alameda Santa Lucía.

Restrooms Most hotels and restaurants will let travelers use their facilities, although they are happiest about providing the service to clients.

Safety Antigua is one of the safest cities in Guatemala, and has a strong police presence. Both regular police and specialized tourist police patrol the city, particularly around the central downtown core. The farther away from Plaza Mayor you venture, the greater your chances of encountering trouble. Be especially careful about hiking to the Cerro de la Cruz without a guide, large group, or tourist police escort. Practice common sense. Don't wear flashy jewelry or wave wads of cash around, be aware of your surroundings, and avoid any people and places that make you feel uncomfortable.

Useful Telephone Numbers For directory assistance, dial ℃ **555-1524**. To get an international outside line, dial ℃ **00** before the country code. To make an international collect call, dial ℃ **147-120**. To make a local collect call, dial ℃ **147-110**. Most of the international phone companies have direct access numbers. If you have a calling plan, you can connect directly to **AT&T** (℃ 9999-190); **MCI** (℃ 9999-189); **Sprint** (℃ 9999-195); **Bell Canada** (℃ 9999-198); and **British Telecom** (℃ 9999-044).

Water Drink only bottled water in Antigua.

3 What to See & Do

Antigua is a fabulous city for a leisurely stroll, and along the way you can visit a museum or do some shopping. If you want to see things on your own, the following descriptions of the main attractions will help you choose what interests you most. There are also a number of tour agencies in town, and most hotels have a tour desk. All of these offer a standard city tour, as well as visits to volcanoes, Chichicastenango market, Lake Atitlán, and one- and multiday trips to Tikal. If you're not happy with the offering at you hotel's tour desk, try **Don Quijote Travel Agency,** 7a Av. Norte, #56 (℃ 502/5611-5670); **Lax Travel Antigua** ✯, 3a Calle Poniente, #12 (℃ 502/7832-1621); **Sin Fronteras** ✯, 5a Av. Norte, #15A (℃ 502/7832-1017); **Rainbow Travel Center** ✯, 7a Av. Sur, #8 (℃ 502/7832-4202; www.rainbowtravelcenter.com); or **Via Venture** ✯✯, 2a Calle Oriente, #22 (℃ 502/7832-2509; www.viaventure.com).

Perhaps the best walking tours are offered by **Antigua Tours** ✯, 3a Calle Oriente, #28 (℃ **502/7832-5821;** www.antiguatours.net), which is based out of the Hotel Casa Santo Domingo. They offer a wide range of tour and hotel booking options, but are most popular for their walking tours with longtime resident and author Elizabeth Bell, whose books about Antigua include *Antigua Guatemala: The City And Its Heritage* (Antigua Tours, 2005). Bell leads a 3-hour walking tour of Antigua almost every Tuesday, Wednesday, Friday, and Saturday beginning at 9:30am. The cost is Q150 ($20/£11). On days when Bell is not available, other well-trained and personable guides lead the tour.

If you're looking for adventure, contact **Old Town Outfitters** ✯✯ (℃ **502/5399-0440;** www.bikeguatemala.com) for mountain biking, hiking, and other activities around Antigua and the country.

Antigua

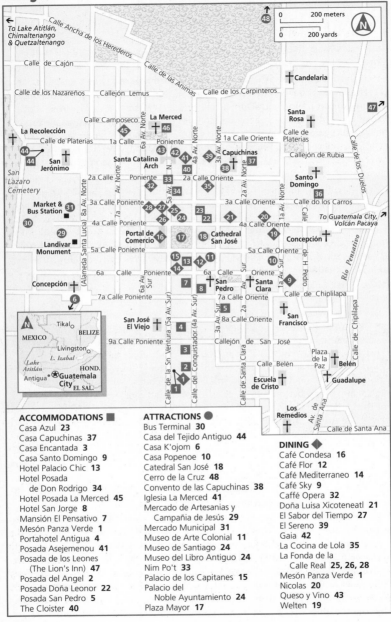

← To Lake Atitlán, Chimaltenango & Quetzaltenango

0   200 meters
0   200 yards

ACCOMMODATIONS ■
Casa Azul **23**
Casa Capuchinas **37**
Casa Encantada **3**
Casa Santo Domingo **9**
Hotel Palacio Chic **13**
Hotel Posada
   de Don Rodrigo **34**
Hotel Posada La Merced **45**
Hotel San Jorge **8**
Mansión El Pensativo **7**
Mesón Panza Verde **1**
Portahotel Antigua **4**
Posada Asejemenou **41**
Posada de los Leones
   (The Lion's Inn) **47**
Posada del Angel **2**
Posada Doña Leonor **22**
Posada San Pedro **5**
The Cloister **40**

ATTRACTIONS ●
Bus Terminal **30**
Casa del Tejido Antiguo **44**
Casa K'ojom **6**
Casa Popenoe **10**
Catedral San José **18**
Cerro de la Cruz **48**
Convento de las Capuchinas **38**
Iglesia La Merced **41**
Mercado de Artesanias y
   Campaña de Jesús **29**
Mercado Municipal **31**
Museo de Arte Colonial **11**
Museo de Santiago **24**
Museo del Libro Antiguo **24**
Nim Po't **33**
Palacio de los Capitanes **15**
Palacio del
   Noble Ayuntamiento **24**
Plaza Mayor **17**

DINING ◆
Café Condesa **16**
Café Flor **12**
Café Mediterraneo **14**
Café Sky **9**
Caffé Opera **32**
Doña Luisa Xicoteneatl **21**
El Sabor del Tiempo **27**
El Sereno **39**
Gaia **42**
La Cocina de Lola **35**
La Fonda de la
   Calle Real **25, 26, 28**
Mesón Panza Verde **1**
Nicolas **20**
Queso y Vino **43**
Welten **19**

126

ATTRACTIONS

The **Plaza Mayor** ⚔️⚔️ is the central axis of all Antigua. In colonial times, this was the city's main market and meeting area. Today, it's a great place to grab a shady seat and watch the parade of life pass before you. The current park was built in the 20th century, and covers a full city block with towering trees, well-tended gardens, various pathways lined with sturdy benches, and a beautiful fountain at its core. Teenage boys get a big kick out of the sculpted sirens lining the inside of the fountain, which is filled by a steady stream of water shooting out of their breasts.

Catedral San José ⚔️   Vowing to learn from the destruction of the cathedral during the earthquakes of 1583, the city (then called Santiago de los Caballeros de Guatemala) began construction of a new, more complex, and supposedly stronger cathedral in 1669. The structure, completed in 1680, contained seven entrances, five naves, 78 arches, 18 chapels, a main sacristy, and a main chamber. Unfortunately, seismology tends to repeat itself, and that cathedral was leveled in the great earthquake of 1773. You can visit the ruins from the south gate on 5a Calle Oeste. The entire structure was rebuilt in the 19th century (the sacrarium is the only piece used from the original). Embedded in the facade are several figures: the Virgen de la Asunción (Virgin of Assumption), Santiago Apóstol (Protector of the City), Padre Eterno (Eternal Father), the Doce Apóstoles (Twelve Apostles), the four Padres de la Iglesia (Church Fathers), as well as the Protectoral Coat of Arms and a shell crossed by swords (a symbol of the Holy Protector). The interior is less impressive but houses a statue of Christ carved by Quirio Cataño, famous for carving the "Black Christ" of Esquipulas (p. 235).

4a Av. Norte, on the east side of Plaza Mayor. No phone. Admission Q5 (65¢/35p) to visit the ruins; free for the main cathedral. Daily 9am–5pm.

Museo del Libro Antiguo   The site of the first printing press in Guatemala (1660), this museum lies within the Palacio del Noble Ayuntamiento. There are three exhibition rooms. The first is an overview of the history of Gutenberg's invention, including a wooden replica of the original printing equipment and works printed on the original Guatemalan press. The second goes into more technical detail about the processes of xylography (printing on wood) and lithography (printing on stone). The last exhibition is dedicated to books decorated with jasper, which gives them a special appearance and texture. The museum's prized possession is a copy of *Explicatio Apologetica,* the first book printed in Guatemala. Because of the fragile state of much of the collection, photography, with or without flash, is prohibited.

4a Calle Poniente, on the north side of the Plaza Mayor, inside the Palacio del Noble Ayuntamiento. (©) 502/7832-5511. Admission Q10 ($1.35/70p). Tues–Fri 9am–4pm; Sat–Sun 9am–noon and 2–4pm.

Museo de Santiago   In 1956, the colonial-era jail in the Palacio del Noble Ayuntamiento was converted into a museum, presenting relics from the glory days of the city to a captive audience. Its five exhibition rooms take visitors back to the city's founding as Santiago de los Caballeros de Guatemala, displaying centuries-old artwork, tools, and other objects. The collection includes sculptures, ceramics, heraldry (official crests of families, cities, or institutions), metalwork, furniture, and weapons. Some of the most popular items are the cannons, shields, and muskets in the collection of arms, some of which visitors can hold in order to feel their impressive weight.

4a Calle Poniente, on the north side of the Plaza Mayor, inside the Palacio del Noble Ayuntamiento. (©) 502/7832-2868. Admission Q10 ($1.35/70p). Tues–Fri 9am–4pm; Sat–Sun 9am–noon and 2–4pm.

Palacio del Noble Ayuntamiento   This 1743 structure was designed by Luis Diez de Navarro, Juan de Dios Aristondo, and Diego de Porras. Its impressive two-story facade is constructed of a double layer of stone archways supported by columns. The eastern wall has one of the few carved stone exteriors surviving from the 18th century. Originally the seat of the Spanish colonial government and a jail, it now houses the *municipalidad,* or city government, the Museo del Libro Antiguo, and the Museo de Santiago.

4a Calle Poniente, on the north side of Plaza Mayor. No phone. Free admission. Daily 9am–4pm.

Palacio de los Capitanes Generales   For 200 years, this was the home of the Spanish Viceroy, making it the seat of power for all of Central America. The original building, modified many times over the centuries, was constructed in the late 1500s and held the court of law, provincial offices, post office, treasury, royal office, servants' quarters, and horse stables within its more than 20,000 sq. m (215,000 sq. ft.). The current two-story structure, with its traditional facade of arches, is home to the INGUAT office and the police station. There's really nothing to see here, but the building remains an important historical site. A short, free bus tour of Antigua leaves from the Palacio every hour from 9am until 2pm Monday through Friday, and from 9am until noon on Saturday.

5a Calle Poniente, on the south side of the Plaza Mayor. No phone. Free admission. Daily 9am–5pm.

NORTH OF THE PLAZA MAYOR

The most distinguishing architectural feature north of Plaza Mayor—even more so than the Convento de las Capuchinas and the Iglesia La Merced (see below)—is the **Arco de Santa Catalina (Santa Catalina Arch).** This high arch spans 5a Avenida Norte, about 3 blocks north of the Plaza Mayor. The arch was built in the mid–17th century to allow nuns to pass from one part of the Santa Catalina Convent to the other without being seen. In the 19th century, a clock was added to a large cupola atop the center point of the beautiful yellow arch. Today, 5a Avenida Norte is often called Calle del Arco.

Cerro de la Cruz ✿   The Cerro de la Cruz, a hill north of the city with a big cross mounted on it, offers the best view of Antigua. You can climb the hill on foot (20–30 min. from the Plaza Mayor), or get there by car or taxi. The trail leading up to the overlook has a well-earned reputation for petty crime, so never go alone. The tourist police will accompany you during certain hours; check in at their office at 4a Avenida Norte, next to the Palacio del Noble Ayuntamiento.

Out beyond 1a Av. Norte. No phone. Free admission. Daily 9am–5pm.

Convento de las Capuchinas ✿✿   The Capuchins are a Roman Catholic order who seek sanctification through a life of work, privation, and continual penitence. Unlike other convents of old, the Convento de las Capuchinas did not require women to donate a dowry to join, though in Antigua that egalitarian outlook kept their ranks at less than 28 nuns. Completed in 1736, the impressive convent was abandoned after an earthquake in 1773 scared the nuns to safer ground. Fortunately the damage was relatively minor, and the well-preserved courtyards, gardens, bathing halls, and nuns' private cells are now open to the public. Mannequins now occupy some of those cells, demonstrating clois-tered life. The roof is a great place to take in a sweeping view of the city.

2a Av. Norte and 2a Calle Oriente. ✆ **502/7832-0184.** Admission Q30 ($4/£2.10), Q15 ($2/£1.05) students and chil-dren under 12. Daily 9am–5pm.

Iglesia La Merced ★★★   This church's central plaza is one of the most important launching points for processions during Holy Week. Built in a baroque style and adorned with stucco pilasters, it's also one of the best restored and preserved in the city. Famous architect Juan de Dios began work on the building in 1749, and completed it in 1767. The facade of the yellow temple is adorned with amazing detail, and several impressive paintings can be found inside, including the well-known work *Jesús Nazareno*. The previous incarnation of the church had, like all the others in town, been destroyed by an earthquake some years before. This incarnation was to suffer the same fate, though it has recently been restored after years of abandonment.

Just to the side of the church are the ruins of the **Convento La Merced**, a 16th-century convent with an enormous star-shaped pond and a beautifully decorated octagonal fountain in the courtyard. There are excellent views from the convent's second floor and rooftop.

1a Calle Poniente and 6a Av. Norte. No phone. Free admission to the church; Q3 (40¢/20p) to visit the convent ruins. Daily 9am–6pm.

SOUTHEAST OF THE PLAZA MAYOR

Casa Popenoe ★   American agriculturalists Dorothy and Wilson Popenoe restored this stylish colonial mansion, which was originally built in 1634 and subsequently damaged by earthquakes. The house is only open 2 hours during the day, but is worth a short visit to peek into the lifestyles of those who once were Antigua's rich and famous. After seeing the beautiful furniture and other goods inside, head to the rooftop for a lovely view.

1a Av. Sur, #2, between 5a and 6a Calle Oriente. ✆ 502/7832-3087. Admission Q10 ($1.35/70p). Mon–Sat 2–4pm.

Museo de Arte Colonial   The Museum of Colonial Art is located on the premises of what was once the University of San Carlos, a building whose cloisters are relatively well-preserved given the city's shaky past. The museum's collection consists largely of paintings and statues commissioned by Spanish *hidalgos* (noblemen) in the 17th century, but includes photographs of contemporary Semana Santa (Holy Week) celebrations.

4a Av. Sur and Calle de la Universidad. ✆ 502/7832-0429. Admission Q25 ($3.35/£1.75). Tues–Fri 9am–4pm; Sat–Sun 9am–noon and 2–4pm.

WEST OF THE PLAZA MAYOR

Casa del Tejido Antiguo ★   This museum will tell you everything you ever wanted to know about textiles. It has a sizeable collection of typical clothing from various

---

You Say Tamal, I Say Tamale

While most folks who come to Antigua seeking an education are learning Spanish, the **Antigua Cooking School**, 5a Av. Norte, #25B (✆ **502/5944-8568;** www.antiguacookingschool.com), offers an alternative to the traditional classroom. Located right under the Santa Catalina Arch, these folks offer regular 4-hour classes in preparing local cuisine. Each class tackles one of five different menus and costs Q375 ($50/£27) per person. Some of the dishes taught include *subanik* (a chicken and beef stew that's served wrapped in a local leaf), *chuchitos* (a small tamal made with corn flour and dried red chiles), and *arroz con leche* (a delicious dessert with rice and cinnamon).

Semana Santa (Holy Week)

The Christian **Semana Santa** ✦✦✦ celebrations in Antigua are an extravagant mix of religious fervor, civic pride, and artistic achievement. Throughout the week there are a score of masses, vigils *(velaciones)*, and public processions. The processions can vary in size, and are often made up of hundreds of worshippers, who include men in regal purple robes, women in white linens and lace, and ubiquitous incense carriers. Other processions feature men in white hooded costumes (whose style was later borrowed by the Ku Klux Klan), women in somber black dresses (as if in mourning), and the occasional horseback-riding members. Most carry large floats *(andas)* with sculptures of Jesus Christ, Mary Magdalene, and other saints.

Some of the *andas* are enormous (as much as 3 tons) and require as many as 100 men to carry each on their shoulders. As these huge floats make their slow way down the rugged streets, they lurch from side to side, often seeming as if they will topple (they *very* rarely do). Individual processions can last for many hours, and you'll notice a complex choreography used to keep the shoulders and legs of those carrying them fresh.

Although the celebrations officially begin on Ash Wednesday, the real spectacle begins on Palm Sunday and peaks on Good Friday. Throughout the week, elements of the Passion, Crucifixion, and Resurrection are reenacted and celebrated. The sheer scope and abundance of the celebrations are hard to describe. The smell of incense and a thick smoke often hang heavy over the whole city.

If you plan on coming during Semana Santa, book your room well in advance, as much as a year or more in some of the more popular hotels here. The real score during Holy Week are rooms overlooking some of the streets on the processional routes. Of the hotels listed below, **Hotel Posada de Don Rodrigo** and the new **Posada del Doña Leonor** both have choice second-floor rooms with balconies fronting one or more of the processional routes. *Warning:* Be careful as you enjoy the Semana Santa celebrations. Pickpockets and petty thieves thrive in the crowded streets. Leave your money and valuables in your hotel safe.

regions of Guatemala. The exhibits of colorful, vintage *cortes* and *huipiles* are complemented by ample information on how they're woven, the history of the process, and the broader cultural significance of Maya cloth. Informative placards explain the exhibits, but guided tours are available and recommended if you're deeply interested in the subject. A gift shop has various handmade items for sale. The selection is good, and the products are guaranteed to be authentic, but you'll probably find better prices elsewhere.

1a Calle Poniente, #51, between Ruinas Recolección and San Jerónimo. ℂ **502/7832-3169.** www.casadeltejido.org. Admission Q5 (65¢/35p). Mon–Sat 9am–5:30pm.

Casa K'ojom   This small museum dedicated to Maya music ("K'ojom" is the word for music in three Mayan languages) is based on the field work of ethnomusicologist Samuel Franco. The extensive multimedia archive contains hours of music and sounds, video footage, and color slides recorded during patron saint festivals and other rituals. A well-made 15-minute documentary film provides a good introduction to the topic, and complements the museum's collection of musical instruments and other related memorabilia. A small gift shop sells crafts, recordings of Guatemalan music, and a few instruments. The museum is in the neighboring town of Jocotenango, a mile from Antigua. Taxis charge between Q20 and Q25 ($2.65–$3.35/£1.40–£1.75) each way. While you're there, check out the neighboring coffee plantation, which has been roasting and harvesting beans since 1883.

At the end of Calle del Cemetario Final, Jocotenango. © 502/7832-0907. Admission Q30 ($4/£2.10). Mon–Fri 8:30am–4pm; Sat 8:30am–2pm.

OTHER ACTIVITIES

There are a host of Spanish-language schools in Antigua. Most offer small group or individual immersion-style classes between 4 and 5 hours daily, as well as various other activities and guided trips and tours. Most offer the option of a homestay with a local family, or a booking at any one of many hotels around the city. The schools I recommend include **Academia de Español Antigüeña,** 1a Calle Poniente, #10 (© **502/ 7832-7241;** www.spanish-iae.com); **Academia de Español Guatemala** ✺, 7a Calle Oriente, #15 (© **502/7832-5057;** www.acad.conexion.com); **Centro Lingüístico Maya** ✺, 5a Calle Poniente, #20 (© **502/7832-0656;** www.clmmaya.com); and **Escuela de Español San José el Viejo** ✺✺, 5a Av. Sur, #34 (© **502/7832-3028;** www.sanjoseelviejo.com).

Rates run between Q1,125 and Q2,250 ($150–$300/£79–£156) per week including classes, excursions, homestay, and airport transfers.

If you want to do volunteer work in the area, check in with **Proyecto Mosaico** ✺, 3a Av. Norte, #3 (©/fax **502/7832-0955;** www.promosaico.org), an organization that formed in the wake of Hurricane Mitch and works as a clearinghouse to connect volunteers with worthy projects and organizations around Guatemala.

4 Where to Stay

Whether you're looking for a budget room in which to plop down your backpack or a top-notch luxury inn in which to kick up your feet, your choices are endless. The high-end boutique hotels here are unmatched in any other area of Guatemala or anywhere else in Central America, for that matter. I've picked the best I can find in each price range and category, but note that new hotels are opening all the time.

VERY EXPENSIVE

On my last visit, work was underway on the **Posada Doña Leonor,** 4a Calle Oriente, #8 (© **502/7832-2281**), housed in the old home of Pedro de Alvarado's daughter Leonor. Owned by the same folks who have **Hotel Atitlán** (p. 153) in Panajachel, this promises to be one of the most luxurious and elegant hotels in town, and it's just a half-block from Plaza Mayor. The first 10 rooms opened in late November 2006.

Casa Santo Domingo ✺✺✺ *(Finds)*   This grandiose hotel lives up to the hype. The hotel is a tourist attraction in and of itself, spread over massive grounds that include the colonial-era ruins of an old convent, a working chapel, several museum-quality display areas, and a large amphitheater. The rooms are all top-notch with comfortable beds, stately decor, and a host of amenities. Most have working fireplaces, and the best have balconies and/or Jacuzzis. Suites and executive level rooms also have separate sitting rooms. I highly recommend the rooms found along the row of nos. 237 to 241, which are wonderfully situated with volcano and sunset views from their private balconies.

Even if you're not staying here, be sure to visit the Casa Santo Domingo, particularly around sunset. The grounds and facilities are impressive, and they have a sunset terrace with a perfect view of the nightly setting behind Volcán de Agua. Stick around for a drink or dinner as night falls, and the whole place is transformed into a candlelit fantasy. The restaurant here is excellent.

3a Calle Oriente, #28. (C) 502/7820-1220. Fax 502/7820-1221. www.casasantodomingo.com.gt. 125 units. Q1,275–Q1,613 ($170–$215/£89–£113) double; Q1,800–Q2,700 ($240–$360/£126–£189) suite. AE, DC, MC, V. Free parking. **Amenities:** Restaurant; bar; large outdoor pool; Jacuzzi; sauna; tour desk; room service; arcade; laundry service. *In room:* TV, minibar, hair dryer, safe.

Mansión El Pensativo ✿   While the hotel itself is small and intimate, the suites here are quite ample. I like room no. 4, which has a massive bedroom with a king-size bed, wood floors, exposed-beam ceilings, and a Jacuzzi in the large bathroom. Most of the rooms have a fireplace, and though the standard rooms all front the street, they can't really compete with the suites. The central garden area is large and well-maintained, and off to one side is a tile pool with a large stone deck area and a shade arbor strung with hammocks. There's no restaurant here, but plenty of good dining options are just a short walk away.

4a Av. Sur, #20. (C) 502/7820-3132. Fax 502/7832-1069. www.aroundantigua.com/hotels. 8 units. Q1,031 ($138/£72) double; Q1,155–Q1,650 ($154–$220/£81–£116) suite. Rates include tax. Lower rates in the off season. DC, MC, V. Free parking. **Amenities:** Midsize outdoor pool; tour desk; laundry service. *In room:* TV.

Mesón Panza Verde ✿✿✿ *(Finds*   Although not nearly as massive in scale, I find this place every bit as captivating and special as the Casa Santo Domingo. The three standard rooms are certainly acceptable, with small semi-private garden terraces, and could put this hotel in the moderate category. However, the rest of the rooms, which are all suites, are why this place is so wonderful—and why it is listed in this price category. All are quite spacious and beautifully decorated, with an eclectic mix of furnishings, artwork, and design touches from Guatemala and around the world. My favorite rooms here are nos. 9 and 10, which are ground-floor suites with large private garden patios and huge bathrooms. Number 12, the Grand Suite, was originally intended to be the owner's residence, and features a private staircase, entrance, and balcony. The restaurant (see review below) is one of the best in Antigua. There's also a small lap pool, adventurous art gallery, and wonderful rooftop terrace that winds around the building with several different places to sit and admire the view.

5a Av. Sur, #19. (C) 502/7832-1745. Fax 502/7832-2925. www.panzaverde.com. 12 units. Q563 ($75/£39) double; Q975 ($130/£69) suite; Q1,125–Q1,875 ($150–$250/£79–£131) master suite. Rates include full breakfast and taxes. Rates lower in the off season and for extended stays; higher during peak periods. AE, DC, MC, V. Free parking. **Amenities:** Restaurant; bar; small lap pool; laundry service. *In room:* TV, coffeemaker, safe.

Portahotel Antigua ✿ *(Kids*   This new, large hotel is designed and decorated in neo-colonial style, with architectural details such as cupolas. All of the rooms are spacious and modern; however, it's worthwhile to upgrade to a deluxe unit, which comes with a private balcony or patio. Most of the rooms have two double beds; about 25 have either one king- or queen-size bed. Some of the rooms come with a working fireplace. You can get a better value and more ambience in the many boutique hotels listed in this section, but if you're looking for a business-class hotel with a wide range of services and amenities, this is still a fine option. These folks also offer babysitting and a children's program, making it a good choice for families.

8a Calle Poniente, #1. © **502/7832-2801**. Fax 502/7832-0807. www.portahotels.com. 97 units. Q1,125–Q1,200 ($150–$160/£79–£84) double; Q1,688 ($225/£119) suite. AE, DC, MC, V. Free parking. **Amenities:** 2 restaurants; bar; midsize outdoor pool; babysitting; room service 7am–10pm; laundry service. *In room:* TV.

Posada del Angel ★★ *Finds*   Yet another wonderful boutique hotel housed in a converted old home, this intimate bed-and-breakfast hosted former U.S. President Bill Clinton. Don't be deceived by the decrepit door letting out onto 4a Avenida Sur. Passing through this faded and falling entrance is part of the charm. All the rooms are artistically decorated, and several feature beautiful showers with a high wooden doorway and hanging star-shaped light fixture. The second-floor suite is very large, with polished wood floors and a vaulted ceiling with exposed worn beams. The suite has a private section of rooftop terrace, but another large section is available for all guests to enjoy. There's a pretty little lap pool in the narrow interior courtyard.

4a Av. Sur, #24A. © **502/7832-5303**. Fax 502/7832-0260. www.posadadelangel.com. 5 units. Q1,425 ($190/£100) double; Q1,800 ($240/£126) suite. Rates include full breakfast and taxes. These are weekend rates, lower rates midweek. AE, DC, MC, V. Free parking. **Amenities:** Lounge; small lap pool; tour desk; laundry service. *In room:* No phone.

Posada de los Leones (The Lion's Inn) ★★ *Finds*   Located just outside the hustle and bustle of downtown Antigua, this elegant hotel seeks to distinguish itself with its excellent service and attention to details. The rooms are all large and quite beautiful, with built-in fireplaces and a refined sense of style. Of the standard rooms, I recommend La Magia, which has its own private garden terrace. The massive Shaharazad Grand Suite features a four-poster king-size bed, a huge walk-in closet, and an oversize bathroom with a combination Jacuzzi-steam bath. The narrow pool is slightly more decorative than functional, but those decorations include a backing wall of stone, brick, and ivy with a three-headed lion fountain filling the pool. Meals can be taken alfresco on a rooftop terrace or in a beautiful dining room with a vaulted brick ceiling.

Calle de los Duelos, Las Gravileas, #1. © **502/7820-7371**. Fax 502/7832-0974. www.lionsinnantigua.com. 6 units. Q1,238 ($165/£89) double; Q1,875 ($250/£131) suite. Rates include full breakfast and taxes. Rates higher during peak periods. AE, DC, MC, V. Free parking. **Amenities:** Restaurant; bar, lounge; small outdoor pool; tour desk; laundry service; free Wi-Fi. *In room:* TV (upon request).

EXPENSIVE

Casa Capuchinas ★   This small bed-and-breakfast sits right across the street from the Convento de las Capuchinas. A large lawn and garden area sits just behind the high wall that runs along 2a Avenida Norte. The hotel is built in an L shape, with a couple of rooms set near the street, and the rest farther back. I recommend room no. 2, a very large second-floor room with a king-size bed, a beautiful mosaic tub and shower, and a great view of the hotel's gardens and the convent. All of the rooms have fireplaces and lively decor, with contrasting pastel walls and local textiles and furniture.

2a Av. Norte, #7. ©/fax **502/7832-0121**. www.casacapuchinas.com. 5 units. Q593–Q690 ($79–$92/£42–£48) double. Rates include full breakfast and taxes. AE, DC, MC, V. **Amenities:** Laundry service. *In room:* TV, coffeemaker.

Casa Encantada ★★ *Finds*   This boutique B&B has a refined air about it, in terms of both the decor and service. Although most rooms are rather compact, what they lack in size they make up for in comfort and style. The best room here is the large, rooftop suite, which has plenty of space and a private Jacuzzi. However, my favorite room is no. 7, which is tucked in the back of the hotel and reached by a rock walkway over a small pool. At night this pathway is lit with candles and is quite romantic.

The whole hotel is really meant for couples and honeymooners, and only one room here—the second-floor room—has two beds; the rest have either one king-size or one queen-size. Breakfast is served on the delightful open-air rooftop, with great views of the red-tile roofs and the surrounding hills and volcanoes. In the afternoons and evenings, the little bar up here is *the* place to be for cocktails and snacks.

9a Calle Poniente Esquina, #1. © 866/837-8900 toll free in the U.S. and Canada, or 502/7832-7903 in Guatemala. www.casaencantada-antigua.com. Q638–Q825 ($85–$110/£45–£58) double; Q1,313 ($175/£92) suite. Rates include full breakfast. These are weekend rack rates. Rates lower midweek and off season; higher during peak periods. AE, DC, MC, V. Parking nearby. **Amenities:** Bar; small pool; tour desk; laundry service; free Wi-Fi. *In room:* TV, minibar, hair dryer, safe.

The Cloister ★ *(Finds* Fabulously located beside the Santa Catalina Arch, this converted convent is about as atmospheric a hotel option as you can find in Antigua, and that's saying a lot. The rooms are spread around the interior of this 17th-century building, and all feature antique tile or stone floors, high exposed-beam ceilings, and a tasteful mix of antiques, local crafts, and textiles. One room fronts the street, but I'd avoid it unless it's Holy Week. A couple of interior courtyards and gardens offer fountains, chairs, and several nooks in which to sit with a book or journal. The hotel doesn't have a restaurant, but they do serve a delicious breakfast.

5a Av. Norte, #12. © 502/7832-0712. www.thecloister.com. 7 units. Q675–Q1,013 ($90–$135/£47–£71) double. Rates include full breakfast. AE, DC, MC, V. Parking nearby. **Amenities:** Tour desk; laundry service; free Wi-Fi. *In room:* No phone.

Hotel Posada de Don Rodrigo ★ This popular, centrally located hotel is spread around the buildings and courtyards of three old houses that have been knit together. At the center of the largest courtyard stands a large pine tree, while fountains and gardens are sprinkled through the rest. Marimba bands play in the restaurant and common areas throughout much of the day, and local artisans make and sell their crafts in the main courtyard. All of the above can give this place a little bit of a kitschy feel. The rooms are simple, with attractive handmade wood furniture and decor that reflects the colonial era. Most are quite spacious, and some have fireplaces. Room nos. 300 to 303 feature small balconies overlooking the street. These rooms are particularly sought-after for Semana Santa.

5a Av. Norte, #17. © 502/7832-0291 or 502/7832-0387. Fax 502/2331-6838. www.hotelposadadedonrodrigo.com. 42 units. Q750 ($100/£53) double. AE, DC, MC, V. **Amenities:** Restaurant; bar; tour desk; room service; laundry service. *In room:* TV.

MODERATE

Casa Azul ★ Unlike the other hotels in Antigua, this place has a modern and eclectic style, with an array of furniture styles from Art Deco to contemporary. The rooms all have very high ceilings, especially those on the second floor. My favorite room in the house is no. 8, a second-floor corner unit with lots of space and great views over the rooftops of Antigua. Casa Azul is very well located, just a half-block from the Plaza Mayor. There's no restaurant here, but breakfast is served, and a host of restaurants are located nearby.

4a Av. Norte, #5. © 502/7832-0961. Fax 502/7832-0944. www.casazul.guate.com 14 units. Q548–Q623 ($73–$83/£39–£44) double. Rates lower in the off season, higher during peak periods. AE, DC, MC, V. Parking nearby. **Amenities:** Small outdoor pool; sauna; Jacuzzi; tour desk; laundry service. *In room:* TV, minibar, safe.

Hotel San Jorge This simple hotel provides clean and comfortable rooms at a reasonable price, but you won't get many frills, and very little in the way of colonial ambience. The rooms, which front a small garden with a fountain and white wrought-iron garden furniture, are all carpeted, feature a working fireplace, have a small desk and chair, and share a common veranda. There's no restaurant here, but a good breakfast is served.

4a Av. Sur, #13. ©/fax **502/7820-3132**. www.hotelsanjorge.centroamerica.com. 14 units. Q398 ($53/£28) double. Rates include tax and continental breakfast. Rates slightly higher during peak weeks. AE, DC, MC, V. Free parking. **Amenities:** Tour desk; laundry service. *In room:* TV, safe.

Hotel Palacio Chico   Parts of this small hotel date back to 1754 and are part of the Palacio de los Capitanes Generales complex, which hosted visiting dignitaries and military brass. The rooms feature antique tile floors and neo-colonial furnishings and decor. Some are a little on the small side (ask to see a couple first if you can), but all are big on ambience. There's a common veranda with various benches and chairs for camping out with a book, and a small central garden with a fountain.

4a Av. Sur, #4. ©/fax **502/7820-0406**. www.palaciochico.enantigua.com. 7 units. Q390 ($52/£27) double. Rates include tax and continental breakfast. Rates slightly higher during peak weeks. AE, DC, MC, V. Free parking. **Amenities:** Tour desk; laundry service. *In room:* TV, no phone.

INEXPENSIVE

Hotel Posada La Merced *Kids*   This economical option is located right near La Merced church. The rooms are spread around a sprawling, converted colonial-style home, and all open on to one of two central courtyard areas. The rooms are simple, clean, and homey. A modest amount of local artwork and neo-colonial wooden furniture liven up the rooms. There are a couple of apartments with kitchenettes for longer stays, and two-bedroom/one-bathroom "suites" that are good for families. There's also a large communal kitchen for all of the guests to use. The owner and staff here are quite personable and helpful.

7a Av. Norte, #43A. © **502/7832-3197** or 502/7832-3301. www.merced-landivar.com. 23 units. Q225–Q338 ($30–$45/£16–£24) double; Q450–Q675 ($60–$90/£32–£47) suite or apt. Rates lower in the off season; higher during peak periods. Rates include taxes. V. Parking nearby. **Amenities:** Tour desk; laundry service; free Wi-Fi. *In room:* Safe.

Posada Asejemenou *Value*   Located near the Santa Catalina Arch, this budget hotel is clean and has a friendly hostel-like vibe to it. Common areas are quite inviting, and are usually filled with fellow travelers reading a book or playing some cards or a board game. The rooms, arranged around an interior courtyard, all feature antique tile floors, minimal furnishings, and double French doors that open onto the central courtyard. (***Note:*** The panels on these doors are the only "windows" in the rooms.) Most of the bathrooms are a good size, with hot showers, where the water is heated at the shower head. There's a small Italian restaurant and pizzeria attached to the hotel.

Calle del Arco, #31. © **502/7820-2670**. asjemenou1@yahoo.com. 12 units (9 with private bathroom). Q214 ($29/£15) double with shared bathroom; Q289 ($39/£20) double with private bathroom. AE, DC, MC, V. Parking nearby. **Amenities:** Restaurant; bar; tour desk; laundry service. *In room:* Safe.

Posada San Pedro *Value*   This simple budget hotel has a calm and almost refined feel when compared to the glut of hostels and hostel-like options in this price range. Most rooms come with one double and one twin bed, and all have private bathrooms. Room nos. 4, 5, and 6 on the second floor are the best rooms here, with good views from their shared veranda. There are two lounge areas with cable television. These folks also have a second branch on the north side of town at 7a Av. Norte, #29.

3a Av. Sur, #15. ©/fax **502/7832-3594**. www.posadasanpedro.net. 10 units. Q263 ($35/£18) double. Rates include tax. AE, DC, MC, V. Parking nearby. **Amenities:** Tour desk; laundry service. *In room:* No phone.

5 Where to Dine

Matching Antigua's abundance of top-notch hotels, boutique inns, and B&Bs, the city has a wide range of excellent dining options. In addition to the places listed below, **Café Mediterráneo**, 6a Calle Poniente, #6A (© **502/7832-7180**), and **Queso y Vino**, 5a Av. Norte, #32 (© **502/7832-7785**), are both excellent Italian restaurants; while **Nicolás**, 4a Calle Oriente, #20 (© **502/7832-0471**), serves quality international fare.

EXPENSIVE

El Sereno ✿ INTERNATIONAL   The dining here is some of the most romantic and atmospheric in Antigua. The restaurant occupies the former home of the Royal Mercedarian Order, who oversaw the construction of the Iglesia La Merced. The fusion-tinged Continental cuisine is certainly acceptable, but often falls short of the surroundings, which include a small rooftop terrace with fabulous views over the town. Even if you don't dine here, be sure to come for a drink. In addition to the terrace, there are a number of elegant dining rooms with fireplaces and rich decor.

4a Av. Norte, #16. © **502/7832-0501**. Reservations recommended. Main courses Q75–Q165 ($10–$22/£5.25-£12). AE, MC, V. Daily noon–3pm and 6–11pm.

La Cocina de Lola ✿✿ SPANISH/TAPAS   This casual Spanish restaurant features a romantic setting, with most of the tables spread around the lush interior courtyard of a classic Antiguan home. This place has been in business more than 15 years—10 of those years in this location. I like to start things off with the carrot soup before moving on to the rabbit stewed in beer. You can opt for a steady stream of tapas, which you can chase down with the homemade sangria or a selection from the good wine list.

2a Calle Poniente, #3. © **502/7832-6616** or 502/7832-3500. Reservations recommended. Main courses Q80–Q140 ($5.60–$9.80/£5.60–£9.80). AE, DC, MC, V. Mon–Fri noon–3pm and 6–10pm; Sat noon–10pm; Sun noon–9pm.

Mesón Panza Verde ✿✿✿ *(Finds* INTERNATIONAL/FUSION   This hotel houses my favorite restaurant in Antigua. The ambience is fabulous, the service professional and attentive, and the food superb. Chef Christophe Pache blends traditional French techniques and training with a wide range of world influences. Try the sea bass with fresh grapes in a white-wine cream sauce, or the Geschnetzeltes Zurich—pork tenderloin in a cognac and demi-glace sauce—from the chef's native Switzerland. Tables are spread around several open-air terraces, assorted rooms, and nooks; my favorite seats are poolside under a vaulted stone roof. Enjoy live jazz Wednesday through Friday nights, and Sunday during brunch. This place has an extensive and reasonably priced wine list, as well as some good top-shelf cognacs, tequilas, rums, and single-malt whiskeys.

5a Av. Sur, #19. © **502/7832-1745**. www.panzaverde.com. Reservations recommended. Main courses Q75–Q150 ($10–$20/£5.25–£1.40). AE, DC, MC, V. Tues–Sat noon–3pm and 7–10pm; Sun 10am–4pm.

Welten ✿✿ *(Finds* INTERNATIONAL   This refined restaurant is an Antiguan institution. Tables are spread through several rooms of a converted old mansion, as well as under verdant vines in an interior courtyard. My favorite seats, however, are under a canvas awning around the edge of a small pool, which is filled with rose petals and floating candles at night. The food is wonderfully prepared and the service excellent. The menu features a broad range of relatively conservative Continental fare with heavy French and Italian influences. You can get a tender steak in green peppercorn sauce, or a fresh fish filet with white wine, cream, and mushrooms. There are several pasta selections, of which I recommend the homemade *annelloni* stuffed with turkey and chicken in a cognac and pepper sauce.

4a Calle Oriente, #21. Ⓒ **502/7832-0630** or 502/7832-6967. www.weltenrestaurant.com. Reservations recommended. Main courses Q94–Q158 ($13–$21/£6.60–£11). AE, DC, MC, V. Sun–Mon and Wed–Thurs noon–10pm; Fri–Sat noon–11pm.

MODERATE

Caffé Opera 🍷 ITALIAN   This place started out as a high-end espresso bar, and has added fine Italian food to its menu over the past few years. With the casual feel of a trattoria, it allows you to order up any number of excellent pasta dishes, traditional panini, or entrees such as tenderloin with arugula or rabbit in red-wine sauce. The wine is excellent, and be sure to save room for dessert and coffee; the espresso and cappuccino are still reason to come here.

6a Av. Norte, #17. Ⓒ **502/7832-0727.** Reservations recommended. Main courses Q45–Q113 ($6–$15/£3.15–£7.90). AE, DC, MC, V. Thurs–Tues noon–10pm.

El Sabor del Tiempo INTERNATIONAL/ITALIAN   You can't find a much cozier place in Antigua than this corner restaurant, which features wood furniture, a chalkboard menu, and dim lighting, even during the day. If you're lucky, or early, you can grab the back table set on a raised platform beside a bay window. There's a range of reasonable pasta dishes and panini. For something more substantial, I recommend the rabbit in rosemary sauce. They also have beer on tap and a good wine list.

3a Calle and Calle del Arco. Ⓒ **502/7832-0516.** Main courses Q45–Q76 ($6–$10/£3.15–£5.30); pastas Q25–Q60 ($3.25–$8/£1.75–£4.20). AE, MC, V. Daily 11am–11pm.

Gaia 🍷 MIDDLE EASTERN   This Middle Eastern restaurant offers a change of pace in Antigua's dining scene. I like to come here in the afternoon for a cooling mint iced tea and a light bite, as well as for a meal in the evening, which could include staples such as falafel, hummus, chicken kabobs, and couscous, and bigger entrees such as a full steak or a grilled chicken plate. Throw pillows are strewn on low benches in the front and back rooms, and the courtyard offers several semi-private gazebos and a few low tables with sturdy ottomans.

5a Av., #35A. Ⓒ **502/7832-3670.** Main courses Q55–Q110 ($7.35–$15/£3.85–£7.75). AE, DC, MC, V. Daily noon–1am.

La Fonda de la Calle Real 🍷 GUATEMALAN   This is *the* place to come in Antigua for authentic Guatemalan cuisine, but don't expect a quiet, laid-back joint. This place has become so popular, in fact, that they now have three branches in town—all within a block of one another. The menu features a range of classic Guatemalan dishes from *pepian,* a spicy chicken dish, to *kac ik,* a filling turkey soup from the Cobán region. All of the branches do a good job of re-creating a sense of colonial ambience with wood furniture and tall-backed chairs. I like the second-floor seating at the original outlet listed below, but the newer space at 3a Calle Poniente, #7, is much more spacious.

5a Av. Norte, #12. Ⓒ **502/7832-0507.** Main courses Q45–Q98 ($6–$13/£3.15–£6.85). AE, MC, V. Daily 8am–10pm.

INEXPENSIVE

Café Condesa 🍷ᵥₐₗᵤₑ INTERNATIONAL   Located just off the central park, this place is a great choice for breakfast, coffee, or a light lunch. Despite the somewhat limited scope of their offerings—there are no true main courses or full plates—there's a wide range of options here. The sandwiches are very creative and come on homemade bread. I like the vegetarian La Tara, with homemade herb garlic cheese and tomato pistou. You can also opt for one of several quiche options or a large salad, and finish with one of the fresh pies or desserts. Sundays feature an all-you-can-eat brunch for Q64 ($8.55/£4.50). Even when this place is packed, which it often is, the service is extremely fast. The restaurant is tucked in the back of a small collection of shops, including one of the best bookstores in town, Librería Casa del Conde, inside the Casa del Conde.

5a Av. Norte, #4. ✆ 502/7832-0038. Breakfast Q24–Q39 ($3.20–$5.20/£1.70–£2.70); salads and sandwiches Q23–Q46 ($3.05–$6.15/£1.60–£3.20); dessert Q15–Q19 ($2–$2.55/£1.05–£1.30). AE, DC, MC, V. Daily 7am–9pm.

Café Flor *(Overrated* THAI/PAN-ASIAN   This place is always packed with backpackers, local language students, and assorted tourists, and while I can find no fault with the welcoming and lively ambience or the prices, the food and service are severe disappointments. Still, if you want a filling and very reasonably priced plate of curried vegetables or chicken in a convivial spot with live piano music, this place is just fine.

4a Av. Sur, #1. ✆ 502/7832-5274. Main courses Q24–Q60 ($3.20–$8/£1.70–£4.20). AE, MC, V. Sun–Thurs 11am–11pm; Fri–Sat 11am–midnight.

Café Sky ✦ *(Finds* INTERNATIONAL   If you're looking for a relaxed restaurant with a great ambience, hearty food, and fantastic views, you can't beat Café Sky. The Bamboo and Sky bars, on the second- and third-floor terraces, serve a simple menu of bar food and Mexican standards, and have good views, making this a great spot around sunset. I love coming here for drinks and appetizers, but their indoor "Saloon" restaurant offers a more substantial menu of grilled steaks, baby back ribs, and more, which are also good.

1a Av. Sur, #15. ✆ 502/7832-7300. Main courses Q23–Q43 ($3.05–$5.75/£1.60–£3). AE, DC, MC, V. Daily 8am–11pm.

Doña Luisa Xicoteneatl GUATEMALAN/BAKERY   This is the original backpacker hangout, and it's still going strong. The crowded bulletin board continues to be a major resource for fellow travelers to leave and receive information. Breakfast is wonderful here, with strong Guatemalan coffee and fresh-baked bread and goodies. Later in the day you can get sandwiches, burgers, burritos, or more substantial main dishes. Try to grab a view table on the second floor, though the fauna-filled open-air courtyard is also delightful.

4a Calle Oriente, #12. ✆ 502/7832-2578. Main courses Q20–Q60 ($2.65–$8/£1.40–£4.20). AE, DC, MC, V. Daily 7am–9:30pm.

6 Shopping ✦✦✦

Antigua is probably the best city for shopping in all of Central America. Options range from high-end jewelry and clothing stores to fine art galleries and open-air street vendors selling locally produced crafts and textiles. There are shops to fit all budgets and tastes.

The streets closest to Plaza Mayor are peppered with souvenir stores hawking T-shirts and key chains, shops selling high-end jewelry, top-notch art galleries, and more. About 3 blocks west of Plaza Mayor is the *mercado municipal,* or public market, as well as an organized handicraft and artisans market.

In general, prices are higher in Antigua than anywhere else in Guatemala. The higher-end stores have set prices, and rarely budge on them. However, the handicraft and souvenir outlets, as well as the larger markets and street vendors, will all bargain.

Tips **Before You Buy**

If you're planning to head to the large and hectic markets—whether here, in Chichicastenango, or around the country—to bargain and shop, it's good to get an idea of what to look for before you dive in. I recommend visiting **Casa de Artes** or **Nim Po't** before setting out in search of any arts, crafts, or textiles. The folks at Casa de Artes carry high-end pieces, and their staff is very knowledgeable, so you can learn the difference between a quality piece of work and something that's mass produced. Be sure to ask where the different styles are from, and see if any specific town or region strikes your fancy. Their selection of *huipiles* is top-notch.

SHOPPING A TO Z

ART

Galería Panza Verde ⋆ This small gallery on the second floor of Mesón Panza Verde features a regularly rotating exhibition of contemporary Guatemalan and international art, as well as a small semi-permanent collection, including excellent works by one of the owners. Open daily 8am to 6pm. 5a Av. Sur, #19, La Antigua. ✆ **502/7832-7920.**

La Antigua Galería de Arte This gallery features artists from all over Latin America and a few from the U.S. and Europe. The works are all well displayed in the rooms of a beautiful colonial-era home. Open daily 10am to 7pm. 4a Calle Oriente, #15. ✆ **502/7832-2124.**

Wer ⋆⋆ *Finds* Owned by local artist Alejandro Wer, this converted 250-year-old home houses a massive collection of contemporary Guatemalan art by more than 100 artists in several of its rooms. Open daily 9am to 5:30pm. 4a Calle Oriente, #27. ✆ **502/7832-7161.**

CANDIES & CHOCOLATE

Chocotenengo ⋆ You'll have to search for this place (it's in the back of a simple convenience store), but it's worth the effort. The homemade chocolates, in particular their truffles, are seriously decadent and delicious. On any day, there may be a dozen or more truffle varieties to choose from. Open daily 9am to 6pm. 3a Calle Poniente, #2. ✆ **502/5500-2457.**

Doña María Gordillo ⋆ This place, which traces its origins to 1874, is an institution, and justifiably so. A glass counter filled with a wide range of homemade sweets—made from marzipan, shredded coconut, dulce de leche, and candied fruit—runs the length of the storefront. You'll have plenty of time to marvel at the extensive collection of children's ceramic savings banks, most in the shape of owls, since this place is almost always packed, and there's little rhyme or reason to their method of dealing with the crowds. Open daily 9am to 6pm. 4a Calle Oriente, #11. ✆ **502/7832-0403.**

CLOTHING

Sudex ⋆ These folks manufacture and sell cotton clothing for men and women featuring their original designs. They have a sister shop in Panajachel. Open daily 9am to 6pm. 6a Av. Norte, between 4a Calle Poniente and 3a Calle Poniente. ✆ **502/7832-4990.**

HANDICRAFTS & SOUVENIRS

Casa de Artes ⑇   If you're looking for the best, this is it—but you'll pay for it. This is probably the art and handicraft shop with the highest-end selection. Different rooms are dedicated to woodcarvings, traditional textiles, ceramics, jewelry, and paintings. Open Monday to Saturday 9am to 1pm and 2:30 to 6:30pm, and by appointment. 4a Av. Sur, #11. ℭ 502/7832-0792. www.casdeartes.com.gt.

Colibrí   This is a good shop for a variety of craft and textile products from around Guatemala, particularly baskets and other woven works. Open daily 9am to 7pm. 4a Calle Oriente, #3B. ℭ **502/7832-0280.**

JEWELRY

There's a glut of shops and street vendors selling jewelry around Antigua. Many specialize in jade and are truly superlative, and at the better shops, you can even design a custom piece.

Jades Imperio Maya ⑇   This shop produces high-quality works in jade, including some interesting and original jewelry designs, which are displayed in a showroom with plenty of light and accessible displays. Open daily 9am to 7pm. 5a Calle Oriente, #2. ℭ **502/7832-0925.** www.jadesimperiomaya.com.

Jades S.A. ⑇   These folks are pioneers of Guatemala's jade industry, and their main factory (listed here) is a museum of their impressive history and dedication to quality production. Wares range from jewelry and replica masks to assorted gift items and sculptures. They have two other storefronts in Antigua, in addition to outlets at the Hotel Casa Santo Domingo and the Marriott and Camino Real hotels in Guatemala City. Open daily 9am to 6:30pm. 4a Calle Oriente, #34. ℭ **502/7832-3841.** www.jademaya.com.

Joyería del Angel ⑇⑇ *Finds*   Custom-made one-of-a-kind pieces are the forte of this place. Though many of the pieces are quite expensive, there are some more moderately priced works, as well as the occasional sale items. Open daily 9am to 6pm. 4a Calle Oriente, #5A. ℭ **502/7832-3189.**

Green with Envy: The History of Jade

The ancient Maya, Olmec, and Aztecs all treasured jade, more so than gold, and because of its durability, it was often considered strong currency in the afterlife. The name comes from the Spanish conquistadors who dubbed it *piedra de ijada* (stone of the kidney, or loins) when they saw the Maya use it to cure kidney disease. This was soon shortened to *jada,* or jade.

There are two distinct silicate rocks that are truly considered jade—nephrite and jadeite. Guatemalan jade is jadeite, which is the harder and more brilliant of the two. It's scarce and thus more valuable. Contrary to popular belief, jade is not always green. In fact, it comes in a wide range of colors, from lavender to black.

Be careful when buying jade, as jewelry made from lesser stones are pawned off as true jade. The more reputable shops in Antigua offer guarantees that their stones are authentic, and many can document the actual mine from which the stone was extracted.

Pauch *&* If you've been jaded by all the, well, jade, try this branch of a Mexican chain, which specializes in amber. They have an excellent and extensive collection of jewelry and gift items. Open daily 9am to 6:30pm. 4a Av. Norte, #2. ℂ 502/7832-0524.

LEATHER

Kuero's & Mucho Más *&* From run-of-the-mill belts to handbags, these are some of the best leather goods I've found around Antigua. Their goods vary in quality, but if you shop carefully, you can find great pieces at very reasonable prices. Their women's handbags and leather and textile luggage pieces are particularly good. They have another location in the Mercado de Artesanías y Compañía de Jesús (see below). Open daily 9am to 5:30pm. 4a Calle Oriente, #5. ℂ 502/7832-5006.

MARKETS

While the prices at Nim Po't are fairly solid (they will offer slight discounts for bulk purchases if you ask), the prices at the other two markets listed here are very negotiable. Be pleasant, but persistent, and you should be able to walk away with your goods and a heavier wallet.

Mercado de Artesanías y Compañía de Jesús *&* This clean and modern facility was built to give a semi-permanent home to the many street vendors who had set up shop around Antigua. It features a tightly packed maze of small souvenir stands selling standard, mass-produced fare aimed at the unsuspecting tourist market. However, there are a few vendors selling quality wares, but you'll have to know your stuff and sift through a lot of junk to get to anything good. Open daily 8am to 7pm. 4a Calle Poniente. ℂ 502/7832-5599. www.munideantigua.com.

Mercado Municipal *Value* Local residents on the west end of the city come here to do their shopping among the numerous stalls connected by narrow passageways. Basic household goods, flowers, vegetables, grains, and spices are all sold here, plus some crafts and textiles. It's worth walking through just to soak in the sights and sounds, but be aware that crowded tight walkways are prime haunts for pickpockets. Open daily 7am to 5pm. 4a Calle Poniente. No phone.

Nim Po't *&&&* *Value* This large indoor market works as a sort of consignment warehouse for local craft and textile cooperatives selling arts, crafts, and textiles from around Guatemala. The prices here are very fair, but the quality of the merchandise varies greatly. You can, however, find excellent *huipiles* and carved masks. Open daily 9am to 7pm. 5a Av. Norte, #29. ℂ 502/7832-2681. www.nimpot.com.

TEXTILES

In addition to the places listed below, the **Casa del Tejido Antiguo** (see "West of the Plaza Mayor" under "Attractions" earlier in this chapter) also has a well-stocked shop. Moreover, all of the listings in the "Markets" section above have ample offerings of traditional Guatemalan textiles.

El Telar *&* The workmanship on these bedspreads, tablecloths, curtains, and other home decor items is superb, but the colors and designs tend to be rather sober. They also sell fabric in bulk. Open daily 9am to 6pm. 5a Av. Sur, #7; and 5a Av. Norte, #18. ℂ 502/7832-3179.

Textura *&&* If you're looking for a bedspread, table settings, or a throw pillow, this is another good option. The different rooms in this store are loosely organized by color (a blue room, a red room, and so on). You can also buy fabrics in bulk here. Open daily 9am to 6pm. 5a Av. Norte, #33. (*C*) **502/7832-5067.**

Tienda Típica Santa María *(Finds)*   Located inside the Mercado de Artesanías (see above), this stall is run by a wonderful Maya woman from Santa María. Hundreds of *huipiles* from around Guatemala are on display and stored in huge piles. While there's a lot of mediocre stuff, you can find some real gems if you're willing to dig a little. I purchased several fabulous *huipiles* from Nebaj and another from Chichicastenango from this stall. Open daily 8am to 7pm. 4a Calle Poniente. (*C*) **502/5929-5083.**

7 Antigua After Dark

You'll find plenty of bars and clubs in Antigua, but overall, the nightlife scene is pretty mellow. In fact, by city ordinance, all bars and clubs must shut down by 1am. Adaptive as always, what follows are several nightly "private" after-hours parties, which are safe for tourists to attend. The parties shift around, and you'll almost certainly be handed a flier "inviting" you to one if you are still hanging around any of the bars in Antigua as the witching hour approaches.

Café 2000 *(*   Contemporary dance, house, trance, and techno, sometimes spun by a DJ, are always on deck here. They often project free films on a large screen. Open daily 7pm to 1am. 6a Av. Norte, #2. (*C*) **502/7832-2981.**

Café No Sé   This small bar is popular with a young crowd and reeks of bohemia. Guitars hang from the walls, and poetry readings are not uncommon. Open daily 11am to 1am. 1a Av. Sur, #11C, between 5a Calle and 6a Calle. (*C*) **502/5501-2680.**

Casbah   Located near the Santa Catalina Arch, this is Antigua's principal dance club. The music ranges from salsa and reggaetón to modern house and dance grooves. Casbah is known for being gay- and lesbian-friendly. Open Thursday to Saturday 6pm to 1am. 5a Av. Norte, #30. (*C*) **502/7832-3553.**

Frida's   While this is a popular Mexican restaurant (with another branch in Guatemala City), I prefer to think of it, and use it, as a drinking establishment. The food is certainly acceptable, but there are better restaurants in town. However, if you want to sit around sipping margaritas and noshing on nachos while a mariachi band serenades you, this is the place to be. Open daily noon to midnight. 5a Av. Norte #29. (*C*) **502/7832-0504.**

La Sin Ventura   Nights here may start off mellow with a late-run movie, but things heat up later in the evening, making this a contender with Casbah (above) for the best dance spot. Most nights you'll find a good mix of locals and tourists grooving to salsa, merengue, and cumbia on the crowded dance floor. Open daily noon to 1am. 5a Av. Sur, between 5a Calle Poniente and 6a Calle Poniente. (*C*) **502/7832-0581.**

Reilly's *(*   The small bar area near the front of this Irish-style pub is often packed, but you'll find more space, as well as some tables and chairs, toward the side and back. This place draws a mixed crowd, but it's popular with expatriates and tourists. Open daily 2pm to 1am. 5a Av. Norte, #31. (*C*) **502/5499-2331** or 502/5672-7910. www.reillysantigua.com.

Riki's Bar   Located inside the Café La Escudilla, this place attracts a lot of expatriates and language students, as well as Guatemala City's visiting hip and well-heeled crowd. Open daily noon to midnight. 4a Av. Norte, #4. (*C*) **502/7832-1327.**

Sangre ✦ Tapas, wine, and cozy lighting are the offerings at this new bar, tucked in the back of a small gallery and boutique. An open courtyard, a dimly lit room, and a small bar are the seating options here, while you can choose both hot and cold tapas from the menu and a variety of wines by the glass from the extensive list. Open Sunday to Monday and Wednesday to Thursday 12:30 to 10pm; Friday to Saturday 12:30pm to midnight. 5a Av. Norte, #33A. © **502/5656-7618.**

Tequila Bar ✦✦ *Finds* You may have to do a shot of house tequila before you're allowed in the door, but once you're in, you'll have your choice of fine and rare tequilas and mescals, which, in addition to beer, are the only things served here. The place is also known as The Mezcal Bar or Bo's Tequila Bar, after a charismatic expatriate named Bo, the late original owner. Located in the back of Café No Sé. Open daily 7pm to 1am. 1a Av. Sur, #11C, between 5a Calle and 6a Calle. © **502/5501-2680.**

8 Outdoor Activities

Most visitors come to Antigua for the history, culture, dining, and shopping, but outdoor enthusiasts will find there's something here for them, too.

BIKING The rural back roads, volcanoes, and mountains around Antigua are perfect for mountain biking. **Old Town Outfitters** ✦✦ (© **502/5399-0440;** www.bike guatemala.com) has quality equipment and offers a variety of rides and tours, ranging from half-day mellow rides to multiday excursions. "The Spinal Chord" journeys along a narrow ridge through the mountains above Antigua. Multiday tours include a 2-day pedal (mountain bike) and paddle (kayak) around Lake Atitlán. Rates average around Q263 ($35/£18) for a half-day tour to Q1,125 to Q1,875 ($150–$250/ £79–£131) for the 2-day excursions.

HIKING & CLIMBING Building on their success in the mountain bike arena, the folks at **Old Town Outfitters** (see above) have also emerged as the best agency for those looking to hike one of the nearby volcanoes such as Acatenango, Pacaya, or Agua (see below) or do some rock climbing. These hikes range from Q225 to Q375 ($30–$50/£16–£26) for a day hike to around Q525 ($70/£37) for overnight camping trips to any of the volcanoes.

HORSEBACK RIDING The same back roads and trails that are so well-suited to mountain biking are also perfect for horseback rides. If you want to explore the region by horseback, contact Fred and Paula at **Ravenscroft Riding Stables,** on the road to Santa María de Jesús (© **502/7830-6669**). Rates run around Q113 ($15/£7.90) per hour.

JOGGING Be careful jogging around Antigua; if the tight streets and unforgiving drivers don't get you, muggers just might. The popular and attractive Cerro de la Cruz makes a great jogging route. However, I know of several incidents in recent years when joggers were attacked. Single women in particular should be on guard.

SPAS & GYMS A few of the higher-end hotels have a small gym or spa. If yours doesn't, and you're looking to burn some calories or get pampered, there are several options around town. For a good workout, head to **Antiguas Gym,** 6a Calle Poniente, #31 (© **502/7832-7554**). Rates for a specific class or day pass run between Q30 and Q75 ($4–$10/£2.10–£5.25).

Head to the **Casa del Conquistador,** 4a Av. Sur, #28 (© **502/7832-9195**) for a wide range of spa treatments. A half-day package with a massage, pedicure, and manicure is just Q263 ($35/£18); a full-day package that also includes a facial and lunch

Going Nuts: Valhalla Macadamia Nut Farm

The **Valhalla Macadamia Nut Farm** (© **502/7888-6308**; www.exvalhalla.net) is an interesting project working toward reversing global warming, assisting local indigenous populations in finding alternative and sustainable sources of food and income, reforesting tropical forests, and providing public education in the areas of conservation and sustainable development.

The folks at this farm offer a free educational tour of their macadamia farm. They also offer up their very famous macadamia pancakes and other macadamia and homemade chocolate products. If you're willing to commit a full month to the task, ask about volunteer opportunities here. The farm is located at Km 52.5 on the route to San Miguel Duenas.

is Q375 ($50/£26). Other options include hot-stone massages and aromatherapy treatments. Use of the pool and Jacuzzi are included when you purchase a massage or other treatment.

SWIMMING If your hotel doesn't have a pool, you can use the one at the **Portotel Antigua,** 8a Calle Poniente, #1 (© **502/7832-2801**), for Q50 ($6.65/£3.50) Monday through Friday, and Q60 ($8/£4.20) Saturday and Sunday. Children under 12 are half-price.

9 Volcanoes near Antigua

There are a handful of both dormant and active volcanoes close to Antigua. You can see several of them from almost any vantage point in the city. A couple are popular destinations for day hikes. Your best bet for hiking any of the volcanoes is to sign up for an organized tour. All of the hotel tour desks in town can set you up, or you can contact **Don Quijote Travel Agency,** 7a Av. Norte, #56 (© 502/5611-5670); **Lax Travel Antigua** ✦, 3a Calle Poniente, #12 (© 502/7832-1621); **Sin Fronteras** ✦, 5a Av. Norte, #15A (© 502/7832-1017); **Rainbow Travel Center** ✦, 7a Av. Sur, #8 (© 502/7832-4202; www.rainbowtravelcenter.com); or **Old Town Outfitters** ✦✦, 5a Av. Sur, #12 (© 502/5399-0440; www.bikeguatemala.com).

VOLCAN PACAYA ✦✦

About an hour-and-a-half from Antigua is the country's most popular volcano destination, **Volcán Pacaya.** Rising to 2,552m (8,370 ft.), Pacaya is in a near constant state of eruption. Tours tend to leave either very early in the morning or around 1pm. I recommend the later tours, especially in the dry season, as you may get to see some of the lava glowing red against the night sky. More likely you'll be treated to the sight, sound, and smell of volcanic gases and steam.

Most ascents of Volcán Pacaya begin at San Francisco de Sales, where you must pay the Q25 ($3.65/£1.75) national park entrance fee. From here you'll hike for about an hour-and-a-half to reach the base of the crater's rim, where the steep hiking trail gives way to a solid slope of loose debris made of lava rocks and ash. This final stretch is a steep and arduous scramble, with loose footings and many mini–rock slides—don't climb directly behind anyone else in your group. On the way down, more adventurous and athletic hikers can "ski" down.

Those who make it to the summit will encounter an otherworldly scene of smoke and gas, with the occasional volcanic belch. Some of the rocks will be very hot to the touch. Very infrequently, Pacaya will let loose with a spectacular eruption. When the skies are clear, the views are amazing.

Be sure to come well-prepared. Sturdy, closed-toe hiking shoes or boots are necessary. You'll also want to bring water, a warm sweatshirt, and (if it's in the forecast) rain gear. Finally, if you're coming on one of the later tours, be sure to either bring a flashlight or make sure your tour agency provides one.

Before you go, get current safety information, in terms of both volcanic and criminal activity, from your tour agency, INGUAT, or the Antigua tourism police. It's sometimes possible to camp here, which is your best chance of seeing the nighttime lava show. If this interests you, many of the tour agencies listed above also offer camping options.

Tour prices range between Q75 and Q225 ($10–$30/£5.25–£16) depending on the size of your group and whether or not lunch and the national park entrance are included. Some of the cut-rate agencies around Antigua will offer the trip for as little as Q38 ($5/£2.65), but I'd recommend going with a reputable agency and paying a few extra dollars.

VOLCAN DE AGUA 🦟

Although higher than Pacaya, the 3,760m (12,333-ft.) **Volcán de Agua** is actually an easier ascent. It's also decidedly less exciting, in large part because Volcán de Agua has been dormant since the mid–16th century. Called Hunapú in the local Kaqchiquel Mayan language, its Spanish name traces back to 1541, when water and mudslides from the volcano wiped out Guatemala's then capital city, today known as Ciudad Vieja. The hike to the summit of Volcán de Agua leaves from the town of Santa Maria de Jesus. The hike is relatively gentle and should take about 4 to 5 hours from Santa Maria to the summit. The hike down is somewhat quicker, but be careful and don't push it.

OTHER VOLCANOS
ACATENANGO 🦟🦟

The tallest of the volcanoes ringing Antigua and the third tallest in Guatemala, **Volcán Acatenango** has two main peaks, Pico Mayor and Tres Marias. Pico Mayor is the taller of the two and peaks out at some 3,975m (13,040 ft.). Tres Marias, which is also known as Yepocapa or Tres Hermanas, rises to 3,880m (12,730 ft.). Acatenango is dormant, although it does have several small craters spewing sulfur gases. Acatenango is very close to Volcán Fuego, and the two are actually connected by a high ridge. This is the best volcano hike in the area for your money, providing spectacular panoramic views on clear days. However, the ascent is long and arduous, taking most climbers between 5 and 6 hours. Overnight trips are common here, and can sometimes be rewarded with a nighttime show from Volcán Pacaya.

FUEGO

Volcán Fuego is very active, and ascents here never get very close to the crater and are entirely dependent on current volcanic activity. Fuego's last major eruption was as recent as 1974. Fuego stands some 12,350 feet (3,760m), although its exact altitude often changes due to volcanic activity. The Kaqchiquel called this volcano Chi Gag.

6

Lake Atitlán

Aldous Huxley famously claimed that **Lake Atitlán** ✦✦✦ was "the most beautiful lake in the world," and that Italy's Lake Como paled in comparison. As one who has been to both and visited Lake Atitlán many times over a span of more than 20 years, I have to agree. Formed thousands of years ago in the crater of a massive volcano, Lake Atitlán is more than 10 miles across at its widest point. It sits at nearly a mile high in altitude, and is surrounded on all sides by steep verdant hills, picturesque Maya villages, and massive volcanoes with striking pointed cones. The views from the lakeshore, the hillsides above the lake, and the boats plying its

waters are all stunning, and seemingly endlessly varied, as the light and cloud cover shift constantly throughout the day.

The shores of Lake Atitlán are sparsely populated with a series of small villages and a few larger towns connected by rugged roads and frequent boat traffic.

The Lake Atitlán region was severely affected by Hurricane Stan in October 2005, and the damage that Stan caused is still palpable, especially in Panajachel and Santiago Atitlán. Landslides, flooding, and overflowing rivers plagued several communities around the lake, their muddy scars visible on the surrounding mountains and hillsides.

1 Panajachel ✦

115km (71 miles) W of Guatemala City; 37km (23 miles) S of Chichicastenango; 80km (50 miles) NW of Antigua

Panajachel is the gateway to Lake Atitlán. It's the largest city on the lake's shore and the most easily accessible by car and bus from the rest of Guatemala. Boats leave from Panajachel throughout the day to the various towns and villages that ring Lake Atitlán. Many, including me, find Panajachel a bit too chaotic and crowded, so the quieter villages and isolated hotels around the lake are your best bet. Still, Pana, as it's most commonly known, offers a wealth of dining, shopping, and tour options, and you can't beat the views, with the three major volcanoes—San Pedro, Toliman, and Atitlán—clearly visible from anywhere along the lakeshore.

Panajachel, and the rest of the north shore of Atitlán, is a predominantly Kaqchiquel Maya area. During the Spanish Conquest, the Kaqchiquel allied themselves with the Spaniards against their Tz'utujil neighbors. The tension is still present, though Maya from the different villages around the region all come to Panajachel to sell their wares.

ESSENTIALS
GETTING THERE
BY BUS   **Transportes Rebuli** (✆ **502/2230-2748**) has buses leaving roughly every hour between 5am and 5pm to Panajachel from 21a Calle 1-34, Zona 1, in Guatemala City. The ride takes around 3½ hours. Fare is Q20 ($2.35/£1.40). The return buses

run along a similar schedule and depart from the crossroads of Calle Principal and Calle Santander.

BY SHUTTLE Panajachel is connected to Guatemala City, Antigua, and Chichicastenango by regular tourist shuttle buses. These range from minivans to standard buses. Fares between Panajachel and Guatemala City run around Q165 ($22/£12); between Panajachel and either Antigua or Chichicastenango is about Q90 ($12/£6.30). Any hotel tour desk or local tour agency can book you one of these shuttles, or you can contact **Atitrans** (© 502/7832-3371 for 24-hr. reservation number; www.atitrans.com) or **Grayline Guatemala** (© 502/2383-8600; www.grayline guatemala.com) directly.

BY CAR To drive to Panajachel and other cities along the lake, take the Pan-American Highway (CA-1) to the junction at Los Encuentros. A few miles north of Los Encuentros is the turnoff to Sololá. In Sololá, follow the signs and flow of traffic to the road to Panajachel. The drive takes a little more than 2 hours from Guatemala City.

GETTING AROUND

Panajachel is relatively compact, so it's fairly easy to walk anywhere in town. In fact, most people spend their time walking up and down the long strip that is Calle Santander. If

Gringotenango

Panajachel was one of the earliest and most popular spots on the "hippie trail" of backpacking travelers who made their way up and down Central America in the 1960s, 1970s, and 1980s. Many stayed, and this prevalent expatriate population has earned Panajachel the rather derogatory nickname of Gringotenango. The suffix *tenango* means "village" or "place of," which makes Gringotenango "the Place of Gringos."

you need a taxi, they are plentiful and can almost always be flagged down anywhere in town. If you need to call one, try **Taxis San Francisco** (© **502/7762-0556**).

If you want to rent a motorcycle, scooter, or bicycle, check out **Emanuel's Moto & Bike Rental,** Calle 14 de Febrero (© **502/7762-2790**). Motorcycles rent for Q60 ($8/£4.20) per hour, or Q250 ($33/£18) for an 8-hour day; scooters run Q70 ($9.35/£4.90) per hour, or Q350 ($47/£25) for an 8-hour day; and modern mountain bikes go for Q5 (65¢/35p) per hour, or Q35 ($4.65/£2.45) for an 8-hour day. You must be over 21 and have a valid motorcycle license to rent a motorcycle, and over 18 with a standard driver's license to rent a scooter.

BY BOAT   Panajachel is connected to all the towns and villages ringing the lake by regular boat taxi service. There are two separate dock areas. The docks below the end of Calle Santander are used by boats heading east around the lake, as well as those going directly to Santiago de Atitlán. The docks at the end of Calle del Embarcadero are used by the boats heading west around the lake, as well as those going directly to San Pedro La Laguna.

There are several types of boats providing service around the lake. The least expensive boats are large and slow, and follow a regular schedule. However, smaller, faster boat taxis leave throughout the day—some by regular schedule, others as they fill up—and are definitely worth the few extra dollars. The slower boat taxis take about an hour to go from Panajachel to either San Pedro La Laguna or Santiago de Atitlán. The smaller, faster boats cut that time in half.

The boats operate from around 5am until 6pm. However, if you're coming back to Panajachel from any of the villages across the lake, you should try to grab a boat by around 4pm, as service after that becomes less frequent and less reliable. Schedules change according to demand, but you should never have to wait more than a half-hour to find a boat heading in your direction.

Boat taxis, their captains, and street touts almost always try to gouge tourists. There is a de facto price differential between what locals pay and what tourists pay, and it's often hard to get a firm sense of what the official rates are or should be. Always ask your hotel or the INGUAT office about current fares before heading to the docks, and then try to be polite but firm in sticking to those guidelines.

In general, a small, fast boat taxi between Panajachel and San Pedro La Laguna or Santiago de Atitlán should cost around Q20 ($2.65/£1.40) each way; between San Pedro and Santiago, or between San Pedro and San Marcos, about Q10 ($1.35/70p). The slow water taxi between Panajachel and either San Pedro or Santiago should cost Q10 to Q15 ($1.35–$2/70p–£1.05). *Note:* Only pay for the leg of the ride you are actually taking. There is absolutely no reason to reserve a return trip in advance, and you run the risk of not meeting up with that specific boat or captain at the appointed time and losing your fare.

Panajachel

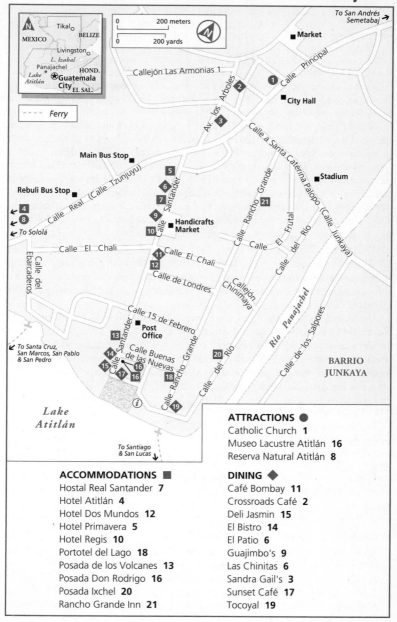

To San Andrés Semetabaj →

Market

MEXICO BELIZE
Tikal
Livingston
L. Izabal
Panajachel
Lake Atitlán
Guatemala City
HOND.
EL SAL.

Ferry

0   200 meters
0   200 yards

Callejón Las Armonias 1

Calle Principal

City Hall

Av. los Arboles

Calle a Santa Caterina Palopó

Main Bus Stop

Rebuli Bus Stop

Calle Real (Calle Tzunjuyu)

Calle Santander

Stadium

To Sololá

Calle Rancho Grande

Calle El Frutal

Calle a Santa Caterina Palopó (Calle Junkaya)

Handicrafts Market

Calle El Chali

Calle El Chali

Calle del Río

Calle Callejón Chinimaya

Calle de Londres

Calle del Ebarcaderos

Calle 15 de Febrero

Post Office

To Santa Cruz, San Marcos, San Pablo & San Pedro

Calle Santander

Calle Buenas de las Nuevas

Calle Rancho Grande

Calle del Río

Río Panajachel

Calle de los Salpores

BARRIO JUNKAYA

Lake Atitlán

To Santiago & San Lucas ↓

ATTRACTIONS ●
Catholic Church **1**
Museo Lacustre Atitlán **16**
Reserva Natural Atitlán **8**

ACCOMMODATIONS ■
Hostal Real Santander **7**
Hotel Atitlán **4**
Hotel Dos Mundos **12**
Hotel Primavera **5**
Hotel Regis **10**
Portotel del Lago **18**
Posada de los Volcanes **13**
Posada Don Rodrigo **16**
Posada Ixchel **20**
Rancho Grande Inn **21**

DINING ◆
Café Bombay **11**
Crossroads Café **2**
Deli Jasmin **15**
El Bistro **14**
El Patio **6**
Guajimbo's **9**
Las Chinitas **6**
Sandra Gail's **3**
Sunset Café **17**
Tocoyal **19**

If you don't want to wait and you've got a small group together, you can always hire an entire boat that will hold between 10 and 12 people. These boats charge around Q150 to Q250 ($20–$33/£11–£18) for a trip to any of the towns around the lakeshore. The higher fares are for those towns farthest away from Panajachel.

ORIENTATION

Panajachel sits on the north shore of Lake Atitlán. As you enter Panajachel from the Pan-American Highway and Sololá, you'll be on Calle Principal (also known as Calle Real), which continues on around the lake toward Santa Catarina Palopó. Soon after you enter Panajachel, you'll come to a major intersection at Calle Santander. The actual center of the town, called the Old Town, or Ciudad Vieja, is about 3 blocks from this intersection and about 10 or so blocks from the lakeshore. This is where you'll find Pana's main church and large market, as well as a few hotels, restaurants, bars, and language schools. By far the majority of the action in Panajachel is centered on Calle Santander, which runs from this intersection directly toward the lake, where it dead-ends. The sidewalks are crowded with street vendors and are such a jumble that most people walk in the center of the street, making way, as necessary, for the sporadic traffic.

FAST FACTS There's an **INGUAT** (Guatemala Tourism Commission) office (© **502/7762-1106**) on Calle Santander 1-87, in the Centro Comercial San Rafael. It's open Monday through Friday from 9am to 5pm. They can give you a map of Panajachel and the Lake Atitlán area, and help you with hotel reservations and figuring out the current bus and boat taxi schedules. To contact the local **tourist police,** dial © **502/7762-1120.**

There are a host of banks on Calle Principal and around the Old Town, including **Banco de Comercio, Banco Industrial,** and **Banco G&T.** There are also scores of Internet cafes around Panajachel, both in the Old Town and along Calle Santander. Most charge between Q3 and Q8 (40¢–$1.05/20p–55p) per hour. The **post office** is located at the corner of Calle Santander and Calle 15 de Febrero. The nearest hospital is the **Hospital Nacional Sololá** (© **502/7762-4121**) in Sololá.

WHAT TO SEE & DO IN PANAJACHEL

The principal activities in Panajachel are strolling along Calle Santander and the lakeshore, shopping, and hanging out in one of the cafes, bars, or restaurants.

The main **Catholic church,** located in the heart of the Old Town, dates back to 1567, and was meticulously restored in 1962. This small church is wonderfully maintained and remains very active to this date. The old stone facade looks almost whitewashed, and the diminutive plaza in front of the church is a major meeting place for locals.

(Moments **Look Out for Lookouts**

There are a couple of lookouts, or *miradores,* on the side of the road just before you enter Panajachel on your way from Sololá. You'll notice them because local crafts vendors are set up waiting to pounce on tourists trying to take in the view, which encompasses Lake Atitlán and a couple of tall volcanoes behind it. These vendors have a wide range of typical tourist wares for sale—jewelry, stone carvings, ceramic goods—but you'll find a much broader selection and better prices in town.

Gone with the Wind

Lake Atitlán has many moods. Mornings are usually calm, and the lake can have a mystical quality with the mirrorlike reflection of clouds and volcanoes in its flat surface. However, most afternoons, sharp winds kick up. These winds are known locally as Xocomil, which translates to "the wind that takes away sin." The lake gets choppy and rough, with steep white caps, which makes the taxi boat crossings wet and almost harrowing at times.

Language schools attract many visitors to Guatemala. While most of the language school action is centered across the lake in San Pedro, there are several Spanish schools in Panajachel. The best of these include **Jardín de América Spanish School** *☆* (*✆* **502/7762-2637;** www.jardindeamerica.com) and the **Pana Atitlán Language School** (*✆* **502/7762-1196**). Rates are around Q938 to Q1,125 ($125–$150/£66–£79) per week for 4 hours of class per day and a homestay with a local family.

Museo Lacustre Atitlán *☆* *(Kids)*   A series of excellent and informative displays explains the geology and geography behind the formation of the lake. The museum also showcases a collection of ceramic pieces discovered in the area, many of which were brought up from the depths of the lake by scuba divers.

At the Posada Don Rodrigo. At the south end of Calle Santander, Zona 2. *✆* **502/7762-2326.** Admission Q35, free for children under 12. Mon–Fri 8am–6pm; Sat–Sun 8am–7pm.

Reserva Natural Atitlán *☆*   A couple of nature trails, a butterfly garden, and botanical gardens are the offerings at this reserve. The trails pass through some areas of dense forest, and feature a few high-hanging bridges to get you up into the canopy. You'll certainly see a range of tropical bird species, and if you're lucky you may see a monkey or two. The reserve has a visitor center, restaurant, and small section of private beach. These folks allow camping down by the beach, and have added a few rooms recently.

In the San Buenaventura valley, just down the road from the Hotel Atitlán (see below). About ¼ mile before Panajachel, on the road in from Sololá. *✆* **502/7762-2565.** www.atitlánreserva.com. Admission Q41 ($5.50/£2.90), Q23 ($3/£1.60) for students; includes a guided tour through the butterfly garden and breeding exhibit. Daily 8am–4pm.

OUTDOOR ACTIVITIES

In addition to the attractions listed above, Panajachel and Lake Atitlán are good bases for active adventures. Most hotels have a tour desk that can arrange most of the activities listed below. You can also book through **Américo's Tours,** Calle Santander (*✆* **502/7762-2641**); **Servicios Turísticos Atitlán (STA)** *☆*, Calle 14 de Febrero 2-81 (*✆* **502/7762-2246;** www.turisticosatitlán.com); or **Toliman Tours,** Calle Santander (*✆* **502/7762-2455**).

BOATING   Boat tours *☆☆* on the lake are one of the most popular activities in Panajachel. All the hotel tour desks and tour agencies in town offer organized tours, most of which depart from Panajachel in the morning and make stops in San Pedro La Laguna, Santiago de Atitlán, and San Antonio Palopó. The tours generally last around 5 to 6 hours. Most cost between Q50 and Q90 ($6.65–$12/£3.50–£6.30), which gets you the guaranteed boat ride and an hour to 90-minute layover in each town. You can also sign on for a more elaborate tour, including a bilingual guide and lunch. These generally run between Q225 and Q375 ($30–$50/£16–£26) per person.

If you prefer to venture on your own, it's easy; see "Getting Around: By Boat" above. As soon as the boat lands in each town, you'll be met by local touts and tour guides offering to show you around. For example, in Santiago de Atitlán, they offer to take you to see Maximón; in Santa Catarina Palopó, they'll take you to see some weaving. For more detailed information on the different towns and villages, see their individual sections below.

FISHING   Fishing for *mojarra* (black bass) is a popular yet somewhat controversial lake activity. The black bass are fairly new to the lake, having been introduced as a game fish in 1958. However, this aggressive fish has decimated many of the native species, and along with them, the local subsistence fishing industry. If you're interested in fishing, ask your hotel or one of the local tour agencies, or simply head down to the waterfront docks.

PARAGLIDING   For a bird's-eye view of the lake and volcanoes, try paragliding. **Roger Lapointe** (panajaro@yahoo.ca), a Canadian paraglide pilot, offers daily rides in a tandem rig from several different takeoff points on the volcanic hillsides surrounding Lake Atitlán. The cost is Q600 ($80/£70) for a 40-minute flight. There are no requirements, but any child 8 and older with enough courage and parental permission could give it a shot.

SCUBA DIVING   Lake Atitlán offers an excellent introduction to the world of high-altitude freshwater diving. This type of diving is slightly more technically challenging than open-water diving at sea level. Because of altitude and decompression, divers must stay in the area for at least 18 hours after diving. Most dives take place in 9 to 11m (30–35 ft.) of water, and because of limited visibility, are rather uneventful. On a good day, you may actually see underwater ruins and relics, as well as volcanic steam vents. The main dive operator here is **ATI Divers** (© **502/7762-2621** or 502/ 5706-4117), which is based out of La Iguana Perdida hotel in Santa Cruz, but also maintains a business office on Calle Santander in Panajachel. A single-tank dive with all equipment costs Q188 ($25/£13). Certification courses are also offered.

SWIMMING   The lakeshore along the front of Panajachel is filled with public beaches. You will almost always find local kids and, to a lesser extent, tourists, swimming here. However, I think the boat and foot traffic and pollution make it unappealing. If you want to swim in the lake, I recommend heading to the beach at the Reserva Natural Atitlán (see above) or San Pedro La Laguna. You could even hire a boat to take you to a more tranquil and picturesque spot.

TWO-WHEEL TOURING   The rugged back roads and mountain trails around Lake Atitlán are well-suited to two-wheel travel, whether by mountain bike or off-road motorcycle. Several tour operators and a couple of rental agencies offer guided tours of this vein. If you're interested, try **Emanuel's Moto & Bike Rental** (© **502/7762-2790**) or **Maco Rent** (© **502/7762-0883**). A full-day tour should run you Q225 to Q413 ($30–$55/£16–£29). For off-road riding, no special license is needed, but Emmanuel's asks that you be 21 or older and have a motorcycle license.

SHOPPING

Calle Santander and the road ringing the lakeshore are crammed with street vendors selling all sorts of Guatemalan handicrafts, ranging from clothing and other textile products to stone and woodcarvings and leather goods. There are also a fair number of stalls selling handmade jewelry and trinkets, but these are relatively run-of-the-mill works that have no real connection to the land or its people and are nothing compared to native arts and crafts.

Just uphill from the Catholic church is the main market area of Panajachel. When I visited in late 2006, it was still being rebuilt after suffering severe damage during Hurricane Stan. By the time this goes to press, the market should be up and running, and definitely worth a visit. Expect to find vendors selling fruits, vegetables, household goods, and flowers mixed in with butchers and some stalls selling arts, crafts, and textiles.

If you're looking for higher quality pieces, check out **Sudex,** Calle Santander 1-83, Zona 2 ✸ (**©️ 502/7762-0302**), which has high-end cotton clothing for both men and women with interesting designs and excellent workmanship. For leather goods—belts, handbags, and shoes—try **Pajayub,** Calle Santander, across from Telgua (**©️ 502/ 7762-0040**).

The nearby towns of **Santiago de Atitlán, Santa Catarina Palopó,** and **Sololá** have deep and highly developed arts, crafts, and textile traditions. It's worth taking a trip to one or all of these towns to shop for the local wares. See below for more information on these towns and how to visit them. In addition, Panajachel makes a perfect base for visiting nearby **Chichicastenango** (p. 171) on market day. All of the tour operators in town offer day trips to Chichi on Thursdays and Sundays.

WHERE TO STAY
VERY EXPENSIVE

Hotel Atitlán ✸✸✸ *(Finds* *(Kids*   Beautiful and luxurious rooms, fabulous grounds, impeccable service, and an excellent restaurant make this my favorite hotel in Panajachel. The hotel is jam packed with colonial-era and local art, sculpture, and religious iconography. The rooms are all distinct and come with a private balcony or garden-front patio. Ask for a third-floor room to get the best lake and volcano views. Room no. 315 is the best standard room in the house, while master suite no. 314 and junior suite no. 308 are slightly better due to their views. The extensive botanical gardens and aviary are true treasures, and the lake-view pool and infinity-edge Jacuzzi may make it hard for you to get up the impetus to tour the lake, towns, and markets just off the hotel's grounds.

Finca San Buenaventura. (**©️ 502/7762-1441** or 502/7762-2060 reservations office. Fax 502/7762-0048. www.hotel atitlan.com. 57 units. Q900 ($120/£63) double; Q1,163 ($155/£81) junior suite; Q1,388 ($185/£97) master suite. AE, DC, MC, V. **Amenities:** Restaurant; bar; lounge; outdoor pool; unlit outdoor tennis court; Jacuzzi; small gym; tour desk; babysitting; laundry service; Wi-Fi; nonsmoking rooms. *In room:* TV, hair dryer.

Portotel del Lago ✸ *(Kids*   This towering, six-story, crescent-shaped, lakefront building feels a bit out of place in Panajachel, since almost no other buildings are more than two stories tall. Rooms are on floors two through five, with the best views in rooms on the higher levels. Standard rooms in the center have better views, as they directly face the lake and volcanoes, while those at the ends (the suites) of the floor have angled views. Most rooms have two double beds, modern decor, and 27-inch televisions, while the suites boast large, wraparound balconies. Suites and executive-level rooms come with extra amenities such as coffeemakers, minibars, and in-room safes. There's also a large pool, midsize gym, and outdoor Jacuzzi. This place is popular with Guatemalan families on weekends, and even has a kids' club.

2a Av. 06-17, Zona 2. (**©️ 502/7762-1555** or 502/7762-1556. Fax 502/7762-1562. www.portahotels.com. 100 units. Q1,050 ($140/£74) double; Q1,125 ($150/£79) executive level; Q1,500 ($200/£105) suite. Rates are all-inclusive, double occupancy. AE, DC, MC, V. **Amenities:** 2 restaurants; 2 bars; lounge; large outdoor pool; 2 Jacuzzis; small gym; sauna; tour desk; children's program; room service; babysitting; laundry service. *In room:* TV.

EXPENSIVE

Posada Don Rodrigo ⚡ (Kids) This lakefront property at the end of Calle Santander is my top choice in the heart of Panajachel. The sprawling grounds, tasteful rooms, fabulous terrace views, and in-house attractions set it apart from the competition. The standard rooms feature dark, colonial decor with heavy wood furniture, stucco walls, and a fireplace. The lakefront rooms are a bit more spacious and worth the modest splurge, which gets you a small private balcony and shared lawn. Tall guests will catch views of the lake and volcanoes over the trees and shrubs. The pool, with a big spiral slide, and a very well-done museum (Museo Lacustre Atitlán) make this an excellent choice for families.

At the south end of Calle Santander, Zona 2. ⓒ **502/7762-2326** or 502/7762-2329. Fax 502/2331-6838. www.hotelposadadedonrodrigo.com. 39 units. Q675–Q825 ($90–$110/£47–£58) double. Rates include full breakfast. AE, DC, MC, V. **Amenities:** Restaurant; bar; lounge; outdoor pool; tour desk; room service; babysitting; laundry service. *In room:* No phone.

MODERATE

Hotel Dos Mundos ⚡ (Value) Not quite as stylish or fancy as the Don Rodrigo (above), this is still an excellent option right on Calle Santander. The rooms, as well as the pool and gardens, are set back off the main drag. All the rooms are spacious and well-kept, and come with a mix of bed options. I prefer room nos. 11 through 23, which front the pool and garden area and share a veranda. The other rooms are a bit closer to the street, though not so close that noise is a problem. The hotel has a good and popular Italian restaurant, as well as a hip cafe and bar right on the street.

Calle Santander 4-72, Zona 2. ⓒ **502/7762-2078** or 502/7762-2865. Fax 502/7762-0127. www.hoteldosmundos.com. 22 units. Q300–Q415 ($40–$55/£21–£29) double. AE, DC, MC, V. **Amenities:** Restaurant; bar; lounge; outdoor pool; tour desk; room service 7:30am–10pm; laundry service. *In room:* TV, safe.

Hostal Real Santander This four-story hotel right on the main drag features clean and comfortable, if somewhat nondescript, rooms. The rooms, all on the second and third floors, feature a large, varnished-wood bay window that lets out on to a shared veranda, a 21-inch flatscreen TV, and faux stucco walls and ceilings. The windows don't offer any real views, but there's an unfinished rooftop terrace for those who want to gaze around.

3a Av. 3-45, Calle Santander, Zona 2. ⓒ **502/7762-2915.** Fax 502/7762-1117. necos@itelgua.com. 12 units. Q320 ($43/£22) double. AE, DC, MC, V. **Amenities:** Tour desk; laundry service. *In room:* TV, no phone.

Hotel Regis This 1934 hotel is run by the granddaughter of the original owner, and the rooms show the bridge between old and new, with some showing their age and others recently updated. (It's worth asking to see a few rooms before booking.) The spacious rooms have tile floors and brightly painted walls, and some even come with a brick fireplace or kitchenette. The most interesting feature here is the two large natural hot spring-fed Jacuzzis.

3a Av. 3-47, Calle Santander, Zona 2. ⓒ **502/7762-1149.** Fax 502/7762-1152. www.hotelregisatitlán.com. 25 units. Q458 ($61/£32) double. AE, DC, MC, V. **Amenities:** Tour desk; 2 Jacuzzis; laundry service. *In room:* TV.

Rancho Grande Inn If you're looking for a clean and comfortable room that's close to the action without feeling like it is, this longtime favorite is a good option. All of the rooms are fairly similar, with plenty of space, a working fireplace, and simple decor. The individual bungalows are the best and biggest options, spread among the grounds, gardens, and pool. If you can, get a room that's away from the street. Despite being more than 60 years old, the hotel has aged remarkably well. There's no restaurant here, but the daily breakfast, in particular their fresh pancakes, are considered by many a large part of the attraction.

Calle Rancho Grande. ℂ 502/7762-2255. Fax 502/7762-2247. www.ranchograndeinn.com. 12 units. Q495 ($66/£35) double; Q675 ($82/£47) suite; Q975 ($130/£68) bungalow for up to 4 people. AE, DC, MC, V. **Amenities:** Small outdoor pool; tour desk; laundry service. *In room:* TV.

INEXPENSIVE

Hotel Primavera *(Value)*   This small hotel is a step above the score of budget options on Calle Santander. Most of the rooms are on the second floor and feature bay windows that overlook the street. The rooms are relatively small and standard, but they are kept immaculate. I like no. 9, which has a private staircase and balcony, and is set back from the busy street.

Calle Santander. ℂ 502/7762-2052. Fax 502/7762-0171. www.primaveratitlan.com. 10 units. Q263–Q338 ($35–$45/£18–£24) double. AE, DC, MC, V. **Amenities:** Restaurant; tour desk; laundry service. *In room:* TV, no phone.

Posada de los Volcanes   This is a good choice among the hoard of budget lodgings in Pana. There are three rooms on each of the four floors, and each floor has a shared veranda with some tables and chairs. The fourth floor offers a glimpse of the lake and a better view all around. The rooms are compact, but clean and modern. The best room in the house is no. 402, which has a picture window with a view of the nearby mountains.

Calle Santander 5-51, Zona 2. ℂ 502/7762-0244. Fax 502/7762-2367. www.posadadelosvolcanes.com. 12 units. Q290–Q345 ($39–$46/£20–£24) double. AE, DC, MC, V (with 10% surcharge). **Amenities:** Tour desk; laundry service. *In room:* TV, no phone.

Posada Ixchel   This bright-white three-story building is just 3 blocks from the lake on a road that runs alongside the river. The rooms are simple and well-maintained, and the hotel has amenities such as a pool, rooftop terrace, small gym, and sauna. The restaurant serves good Guatemalan fare at reasonable prices.

Calle del Río. ℂ 502/7762-2375. Fax 502/7762-1016. posadaixchel@yahoo.com. 15 units. Q200–Q350 ($27–$47/£14–£25). AE, DC, MC, V. **Amenities:** Restaurant; small outdoor pool; small gym; sauna; tour desk; laundry service. *In room:* TV, no phone.

WHERE TO DINE

In addition to the places listed below, **Guajimbo's,** Calle Santander (ℂ **502/7762-0063**), is a popular Uruguayan-style steakhouse that often has live music, while **Las Chinitas,** Calle Santander (ℂ **502/7762-0063**), is the town's most popular Asian restaurant, with a mix of Chinese, Thai, and Indian options. **El Patio,** Calle Santander (ℂ **502/7762-2041**), isn't known for its food, but it has some of the best people-watching on its open-air patio just off Calle Santander. For a casual meal, try **Deli Jasmín,** Calle Santander (ℂ **502/7762-2586**).

Since my last visit, the long-standing landmark restaurant Al Chisme has been converted into **Sandra Gail's,** Avenida Los Arboles (ℂ **502/7762-2063**), a "Texas-style restaurant" with barbecue ribs, chicken-fried steak, and massive burgers. The early reports I've received are good.

For a coffee break and something sweet, try the **Crossroads Café,** Calle del Campanario 0-27 (ℂ **502/5292-8439**).

EXPENSIVE

Hotel Atitlán *☆☆* *(finds)* INTERNATIONAL   This hotel restaurant is by far the most elegant dining option in Panajachel. Wood tables and chairs, beautiful place settings and glassware, and candles and a fireplace contribute to the ornate setting, while patio tables add lake and volcano views to the menu. Standout entrees include grilled salmon braised with pesto and filet mignon with Roquefort sauce. They also offer a selection of pastas and a few refined takes on Guatemalan classics, including *pupusas* (cornmeal patties usually stuffed with beans, cheese, or meat) and the typical Chapin plate of grilled meat, fried plantain, refried beans, and local cheese. For lunch, you can get hearty sandwiches and burgers in addition to the regular menu, and the Sunday brunch buffet is justifiably popular.

Finca San Buenaventura. *©* **502/7762-1441.** Reservations required. Main courses Q56–Q1,557 ($7.45–$21/ £3.90–£62). AE, DC, MC, V. Daily 6:30am–10pm.

MODERATE

El Bistro *☆* ITALIAN   This long-standing local favorite serves up excellent pastas and entrees in a convivial open-air setting. While there's some indoor seating, the best tables are found in a large covered courtyard just off Calle Santander that's lined with plants, palms, and bamboo. The proper tablecloths and candlelight are offset by the plastic lawn chairs. The homemade fettuccine is available with more than 15 different sauces, and other pasta options include lasagna and cannelloni. For something heartier, opt for grilled fish, chicken parmigiana, or steak pizzaola. When you order, the waiter will ask if you want your pasta "al dente" or "normal." "Normal" would be overcooked for most people accustomed to good Italian cooking. This place also serves up good, standard breakfast fare most days.

Southern end of Calle Santander. *©* **502/7762-0508.** Reservations recommended. Pasta Q45–Q50 ($6–$6.65/ £3.15–£3.50); main courses Q45–Q75 ($6–$10/£3.15–£5.25). AE, DC, MC, V. Tues–Sun 7:30am–10pm; Mon noon–10pm.

Sunset Café GUATEMALAN/MEXICAN   As the name suggests, sunset is a good time to come here, when you can marvel at the reflection of the moon in Lake Atitlán and the flickering of the lights in San Pedro. The spectacular setting here makes the standard Mexican fare acceptable, but I still like the *fajitas de pescado* (fish fajitas) and *enchiladas verdes* (chicken enchiladas in a green tomatillo sauce). There's live music here most nights, so grab a drink, a plate of nachos, and a seat under the tree (heavily hung with orchids and bromeliads) that grows through the thatch roof.

Calle Santander and Calle del Lago. *©* **502/7762-0003.** Reservations recommended for large groups. Main courses Q32–Q80 ($4.25–$11/£2.25–£5.60). AE, DC, MC, V. Daily 11am–midnight.

Tocoyal GUATEMALAN   The front wall of picture windows allows great views of the lake, but passing traffic and souvenir stands sometimes get in the way. The food here is well-prepared and attentively served by waiters in starched white shirts, black bow ties, and red Guatemalan vests. The restaurant is named after a traditional headdress made from a very long ribbon tightly wound around itself and worn almost like a halo by Maya women.

Calle del Lago, Playa Publica, Zona 2. *©* **502/7762-1555.** Main courses Q24–Q107 ($3.20–$14/£1.70–£7.50). AE, DC, MC, V. Daily 8am–9pm.

INEXPENSIVE

Café Bombay *☆* *(Value)* INDIAN/VEGETARIAN   The name of this place would indicate Indian cuisine, which you'll find here, but you'll also get everything vegetarian from pad Thai and tacos to lasagna and falafel. Excellent sandwiches, soups, and smoothies are also served, as well as vegan fare. The atmosphere is casual, and on a nice day you can grab a seat on one of the umbrella-covered tables just off Calle Santander.

Calle Santander. ℂ **502/7762-0611.** Reservations not accepted. Main courses Q43–Q52 ($5.75–$6.95/£3–£3.65); sandwiches Q14–Q28 ($1.90–$3.75/£1–£2). No credit cards. Wed–Mon 11am–10pm.

PANAJACHEL AFTER DARK

Panajachel has a fairly active nightlife. For the past 15 years, my favorite place has been the **Circus Bar** 🅦🅦, Avenida Los Arboles (ℂ **502/7762-2056**), which has a relaxed vibe, simple menu, and decor to match the joint's name. They also frequently have live music. This is also the first place I ever tried **Ron Zacapa** 🅦🅦🅦, Guatemala's world-class 23-year-old aged rum. Circus Bar, just north of Calle Principal, is located in what's considered Panajachel's mini–Zona Viva.

Of the bars on Calle Santander, I like the new **Maktub'ar Café,** which has a relaxed, almost beach-bar feel, and **Pana Rock Café** (ℂ **502/7762-2194**), which is a takeoff on the Planet Rock chain.

For a mellow night, **La Terraza,** Calle Santander (ℂ **502/7762-0041**), has a second-floor tapas bar with a balcony overlooking Calle Santander.

For loud and late-night dancing, try **Sócrates Disco,** Calle Principal (ℂ **502/ 7762-1015**); **El Aleph,** Avenida Los Arboles (ℂ **502/7762-0192**); or **El Chapiteau Discoteque,** Avenida Los Arboles (ℂ **502/7762-0374**).

2 San Pedro La Laguna 🅧

8km (5 miles) SW of Panajachel across the lake

Panajachel has become more commercial and upscale over the years, so the hippie and backpack crowd moved across the lake to San Pedro La Laguna. However, with a growing number of budget lodgings, Spanish schools, international restaurants, and late-night bars, San Pedro is starting to give Pana a run for its money. San Pedro has a more relaxed and less commercial vibe to it than Panajachel, but more of a foreign influence than Santiago de Atitlán or Santa Catarina Palopó.

ESSENTIALS

GETTING THERE

BY BOAT   From Panajachel, the docks for boats to San Pedro are found at the end of Calle del Embarcadero. The boats operate roughly every half-hour from around 5am until 6pm. However, if you're coming back to Panajachel, try to grab a boat by around 4pm, as service after that becomes less frequent and less reliable. Schedules change according to demand, but you should never have to wait more than a half-hour to find a boat heading in your direction. These boats ply a route that stops at Santa Cruz La Laguna, Jaibalito, and San Marcos La Laguna en route to San Pedro La Laguna. In addition, they will stop at any number of other smaller docks, whether they are for tiny communities, individual homes, or hotels.

Boat taxis, their captains, and street touts almost always try to gouge tourists. There is a difference between what locals pay and what tourists pay, and it's often hard to get a firm sense of what the official rates are or should be. Always ask your hotel or the INGUAT office about current fares before heading to the docks, and then try to be polite but firm in sticking to those guidelines.

A boat taxi between Panajachel and San Pedro La Laguna should cost around Q20 ($2.65/£1.40) each way. Between San Pedro and Santiago or San Pedro and San Marcos should run Q10 ($1.35/70p). **Note:** Only pay for the leg of the ride you are actually taking. There is absolutely no reason to reserve a return trip in advance, and you run the risk of not meeting up with that specific boat or captain at the appointed time and losing your fare. The slow water taxi between Panajachel and San Pedro leaves about twice a day from the docks below the end of Calle Santander and should cost Q10 to Q15 ($1.35–$2/70p–£1.05). However, I recommend you take the much faster and more frequent boats from the end of Calle del Embarcadero, which charge Q20 ($2.65/£1.40) each way.

You can always hire an entire boat to make the trip for around Q250 ($33/£18). These boats hold between 10 to 12 people, so if you can round up a group, it's not too expensive.

BY CAR   To reach San Pedro La Laguna by car, take the exit for Santa Clara La Laguna and San Pedro La Laguna off the Pan-American Highway (CA-1) about 20km (13 miles) west of Los Encuentros. Don't take the exit for Sololá and Panajachel. San Pedro La Laguna is also connected to Santiago de Atitlán by a paved road.

BY BUS   There are no express or luxury buses to San Pedro. If you're coming by bus, your best bet is to head Panajachel first (see "Panajachel: Getting There: By Bus," earlier in this chapter), and then catch a boat taxi to San Pedro (above). However, San Pedro does have regular "chicken bus" service (cheap, local, commuter buses) to and from both Guatemala City and Quetzaltenango. Ask your hotel, or contact **Asistur** (© **1500**) for current schedules.

GETTING AROUND
Although distances are short, the hill between the docks and the center of town is formidable. You can usually find a taxi or tuk tuk near either dock to take you to the center of town for around Q5 (65¢/35p). Alternately, you can pile into one of the collective pickups that provide this service for just Q2 (25¢/15p).

For information about getting around the lake by boat, see "San Pedro La Laguna: Getting There: By Boat" and "Panajachel: "Getting Around: By Boat," above.

ORIENTATION
San Pedro La Laguna is located on the southwestern shore of Lake Atitlán. The center of the town sits on a small plateau a steep climb up from the shores. This is where you'll find San Pedro's Catholic church and central plaza, as well as most of the town's shops and services. From this plateau, streets run down on either side of a steep ridge. The roads heading down the west side of this ridge lead toward the *muelle municipal,* which is the main dock for boats arriving from and departing to Panajachel. The roads heading down the east side of this ridge lead toward an area known as *la playa,* or "the beach," and the *muelle santiago,* the main dock for boats arriving from and departing for Santiago de Atitlán.

FAST FACTS   There is a **Banrural** office (3a Av. 1-51, Zona 3) in the center of town just up from the church. You'll also find the **post office** and a **Telgua** telephone office on the street behind the church. To contact the local **police,** dial © **502/7762-4000.** There's no hospital or major medical clinic in San Pedro. In the event you need medical care, ask your hotel. There are a handful of Internet cafes around San Pedro. I like **Planeta En Línea** (© **502/5414-4959**) and **Dnoz.com** (© **502/7721-8078**). Most hotels and several private operations will launder your clothes. If you can't have it done at your hotel, try **Laundry Karina** (© **502/7721-8194**).

To San Pablo, San Marcos & Santa Cruz

To Panajachel

To San Juan

Evangelical School

Lake Atitlán

To Santiago de Atitlán

Bus Stop

Market

Bank

Post Office

Ferry
Trail

Cemetery

0   500 meters
0   500 yards

DINING & NIGHTLIFE ◆
Café Munchies **10**
Chile's **3**
El Barrio **13**
Freedom **2**
Nick's Place **5**
Punto Rojo **7**
Shanti **1**
The Alegre Pub **6**

ATTRACTIONS ●
Boats to Panajachel **4**
Boats to
   Santiago de Atitlán **17**
Catholic church **15**
Los Thermales **11**
Volcán San Pedro **16**

ACCOMMODATIONS ■
Casa Elena **9**
Hotel Gran Sueño **8**
Hotel Mansion
   del Lago **14**
Hotelito El Amanacer
   Sak'cari **12**

FUN ON & OFF THE LAKE

San Pedro is a laid-back lakeside town, with most visitors opting to spend the day at a cafe or restaurant. However, if you want to get active, there are plenty of options. To set up any sort of organized tour, head to **Big Foot Tourist Info Center** (✆ **502/ 7721-8202**) or **Casa Verde Tours** (✆ **502/7721-8090**). If you happen to be here on June 29, take part in the feast day of San Pedro, when the town pulls out all the stops with a major street fair, bullfights, carnival rides, and live music and dancing.

KAYAKING & CANOEING   You can rent canoes and kayaks from several operators in town. Just head down to either one of the main docks. Rates run around Q10 ($1.35/70p) per hour and Q25 to Q35 ($3.35–$4.65/£1.75–£2.45) per day. If you're in good shape, you can paddle to one of the nearby towns or villages. Be careful of the

---

Tips   Be Careful

The beautiful countryside and volcanic peaks around Lake Atitlán are quite enticing to climbers and hikers. However, due to the current security situation, poverty, and a history of violence, it's often not safe for tourists to be on isolated trails or back roads. It's best to sign up for a guided tour if you want to scale a volcano or hike to one of the nearby villages or lookouts.

---

regular boat taxis, and try to avoid spending too much time near the busy dock areas. Also, remember that the winds and chop tend to kick up in the afternoons.

HIKING   At 3,020m (9,905 ft.), **Volcán San Pedro** towers over and behind the town. The trail is generally wide and well-maintained, and the round-trip hike should take between 5 and 6 hours. Tour desks all over town offer guided hikes to the summit for around Q38 to Q75 ($5–$10/£2.65–£5.25) per person. Other hikes around San Pedro head to **Cerro de la Cruz,** a beautiful hilltop with great views, and to **La Nariz del Indio (Indian's Nose),** another lookout spot that allegedly looks like a Maya profile from afar.

HORSEBACK RIDING & MOUNTAIN BIKING   Horseback and mountain bike tours can be set up by any hotel tour desk or in-town tour agency. You'll also find horses for rent near the Santiago dock. If you want to rent a bike on your own, check in with **Bici Amistad,** 4a Calle 3-08, Zona 2 (✆ **502/7721-8032**).

LANGUAGE LESSONS   San Pedro has become a hot spot for foreign students looking to learn or brush up on some Spanish. There are a half-dozen or more language schools in San Pedro. Most offer either individual or small class intensive instruction combined with a homestay with a local family and various organized activities and tours. Try **Atitlán Spanish School** (✆ **502/7721-8151;** www.atitlánspanish school.net), **Corazón Maya Spanish School** (✆ **502/7721-8160;** www.corazon maya.com), or **San Pedro Spanish School** (✆ **502/5715-4604;** www.sanpedrospanish school.com). Rates run around Q750 to Q1,125 ($100–$150/£53–£79) per week for 4 hours of class per day and a homestay with a local family. More adventurous students might want to learn some of the Tz'utujil Mayan dialect. Ask at any of the language schools, and they'll be able to set you up with a local instructor.

A SOAK & A SAUNA   If you have sore muscles from hiking to the summit of Volcán San Pedro or horseback riding around the shores, book yourself a tub and sauna at **Los Thermales** (✆ **502/5897-5319**). Solar heated water is used to fill several large hot tubs. They also have a wood-fired sauna. Open daily 8:30am to midnight. Rates run around Q25 ($3.35/£1.75) per person.

WHERE TO STAY IN SAN PEDRO LA LAGUNA
INEXPENSIVE

Casa Elena *Value*   Most of the rooms at this popular budget option are bare-bones concrete-block affairs, with minimal furnishings, shared bathrooms, and little ambience. However, room nos. 9 and 10, at the end of the third and fourth floors, are real steals. Less than $10 gets you a private bathroom and large picture windows with fabulous views overlooking the lake.

7a Av. 8-61, Zona 2. ⓒ **502/5980-4400.** 20 units (7 with private bathroom). Q35 ($4.65/£2.45) double with shared bathroom; Q70 ($9.35/£4.90) double with private bathroom. AE, DC, MC, V. **Amenities:** Laundry service. *In room:* No phone.

Hotel Gran Sueño   This new hotel is clean and well-run. The rooms are on the small side, but all come with cable TV, rough stucco walls, and a private bathroom with heated shower head. Most of the rooms have just one double bed and feature a large round picture window with intricate wood and brick framing.

8a Calle 4-40, Zona 2. ⓒ **502/7721-8110.** 7 units. Q75 ($10/£5.25) double. AE, DC, MC, V. **Amenities:** Tour desk; laundry service. *In room:* TV.

Hotelito El Amanacer Sak'cari ⍟ *Value*   This modern hotel is probably my favorite option in San Pedro. The second-floor rooms are the best, with a shared veranda overlooking the lake, though the few individual bungalows are also good options. Only three of the rooms have queen-size beds, so be sure to request one of these if you're traveling as a couple. The hotel also has a large, clean steam bath. The name is a little redundant since "amanacer" and "sak'cari" mean sunrise in Spanish and Tz'utujil, respectively.

7a Av. 2-10, Zona 2. ⓒ **502/7721-8096** or 502/5512-0038. www.hotelsakcari.com. 16 units. Q120 ($16/£8.40) double. AE, DC, MC, V. **Amenities:** Tour desk; laundry service; steam bath. *In room:* No phone.

Hotel Mansión del Lago   This hotel is set on the hillside above the *muelle municipal,* and the rooms on the top floor have the best views, especially from their shared veranda. Most rooms, which are named after different cities and archaeological sites around Guatemala, are rather small, and lack anything in the way of style, but all come with a small television and private bathroom. There are two bare concrete rooftop terraces, and one of these has an unheated Jacuzzi. These folks have a good Internet cafe on-site.

4a Av. and 8a Calle, Zona 2. ⓒ **502/7721-8041** or 502/7721-8124. 17 units. Q150 ($20/£11) double. AE, DC, MC, V. **Amenities:** Jacuzzi; tour desk; laundry service. *In room:* TV, no phone.

WHERE TO DINE IN SAN PEDRO LA LAGUNA

In addition to the places listed below, **Shanti,** 8a Calle 3-93, Zona 2 (ⓒ **502/5561-8423**), is a popular and laid-back breakfast and sandwich joint, with a good lake view. Vegetarians will like **Café Munchies,** 7a Av. 3-32, Zona 2 (ⓒ **502/5875-2461**).

INEXPENSIVE

Chile's ⍟ *Value* INTERNATIONAL   Good food and a nice view of the lake make this one of the best and most popular options in San Pedro. The menu ranges from pizzas and pastas to beef in orange sauce and red curry chicken with rice. There are several different vegetarian dishes, as well as a selection of salads and hearty sandwiches. Everything is very well prepared, and the service is attentive and jovial. The best seats are on the open-air deck and covered patio closest to the water. After you're stuffed, stick around for dance class. (Tues and Sat introductory lessons are free.)

4a Av. 8-12, Zona 2 (above the *muelle municipal*). ⓒ **502/5594-6194.** Reservations not accepted. Main courses Q30–Q45 ($4–$6/£2.10–£3.15). AE, DC, MC, V. Daily 7am–1am.

Nick's Place *Value* PIZZA/INTERNATIONAL   Nick's has a little of everything: a good lake view, a long-standing reputation, and a broad menu that includes steak, pasta, hamburgers, nachos, and pizza. The delicious thin-crust pizzas here are particularly popular.

The large open-air dining room features wood tables and chairs, and plenty of hanging plants to liven up the ambience.

4a Av. 8-16, Zona 2 (above the *muelle municipal*). © 502/7721-8065. Main courses Q30–Q55 ($4–$7.35/ £2.10–£3.85). AE, DC, MC, V. Daily 7am–midnight.

SAN PEDRO AFTER DARK

San Pedro is a great town to bar crawl, since everything is within walking distance. Most of the nightlife centers around the *muelle municipal*. On any night you might find things happening at **El Barrio** (© 502/5577-2601), **The Alegre Pub** (© 502/ 7721-8100), **Punto Rojo** (© 502/5569-7020), or **Freedom** (© 502/5392-5942). Most tourists and language students tend to do a simple pub crawl and congregate at whichever spot is most happening on that night. El Barrio and The Alegre Pub shoot for an Anglo-American pub vibe, and The Alegre Pub shows American sporting events, including Sunday afternoon American football. Freedom and Punto Rojo have a more European feel, while Freedom sometimes has live music, which might be anything from rock to Latin Folk.

3 Santiago de Atitlán ★★

8km (5 miles) S of Panajachel across the lake

Set on the southern shores of Lake Atitlán, near the start of a long narrow bay, Santiago de Atitlán is a picturesque Tz'utujil town with a distinct character and fiercely independent streak. Santiago de Atitlán was the site of a horrible massacre during the civil war and one of the first villages to organize against the paramilitary and military forces.

The town was severely ravaged by the effects of Hurricane Stan in October 2005, and mudslides from the Toliman volcano killed more than 70 people in and around Santiago.

The Santiago de Atitlán *huipil* and men's pants are unique and highly prized by foreigners buying indigenous textiles. The cult of Maximón (see the box, below) is very strong in Santiago, and as soon as you step off of any boat here, you'll be met with offers from local kids and touts to take you to see him. You'll definitely want to visit Maximón, but don't feel obligated to go along with the first person who approaches you.

ESSENTIALS
GETTING THERE
BY BUS   There are no express or luxury buses to Santiago de Atitlán. If you're coming by bus, your best bet is to head to Panajachel first (see "Panajachel: Getting There: By Bus," earlier in this chapter), and then catch a boat taxi to Santiago de Atitlán (below). Santiago does have regular "chicken bus" service to and from Guatemala City. From Santiago, they leave from in front of the main plaza, roughly every hour between 4am and 3pm. Ask your hotel, or contact **Asistur** (© **1500**) for current schedules.

BY BOAT   From Panajachel, the docks for boats to Santiago de Atitlán are found at the public docks and beach area below the end of Calle Santander. The boats operate roughly every hour from around 6am until 5pm; however, if you're coming back to Panajachel, try to grab a boat by 4pm, as service after that becomes less frequent and less reliable. Schedules change according to demand, but you should never have to wait more than an hour to find a boat heading in your direction. Alternatively, you can hire an entire boat (which holds 10–12 people) to make the trip for around Q250 ($33/£18).

Boat taxis, their captains, and street touts almost always try to gouge tourists. There is a price difference between what locals pay and what tourists pay, and it's often hard to get a firm sense of what the official rates are or should be. Always ask your hotel or the INGUAT office about current fares before heading to the docks, and then try to be polite but firm in sticking to those guidelines.

A boat taxi between Panajachel and Santiago de Atitlán should cost around Q20 ($2.65/£1.40) each way. Between Santiago and San Pedro the ride should run Q10 ($1.35/70p). *Note:* Only pay for the leg of the ride you are actually taking. There is absolutely no reason to reserve a return trip in advance, and you run the risk of not meeting up with that specific boat or captain at the appointed time and losing your fare.

BY CAR   The best route to drive here from Guatemala City is via the Pacific Highway (CA-2). From the Coastal Highway, turn right at Cocales, through the towns of Patutul and San Lucas Tolimán.

Driving from Antigua, the best route is via the Pan-American Highway (CA-1). Take this road to Las Trampas, where you'll turn left toward Godinez. Drive through Aguas Escondidas and on to San Lucas Tolimán.

GETTING AROUND

Santiago is quite compact, and aside from the challenge presented by its steep hill, you should be able to walk anywhere in town. Still, you can always find a taxi or tuk tuk near the dock to take you to the center of town for around Q5 (65¢/35p). A taxi to Posada Santiago or El Bambu should run you Q10 (75¢/70p).

ORIENTATION

The boat taxis all land at a busy dock area at the foot of town. Just off the dock area and all along the steep cobblestone road leading up to the center of town, you'll find scores of makeshift stands and stores selling local arts and crafts. The main church and central plaza are at the top of this steep road. There are **Banrural** and **Banco G&T Continental** branches near the main plaza in Santiago; both have ATMs.

WHAT TO SEE & DO

La Iglesia Parroquial Santiago Apóstol was built in the late 16th century, and features a plaque and statue dedicated to **Father Stanley Rother,** an American priest who was murdered by a right-wing group in 1981. The main structure consists of large intricately carved altars with numerous niches, each filled with a carved figure of a saint or holy person, many of whom are adorned in traditional Maya clothing.

Outdoor enthusiasts will be happy to know that one of the best ways to tour the countryside around Santiago de Atitlán is on horseback. Longtime residents **Jim & Nancy Matison** (© 502/5811-5516; wildwestgua@yahoo.com) offer a range of rides in the area, including a full-day tour with lunch for Q375 ($50/£26) per person; shorter rides for Q113 ($15/£7.90) per person per hour, plus Q38 ($5/£2.65) per hour for the guide; as well as various treks and hikes.

Dolores Ratzan is a Tz'utujil woman who has dedicated herself to the study of traditional Maya healing and religion. She also conducts wonderful tours to the studios and workshops of local artists and weavers.

If you don't want to swim in the lake, you can use the pool and facilities at **Turicentro Tiosh Abaj** (see below) for Q24 ($3.35/£1.70) per day.

SHOPPING

The local **Santiago de Atitlán** *huipil* 🐦🐦 is distinctive and beautiful, featuring large embroidered birds and flowers, usually densely displayed around the neck and chest area, on a plain white cloth with thin, blue vertical stripes or a checkerboard pattern. You'll find these at the numerous stands that line the main road between the dock and center of town. Santiago is also a good place to shop for carved-wood masks, as well as local paintings done in a "primitive" style. Friday and Saturday are the principal market days, and you'll find a greater selection on those days, with sellers coming into town from surrounding villages. However, the shopping scene is good here just about any day.

Father Rother & the Santiago Massacre

For 13 years, Father Stanley Rother of Oklahoma worked in the Santiago de Atitlán, translating the Bible and reciting Mass in the local Tz'utujil language, and establishing a small hospital to serve the community. He was first assigned to Santiago de Atitlán in 1968 after he was ordained Catholic priest of the Oklahoma Archdiocese.

Despite, or perhaps because of, his work, he received death threats, and Rother was summoned back to Oklahoma in January 1981, only to return days later. On July 28, 1981, four men entered the church rectory and shot him. Rother was one of 10 priests murdered in Guatemala that year, and parish members built a memorial in his living quarters.

Throughout the 1980s, Santiago suffered heavily under the military campaign to combat alleged subversives, guerrillas, and communists. More than 1,000 people from Santiago were killed or disappeared during this time.

On December 1, 1990, a group of drunk soldiers in civilian dress went to the home of a shopkeeper and threatened to break the door down. The family's screams were overheard by neighbors who, perhaps emboldened by the memory of Father Rother, chased the soldiers away. Someone rang the town bell, and nearly the entire village gathered in the plaza, where they met for several hours.

At 4am, 3,000 shouting people woke the soldiers sleeping at the nearby military base. When a couple of villagers threw rocks over the barbed-wire fence, the army opened fire, killing 11 villagers (of whom 3 were children) and wounding 17.

Government officials who arrived the next day were presented with a petition signed by more than 20,000 people. The petition demanded that the army withdraw from the area. The killings and the villagers' response had drawn international attention, and the government chose to remove the troops rather than risk an international scandal and the loss of considerable amounts of tourist and foreign aid dollars. To this day, the Guatemalan military is banned from establishing any sort of presence in Santiago.

The site of the massacre is now a small park called Parque del La Paz, or Peace Park. A memorial celebration is held here each year on December 2.

Maximón

The Mayas' introduction to Catholicism often came with the threat of immolation, hanging, or beheading, and they soon rationalized that this new religion could easily be superimposed with their own. When they saw the statue of Mary crushing a snake under her foot, they prayed to Gukumatz, the creator snake god.

The Maya also brought their own saint to their brand of Catholicism. Maximón (pronounced "Mashimon") was a pre-Columbian Maya god of the underworld known as Maam, or Grandfather. The modern name is a blend of Maam and his other name, San Simon. Maximón symbolizes male sexual virility and brings rain to fertilize the earth. He's known as the saint of gamblers and drunkards, and is thought to give wealth and worldly success to his followers.

Despite the Catholic church's attempt to demonize the dark-skinned Maximón by equating him with Judas, he is still found in churches, shops, and homes across Guatemala. He is now depicted as a 20th-century mustached man wearing a black suit, red tie, and wide-brimmed hat, and is represented in life-size wood statues, small dolls, or pictures on votive candles. He's given offerings of tobacco, alcohol, Coca-Cola, and a tropical plant with orange-red berries.

Maximón's feast day is October 28. On this day, and on the Wednesday of Holy Week, he's carried through the streets on the shoulders of his followers. In some villages he's hung from the main church's cross at the end of the ceremony. Maximón's more scandalous side forces most followers to keep him out of public view for the rest of the year, for fear that his famed sexual desires may run amok. He is kept in the house—and sometimes the outhouse—with his whereabouts changing regularly. In most towns with strong Maximón traditions (including Santiago de Atitlán and Zunil), locals will bring you to see him for a small tip. If you go, be sure to bring a cigar or some rum to leave in offering. In most cases, you'll also have to pay a small fee for each photo you take. Most touts want Q5 to Q10 (65¢–$1.35/35p–70p) to take you to see Maximón. You may be charged an extra Q1 to Q5 (15¢–65¢/10p–35p) per photo, depending upon who's minding the saint and how much he thinks he can get from you.

Note: It's become common practice to take old *huipiles,* particularly those from Santiago, and dip them into a large dye vat of either blue or ocher. This gives the *huipil* an interesting look, but it's very far from traditional, and often serves to mask an inferior piece of work.

WHERE TO STAY & DINE IN SANTIAGO DE ATITLAN

Santiago de Atitlán is not a dining destination, but **Posada de Santiago** and **Bambú Hotel & Restaurant** (see below) have the best offerings in town. You can also get good, simple Guatemalan fare at **El Gran Sol,** located on the main road between the docks and center of town. All hotel rates listed below include the 22% hotel tax.

MODERATE

Bambú Hotel & Restaurant ✦ *(Finds)*   Though the Bambú sits above the lake just out of town, I still say it's my favorite hotel in Santiago de Atitlán. Rooms include two bungalows with private patios near the water's edge and those in the two-story building set a bit farther back from the lake. Both options are spacious and artistically decorated with warm earth tones and beautiful artwork. The hotel has a pool and an excellent Nuevo Spanish-influenced restaurant with lake and volcano views. The staff is trained by a chef from Barcelona who makes periodic visits. The town is just a 15-minute walk or short cab ride away, and any of the boat taxis from Panajachel or San Pedro will drop you off at the hotel's private dock.

Carretera San Lucas Toliman, Km 16. © **502/7721-7332.** Fax 502/7721-7333. www.ecobambu.com. 11 units. Q413 ($55/£29) double. Rates include full breakfast. AE, DC, MC, V. **Amenities:** Restaurant; bar; midsize outdoor pool; sauna; tour desk; laundry service. *In room:* No phone.

Posada de Santiago 🍴 While the rooms could use some sprucing up, the setting on a lush hillside above the lake makes this a great choice. The best rooms are the six individual stone cottages, which each come with a queen- and twin-size bed and a private patio or terrace with a hammock. Casa Maya has a private gazebo and bit of lawn. There are three suites, of which I like Casa Rosa, which has a stone headboard with a Maya-styled face over the queen-size bed. There are also a couple of budget cottages with basic rooms that share a common kitchen, living area, and bathroom. All but the budget rooms have a fireplace, and the two suites come with TVs. The best feature here is the pool and barbecue area, which has a fabulous perch overlooking the lake, as well as a separate hot tub and sauna. The restaurant is also very good, and serves a mix of traditional Guatemalan food (thanks to the chefs) and American/international dishes (thanks to the American owners). A taxi or tuk tuk here should cost around Q10 ($1.35/70p).

1.5km (2 miles) south of the dock. © **502/7721-7366** or 502/5784-9111. Fax 502/7721-7365. 15 units (10 with private bathroom). Q210–Q375 ($28–$50/£15–26) double with shared bathroom; Q413 ($55/£29) double with private bathroom; Q638–Q713 ($85–$95/£45–£50) suite. AE, DC, MC, V. **Amenities:** Restaurant; bar; midsize outdoor pool; Jacuzzi; sauna; tour desk; laundry service. *In room:* No phone.

Turicentro Tiosh Abaj 🍴 This hotel introduced swank to Santiago, but it lacks the personality and charm of the hotels listed above. Still, if you want a large, comfortable room with modern amenities that's in the heart of town, this is a good choice. Most of the rooms come with a king-size bed, and all have a 27-inch flatscreen TV and a private balcony or patio (only a few on the fourth floor have a view of the lake). Walls are painted in soft tones and decorated with local handicrafts and textiles. The suites are massive, and come with a fireplace and even larger flatscreen TV. The pool here is shaped like a fish and features a children's end and two water slides.

Downtown. © **502/7721-7656.** Fax 502/7721-7165. www.turicentrotioshabaj.com. 30 units. Q488 ($65/£34) double; Q1,013 ($135/£71) suite. AE, DC, MC, V. **Amenities:** Restaurant; bar; large outdoor pool; tour desk; laundry service. *In room:* TV.

4 Other Villages around Lake Atitlán 🌟🌟

A dozen or more small towns and villages ring the shores of Lake Atitlán. All are easily accessible by car, taxi, tuk tuk, or boat. Some, in fact, are only accessible by boat. While all of these towns and villages are good destinations for day trips, they also make great places to stay, especially if you want to get away from the heavily beaten tourist path.

SANTA CATARINA PALOPO & SAN ANTONIO PALOPO ⊛

These two Kaquichel Maya towns on the northeastern shore of the lake are connected to Panajachel by a well-paved road, and are also accessible by regular water taxi service. **Santa Catarina Palopó** ⊛ is particularly well-known for its distinctive *huipil* of dark blues and greens with intricate embroidery. **San Antonio Palopó** ⊛ is where the paved road ends and a dirt road continues around the lake. Both towns have tight streets packed with homes and businesses that rise from the lake shore, as well as churches in their town centers. The brilliantly whitewashed church in San Antonio Palopó is especially pretty, with an enviable perch and fantastic view over Lake Atitlán. San Antonio Palopó is often a featured stop in the organized lake tours sold out of Panajachel.

Although the walk isn't particularly picturesque, and you have to be careful of passing traffic, you can walk from Panajachel to San Antonio. There are some great views from the side of the road as you arrive in San Antonio Palopó. Whether you're walking or driving, be sure to stop here. It takes between 2 and 2½ hours to walk one-way. You could walk there and back, or simply walk one-way and grab a taxi or hitchhike back. Hitchhiking between San Antonio Palopó and Panajachel during the day is relatively safe, but avoid doing so at night or at any other places around the lake.

WHERE TO STAY & DINE
VERY EXPENSIVE

Casa Palopó ⊛⊛⊛   This small hotel exudes elegance, from the stone tiles on the pool deck to the original art adorning the walls. Most of the rooms have king-size beds, large bathrooms with beautiful Mexican majolica sinks, and large terraces with gorgeous views. My favorite is suite no. 1, whose large terrace is reached through French doors. There's a private villa above the main building with two gorgeous master suites, a Jacuzzi, a full kitchen, dining and living rooms, and a private infinity-edge pool. The villa also comes with a personal butler and cook. Back down at the hotel, the restaurant is worth a visit even if you're not a guest here, and the pool with wood gazebo is a good place to unwind.

Carretera a San Antonio Palopó, Km 6.8, Santa Catarina Palopó. ℂ 502/7762-2270. Fax 502/7762-2721. www.casa palopo.com. 8 units. Q938–Q1,373 ($125–$175/£66–£96) double; Q1,403–Q1,688 ($187–$225/£98–£118) suite; Q5,925 ($790/£415) villa. Rates higher during peak periods, lower during the off season. No children under 15 allowed. AE, DC, MC, V. **Amenities:** Restaurant; bar; small outdoor pool; small gym; tour desk; laundry service. *In room:* Minibar.

MODERATE

Villa Santa Catarina ⊛   This pretty hotel is located in the Heart of Santa Catarina Palopó, just up from the lake. All of the rooms are spacious, with tile floors and tasteful local decor, and though the lake is nearby, the shape of the building compromises the views from most of the rooms. The best bed in the house is room no. 51, a junior suite with a mosaic-tile bathroom, a balcony with both lake and mountain views, and a large picture window with a full-on view of the water. Of the standard rooms, no. 3 has the best view.

Santa Catarina Palopó. ℂ 502/7762-1291 at the hotel, or 502/2334-1818 reservations in Guatemala City. Fax 502/ 2334-8134. www.villasdeguatemala.com. 36 units. Q420 ($56/£29) double; Q638 ($85/£45) junior suite. AE, DC, MC, V. **Amenities:** Restaurant; bar; outdoor pool; tour desk; room service 7am–10pm; laundry service. *In room:* No phone.

(Tips   Safety First

Dirt paths and roads running close to the lakeshore connect all of the towns and villages along the northwestern shore of Lake Atitlán. Walking between the towns can be an excellent way to spend a day. However, be careful and always ask your hotel or the INGUAT office about the current security situation along these paths. The town of San Pablo La Laguna, in particular, has been known in the past for attacks on tourist hikers.

INEXPENSIVE

Hotel Terrazas del Lago   Simple and relaxed is the best way to describe this place on the eastern edge of San Antonio Palopó. Most of the rooms are on the top floor of this two-story building, and all have terra-cotta tile floors, stone walls, simple furnishings, private bathrooms, and heavy wool blankets on the beds. Room no. 12 is the pick of the litter: a second-floor end unit with a great view of the lake. This hotel feels very isolated, though they have their own boat dock and are just a short walk to town.

San Antonio Palopó. ⓒ **502/7762-0157.** Fax 502/7762-0037. www.hotelterrazasdellago.com. 10 units. Q195 ($26/£14) double. AE, DC, MC, V. **Amenities:** Restaurant; bar; laundry service. *In room:* No phone.

THE NORTHWEST SHORE OF LAKE ATITLAN

Many of the boats leaving Panajachel for San Pedro La Laguna make a series of stops at a handful of small villages and isolated hotels that line the northwestern shore of Lake Atitlán.

San Marcos La Laguna and **Santa Cruz La Laguna** are two small communities on the northwestern shores of Lake Atitlán. Both are set on high hillsides above the lakeshore. However, each has a selection of small hotels spread along the water's edge. For some reason, these two towns have developed as hot spots for yoga retreats and holistic getaways, with several hotels in each town catering to this niche. The most serious and long-standing yoga retreat and meditation center in the area is **Las Pirámides** (ⓒ **502/5205-7151**), which was inaugurated on the summer solstice more than 15 years ago and continues to offer a full range of retreats, classes, and treatments.

One of the smallest towns along the lakeshore, **Jaibalito** is home to the hotel **La Casa del Mundo** (see below).

WHERE TO STAY & DINE

Most folks eat all their meals at their hotels, but if you do venture out, there are a couple of good options in each of the towns. In San Marcos, I recommend grabbing a lake-view table at the French-run **Tul y Sol;** or try the pizzas, pastas, and vegetarian fare at **Il Giardino.**

In addition to the places listed below, I've received good reports about the new **Hotel Jinava** (ⓒ **502/5299-3311;** www.hoteljinava.com) in San Marcos. In Santa Cruz, backpackers and adventure travelers tend to congregate and stay at **La Iguana Perdida** (ⓒ **502/5706-4771;** www.laiguanaperdida.com), located just above the town's main dock.

Moderate

La Casa del Mundo ⓡ *Finds*   When the boat drops you off here, you'll feel like you're entering some sort of movie set. The hotel sits at the top of several steep flights of steps on a rocky outcropping that juts into the lake. The rooms' distinctive decor mixes local arts and crafts with a European sense of style. Every room has a view of the lake, and a few have private balconies with lake and volcano views. There are also several open-air tiled terraces spread around the grounds, all with great views. On one of these terraces, down near the water, is the hotel's wood-fired hot tub, wonderfully located to allow you to alternate between the hot tub and the cool lake. However, use of the hot tub requires advance notice and a bit of a surcharge. Excellent meals are served family style, allowing you to mingle with the rest of the guests at this enchanted retreat.

Jaibalito. © 502/5218-5332. www.lacasadelmundo.com. 15 units (9 with private bathroom). Q203 ($27/£14) double shared bathroom; Q375–Q450 ($51–$60/£26–£32) double with private bathroom. Rates slightly higher during peak periods. AE, DC, MC, V. **Amenities:** Restaurant; bar; tour desk; kayak rentals; laundry service. *In room:* No phone.

Villa Sumaya ★★ *Finds*   If you're looking for spiritual and physical rejuvenation, this is the place for you. The individual cabins are beautifully done with tile floors, soft cotton comforters, local crafts, and a large veranda with several chairs and a hammock. All rooms face the lake, with the towering silhouettes of volcanoes in the background. The hotel's Blue Tiger Temple is a wonderful wood-floored yoga and meditation room that often attracts visiting instructors and retreat guests, and there's always a massage therapist on call. There's a good beach for swimming, and the grounds are lush with tropical flowers. This place is pretty isolated, so unless you're out touring for the day, you'll probably be taking all your meals here. A meal plan runs around Q262 ($35/£18) per day.

San Marcos La Laguna. © 502/5617-1209 or ©/fax 502/5810-7199. www.villasumaya.com. 8 units. Q300–Q600 ($40–$80/£21–£42) double. AE, DC, MC, V. **Amenities:** Restaurant; bar; sauna; tour desk; laundry service. *In room:* No phone.

Inexpensive
Posada Schumann ★   This lodge has a series of private and duplex bungalows spread over lush grounds that slope down to the lake. You'll pay a little more for the best bungalows, which are those closest to the water. Some come equipped with kitchenettes and/or minifridges. Kayaks can be rented for tooling around on the lake. The whole complex is tied together by large stone walkways.

Barrio Tres, San Marcos La Laguna. © 502/5202-2216. Fax 502/2473-1181. www.posadaschumann.com. 14 units. Q150–Q300 ($20–$40/£11–£21) double. AE, DC, MC, V. **Amenities:** Restaurant; bar; sauna; tour desk; kayak rentals; laundry service. *In room:* No phone.

SOLOLA
Sololá sits at a strategic point between Lake Atitlán and the Pan-American Highway. Even before the highways were built and the Spanish arrived, Sololá was a major trading post connecting various coastal, lake, and highland communities. To this day, **Sololá's Tuesday and Friday markets** ★ are some of the largest in the highlands. The markets are anything but the typical tourist haunt, and are primarily for buying and selling among the various highland communities. However, you can find excellent textile products and some arts and crafts here. Sololá is one of the few towns where the men still wear the elaborate traditional garb, with shirts featuring intricate embroidery over multicolored cloth; the cut of the shirt looks like something out of the American Old West.

Very few tourists stay in Sololá, but if you want to stay and get a feel for this traditional Kaquichel town, try the **Hotel Belén,** 10a Calle 4-36, Zona 1 (© **502/7762-3105**).

Sololá is located on a well-paved road 8km (5 miles) from Panajachel. A taxi from Panajachel should cost around Q25 to Q35 ($3.35–$4.65/£1.75–£2.45). You can also hitch a ride here on any number of buses plying the route between Panajachel and Los Encuentros.

IXIMCHE & TECPAN

When Iximché as founded in 1465, the Kaqchiquel were at war with the Ki'ché, and the town's location, atop a long narrow plateau with steep ravines on either side, was chosen for its natural defenses. Today, the ruins at Iximché are made up of four large plazas that demark distinct religious and residential areas. There's one particularly well-maintained ball court and several large temple structures. At one end of the site there's a mound that remains an active site of Maya worship, and it's quite common to see locals lighting candles and incense and making offerings.

When the conquistador Pedro de Alvarado founded the first capital of Guatemala in 1524, he placed it next to Iximché, a Kaqchiquel capital city, near the present-day town of Tecpán. However, Kaqchiquel unrest and uprisings soon forced Alvarado to move the Spanish capital to the site of present-day Ciudad Vieja.

While nowhere near as spectacular as Tikal or Copan, Iximché is very well preserved, and a visit here is definitely worthwhile for anyone interested in ancient Maya culture and architecture.

The archaeological site is open daily from 8am until 5pm. Admission is Q25 ($3.35/£1.75). Tecpán is located just off the Pan-American Highway about halfway between Los Encuentros and Chimaltenango. From Tecpán it's just 5km (3 miles) along a well-paved road to the ruins. The best way to visit the site is as part of a guided tour. All of the agencies in Panajachel offer guided tours to Iximché and Tecpán. Rates run around Q150 to Q225 ($20–$30/£11–£16) for a half-day tour including transportation and a light lunch.

7

Western Highlands

The rugged geography of Guatemala's Western Highlands is a dense patchwork of volcanic mountains and lakes populated mostly by small, and often isolated, villages of the country's many Maya people. Some of the primary tribes who call this area home include the Ki'che, Mam, Kekchi, Tz'utujil, Ixil, Kaqchiquel, and Jacaltec. Most still practice small-scale plot farming on *milpas,* which are usually predominantly sown with corn. Locals live on a mix of subsistence farming and bartering. Aside from the food they grow, they also produce intricately designed and brightly colored woven textiles.

In Spanish, the Western Highlands are called the Altiplano, comprised of seven distinct provinces: Quetzaltenango, Sololá,

Huehuetenango, Quiché, San Marcos, Totonicapán, and Chimaltenanago.

Aside from the area around Lake Atitlán, which is covered in-depth in chapter 6, other highlights of the Western Highlands include the small city of **Chichicastenango** and its remarkable market; the university and language-school hub of **Quetzaltenango;** and the northern outpost of the almost border-town **Huehuetenango.** Surrounding these larger cities are many small beautiful villages worth exploring. In addition, the area presents opportunities for hiking **volcanoes,** soaking in **hot springs,** or trekking through the isolated region known as the **Ixil Triangle.**

1 Chichicastenango

144km (89 miles) NW of Guatemala City; 37km (23 miles) N of Panajachel

Santo Tomás de Chichicastenango is a small, highland city with perhaps the most impressive—and certainly the most famous—open-air market in all of Guatemala. Although the twice-weekly market and the city have adapted to the flood of tourists, they both maintain a sense of tradition and the indelible mark of Maya culture that stretches back for millennia. The city center is made of narrow, cobblestone streets, and just outside the center, the landscape is one of deep ravines and sparsely populated hillsides. In fact, one local name for Chichicastenango is Tziguan Tinamit, which translates roughly as "surrounded by ravines." However, most people simply refer to it as Chichi.

The town's name derives from a local purple flower, the *chichicaste.* The locals often refer to themselves as Maxeños, with the "x" pronounced as a soft "sh" sound. The Ki'che Maya are the principal linguistic group found in Chichicastenango, although on market days, the town is filled with a cacophony of Mayan dialects, mixed with Spanish and the bargaining banter of Americans, Europeans, and other Central and South Americans.

North of Chichicastenango are several small towns and villages worth visiting, including Santa Cruz del Quiché, Nebaj, and the Ixil Triangle.

(*Fun Fact*   **Seeing Fireworks**

Don't be surprised or scared, it's not gunfire, and it's not a bomb—although they are called *bombas*. Guatemalans have an ongoing fascination with fireworks. In many of the major cities (particularly Chichicastenango on market day), you're likely to hear fireworks going off almost any day or night.

ESSENTIALS

GETTING THERE

BY BUS   **La Masheñita** (© 502/2232-4868) buses leave Guatemala City from 10a Calle 10-03, Zona 1, roughly every 15 to 20 minutes between 3am and 6pm. **Veloz Quichelense** (no phone) buses leave from the main Terminal de Autobuses in Zona 4, on roughly the same schedule. The ride takes 3 hours and the fare is Q15 ($2/£1.05). You can also take any bus to Santa Cruz de Quiché from the Terminal de Autobuses and get off in Chichicastenango.

If you're coming from anywhere else on a bus along the Pan-American Highway, get off in Los Encuentros, and hop on the next bus heading north to Chichicastenango.

On market days, tourist shuttles flock to Chichi from Guatemala City, Panajachel, Antigua, and Quetzaltenango. If you're staying at any of these other towns or cities, ask your hotel or any tour agency to find out current schedules and fares.

BY CAR   To drive to Chichicastenango, take the Pan-American Highway (CA-1) north out of Guatemala City and the turnoff at Los Encuentros. Follow the exit sign for Chichicastenango and Santa Cruz del Quiché. The drive takes about 2 to 3 hours from Guatemala City; from Panajachel the trip is under an hour.

GETTING AROUND

Chichicastenango is extremely compact, so it's easy to walk just about anywhere in the downtown area. Taxis and tuk tuks can be flagged down all around the central plaza. If you can't readily find one, have your hotel call one for you.

ORIENTATION

The large main plaza is Chichi's central hub. This is ground zero of the market, and where you'll find the city's two main churches, museum, and municipal office buildings. Almost all of the hotels, restaurants, banks, shops, and other services can be found within a 4- or 5-block radius of the central plaza.

FAST FACTS   There's an **INGUAT** tourist office just off the main plaza on 7a Calle (© 502/7756-2022). The **post office** is located on 7a Av. 8-47. **Banco Industrial, Banrural, Banco G & T,** and **Banco de Comercio** all have branches with ATMs just off the central plaza. There are several Internet cafes around the downtown section of Chichi. I like **Cyber Center,** 6a Avenida, between 4a Calle and 5a Calle (© 502/ 5748-8244). The local heath clinic (© 502/7756-1356) is just off the main plaza. If you need to contact the local **police,** dial © 502/7756-1365.

WHAT TO SEE & DO

By far the main attraction in Chichicastenango is its twice-weekly market. In fact, Chichi is almost a ghost town on non-market days, with a few vendors set up in permanent stalls on the town's main plaza.

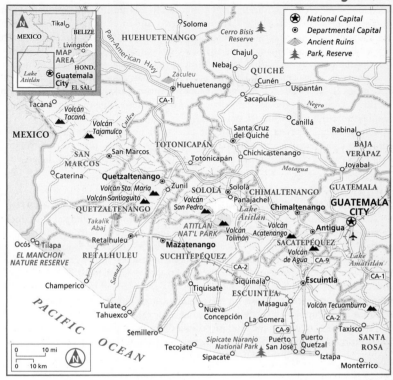

One of the city's only other official attractions is the **Museo Regional,** 5a Av. 4-47, Zona 1 ✆ **502/7756-1015**), located cater-cornered to the Iglesia de Santo Tomás (see below). This small museum has some decent ancient artifacts in jade, stone, and ceramic. The rooms are dimly lit, and the explanatory material is all in Spanish. This place is also sometimes called the Museo Arqueológico Rossbach because much of the collection was donated by the German priest Idelfonso Rossbach. The museum is open Monday and Wednesday through Saturday from 8am to 4pm, and Sunday from 8am to 2pm. Admission is Q10 ($1.35/70p).

Chichicastenango's **cemetery** is filled with brightly painted mausoleums and above-ground crypts. While very photogenic and atmospheric, there have been reports of attacks on tourists here, so be careful and only visit the cemetery as part of a group or with a tour guide. The cemetery is located along the western end of 8a Calle.

THE MARKET ✦✦✦

Thursday and Sunday are market days in Chichi, and on these days, the city is a mad orgy of sights, sounds, and smells. Maya craft sellers from across the highlands set up makeshift booths around the central plaza, spilling over on to sidewalks, the church steps, and up various side streets. A broad selection of Guatemalan handicrafts is available, including carved-wood masks and religious figures, ceramic wares, and an immense selection of the country's amazing native textiles. In addition to the craftworks, vendors sell fruits, vegetables, flowers, medicinal herbs, and more. *Note:* While a discerning shopper can find quality goods in Chichicastenango's market, much of what is offered is now machine-made and geared toward the mass tourist market. Despite the seeming chaos, there's actually a historical order to the setup, with vendors selling certain products in specific areas that have been designated for as long as anyone can remember. In fact, while tourists might think the entire market is geared toward them, the market is actually the central meeting place for inter-village trade and commerce among the various highland Maya.

Vendors begin arriving in Chichi the afternoon before market day, and set up throughout the evening and into the early morning. The best time to shop is either very early, before the tour buses from Guatemala City and Lake Atitlán begin arriving, or in the afternoon, after everyone's cleared out.

CHURCHES & SHRINES

The **Iglesia de Santo Tomás** ✿✿ was built by Dominican priests more than 450 years ago on top of an ancient Maya worship site. It remains the heart and soul of Chichicastenango and—to this day—is used as much for traditional Maya ceremonial purposes as it is for Catholic Mass. Local Maya can almost always be found on the steps leading up to the church, burning copal incense and candles, and offering prayer. Each of the 18 steps represents one of the months in the Maya calendar. Rather than the expected pews, you'll find make-shift shrines and altars spread out on the floor with pine needles and candles. It was in the church's convent that the oldest known copy of the ancient **Popol Vuh** text was discovered.

The church is located on the southeast corner of the main plaza. *Note:* Out of respect, the front door of the church is informally reserved for locals and high church officials. Visitors are encouraged to use the side door.

The Popol Vuh

The Popol Vuh, often referred to as the Maya Bible, is one of the most important Maya texts. It was first discovered around 1702 by Dominican Father Francisco Ximénez, who found it in the Santo Tomás convent and translated it into Spanish. Not only did he translate the text, but he made a copy of the original, ensuring that a direct connection to the ancient hieroglyphic and oral texts would exist to this day. It was also transliterated into the Ki'che language using Latin letters sometime in the 16th century.

The Popol Vuh contains a treasure-trove of ancient Maya myth, including tales of the twin heroes Hunahpu and Xbalanque and their battles with the lords of Xibalba, or the underworld. Like the Judeo-Christian Bible, the Popol Vuh begins with the creation myth of the Ki'che people.

In 1972, the Popol Vuh was declared Guatemala's national book. Several good English translations exist, including Dennis Tedlock's *Popol Vuh: The Definitive Edition of the Mayan Book of the Dawn of Life and the Glories of Gods and Kings* (Touchstone Press, 1996), and Allen J. Christenson's *Popol Vuh: The Sacred Book of the Mayas* (O Books, 2004).

Chichicastenango

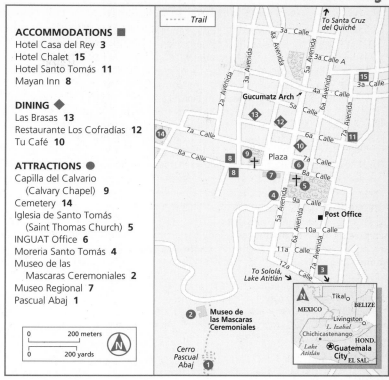

ACCOMMODATIONS ■
Hotel Casa del Rey **3**
Hotel Chalet **15**
Hotel Santo Tomás **11**
Mayan Inn **8**

DINING ◆
Las Brasas **13**
Restaurante Los Cofradías **12**
Tu Café **10**

ATTRACTIONS ●
Capilla del Calvario
  (Calvary Chapel) **9**
Cemetery **14**
Iglesia de Santo Tomás
  (Saint Thomas Church) **5**
INGUAT Office **6**
Moreria Santo Tomás **4**
Museo de las
  Mascaras Ceremoniales **2**
Museo Regional **7**
Pascual Abaj **1**

Capilla del Calvario ✪ is the smaller and less active of the two churches on Chichi's main plaza. Inside you'll find hand-painted murals and an intricate wood altar with a carved Christ in a glass coffin in front. You'll notice a dark room off the main body of the church; this holds a second Christ in a glass coffin, and is where many locals prefer to pray.

The Maya shrine, **Pascual Abaj,** is located on a hilltop south of Chichi. A carved stone idol, said to be hundreds of years old, is the centerpiece of the shrine. This is an active site of worship for many locals, who come here to make offerings and pray. Candles, incense, flowers, food, and even booze offerings are brought here to please the gods. Be respectful of the spiritual significance of this site, and don't take pictures or interfere with the worship.

On the way to Pascual Abaj, it's worth stopping at the **Museo de las Máscaras Ceremoniales** ✪ (© **502/7756-1915**). The museum has been run by the same family since it opened in 1880, and is located near the end of 9a Calle, just up the path to Pascual Abaj. Closer to downtown, you'll find **Morería Santo Tomás,** 5a Avenida and 9a Calle (© **502/7756-1882**). Both of these places are actually known as *morerías,* the name for shops where ceremonial masks and costumes are made and stored.

While many tourists visit Pascual Abaj on their own, I recommend you go with a guide, which can be arranged through your hotel or INGUAT. It can be unsafe for

Las Cofradías

While the Catholic church and its appointed priests are prominent in Chichicastenango, the city's real seat of religious power rests with the *cofradías* (brotherhoods). There are 14 *cofradías* in Chichi. Each *cofradía* has between six and eight members with specific ranks and responsibilities, which are clearly denoted by their ceremonial dress. The *cofradías* attend church together in their ornate regalia every Sunday, and each *cofradía* is responsible for the care and celebration of their namesake saint. On the celebration day of their saint, the *cofradía* marches in a loud procession through the town. Being the city of Santo Tomás de Chichicastenango, the Santo Tomás *cofradía* is the most important in town. Throughout the week leading up to Saint Thomas's feast day of December 21, Chichicastenango is abuzz in religious fervor, with numerous processions and traditional dances, including the **Palo Volador,** in which dancers descend in flying arcs suspended by their ankles from a high pole or tower.

solo tourists or small groups, and a local guide provides insurance against robbery as well as informing visitors of cultural sensitivities including local customs and sacred ground.

WHERE TO STAY

Hotels in Chichicastenango fill up Wednesday through Thursday and Saturday through Sunday. On these days it's essential to have a reservation, and the hotels will charge top dollar. On other days, the hotels are empty and usually very willing to negotiate a lower rate.

EXPENSIVE

Hotel Santo Tomás *Finds*　This hotel has the best location—just 2 blocks from the central plaza and market—and is easily my top choice in Chichicastenango. The colonial-era mansion has expanded to a sprawling operation, but still maintains its style and ambience. Several large interior courtyards, common verandas, garden fountains, and assorted nooks tie the whole thing together. The rooms are all fairly large and are outfitted with two queen-size beds, wood furnishings, and a fireplace. There's a large terrace with a pool and separate Jacuzzi, and a gym with steam bath and sauna. The restaurant and bar are both stately and popular. There's a fabulous panoramic view of all of Chichi from the hotel's rooftop terrace.

7a Av. 5-32, Zona 1. 502/7756-1061 or 502/7756-1269. Fax 502/7756-1306. 75 units. Q863–Q975 ($115–$130/£61–£68) double Wed–Thurs and Sat–Sun. Rates lower on other days. AE, DC, MC, V. **Amenities:** Restaurant; bar; small outdoor pool; Jacuzzi; small gym; tour desk; laundry service. *In room:* Hair dryer.

MODERATE

Hotel Casa del Rey　Though this is the most modern hotel in Chichicastenango, the basic rooms show their age. Some have good views of the town below; the best are in the 300 and 400 block of rooms. It's worth the extra money to upgrade to a suite, which is much larger and comes with a spacious sitting room, fireplace, and private porch. The hotel has a pool with a large waterfall, and a separate children's pool and Jacuzzi.

Km 144, on the road into Chichicastenango. 502/7756-1053. Fax 502/7756-1140. www.hotelcasadelrey.com. 68 units. Q450–Q600 ($60–$80/£32–£42) double Wed–Thurs and Sat–Sun. Rates lower on other days. AE, DC, MC, V. **Amenities:** Restaurant; bar; midsize outdoor pool; tour desk; laundry service. *In room:* TV, no phone.

Mayan Inn   This hotel, just off the central plaza behind El Calvario, is certainly acceptable, but it's in desperate need of a face-lift or even some fresh paint. Rooms are divided among two facing buildings, and come with two twin beds. I'd definitely ask to see a few first before making my choice. The best standard rooms are nos. 12, 14, and 15, while no. 11, a second-floor suite, has great views, tons of space, and two double beds. Each building has a garden courtyard, and Maya glyphs are painted on the walls, mixing somewhat awkwardly with the colonial-era decor.

8a Calle and 3a Av., Zona 1. © **502/7756-1176.** Fax 502/7756-1212. www.mayaninn.com.gt. 30 units. Q585 ($78/£41) double Wed–Thurs and Sat–Sun. Rates lower on other days. AE, DC, MC, V. **Amenities:** Restaurant; bar; tour desk; laundry service. *In room:* No phone.

INEXPENSIVE

Hotel Chalet *(Value)*   This bed-and-breakfast is located a few blocks away from the center of the action. The rooms are basic and small, as are the bathrooms, but they have good firm beds, either one queen-size or two twins, and the management is very amiable and helpful. If possible, try for room no. 18, which is on the third floor and features a queen-size bed and a bit of a view. There's a pleasant rooftop terrace where breakfast is often served.

3a Calle C, 7-44, Zona 1. © **502/7756-1360.** Fax 502/7756-1763. 6 units. Q160 ($21/£11) double. AE, DC, MC, V. **Amenities:** Laundry service. *In room:* No phone.

WHERE TO DINE

In addition to the places listed below, **Restaurante Los Cofradías,** at the corner of 5a Avenida and 6a Calle (© **502/7756-1643**), is a good option for local food in a pleasant setting; their second-floor corner location offers a view of the activity below.

There are a host of stalls set up on the main plaza serving grilled meats with fresh tortillas and other Guatemalan fast food. The food here is hearty and very inexpensive, but only those with well-adapted digestive tracts should partake.

INEXPENSIVE

Las Brasas *⊛* GUATEMALAN/STEAKHOUSE   Get hearty steaks and Chapin fare at very reasonable prices, in addition to thick cuts of beef, shish kabobs, fire-roasted chicken, and a very tasty pork *adobado,* a tangy local tomato-based sauce. The large dining room is sparsely, yet eclectically, decorated, with locally carved masks, drums, and deer skin. Try to grab a table overlooking the street.

6a Calle 4-52, Zona 1, at the entrance to Hotel Giron. © **502/7756-2226.** Main courses Q28–Q65 ($3.75–$8.65/£2–£4.55). MC, V. Daily 7:30am–10pm.

Tu Café *⊛ (Value)* GUATEMALAN   Tucked into a little space fronting the main plaza and market, this pleasant restaurant and cafe serves well-prepared Guatemalan fare at reasonable prices. Try the grilled chicken smothered in sautéed onions with delicious vegetables and rice on the side. There's always a daily special, which is a full three-course meal, for around Q25 ($3.35/£1.75).

5a Av. 6-44, Zona 1, fronting the main plaza. © **502/7756-1448.** Main courses Q25–Q40 ($3.35–$5.35/£1.75–£2.80). No credit cards. Daily 7:30am–8pm.

CHICHI AFTER DARK

Chichicastenango is a sleepy town, with almost no nightlife apart from what you'll find at the bars in the various hotels. On the nights before market day, the central market is abuzz with activity, and you may actually find a marimba band set up entertaining the crowds.

GOING BEYOND CHICHICASTENANGO
SANTA CRUZ DEL QUICHE & K'UMARCAAJ

Located some 19km (12 miles) north of Chichicastenango is the small mountain city of Santa Cruz del Quiché, or simply Quiché. Slightly off the main circuit, Santa Cruz del Quiché (the capital of the Quiché province) is much more representative of a modern highland Maya city than its more touristy neighbor. The pace of life here is quite slow, except on Saturday market days.

Quiché is also the gateway to the post-Classic Maya city of **K'umarcaaj,** also known as **Utatlán,** and sometimes spelled Q'uma'rka'aaj. **K'umarcaaj** was the ancient capital of the Quiché region, and is even mentioned in the Popol Vuh. The Maya K'iche offered some of the fiercest resistance ever encountered by the Spaniards. However, they were technologically outmatched and eventually defeated. K'umarcaaj was captured and mostly destroyed in 1524 under the orders of Pedro Alvarado, who had recently defeated the Maya Ki'che King Tucún Umán outside of Quetzaltenango. In fact, the story goes that the surviving Maya Ki'che had put forth a cordial invite for Pedro Alvarado to visit K'umarcaaj, where they planned to ambush him, but he wised up to the plan and sacked the city instead.

The ruins sit on a hilltop surrounded by steep ravines, a testament to the city's strategic wartime position. There has been little done here in the way of excavation, but the ruins of several temples, a ball court, and some well-maintained plazas can be visited. K'umarcaaj is still considered a sacred site by modern Maya, and it's not uncommon to find them performing rituals here. This is particularly true of a long tunnel or cave, known locally as *la cueva*. It's wise to plan ahead, bring a flashlight, be respectful, and definitely ask permission of the park guards and anyone you encounter there in prayer before entering the cave.

K'umarcaaj is located just 3km (2 miles) outside of Quiché. The ruins are open daily from 8am to 5pm. Admission is Q10 ($1.35/70p). There's a small museum (© 502/7702-0362) near the entrance with a detailed scale model of the city. A taxi from Santa Cruz del Quiché should cost around Q75 ($10/£5.25) round-trip, with an hour or more set aside to explore the ruins.

Quiché is serviced by frequent buses from Chichicastenango and Guatemala City. If you need or want to spend the night here, check into the **Hotel Rey Ki'che,** 8a Calle 0-39, Zona 5 (© 502/7755-0827).

NEBAJ & THE IXIL TRIANGLE 🎇🎇

The Ixil Triangle is a remote region of northern Quiché populated by the Maya Ixil people. The people of this region are deeply tied to their Maya roots, and many speak only their local dialect and little or no Spanish. The small village of Nebaj is the heart of the Ixil Triangle. The town has cobblestone streets and a lovely colonial-era church. The two other principal towns forming the triangle are Chajul and Cotzal. This mountainous region is surrounded by tiny villages and communities, which are tied together by heritage and an active barter economy.

The Ixil Triangle suffered brutal repression during the Civil War, particularly under the reign of General Ríos Montt (1982–83). Despite this past, the area is actually one of the safer regions for independent travelers. The local populations tend to be relatively open and friendly to foreigners, although you should still be very respectful and always ask permission before taking anyone's photograph.

The distinctive Nebaj *huipiles* are some of the most beautiful in Guatemala. Predominantly fashioned of purples, greens, and yellows, they feature incredibly tight

Rigoberta Menchú

Rigoberta Menchú is one Guatemala's best-known and most powerful public figures. Born in 1959 in Chimal, a Quiché village, Menchú is a diminutive woman who almost always dresses in the traditional garb of the Highland Maya. With just a sixth-grade education, she is a Nobel Prize winner and best-selling author.

As an adolescent, Menchú worked with Catholic social reform groups, and in 1979, she became an activist with the Peasant Unity Committee. The following year, Menchú's brother was murdered by the military, and in 1980, her father died, along with 36 others, when the military set fire to the Spanish embassy. The group had sought refuge in the embassy after publicly denouncing the ongoing atrocities. Later that same year, Menchú's mother was taken by paramilitary forces, never to be seen again.

In 1981, Menchú went into hiding after receiving death threats for her work to organize the Maya people against the rampant violence and oppression in Guatemala. She fled the country, remaining in exile for 12 years. During her exile, Menchú returned clandestinely to Guatemala several times in an attempt to continue her work, but was always forced to leave because of death threats and personal danger.

I, Rigoberta Menchú, based on a series of recorded interviews with the Maya activist, was published in 1983. The book had an immense impact in bringing the atrocities being committed by the military against the Maya in Guatemala to the attention of the international community. In 1992, Menchú was awarded the Nobel Peace Prize for her work promoting indigenous rights. The other Guatemalan Nobel laureate, Miguel Angel Asturias, won the Nobel Prize for Literature in 1967 for his novels condemning the injustice that Menchú was to experience, fight, and speak out against later.

Menchú's selection was criticized by some because she had been a member of organizations that advocated violence. In 1999, further controversy arose when an academic researcher disputed the accuracy of some of the details in her book. Menchú eventually admitted that some of the events and atrocities described in the book were generalized and composite accounts of what was occurring in Guatemala throughout the period, although they may not have occurred on the dates or in the places originally claimed. A member of the Nobel committee stated that Menchú's award was not based exclusively on her autobiography, and he dismissed any suggestion that the Committee should consider revoking her prize.

With the funds from the Nobel prize, Menchú formed a foundation to work for indigenous rights internationally (the rights of women in particular), attempted to have Guatemalan military leaders extradited and tried for crimes against humanity, and became president of a company that distributes low-cost generic medications to the poor. Menchú was named a Goodwill Representative for the 1996 Guatemalan Peace Accords by then President Alvaro Arzu. She is also a representative of the United Nation's Educational, Scientific and Cultural Organization (UNESCO).

embroidery of human and animal figures as well as complex geometric designs. The women wear a headdress of colorful ribbons with fluffy pompoms. As in Chichicastenango, market days here are Thursday and Sunday.

Most of your travel needs in and around Nebaj can be arranged with the folks at **El Descanso** restaurant and their sister operation **Guías Ixiles** (© 502/5311-9100; www.nebaj.com). This place is the central hub for many travelers into and around the Ixil Triangle. Multiday and overnight hikes and mountain-biking tours are offered around the Ixil Triangle, the most popular in the nearby villages of **Acul** and **Cocop.**

If you need to spend the night here, check out the new **Hotel Villa Nebaj,** Calzada 15 de Septiembre 2-37 (© **502/7756-0005** or 502/5614-2506; www.villanebaj.com), a modern hotel in the heart of Nebaj. A room with private bathroom and cable TV is less than Q900 ($120/£63) double occupancy. Backpackers and budget hounds should head to **Hotel Ixil** (© **502/7756-0036**) or **MediaLuna MedioSol Hostal,** at the corner of 3a Calle and 4a Avenida (© **502/5311-9100;** www.nebaj.com). For meals, I recommend **El Descanso** (see above) or **Papi's** (© **502/5906-5780**).

Nebaj is located 95km (59 miles) north of Santa Cruz del Quiché. Buses between Santa Cruz del Quiché and Nebaj leave roughly every hour or two. The ride takes around 3 hours and costs Q10 ($1.35/70p).

2 Quetzaltenango (Xela) ⓧ

201km (125 miles) NW of Guatemala City; 90km (56 miles) S of Huehuetenango

The highland burg of **Quetzaltenango** is the second-largest city in Guatemala, with a population of more than 300,000. Like Chichicastenango, this was and still is a principal center of the Maya Ki'che of Guatemala—and many locals still refer to the city by its Ki'che name **Xelajú.** In fact, most people simply call the place **Xela** (pronounced "*sheh*-la"). Xelajú is close to the sight where Ki'che King Tecún Umán was killed in battle against the Spanish conquistador Pedro de Alvarado. Following Tecún Umán's defeat in 1524, the city was renamed Quetzaltenango, or "place of the Quetzal," which is what Alvarado's Nahuatl mercenaries called it. In 1848, Quetzaltenango declared itself "El Sexto Estado del los Altos," independent from Guatemala. However, while the city retains an independent streak, its political independence lasted only 2 years, and the Guatemalan military quickly brought the rogue state back into the fold.

Thanks to the presence of a large national university and scores of language schools and foreign volunteer programs, there are several good coffee shops and used bookstores in Xela, and even a couple of art-movie houses. You'll also find more nightlife here than anywhere else in the country outside of Guatemala City.

Quetzaltenango makes an excellent base for visiting a host of nearby towns and attractions, including **hot springs,** small villages with impressive **markets and churches,** and towering **volcanoes** waiting to be hiked. The city also serves as a convenient gateway to both Mexico and the Pacific coast of Guatemala.

ESSENTIALS
GETTING THERE
BY BUS   Several bus lines provide regular service in comfortable modern buses throughout the day between Xela and Guatemala City. **Líneas Américas** (© **502/ 2232-1432** in Guatemala City, or 502/7761-4587 in Xela) has buses leaving from 7a Av. 3-33, Zona 2 in Guatemala City, at 5, 9:15, and 11:30am; and at 3:15, 4:30, 6,

Quetzaltenango

Calle Rodolfo Robles
Calle Rodolfo Robles
16a Avenida
15a Avenida
14a Avenida A
14a Avenida
13a Avenida
12a Avenida
11a Avenida
10a Avenida
9a Avenida
8a Avenida
7a Avenida
15a Avenida

To San Marcos
Calle Cajola
Teatro Roma 2
Teatro Municipal 3
2a Calle
3a Calle
1a Calle
2a Calle
3a Calle
4a Calle
5a Calle
6a Calle
7a Calle
8a Calle
Diagonal 13

Parque Centro America
Museo del Ferrocarril
Catedral Metropolitano de los Altos

To Guatemala City, Chichicastenango
To Retalhuleu

Bus Station
(To Almolonga & Zunil)

Inset map: N — MEXICO — BELIZE — Tikal — Livingston — Quetzaltenango — HOND. — Lake Atitlán — ★Guatemala City — EL SAL.

ACCOMMODATIONS
Casa Doña Mercedes 21
Casa Florencia 10
Casa Mañen 15
Hotel Bonifaz 11
Hotel Modelo 6
Hotel Villa Real Plaza 12

DINING
Al Andalus 4
Café Bavaria 13
Café La Luna 16
Café Q 22
Casa Antigua 9
El Alquimista 1
El Balcón de Enriquez 12
Giuseppe's 7
Restaurante Il Giardino 22
Royal Paris 8
Sabor de la India 5

ATTRACTIONS
Casa de la Cultura 19
Catedral Metropolitano de los Altos 17
INGUAT 19
Museo de Historia Natural 19
Museo del Ferrocarril 20
Parque Centro America 18
Teatro Municipal 3
Teatro Roma 2

0   100 meters
0   100 yards

What's in a Name?

The complete Ki'che Mayan name of the city is Xelajú Noj, which translates roughly as "under the 10 mountains," in reference to the surrounding mountains and volcanoes.

---

and 7:30pm. The return buses leave Xela from 7a Av. 3-33, Zona 2 at 5:15, 9:30, and 11am; and at 1, 2, and 3:30pm.

Transportes Galgos (✆ **502/2471-4116** in Guatemala City, or 502/7761-2248 in Xela) has buses leaving Guatemala City for Xela at 8:30 and 11am, and 2:30 and 5pm. The return buses leave Xela from Calle Rodolfo Robles 17-43, Zona 1, at 4 and 8:30am, and at 12:30 and 3pm.

The trip on either bus line takes about 4½ to 5 hours. The fare is around Q50 ($6.65/£3.50) each way.

BY CAR   To drive to Quetzaltenango, take the Pan-American Highway (CA-1) north out of Guatemala City. At Cuatro Caminos, take the turnoff for Quetzaltenango, which lies 13km (8 miles) to the southwest, after the small city of Salcajá. The trip takes about 4 hours from Guatemala City. Quetzaltenango is also connected to the southern Pacific Coast Highway, which visitors would use to go down to Retalhuleu and the Pacific beaches.

GETTING AROUND

Taxis and tuk tuks are plentiful in Xela. You can always find one around Parque Centro America. Fares around town should run between Q10 and Q25 ($1.35–$3.35/70p–£1.75). If you can't flag one down, have your hotel call one for you, or call **Taxi del Enríquez** (✆ **502/7765-2296**).

If you want to rent a car for the day, or longer, contact **Renta Autos del Enríquez** (✆ **502/7765-2296**). Rates run around Q338–Q450 ($45–$60/£24–£32) per day for a compact car.

If you want to rent a bicycle for getting around town, check out **Vrisa Bookshop** (✆ **502/7761-3237**). These folks charge Q40 ($5.35/£2.80) per day, or Q100 ($13/£7) per week. However, I find the congested streets and hilly terrain to be very inhospitable to bicycles.

ORIENTATION

The long, narrow **Parque Centro América** is the central hub of Xela. You'll find most of the hotels, restaurants, language schools, and offices, and the main Catholic church either right on this central plaza or within a few blocks. You can see the massive cone of the Santa Maria Volcano 3,677m (12,256 ft.) towering over the southern horizon from almost anywhere in town.

Xela sits at 2,334m (7,656 ft.) above sea level. The climate here is relatively cool, and sometimes damp, particularly from May through mid-November. Be sure to have a light jacket or sweater for the evenings.

FAST FACTS   There's an **INGUAT** office (✆ **502/7761-4931**) fronting the Parque Centro America in the Edificio Casa de la Cultura. They can provide you with a city map and basic information on tours and attractions in and around Xela. The main **post office** (✆ **502/7761-7608**) is located about 4 blocks west of the central park at

4a Calle 15-07, Zona 1. There's also a **DHL** office, 12a Av. C-35, Zona 1 (© **502/ 7763-1209**), if you want to send anything of value or with a greater measure of safety and speed.

Banco de Occidente (© **502/7761-2861**), **Banrural** (© **502/7761-3633**), and **Banco Industrial** (© **502/7761-6383**) all have branches right on Parque Centro America, and there are dozens of other bank branches around town. Since this is a university and language school city, you'll also find an abundance of Internet cafes in Xela. Most charge between Q3 and Q8 (40¢–$1.05/20p–55p) per hour. If your hotel doesn't provide the service, there are several coin-operated and self-service laundromats, and most of these will also wash and fold for you. I like **Pila's Laundry**, 15a Av. 3-51, Zona 1, inside the Plaza Centro (© **502/7765-3220**), which has three locations around the city.

In the event of a medical emergency, the **Hospital La Democracia**, 13a Av. 6-51, Zona 3 (© **502/7763-6760**), is a well-equipped, modern hospital. You might also try **Hospital Privado Quetzaltenango**, Calle Rodolfo Robles 23-51, Zona 1 (© **502/ 7761-4381**), a well-equipped private hospital. To reach the **Red Cross**, dial © **502/ 7761-2746**; for the **National Police** dial © **502/7765-4991.** However, for most tourist needs, whether it be for information or an emergency, you should call **Asistur** (© **1500**), which is a toll-free call.

WHAT TO SEE & DO

It won't take you long to visit Quetzaltenango's principal attractions. The **Parque Centro América** ✈, with its open-air gazebo, is the town's focal point. On the southeastern side of the park you'll find the **Catedral Metropolitano de los Altos**, which is actually two churches. Fronting the park is the ornate facade of the **Catedral del Espíritu Santo** ✈, which is all that remains of the city's original 16th-century baroque church. Behind this facade is the more modern, and much larger, **Catedral de la Diócesis de los Altos,** which was inaugurated in 1899.

Also fronting the Parque Centro America is the **Museo del Ferrocarril (Train Museum),** which documents, mostly in photographs, the construction and functioning of the electric train built in the late 19th and early 20th centuries to connect Quetzaltenango with Retalhuleu and the Pacific coast.

Just north of the park center is the **Teatro Municipal (Municipal Theater)** ✈, 14a Avenida and 1a Calle (© **502/7761-2218**), a wonderfully restored theater built between 1884 and 1908. The theater hosted its first concert in 1903 and is still functioning today. It's worthwhile to catch a show if there's one while you're in town. Just across from the Teatro Municipal is the equally well-restored **Teatro Roma,** 14a Avenida A (© **502/7761-4950**), the city's first cinema. While they no longer show movies here, they do have occasional performances, which are worth a visit.

On the south side of the park sits the **Casa de la Cultura,** 7th Calle 11-09, Zona 1 (© **502/7761-6031**), a large building that houses the INGUAT offices and the Museo de Historia Natural (Natural History Museum), which, in my opinion, can be missed. It gets a fair amount of press in the local tourist propaganda, and is housed in the popular Casa de la Cultura, next to the INGUAT office. Should you decide to visit the exhibits, which include dinosaur bones, Maya artifacts, and a room dedicated to the marimba (a large wooden xylophone and the bands that play them), the museum is open Monday through Friday from 8am to noon and 2 to 6pm; and Saturday from 9am to 1pm. Admission is Q10 ($1.35/70p).

TOURS, TREKS & ATTRACTIONS AROUND QUETZALTENANGO

While there is little to see in Xela itself, there are a host of tour and activity options within easy reach of the town. All of the hotels and tour agencies listed in this section can arrange any of the tours or excursions listed below.

In addition to the attractions listed here, many visitors use Xela as a jumping-off point to visit the **IRTRA** amusement and theme park complex, the Maya ruins of **Takalik Abaj,** and the lowland city of **Retalhuleu,** continuing on to the beaches of the Pacific coast. For information on all of these places, see chapter 11. All of the tour companies listed here also use Xela as a base for trips to **Nebaj** and **Todos Santos Chuchumatán,** which are both mentioned later in this chapter.

The best and longest-running agencies in Xela include **Adrenalina Tours** ✸ (ⓒ **502/7761-4509;** www.adrenalinatours.com), which has its offices in the Pasaje Enriquez building just off Parque Centro America; and **Chilli Tours,** 14a Av. A 4-85, Zona 1 (ⓒ **502/7765-8114;** www.chillitoursguate.com). For more adventurous multi-day treks, check out the socially conscious **Quetzal Trekkers** ✸, Casa Argentina at 12a Diagonal, 8-37, Zona 1 (ⓒ **502/7765-5895;** www.quetzaltrekkers.com). Among the treks offered by these folks are a 6-day trip through **Nebaj** and **Todos Santos Chuchumatán;** a 3-day hike from **Xela** to **Lake Atitlán;** and a 2-day trek to the summit of **Tajumulco** volcano; at 4220m (13,842 ft.), it's the highest point in all of Central America. They also offer several volunteer programs.

ZUNIL & FUENTES GEORGINAS

Zunil ✸ is a picturesque little town on the shores of the Salamá River and is surrounded by verdant agricultural fields. It has a beautiful whitewashed church and narrow, cobblestone streets that wind up the hills from the river. Zunil is famous for its worship of Maximón (p. 165), who is known as San Simon here in Zunil. San Simon is housed in different local homes at different times, and you can ask anyone it town where to find him. A small tip is expected for taking you to see the saint's statue. Monday is market day in Zunil, and while small, it's still a colorful and vibrant market.

Hot springs can be found in several places on the way to Zunil, including Los Vahos, El Recreo, and Los Cirilos, but they all pale in comparison to **Las Fuentes Georginas** ✸ (ⓒ **502/5704-2959**), a hot springs resort just beyond Zunil. The large pool here is set near a crook and surrounded by steep hills. The hottest water is found closest to the hillside in the center of the crook, and gets cooler as you move farther away. There's a restaurant, some changing rooms, and a few basic cabins for overnight stays, but I don't recommend them, as they're very musty and in desperate need of upkeep. Las Fuentes Georginas is open daily from 8am to 6:30pm. Admission is Q20 ($2.65/£1.40) for adults, Q10 ($1.35/70p) for children under 12. Parking is an extra Q10 ($1.35/70p) if you come in your own car.

Zunil is located 9km (5½ miles) south of Xela on the road to Retalhuleu and the Pacific coast. Las Fuentes Georginas is another 8km (5 miles) beyond Zunil up a beautiful, winding road that heads into the mountains. A taxi from Xela to Zunil should charge around Q40 ($5.35/£2.80) each way. The fare is about the same from Zunil to Las Fuentes Georginas.

VOLCAN SANTA MARIA ✸✸

The skyline south of Quetzaltenango is dominated by the 3677m (12,256-ft.) **Volcán Santa María.** All of the tour agencies listed above lead hikes to the summit, and most leave Xela before dawn by car or minivan to the town of Llanos del Pinal. From here it takes between 3 and 4 hours of strenuous hiking to reach the summit. On a clear day, you can see as far as Mexico. You can also see a host of other Guatemalan volcanoes, including Tajumulco, Siete Orejas, and Acatenango, as well as the volcanoes surrounding Lake Atitlán and the volcanoes Fuego and Agua just outside of Antigua. The best view here, however, is of the crater of Santa María's very active sister volcano, **Santiaguito.** Santa María had a major eruption in 1902, which covered much of Quetzaltenango in thick ash and killed more than 1,500 people in the region. It was during this eruption that Santiaguito was born. Santiaguito is in an almost constant state of eruption, belching out gases, volcanic ash, and molten lava. Guided tours run between Q75 and Q225 ($10–$30/£5.25–£16) per person, depending upon group size. During the dry season, it's possible to camp near the summit, which is worth it for the amazing sunrise and sunset views.

SALCAJA

While this small town boasts the oldest Spanish church in Guatemala, it's better known for the private and established vendors lining the streets, particularly the highway leading to Quetzaltenango, with used cars for sale. Of these, the majority seem to be Toyota pickup trucks.

The **Iglesia de San Jacinto** may be small, but it's well-maintained and worth a visit. Established in 1524 during Pedro de Alvarado's conquest of the region, the church boasts an ornate altar and some antique paintings.

Salcajá is also famous for its *jaspé* or *ikat* textile weaving. This complex dyeing and weaving process produces intricate abstract designs, although they've been weaving these cloths here since the 1860s. Salcajá is also known for two locally produced liquors—*caldo de frutas* and *rompopo. Caldo de frutas* (literally, fruit soup) is a strong brew of fermented fruits and rum or cane alcohol. Rompopo is a somewhat milder concoction of rum, milk, and egg yolks.

Salcajá is located 7km (4 miles) from Xela on the road to Cuatro Caminos.

SAN ANDRES XECUL

The ornate church here is definitely worth a visit. Try to come in the afternoon, when the sun hits the church's facade, as it's much harder to get a good photo in the morning, when the sun is behind the church. Up the hill from the main church is a much smaller church worth a visit for two reasons. First, the high perch here offers a wonderful view of the main church and town. Second, this church, and the plot of land beside it, are still actively used for Maya ritual prayers and ceremonies, and you can almost always find local Maya worshiping here.

San Andrés Xecul is located 9km (5½ miles) from Xela, just beyond Slacajá, and off the road to Cuatro Caminos.

Getting Involved & Giving Back

Those interested in volunteering have several excellent options in and around Quetzaltenango. Your best bet is to contact **Entre Mundos** (© 502/7761-2179; www.entremundos.org), which functions as bridge between a host of nongovernmental organizations and community projects. They specifically work to connect foreign volunteers with appropriate community, social, health, and educational projects.

Getting Schooled

Quetzaltenango offers a number of Spanish schools, most with immersion-style lessons, small classes, excursions, and homestay accommodations with a local family. The best among the choices are **Casa Xelaju,** Callejón 15 D, 13-02, Zona 1 (✆ **502/7761-5954;** www.casaxelaju.com); **Celas Maya Spanish School,** 6a Calle 14-55, Zona 1 (✆ **502/7761-4342;** www.celasmaya.edu.gt); **Proyecto Lingüístico Quezalteco** ✦, 5a Calle 2-40, Zona 1 (✆ **502/7763-1061;** www. hermandad.com); **Ulew Tinimit Spanish School** ✦, 7a Av. 3-18, Zona 1 (✆ **502/ 7761-6242;** www.spanishguatemala.org); and **Utatlán Spanish School,** 12a Av. 4-32, Zona 1 (✆ **502/7763-0446**). Rates run between Q1,125 and Q1,500 ($150–$200/£79–£105) per week, including homestay, most meals, and some organized excursions.

If you want to learn how to dance salsa and merengue, check out the **Trópica Latina Dance School,** 13a Av. 5-38, Zona 1, in the Mansión Marilyn (✆ **502/5790-0561**). Regular group lessons are Q30 ($4/£2.10) per hour; private lessons are Q75 ($10/£5.25) per hour.

SAN FRANCISCO EL ALTO

While Chichicastenango's market gets most of the press and acclaim, insiders know that **San Francisco El Alto's Friday market** ✦✦ is the place to shop the best and largest selection of textiles and garments in Guatemala, plus take in some good views from the hillside location. As in Chichi, San Francisco's central plaza is taken over on market day and packed with merchants from all over the highlands. However, far fewer tourists come here. Instead, large wholesalers and local barterers are the principal buyers. Animal activists should be aware that part of the market here is reserved for live animals, everything from dogs and cats to pigs and chickens. You'll also see caged birds and the occasional captured monkey. San Francisco El Alto is located 17km (11 miles) from Xela beyond Cuatro Caminos on the way to Huehuetenango.

LAGUNA DE CHICABAL

The **Laguna de Chicabal** ✦ is a gorgeous lake formed in the crater of an extinct volcano. The cone of the lake rises to 2900m (9,514 ft.), and the emerald-green lake, considered sacred to the Maya, lies a few hundred feet below the rim, surrounded by lush cloud forests. Even if there are no active ceremonies taking place when you visit, you'll notice the many altars around the lakeshore and the ashes, burned candles, and past offerings from recent devotees.

Laguna de Chicabal is accessed from the village of San Martin Sacatepequez, which is also called San Martin Chile Verde. The hike from San Martin takes about 2 hours. Alternatively, you can drive to a parking lot that is just a 40-minute hike from the lake. The best way to visit the lake is on a guided tour out of Xela. The lake is open daily from 8am to 5pm. Admission is Q10 ($1.35/70p), and parking is an additional Q10 ($1.35/70p). Camping is allowed for Q25 ($3.35/£1.75) per person.

SHOPPING

The shopping scene is rather uninspired in Xela, but because of the large university and language school presence here, there are several good used bookstores in town, with selections of both English- and Spanish-language books. **Vrisa Bookshop,** 15a Av. 3-64, Zona 1 (© 502/7761-3237); **North & South Bookstore,** 8a Calle and 15 Av. 13-77, Zona 1 (© 502/7761-0589); and **El Libro Abierto,** 15 Av. A, 1-56, Zona 1 (© 502/7761-5195), are all good choices.

If you want to bring home some fresh-roasted Highland coffee, head to **El Bazar del Café,** 13a Av. 5-38, Zona 1, in the Mansión Marilyn (© **502/7761-4980**). For Guatemalan textiles or craftwork, your best bet is to head to the Friday market at San Francisco El Alto (see above).

WHERE TO STAY
MODERATE

Casa Mañen ★★ *Finds*   The immaculately restored building that houses this B&B might be pushing 200 years, but it's still my top choice in Xela. The rooms all feature thick, antique terra-cotta floors, heavy hand-woven wool blankets and rugs, firm and comfy beds, and a wealth of local art and craft works for decoration; most also have working fireplaces. I prefer the second- and third-floor rooms, which are above the street and away from the action, but room no. 2 on the first floor is an excellent choice and features a large living room, 32-inch flatscreen TV, and a queen-size bed in a sleeping loft. The hotel's terrace offers great views of the city. Breakfasts are delicious and filling, and full dinners are available for guests upon request.

9a Av. 4-11, Zona 1. © **502/7765-0786.** Fax 502/7765-0678. www.comeseeit.com. 9 units. Q325–Q488 ($50–$65/ £23–£34) double; Q525–Q750 ($70–$100/£37–£53) suite. Rates include full breakfast. AE, DC, MC, V. **Amenities:** Laundry service. *In room:* TV.

Hotel Bonifaz ★   If you're looking for a host of modern amenities, including free Wi-Fi and a pool, this is definitely the place for you. The hotel is also called Pension Bonifaz, which is written in large letters above the entrance. The hotel is a rambling, mazelike structure with rooms spread across five floors, accessed via various staircases, and an assortment of lounges and common areas tying the whole thing together. Most of the rooms are spacious and well-maintained, and many have good-size private balconies. Those on the fifth floor feature exposed wood-beam ceilings. My favorite room is no. 508, a suite with a large sitting area, fireplace, and good views. The somewhat misnamed Presidential Suite is also a good choice, and features a large bathroom with a Jacuzzi tub and a small private outdoor patio. A large atrium on the fourth floor houses a pool and separate Jacuzzi.

4a Calle 10-50, Zona 1. © **502/7765-1111.** Fax 502/7763-0671. bonifaz@intelnet.net.gt. 75 units. Q600–Q675 ($80–$90/£42–£47) double; Q800–Q1,000 ($107–$133/£56–£70) suite. AE, DC, MC, V. **Amenities:** Restaurant; bar; small enclosed rooftop pool; Jacuzzi; tour desk; room service 7am–9pm; laundry service; free Wi-Fi in the lobby area. *In room:* TV, hair dryer, safe.

INEXPENSIVE

In addition to the places listed below, **Casa Florencia,** 12a Av. 3-61, Zona 1, near the Parque Centro America (© **502/7761-2326**), is another good choice.

Casa Doña Mercedes *Value*   There are tons of budget options in Xela, but I prefer this joint. The converted old home is located just 2 blocks from the Parque Centro America. The rooms are cheerful and immaculate, there's a shared kitchen, and the service is friendly and efficient.

6a Calle and 14a Av. 13-42, Zona 1. © **502/5569-1630** or 502/7765-4687. www.geocities.com/guest_house_ mercedes. 3 units. Q150 ($20/£11) double. No credit cards. **Amenities:** Tour desk; laundry service. *In room:* No phone.

Hotel Modelo   The rooms here are all clean and spacious, have tile or wood floors, are flooded with natural light, and come with 21-inch flatscreen televisions. The bathrooms tend to be on the small side, and the hotel is very close to Quetzaltenango's lively Zona Rosa, which is convenient if you want to take advantage of the nightlife, but makes those rooms that front the street a bit too noisy. Most of the rooms are housed in the main hotel building, with the least expensive one in a newer annex across the street. Both buildings have small open-air interior courtyards.

14a Av. A 2-31, Zona 1. ℂ 502/7761-2529 or 502/7763-0216. Fax 502/7763-1376. 29 units. Q220–Q300 ($29–$40/£15–£21) double. AE, DC, MC, V. **Amenities:** Restaurant; bar; tour desk; laundry service. *In room:* TV.

Hotel Villa Real Plaza   While excellently located on a busy corner fronting the Parque Centro America, don't expect much from the basic rooms. All are carpeted and fairly large, and the fireplaces found in many are purely decorative. Several rooms have small balconies overlooking the park, but if you choose one of these, be prepared for the trade-off—you get a great view of the action, but also plenty of street noise. If you want a quiet night's sleep, be sure to ask for an interior room. The ground-floor restaurant features some seating in a pleasant atrium.

4a Calle 12-22, Zona 1. ℂ 502/7761-4045 or 502/7761-6270. Fax 502/7761-6780. 54 units. Q325 ($50/£23) double; Q525 ($70/£37) suite. AE, DC, MC, V. **Amenities:** Restaurant; bar; tour desk; laundry service. *In room:* TV.

Las Cumbres *(Kids) (Finds)*   This hotel centers around the hot sulfur springs and steam vents it sits upon, is and is located just out of Zunil on the road to Retalhuleu. Each spacious room comes with its own Jacuzzi fed by a hot spring. Some rooms have beautiful stone floors and four-poster beds, and four also have their own sauna. However, I prefer the rooms with a view (which don't have their own saunas). My favorites are "Quetzaltenango" and "Cantel," which have beautiful views over the Salamá river valley. The restaurant here is excellent, and there are seven individual steam baths and saunas open to guests and the paying public.

Km 210, Zunil. ℂ 502/5399-0029 or 502/7767-1746. Fax 502/5304-2102. 11 units. Q250–Q350 ($33–$47/£18–£25) double. AE, DC, MC, V. **Amenities:** Restaurant; bar; small gym; saunas; tour desk, laundry service; steam baths; squash court. *In room:* TV.

WHERE TO DINE

In addition to the Italian restaurant listed below, **Giuseppe's,** 15a Avenida and 4a Calle, Zona 1 (ℂ **502/7761-2521**) is also excellent and a local favorite. Vegetarians will want to check out **Café Q,** Diagonal 12 and 6a Calle (ℂ **502/7761-1636**), and **El Alquimista,** at the end of 13a Avenida (ℂ **502/5399-0020**), a 15-minute walk from Parque Centro America.

For breakfast it's hard to beat the views from **El Balcón de Enríquez,** 4a Calle 12-33, Zona 1 (ℂ **502-7765-2296**). If you're looking for a light meal or simple coffeehouse, try **Café La Luna** *(Kids)*, 8a Av. 4-11 (ℂ **502/7761-2242**), with its hodgepodge of antiques; **Casa Antigua,** 12a Av. 3-26, Zona 1 (ℂ **502/7765-8048**), with its more elegant decor; or **Café Bavaria,** 5a Calle 13-14, Zona 1 (ℂ **502/7763-1855**), which has a wonderful Sunday brunch featuring live jazz.

On my last visit, work was underway on **Restaurante y Cantina Dos Tejanos,** 4a Calle 12-33, Zona 1 (ℂ **502-7765-4360**), a new Texas-style barbecue restaurant on the ground floor of the Pasaje Enriquez building, across from the popular **Salon Tecún** (see below). It's owned and operated by the same folks who have Casa Mañen (see above), so I expect this place to be pretty good.

Al Andalus *(finds)* SPANISH/TAPAS   This new restaurant is set in an old colonial house near the center of town. They have a wide range of traditional Spanish fare to choose from, including a host of tapas and various paellas for groups with an appetite. The sangria is delicious, and the atmosphere, with candlelight and a courtyard patio, is elegant and romantic by Xela standards.

2a Calle 14A-30, Zona 1. (℃) 502/5689-9692. Reservations recommended. Main courses Q30–Q85 ($4–$11/ £2.10–£5.95). AE, MC, V. Tues–Sun 10am–10pm.

Restaurante Il Giardino ITALIAN/PIZZA   This place is rapidly gaining a reputation as having the best Italian food in Xela. The thin-crust pizzas are excellent and offered with a wide array of toppings. There's also a long list of pasta dishes, which are cooked to perfection, and a pretty decent wine list. The best tables are in a small garden area. You'll find the restaurant just outside the center of town, near Las Flores market.

19 Callejón 8-07, Zona 1. (℃) 502/7765-8293. Pizza Q20–Q45 ($2.65–$6/£1.40–£3.15); main courses Q30–Q65 ($4–$8.65/£2.10–£4.55). AE, MC, V. Wed–Mon 10am–10pm.

Royal Paris *𝒢* FRENCH/INTERNATIONAL   This restaurant has the reputation of being the fanciest dining option in town, but the pretence and prices are mellow enough to attract a good share of the local student crowd. Channel the fancy French restaurant by ordering the lobster, or go the bistro route for lunch with one of the excellent sandwiches, made on homemade baguette or whole wheat bread. Find live music here most weekend nights.

14a Av. A 3-06, Zona 1, 2nd floor. (℃) 502/7761-1942. Reservations recommended. Main courses Q30–Q110 ($4–$15/£2.10–£7.70). AE, DC, MC, V. Tues–Sun 11am–3pm and 6–10:30pm; Mon 6–10pm.

Sabor de la India *𝒢 (finds)* INDIAN   Finding this place is half the battle—it's hard to find from the street and sometimes it's necessary to let yourself in through the gate— but once you do, you'll be treated to delicious, hearty fare that's a welcome change from the other food options in Guatemala. Fish and shrimp curries are on the menu, as are chicken *tikka masala* and *aloo gobi* (potato and cauliflower). Meals are accompanied by lentils, Indian bread, and a thick and tasty yogurt. At Q30 ($4/£2.10), the massive combo plates are a great bargain. While the food is good, the ambience is lacking, with three bare dining rooms, vinyl tablecloths, and plastic lawn chairs.

2a Calle and 15a Av. A 19, Zona 1. (℃) 502/7765-0101 or 502/5567-0731. Reservations recommended. Main courses Q15–Q50 ($2–$6.65/£1.05–£3.50). MC, V. Tues–Sat 11am–9pm; Sun 5–9pm.

XELA AFTER DARK

Xela has a very active nightlife. Many start things off at the very popular **Salon Tecún** *𝒢* (℃ 502/7761-2832) in the interior passageway of the Enríquez building, fronting the Parque Centro América. The long wooden tables with bench seating fill up most nights with a mix of locals and language students. A better option is **El Balcón de Enríquez** *𝒢𝒢* (℃ 502/7765-2296), which is in the same building but has second-floor outdoor seating that overlooks the park below.

Most of the bars and discos are concentrated within 2 blocks around 14a Avenida A, which is known as Xela's Zona Viva (Live Zone). This is the place to come if you want to bar-hop. Of the bars along this stretch, the most happening include **Bukanas,** 14 Av. A A-80 (℃ 502/7761-5602); **La Tasca,** 14 Av. A 1-49 (℃ 502/7761-2079); **El Zaguan,** 14 Av. A A-70 (℃ 502/7761-8310); **Hektisch,** 1a Calle 14a-11 (℃ 502/ 7761-3546); and **El Duende,** 14 Av. A 1-70 (℃ 502/5547-6197).

Other popular bars include **Casa Verde** (★, 12 Av. 1-40, Zona 1 ((© **502/7763-0271**); **Rusticuela,** 16a Av. 7-68, Zona 3 ((© **502/5398-4850**); and **Kokoloko's,** 15a Avenida and 4a Calle ((© **502/5672-9881**).

For a mellower ambience, try **El Viñedo,** 15a Av. A 3-05 ((© **502/7761-8844**), or **La Taberna** (★, 4a Calle 16-11 ((© **502/5682-9395**).

A couple of informal cinemas cater to Xela's student population, showing DVDs on a large flatscreen TV or projected onto a screen. **Cine Sofía,** 7a Calle 15-18, Zona 1 ((© **502/7761-7815**), has beanbag chairs and features late-run American movies, while **Cínema Paraíso,** 1a Calle 12-20, Zona 1 ((© **502/7761-3546**), tends to show more Latin American and art films. Both charge Q10 ($1.35/70p). Ask around town, or pick up a copy of the free weekly *Xela Who* (www.xelawho.com) to find the current schedule.

3 Huehuetenango

266km (165 miles) NW of Guatemala City; 90km (56 miles) N of Quetzaltenango; 84km (52 miles) S of La Mesilla (border with Mexico)

Huehuetenango has a reputation as an unattractive and neglected border outpost, but it's actually a pretty city, set at the foot of the impressive Sierra de los Cuchumatanes. Commonly known as Huehue (pronounced "*weh*-weh"), the city functions for tourists primarily as an entry and departure point for those coming from or continuing on to Mexico—even though the city is a good hour away from the border by car or bus. Aside from the Maya ruins of **Zaculeu,** the city has few attractions, but it serves as an excellent jumping-off point for the isolated mountain hamlet of **Todos Santos Chuchumatán.**

ESSENTIALS
GETTING THERE
BY BUS   Los Halcones buses ((© **502/2238-1929** in Guatemala City, 502/7764-2251 in Huehuetenango) leave Guatemala City from 7a Av. 15-27, Zona 1 at 7am, 2pm, and 5pm. Return buses leave Huehue from 7a Av. 3-62, Zona 1, at 4:30 and 7am, and at 2pm. The trip takes 5 to 6 hours. The fare is around Q55 ($7.35/£3.85) each way. There are also several first-class buses throughout the day from Mexico to Guatemala City that stop in Huehue. If there's room, you can always hop on one of these. Ask your hotel for current schedules.

Transportes María Victoria ((© **502/5972-2650**) has service between Huehuetenango and Quetzaltenango roughly every hour between 6am and 5pm.

Huehuetenango's **main bus terminal** is located about a mile outside of downtown on the way to the Pan-American Highway, although **Los Halcones** (see above) has its own terminal. There are frequent local buses between the bus terminal and downtown. Ask for any bus to El Centro. Fare is Q2 (25¢/15p). A taxi to the center should cost around Q15 ($2/£1.05).

(*Fun Fact* **Pre-Columbian Palm Springs**

Huehuetenango has been inhabited since at least 1500 B.C., and its name is a Haxcalteca word meaning "Place of Old People."

Huehuetenango

ACCOMMODATIONS ■
Hotel Casa Blanca **10**
Hotel Cascata **11**
Hotel Los Cuchumatanes **11**
Hotel Zaculeu **1**

DINING & NIGHTLIFE ◆
Bob's Bar **3**
Copacabana
   Sports Bar **8**
Flash Dance **9**
Jardin Café **7**
Las Brasas **2**
Le Kaf **12**

ATTRACTIONS ●
Catholic Church **6**
Central Plaza **5**
El Centro Cultural
   La Democracia **11**
Post Office **4**

BY CAR To drive to Huehuetenango, take the Pan-American Highway (CA-1) north out of Guatemala City. At Cuatro Caminos, keep going straight.

GETTING AROUND

The downtown center of Huehuetenango is very compact, and you should have no trouble walking most places. However, taxis and tuk tuks are plentiful. If you can't easily flag one down, call **Taxis Palacios** (© 502/7764-9520) or **Taxis Unidos** (© 502/7764-2218).

ORIENTATION

Like most cities across Guatemala and throughout Central America, Huehuetenango features a popular central plaza or park, fronted by the city's Catholic church. To the north, Sierra de los Cuchumatanes are clearly visible from almost any vantage point.

FAST FACTS The **post office** (© 502/7764-1123) is located about a half-block east of the central plaza at 2 Calle 3-54, Zona 1. You'll also find a cluster of banks within a block or two of the central plaza, including **Bancafé** (© 502/7769-1101); **Banco G&T Continental** (© 502/7764-1290); **Banco Industrial** (© 502/7764-3128); and **Banco de Occidente** (© 502/7764-3196). There's an INGUAT information office (© 502/7764-9354) in the Edificio de Gobernacion just east of the central plaza, before the post office. Huehue's main hospital, the **Hospital Nacional de Huehuetenango** (𝄯 **502/7764-1849**), is located on the outskirts of downtown, in Zona 10. There are several good Internet cafes around central Huehue. I like **Inter-huehue,** 3a Calle 6-65, Zona 1 (𝄯 **502/7764-6382**).

WHAT TO DO IN & AROUND HUEHUE

Huehuetenango doesn't have much to offer tourists, with the exception of a pretty fountain and a Catholic church, which, after suffering great hardships (it suffered massive destruction in the 1902 and 1976 earthquakes, and the church's patron saint, **La Virgen de la Concepción Inmaculada,** was destroyed by fire in 1956), was rebuilt, and once again anchors the plaza with two prominent bell towers and eight white columns dominating its facade.

Most visitors stop here on their way to **Zaculeu,** the post-Classic city that was once the center of power for the Mam Maya group. It's no coincidence that the city sits on a hilltop with steep ravines on three sides. Zaculeu was occupied for more than 10,000 years until its defeat by Spanish conquistadors in 1525. Not even the Spaniards were able to breech the city's defenses, so they simply laid siege, and in a couple of months starved the Mam into submission.

The city was restored by the United Fruit Company in the 1940s, so the main temple is in good shape, although the rather heavy-handed use of concrete and plaster in the restoration have garnered scorn over the years. There's also a ball court and a small museum.

Zaculeu is located 5km (3 miles) west of Huehuetenango. The site is open daily from 8am to 5pm. Admission is Q30 ($4/£2.10). A taxi from town should cost around Q25 ($3.35/£1.75)

WHERE TO STAY

Hotel Casa Blanca 𝍏 𝘝𝘢𝘭𝘶𝘦   The rooms and facilities at this downtown hotel are a bit bigger and better maintained than those at Hotel Zaculeu (below). I'd opt for a third-floor room with a view. The hotel's restaurant has some delightful open-air seating in the courtyard, and it's worth trying even if you're not staying here.

7a Av. 3-41, Zona 1. 𝄯/fax **502/7764-2586** or 502/7769-0777. 15 units. Q225–Q375 ($30–$50/£16–£26) double. AE, DC, MC, V. **Amenities:** Restaurant; bar; tour desk; laundry service. *In room:* No phone.

Hotel Cascata   This place is outside of downtown, near the bus station. The building is a modern, with more steel and glass than you'd expect to find in this isolated town. The hotel takes its name from a beautiful nearby waterfall, which they have tried to mimic with a small artificial waterfall built under a stairway in the narrow lobby area. The carpeted rooms are sparsely decorated, with diminutive 13-inch televisions, but they're clean and comfortable. Try to land a second-floor room (some of these have excellent balconies). The hotel has its own Internet cafe, and provides free Wi-Fi to guests.

Calzada Kalbil Balam, Lote 4, 4-42 Zona 5, Colonia Alvarado. 𝄯 **502/7769-0795.** Fax 502/7764-1188. www.hotel cascata.ya.st. 15 units. Q195 ($26/£14) double. AE, DC, MC, V. **Amenities:** Restaurant; bar; tour desk; laundry service; free Wi-Fi. *In room:* TV, no phone.

Hotel Los Cuchumatanes 𝍏 𝘒𝘪𝘥𝘴   Not many people come to Huehue looking for a resort-style hotel, but if you're one who does, this is your best bet in town. The 55 rooms are all spacious, comfortable, and almost modern in decor and feel. The hotel has a good-size outdoor pool and a game room. It's also popular with vacationing Guatemalan families, making it a good choice if you've got kids along.

2km south of downtown, Sector Brasilia Zona 7. ℂ **502/7764-1951.** Fax 502/7764-2816. castitell@hotmail.com. 55 units. Q300–Q525 ($40–$70/£21–£37) double. Rates include breakfast. AE, DC, MC, V. **Amenities:** Restaurant; bar; midsize outdoor pool; tour desk; laundry service. *In room:* TV.

Hotel Zaculeu   Located just a half-block off the central plaza, this place has been welcoming guests for more than 100 years, which is apparent in some of the front rooms, which can be a bit musty. However, newer, bigger rooms are farther from the street, and are a bit more comfortable. All the rooms are simple, but decorated nicely with local fabrics, furniture, and craftworks. The central courtyard is a lush oasis of tropical flora, and the restaurant serves good local cuisine at excellent prices.

5a Av. 1-14, Zona 1. ℂ **502/7764-1086.** Fax 502/7764-1575. 38 units. Q225–Q375 ($30–$50/£16–£35) double. Rates include breakfast. AE, MC, V. **Amenities:** Restaurant; bar; tour desk; laundry service. *In room:* TV.

WHERE TO DINE

Jardín Café GUATEMALAN/INTERNATIONAL   This popular and pleasant lit-tle restaurant is a good choice any time of the day. The full Chapin breakfast here, or fresh pancakes, are a great way to start the day. There's always a very economical plate of the day for lunch. The bulk of the menu consists of standard Guatemalan and Mexi-can dishes, ranging from whole grilled steaks to burritos and fajitas.

4a Calle and 6a Av. ℂ **502/7769-0769.** Main courses Q20–Q55 ($2.65–$7.35/£1.40–£3.85). No credit cards. Daily 6:30am–10pm.

Las Brasas ⚜ STEAKHOUSE/INTERNATIONAL   This is arguably the fanciest restaurant in Huehue, which isn't saying much. Still, they do a good job with their extensive menu. I recommend sticking with the house specialty of grilled steaks, which are expertly prepared over an open-flame grill. However, you can also order from a variety of Chinese dishes, ranging from chow mein to kung pao chicken. Por-tions are large, so feel free to share.

4a Av. 1-55. ℂ **502/7764-2339.** Main courses Q30–Q110 ($4–$15/£2.10–£7.70). AE, DC, MC, V. Daily 7am–10pm.

Le Kaf *Finds* INTERNATIONAL   While Las Brasas may be the most elegant restau-rant in Huehue, this is certainly the hippest. Le Kaf is popular with local students and travelers. The massive menu ranges from nachos and pizza to grilled meats and poul-try. There's live music most weekend nights, making this a good place to come for drinks, a light meal, and some entertainment.

6a Calle 6-40. ℂ **502/7764-3202.** Main courses Q30–Q75 ($4–$10/£2.10–£5.25). MC, V. Tues–Sun 11am–11pm.

HUEHUE AFTER DARK

Huehuetenango is pretty mellow. **Bob's Bar,** 2a Avenida, across from the post office, Zona 1; and **Copacabana Sports Bar,** 6a Avenida and 4a Calle, Zona 1, are two spots that attract foreign visitors and expatriates. For dancing, head to **Flash Dance,** 4a Calle and 8a Avenida, Zona 1.

If chamber concerts, dance performances, and poetry readings interest you, see if there's anything happening at **El Centro Cultural La Democracia** (ℂ **502/7773-8126**).

A SIDE TRIP OUT OF HUEHUE
TODOS SANTOS CHUCHUMATAN ⚜

Todos Santos Chuchumatán is a beautiful and remote mountain town that remains a major Mam Maya center. Todos Santos suffered some serious atrocities during the civil war, and an army massacre in 1981 is still fresh in the minds of many here.

Both men and women in the area still wear traditional dress. In fact, the *huipiles* and other textile products from Todos Santos are famous throughout Guatemala, and even the men are known for their crocheted handbags. The market, open Saturday and Wednesday, is a great place to purchase the local wares. Todos Santos Chuchumatán is very small, but still attracts a fair number of backpackers and adventurous tourists. There are a few schools catering to foreign tourists looking to learn a Mam, Spanish, or traditional weaving technique.

The town's greatest fame comes from its **drunken horse race,** held each year on All Saint's Day, November 1. The *corrida,* or "horse race," dates back to the days of the conquistadors, and is a combination of a drinking game, horse race, and endurance event. Local riders, usually already drunk before the early morning start, race back and forth along a course, drinking after each leg. Racers keep going until they literally fall off their horses, at which point they are dragged to the perimeter to wallow and retch. Over the years there have been deaths and serious injuries. The spectacle is a bit tough to watch for some, as the humor of it all gives way to drunken danger and debauchery. If you plan to come for the corrida, be sure to arrive several days early in order to nail down a room, as the limited accommodations in town go fast for these festivities, and it's nearly impossible to reserve anything in advance.

At other times of the year, Todos Santos Chuchumatán serves as a good base for some beautiful hiking. The town sits at 2,500m (8,200 ft.), and the surrounding mountains are much higher. It's often cold here, especially at night, so be sure to bring appropriate clothing. Some popular hiking destinations include the 3,837m (12,585-ft.) summit of **La Torre,** which offers amazing views on clear days. The small village of **San Juan Atitlán** is another popular destination.

Todos Santos is also known for its hot steam baths, or *chuj.* Found in most homes, and often available to tourists for a few *quetzales,* the chuj are mud-brick structures with a fire pit at the center. Rocks are heated, and then the bather pours cold water over the rocks and themselves, enjoying the mix of hot steam and refreshing water.

All of the hotels in town are very simple, and none have a phone for reservations. Among those I recommend are **Casa Familiar, Hotel La Paz,** and **Hotelito Todos Santos.**

Todos Santos Chuchumatán is located 45km (28 miles) northwest of Huehu, and periodic buses connect the two. Buses leave every couple of hours between 6am and 6pm from the main Huehuetenango bus terminal. Ask your hotel in Huehue for the current schedule, which changes according to demand. Fare is around Q10 ($1.35/70p). The ride takes about 3 hours due to the rough road. It's also possible to hike from Huehuetenango or Xela to Todos Santos; all the hotel tour desks and tour companies mentioned above can help arrange this.

8

Tikal & the Petén

Occupying the entire northeastern section of Guatemala, the Petén is the country's largest and least populated province. Most of the Petén is forest—thick tropical rainforest—and its lush and wild landscape contains some of Mesoamerica's richest archaeological treasures. In 1990, the government of Guatemala officially established the **Maya Biosphere Reserve,** a tract of 1 million hectares (2.5 million acres) that includes most of Petén province. The Maya Biosphere Reserve adjoins the neighboring **Calakmul**

Biosphere Reserve in Mexico and the **Río Bravo Conservation Area** in Belize, comprising a joint protected area of more than 2 million hectares (5 million acres).

The Petén Province is home to perhaps the most impressive and best preserved of all ancient Maya ceremonial cities, **Tikal,** as well as other less excavated sites, including **Yaxhá, El Ceibal, El Mirador,** and **Uaxactún.** The area is also a rich and rewarding destination for bird-watchers and ecotourists.

1 Tikal ⟨★⟨★⟨★

548km (340 miles) NE of Guatemala City; 65km (40 miles) N of Flores; 100km (62 miles) NW of the Belize border

Tikal is the greatest of the surviving classic Maya cities, and is estimated to have once supported a population of about 100,000 people. Archaeologists have identified more than 3,000 structures, and in its heyday, the city probably covered as much as 65 sq. km (25 sq. miles). Tikal is more extensively excavated than any ruins in Belize, and unlike the grand cities and excavations in Mexico, Tikal rises out of dense jungle. The pyramids here are some of the most perfect examples of ceremonial architecture in the Maya world. Standing atop Temple IV, you are high above the rainforest canopy. The peaks of several temples poke through the dense vegetation, toucans and parrots fly about, and the loudest noise you'll hear is the guttural call of howler monkeys.

ESSENTIALS
GETTING THERE
BY PLANE   TACA Regional Airline (© 502/2279-5821 or 502/2470-8222; www. taca.com) has two daily flights to Flores Airport (FRS) from La Aurora International Airport in Guatemala City. Flights leave at 6:30am and 5:55pm, and return at 8:05am and 7:15pm. The 50-minute round-trip is around Q1,700 ($225/£119), and extra flights are sometimes added in the high season (Dec to early Apr, and sometimes July–Aug).

   TAG Airlines (© 502/2360-3038; tagventas@turbonett.com) has one daily flight from La Aurora International Airport in Guatemala City to Flores at 6:30am, returning at 5pm. The fare is Q1,650 ($220/£116) round-trip. *Note:* Travelers with fears of smaller, propeller-driven commuter craft will want to go with TACA, which flies an Airbus A-319 jet.

The Flores airport is on the road to Tikal, about 1½ miles (2.4km) east of Santa Elena. A taxi from the airport into Santa Elena or Flores should cost you around Q15 ($2/£1.05), or you can take a local bus (usually an old Bluebird school bus) for around Q1 (15¢/10p). Collective taxis and minivans to Tikal are usually waiting at the airport and charge around Q30 to Q45 ($4–$6/£2.10–£3.15) per person each way. You can sometimes bargain, and can often get a slight discount if you purchase a round-trip fare right from the start. A private taxi can be hired for Q250 to Q400 ($33–$53/£18–£28).

BY BUS   Autobuses del Norte (ADN; ☎ 502/2221-2515 in Guatemala City, or 502/7924-8131 in Santa Elena; www.adnautobusesdelnorte.com) has two daily buses between Guatemala City and Santa Elena/Flores departing at 10am and 9pm in each direction. The fare is Q165 ($22/£12) one-way, Q285 ($38/£20) round-trip on the first departure; and Q218 ($29/£15) one-way, Q375 ($50/£26) round-trip on the later bus. Children under 10 and adults over 70 pay half-price. The buses stop in Río Dulce in both directions. Their terminal in Guatemala City is Estación Central, 8a Av. 16-41, Zona 1. In Santa Elena, they arrive at and depart from the main bus terminal.

Línea Dorada (☎ 502/2232-5506 in Guatemala City, or 502/7926-0070 in Santa Elena; www.tikalmayanworld.com) also has two daily buses between Guatemala City and Santa Elena-Flores departing at 10am and 9pm in each direction. Their fares run Q225 ($30/£16) one-way, Q415 ($55/£29) round-trip. Their terminal in Guatemala City is at 16a Calle 10-03, Zona 1, and they also arrive at and depart from the main bus terminal in Santa Elena. Linea Dorada also has direct daily buses to Belize City.

Tips **Shameless Plug**

If you're going on to Belize, you'll want to pick up a copy of *Frommer's Belize*.

The trip on either bus line takes around 8 to 9 hours. If you arrive by bus, you'll have to arrange a taxi, collective taxi, or minivan ride out to Tikal. See "Getting There: By Plane," above, and "Getting Around," below, for more details.

BY CAR   To drive to Tikal from Guatemala City, you must first drive to Santa Elena. The best and fastest route is via Río Dulce. Take the Carretera al Atlántico (CA-9) out of Guatemala City to La Ruidosa crossroads at Km 245. From here it's 34km (21 miles) north on highway CA-13 to Río Dulce and another 180km (112 miles) from Río Dulce to Santa Elena. From Santa Elena, you'll need to drive 32km (20 miles) to the crossroads at Ixlú (El Cruce), and turn north toward Tikal, which is 65km (40 miles) away. The route and turnoffs are all well-marked, and the drive should take about 8 hours.

Warning: It's strongly advised that you do not drive at night. It's a sad fact that armed groups occasionally set up roadblocks along these isolated, yet frequently trafficked, roads. While this is a rare occurrence, it's better to be safe than sorry.

BY ORGANIZED TOUR   Organized day trips leave daily for Tikal from Guatemala City and Antigua. Costs for these all-inclusive trips are approximately Q1,650 to Q2,250 ($220–$300/£116–£158) per person including round-trip airfare, ground transportation, park entrance fees, a guide, and lunch. These tours generally leave at around 5am and get back to Guatemala City or Antigua at around 6pm. Budget an additional Q375 to Q1,125 ($50–$150/£26–£79) per person per day for multiday

excursions, depending on the level of accommodations chosen. In Guatemala City, call **Maya Vacations** ✦ (© **502/2339-4638;** www.mayavacations.com), **Clark Tours** (© **502/2412-4700;** www.clarktours.com.gt), or **Grayline Guatemala** (© **502/2383-8600;** www.graylineguatemala.com). From Antigua, **Via Venture** ✦✦ (© **502/7832-2509;** www.viaventure.com) offers a 2-day/1-night tour to Tikal, with a private 5-hour guided tour of the park, overnight at La Lancha, round-trip airfare, and all transfers, for Q4,455 ($594/£132) per person, double occupancy.

GETTING AROUND

BY TAXI OR MINIVAN   Minivans and collective taxis leave throughout the day plying the route between Tikal and Santa Elena/Flores, charging between Q30 and Q45 ($4–$6/£2.10–£3.15) per person. From Santa Elena, you can catch a bus back to the border. A private cab from Tikal to Santa Elena/Flores will run around Q250 to Q400 ($33–$53/£18–£28); between Tikal and El Remate (later in this chapter), the fare is about Q100 to Q200 ($13–$27/£7–£14).

BY CAR   Hertz (© **800/654-3131** in the U.S., or 502/7926-0415 in Flores; www.hertz.com.gt) has an office at the Flores airport, as well as at the Camino Real Tikal (later in this chapter). There are also several local agencies at the airport of which **Tabarini Rent A Car** (© **502/7926-0277;** www.tabarini.com) is a good choice. Most rent small jeeps and SUVs. Rates run from Q340 to Q675 ($45–$90/£24–£47) per day. *Note:* Be sure to get a 4WD vehicle; even though you may never need the traction or off-road ability, the extra clearance will come in handy.

ORIENTATION   There is no village or town inside Tikal National Park. After having paid your Q50 ($6.65/£3.50) admission at the entrance booth 18km (11 miles) south of the ruins, you'll eventually come to a large central parking area and visitor center. This is where you'll find the three hotels and campsite reviewed in "Where to Stay," later in this chapter, as well as the two museums, a collection of simple restaurants, and the trail entrance, from which the ruins are about a 15- to 20-minute walk through the forest.

There's a **post office** and **telegraph** office on the left as you arrive at the parking area. You'll find a **public phone** in the Stelae Museum. There's no bank or ATM in Tikal, and most of the little restaurants and gift stands only accept *quetzales*. While some of the hotels here do accept credit cards, the phone connections are spotty, and they sometimes have problems getting the authorizations, so it's best to bring *quetzales* to pay for your entire stay. Also, be sure to bring plenty of insect repellent with you—the bugs here are rapacious.

Tikal National Park is open daily from 6am to 6pm. If you'd like to stay in the park until 8pm (for sunset and nocturnal wildlife viewing), get your admission ticket stamped at the office behind the Stelae Museum. If you arrive after 3pm, your admission is good for the following day as well, and if you're staying multiple days, you must pay the admission fee each day. The best times to visit the ruins are in early morning and late afternoon, which are the least crowded and coolest times of day.

(*Fun Fact* **Camera-Ready**

Tikal's landscape is so stunning that it was chosen for an exterior shot in George Lucas's *Star Wars* and as the site for a series of famous Nike commercials.

FAST FACTS   There are no banks, medical facilities, laundromats, or other major services available at Tikal. All of these can be found in Flores and Santa Elena, some 65km (40 miles) away (see "Flores & Santa Elena," later in this chapter).

If you arrive by air, you can exchange money at **Banquetzal** (✆ 502/7926-0711) in the departure area of the small airport. It's open daily from 7am to noon and 2 to 5pm. You'll also find individuals offering to exchange money (which is safe), but you're better off heading into Santa Elena or Flores if the Banquetzal branch isn't open. Most of the hotels and restaurants in Tikal, in fact, will exchange dollars for *quetzales,* though they may give you a slightly less favorable rate than you would get at a bank.

EXPLORING TIKAL

Tikal is one of the largest Maya cities ever uncovered, and houses the most spectacular ruins in Guatemala, which are comparable to Mexico's Chichén Itzá in pre-Columbian splendor. However, unlike at Chichén Itzá, the ruins of Tikal are set in the middle of a vast jungle through which you must hike from temple to temple. The many miles of trails provide numerous opportunities to spot interesting birds such as toucans and parrots, and wild animals including coatimundis, spider monkeys, howler monkeys, and deer.

Moments   Sunrise, Sunset

Tikal is a place of magic and mystique, which many say is heightened around sunrise and sunset. Sunsets are easier to catch and a more dependable show, while sunrises tend to be more a case of the sun eventually burning through the morning mist than of any impressive orb emerging. However, afternoons are usually clear, especially during the dry season, allowing for excellent sunset viewing from the tops of the main temples. Staying at the ruins increases your chances of catching the sunrise, since visitors staying inside the park are often admitted to Tikal as early as 5am. However, mini-vans and collective taxis do leave Flores and El Remate early enough to get you to the Tikal entrance gate at 6am when it opens. This will generally enable you to get to the top of one of the main temples by 6:30am, which is usually early enough to catch the sunrise.

No one's sure just what role Tikal played in the history of the Maya, whether it was a ceremonial center for priests, artisans, and the elite, or a city of industry and commerce. In the 16 sq. km (6 sq. miles) of Tikal that have been mapped and excavated, only a few of the buildings were domestic structures; most were temples, palaces, ceremonial platforms, and shrines. So far, archaeologists have mapped about 3,000 constructions, 10,000 earlier foundations beneath surviving structures, 250 stone monuments (stelae and altars), and thousands of art objects found in tombs and cached offerings. There is evidence of continuous construction at Tikal from 200 B.C. through the 9th century A.D., with some suggestion of occupation as early as 600 B.C. The Maya reached their zenith in art and architecture during the Classic Period, which began about A.D. 250 and ended abruptly in about A.D. 900, when for some reason Tikal and all other major Maya centers were abandoned. Most of the visible structures at Tikal date from the Late Classic Period, from A.D. 600 to A.D. 900.

Workers are presently excavating the countless mounds on the periphery of the mapped area, and have been finding modest houses of stone and plaster with thatch roofs. Just how far these settlements extended beyond the ceremonial center and how many people lived within the domain of Tikal are yet to be determined.

MAKING THE MOST OF YOUR VISIT

Tikal is such an immense site that you really need several days to see it thoroughly. However, you can visit many of the greatest temples and plazas in 1 day. First-time visitors should hire a guide, which are available at the visitor center and charge around Q150 ($20/£11) for a half-day tour of the ruins. In addition, most hotels and all tour agencies in the region offer guided tours for a similar price.

There are a host of excellent books on the Maya, some specifically about Tikal. *Tikal: An Illustrated History of the Ancient Maya Capital,* by John Montgomery (Hippocrene Books, 2001), is a good place to start. *The Lords of Tikal: Rulers of an Ancient Maya City,* by Peter D. Harrison, et al. (Thames & Hudson, 2000), is a similar option. For a more comprehensive view of the ancient Maya, try *A Forest of Kings: The Untold Story of the Ancient Maya,* by David Friedel (William Morrow & Co., 1992). Although out of print, you might want to try to find a copy of *Tikal: Handbook of the Ancient*

Tikal

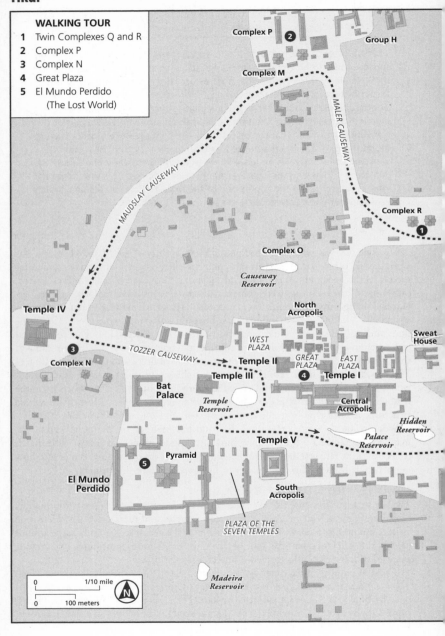

WALKING TOUR

1 Twin Complexes Q and R
2 Complex P
3 Complex N
4 Great Plaza
5 El Mundo Perdido
  (The Lost World)

Complex P ②

Group H

Complex M

MALER CAUSEWAY

MAUDSLAY CAUSEWAY

Complex R ①

Complex O

Causeway Reservoir

Temple IV

TOZZER CAUSEWAY

③

Complex N

North Acropolis

Sweat House

WEST PLAZA

Temple II

GREAT PLAZA

EAST PLAZA

④

Temple I

Temple III

Bat Palace

Temple Reservoir

Central Acropolis

Hidden Reservoir

Temple V

Palace Reservoir

⑤

Pyramid

El Mundo Perdido

South Acropolis

PLAZA OF THE SEVEN TEMPLES

0   1/10 mile
0   100 meters

N

Madeira Reservoir

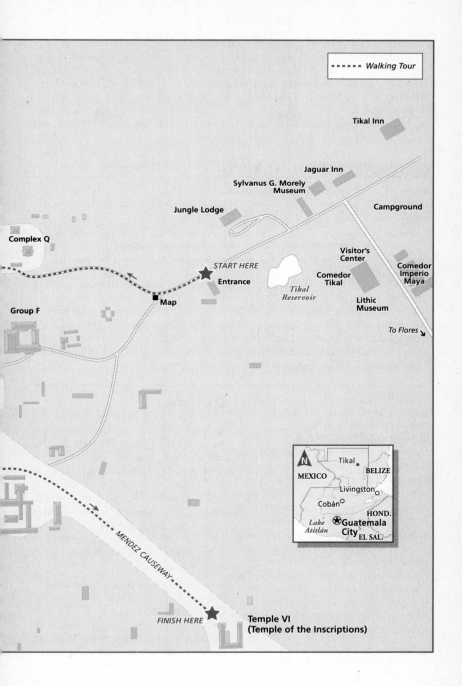

Walking Tour

Tikal Inn

Jaguar Inn

Sylvanus G. Morely Museum

Jungle Lodge

Campground

Complex Q

START HERE

Visitor's Center

Comedor Imperio Maya

Entrance

Tikal Reservoir

Comedor Tikal

Map

Lithic Museum

Group F

To Flores

N

Tikal
BELIZE
MEXICO
Livingston
Cobán
HOND.
Lake Atitlán
Guatemala City
EL SAL.

MENDEZ CAUSEWAY

FINISH HERE

Temple VI
(Temple of the Inscriptions)

Maya Ruins, by William R. Coe, written under the auspices of the University Museum of the University of Pennsylvania. Archaeologists from the university, working in conjunction with Guatemalan officials, did most of the excellent excavation work at Tikal from 1956 to 1969. Birders will want to have a copy of *The Birds of Tikal: An Annotated Checklist,* by Randall A. Beavers (Texas A&M University Press, 1992), or *The Birds of Tikal,* by Frank B. Smithe (Natural History Press, 1966). The latter three books are hard to find, but you should be able to order used copies in the U.S., or you can usually find copies of all of these in Flores or at Tikal.

WALKING TOUR   TIKAL RUINS

Start:	**Visitor Center and Stelae Museum.**
Finish:	**Temple VI.**
Time:	**3 to 4 hours.**
Best Time:	**Before or after the crowds gather at the Great Plaza. Feel free to reverse the order of this walking tour if it will help you avoid the masses.**
Worst Time:	**Between 10am and 2pm, when crowds and tour buses stop at the Great Plaza.**

A full tour of Tikal will require an extensive amount of walking—as much as 10km (6 miles). The itinerary described here will take you to most of the major temples and plazas, and can be accomplished in about 3 to 4 hours. If your time is really limited, you should follow the signs and head straight to the Great Plaza. To orient yourself, begin your tour at the visitor center and neighboring Stelae Museum. Here you'll find some informative exhibits and relics, as well as an impressive relief map of the site. See "The Museums," below, for more information on the museum.

From the museum, walk along the road that goes west toward the ruins, and turn right at the first intersection to get to:

❶ Twin Complexes Q & R

Seven of the twin complexes at Tikal have been discovered and mapped (only a few have been excavated), but their exact purpose is still a mystery. Each complex has two pyramids facing east and west; at the north is an unroofed enclosure entered by a vaulted doorway and containing a single stela and altar; at the south is a small palace-like structure. Of the two pyramids here, one has been restored and one has been left as it was found (the latter will give you an idea of just how overgrown and ensconced in the jungle these structures had become).

At the end of the Twin Complexes is a wide road called the Maler Causeway. Turn right (north) onto this causeway, and walk 15 minutes to get to:

❷ Complex P

Some restoration has been done at this twin complex, but the most interesting points are the replicas of a stela (no. 20) and altar (no. 8) in the north enclosure. Look for the beautiful glyphs next to the carving of a warrior on the stela, which are all in very good condition. The altar shows a captive bound to a carved-stone altar, his hands tied behind his back—a common scene in carvings at Tikal. Both these monuments date from about A.D. 751.

From Complex P, head south on the Maudslay Causeway to:

❸ Complex N

This complex is the site of **Temple IV (Temple of the Two-Headed Serpent).** Finished around A.D. 740, Temple IV is the tallest structure in Tikal at 64m (212 ft.) from the base of its platform to the top. The first glimpse you get of the temple from the Maudslay Causeway is awesome, for the temple has not been restored, and all but the temple proper (the enclosure) and its roof comb are covered in foliage. The stairway is covered in earth and roots, but you can get to the top of the temple using a system of roughly made wood ladders set against the steep sides of the pyramid. The view of the setting and layout of Tikal—and all of the Great Plaza—is magnificent. From the platform of the temple, you can see in all directions and get an idea of the extent of the Petén jungle. **Temple III (Temple of the Great Priest)** is in the foreground to the east; **Temples I** and **II** are farther on at the Great Plaza. To the right of these are the **South Acropolis** and **Temple V.**

Temple IV, and all the other temples at Tikal, are built on this plan: A pyramid is built, upon which a platform is constructed. The temple proper rests on this platform and is composed of one to three rooms, which are usually long and narrow and used for priestly rites rather than for habitation. Most temples had beautifully carved wooden lintels above the doorways. The one from Temple IV is now in the Völkerkunde Museum in Basel, Switzerland.

From Temple IV, walk east along the Tozzer Causeway for 10 minutes to get to:

❹ Great Plaza

Along the way you'll pass the twin-pyramid Complex N, the **Bat Palace,** and **Temple III.** Take a look at the altar and stela in the complex's northern enclosure—two of the finest monuments at Tikal—and also the altar in front of Temple III, showing the head of a deity resting on a plate. The crisscross pattern shown here represents a woven mat, a symbol of authority to the Mayas.

Entering the Great Plaza from the Tozzer Causeway, you'll be struck by the towering stone structure that is **Temple II,** seen from the back. It measures 38m (125 ft.) tall now, but is thought to have been 140 feet (42m) high when the roof comb was intact. Also called the Temple of the Masks, because of a large face carved in the roof comb, the temple dates from about A.D. 700. Walk around this temple to enter the plaza proper.

Directly across from Temple II you'll see **Temple I (Temple of the Great Jaguar),** the most striking structure in Tikal. Standing 44m (145 ft.) tall, the temple proper has three narrow rooms with high corbeled vaults (the Maya "arch") and carved wooden lintels made of zapote wood, which is rot-resistant. One of the lintels has been removed for preservation in the Guatemala National Museum of Archaeology and Ethnology in Guatemala City. The whole structure is made of limestone, as are most others at Tikal. It was within this pyramid that one of the richest tombs in Tikal, believed to be the tomb of Tikal ruler Hasaw Chan K'awil, was discovered. When archaeologists uncovered it in 1962, they found the former ruler's skeleton surrounded by some 180 pieces of jade, 90 bone artifacts carved with hieroglyphic inscriptions, numerous pearls, and objects in alabaster and shell. *Note:* Tourists can no longer scale temples I or III. However, those in need of serious cardio workouts will get their fill by climbing some of the other temples.

The **North Acropolis** (north side of the Great Plaza) is a maze of structures from various periods covering an area of 8 hectares (21 acres). Today it stands 9m (30 ft.) above the limestone bedrock and contains vestiges of more than a hundred different constructions dating from 200 B.C. to A.D. 800. At the front-center of the acropolis (at the top of the stairs up from the Great Plaza) is a temple numbered **5D-33.** Although much of the 8th-century temple was destroyed during the excavations to get to the Early Classic period temple (A.D. 300) underneath, it's still a fascinating building. Toward the rear of it is a tunnel leading to the stairway of the Early Classic temple, embellished with two 3m-high (10-ft.) plaster polychrome masks of a god—don't miss these.

Directly across the plaza from the North Acropolis is the **Central Acropolis,** which covers about 1.6 hectares (4 acres). It's a maze of courtyards and palaces on several levels, all connected by an intricate system of passageways. Some of the palaces had five floors, connected by exterior stairways, and each floor had as many as nine rooms arranged like a maze.

Before you leave the Great Plaza, be sure to examine some of the 70 beautiful stelae and altars right in the plaza. You can see the full development of Maya art in them, for they date from the Early Classic period right through to the Late Classic period. There are three major stylistic groups: the stelae with wraparound carving on the front and sides and text on the back; those with a figure carved on the front and text in glyphs on the back; and those with a simple carved figure on the front, hieroglyphs on the sides, and a plain back. The oldest stela, no. 29 (now in the Tikal Museum), dates from A.D. 292; the most recent is no. 11 in the Great Plaza, which dates from A.D. 869.

If you head southwest from Temple II, you'll come to the area known as:

⑤ El Mundo Perdido (The Lost World)

This plaza contains the **Great Pyramid,** which stands 34m (114 ft.) high and is the oldest excavated building in Tikal. This pyramid is one of the most popular spots for watching the sunset. If you've timed it right, you might be able to hang out here and watch the show; otherwise, make a mental note to get your bearings and come back later. Directly east of the Great Pyramid is the **Plaza of the Seven Temples,** which dates to the Late Classic period. Bordering this plaza on the east side is an unexcavated pyramid, and behind this is **Temple V.** This entire area is known as the **South Acropolis.** You can climb Temple V, but be forewarned: While the view from above is beautiful, the climb, both up and down, is on a very steep and rather rickety wood stairway, which can be scary.

If you cross through the South Acropolis to the east and then turn north in the general direction of the Great Plaza, you'll come to the East Plaza. From here you can walk southeast on the Méndez Causeway to **Temple VI (Temple of the Inscriptions),** which contains the most extensive hieroglyphics in Tikal, although they are nearly illegible. It's worth coming out this way just for the chance to spot some wild animals, which seem to be fairly common in this remote corner of the park.

THE MUSEUMS

The most formal museum here has been officially christened the **Sylvanus G. Morely Museum,** but is also known as the **Tikal** or **Ceramic Museum.** This museum, located between the Jungle Lodge and the Jaguar Inn, has a good collection of pottery, mosaic masks, incense burners, etched bone, and stelae that are chronologically displayed. Of note are the delicate 7.6-to-13-centimeter (3-to-5-in.) mosaic masks made of jade, turquoise, shell, and stucco. There's a beautiful cylindrical jar from about A.D. 700 depicting a male and female seated in a typical Maya pose. Also on exhibit are a number of jade pendants, beads, and earplugs, as well as the famous **stela no. 31,** which is carved on all four sides. Two sides show spear throwers, each wearing a large feathered headdress and carrying a shield in his left hand; on the front is a complicated carving of an individual carrying a head in his left arm and a chair in his right. This Early Classic period stela is considered one of the finest. Be sure to check out the reconstruction of the tomb of Hasaw Chan K'awil, who was also known as Ah Cacao, or "Lord Chocolate."

The second museum is known as the **Lithic** or **Stelae Museum,** and is in the large new visitor center, which is on your left as you arrive at the parking area coming from Flores. The spacious display area contains a superb collection of stelae from around the ruins. Just outside the front door of the museum is the scaled relief map (mentioned above) that will give you an excellent perspective on the relationships between the different ruins at Tikal. Both museums are open daily from 9am to 5pm, and a Q10 ($1.35/70p) admission will get you into both.

Tip: Only visit the museums if you have extra time or a very specific interest in either the stelae or ceramic works. The ruins themselves are by far much more interesting and interactive.

WHERE TO STAY

There are only three hotels and a campground in the little Tikal village near the entrance to the ruins. Unless you have more than 2 days to spend exploring the region, I highly recommend staying near the ruins, as it allows you to enter early and stay late, and helps you avoid the Great Plaza and North Acropolis during the peak period when they are swarmed with day-trippers.

Although the ruins are officially open from 6am to 6pm, those staying at the site can sometimes finagle their way in earlier. Better yet, those staying at the site can have their admission ticket stamped, allowing them to stay inside the park until 8pm and a chance to catch both the sunset and moonrise from the top of one of the temples.

Note: Rooms are often difficult to get at the park, and making reservations is essential during the high season, which runs December through mid-April, coinciding with the winter months in most northern countries. There's also a mini–high season during the months of July and August. Some hotels charge their high-season rates during these months. Communication with the hotels here is difficult and undependable, and many reserve all of their high-season bookings for groups and prepaid package tours. Overbooking on behalf of these hotels is also not uncommon. If you're only coming for a couple of nights, book an organized tour to save yourself some hassle. If you plan to spend more time in the area and don't mind possibly spending a night in Flores or Santa Elena if necessary, you can probably make your arrangements once you're in Tikal.

VERY EXPENSIVE

Jungle Lodge ✦ Also known as *Posada de la Selva,* this is the largest and most comfortable hotel at the park. However, at times there can be a cattle-car feel to the

Play Ball!

Imagine a game that combines the ball and hoop of basketball, the protective pads and jarring contact of American football, and the no-hands policy of soccer.

This is the 3,000-year-old Maya ballgame of Pak-a-Tuk ("Juego de Pelota" in Spanish, "Uluma" in the indigenous Nuahtl language of Mexico). It is depicted in one form or another on thousands of artifacts, murals, and descriptive carved stelae found at archaeological sites.

Experts think the sport's primary purpose was ritualistic, or that it was a metaphor for the Maya dialectic cosmology. Perhaps it was just pure entertainment.

Other questions remain. Was it a game played by two nobles from different kingdoms, or by two teams of various numbers? Did the match last for hours or for days? And when the game was finally over, was the losing team sacrificed to the gods for its failure, or did the winning team lose their heads as a reward for pleasing the gods with their skill?

There are numerous ball courts to be found in Guatemala. They can be found at the archaeological sites of Cancuen, Nakbe, Naranjo, and Quirigua. At Tikal, in the jungles of the Petén, there are seven, and several more are found throughout the rest of the country. Nearly every pre-Columbian city of any significant size appears to have had at least one, and more than 700 ball courts are found as far north as Arizona. The ball courts vary in size; some have open ends, while others have closed ends.

Despite the extensive findings by hundreds of archaeologists and the score of competing theories, there is no universal agreement as to the reasons, rules, regulation sizes, or results of this mysterious game.

operation. The majority of the rooms, and the best ones, are housed in duplex bungalows with high ceilings, white tile floors, two double beds with mosquito netting, and a ceiling fan. Each has its own porch with a couple of chairs, which are great places to sit and read a book or do some bird-watching. Two new junior suites feature king-size beds, a large Jacuzzi-style tub (but without jets), and private patios in both the front and back of the room. There are also 12 older rooms with polished cement floors and shared bathroom facilities, which are certainly more comfortable than camping. It's hot and steamy here in the jungle, but after you've spent the day traipsing up and down pyramids, you'll be thankful you can cool off in the hotel's pool, which is built on a rise and shaped like a Maya pyramid. Meals in the large dining rooms are some of the best you can find in Tikal.

Tikal village. © 502/7861-0447 or 502/2476-8775. Fax 502/7861-0448. www.junglelodge.guate.com. 50 units (38 with private bathroom). Q1,200 ($160/£84) bungalow; Q300 ($40/£21) double with shared bathroom. MC, V. **Amenities:** Restaurant; bar; small pool; tour desk; laundry service. *In room:* No phone.

Tikal Inn   Set back amid the trees, the Tikal Inn is the farthest hotel from the entrance to the ruins. The best rooms here are the individual bungalows, which feature high thatch roofs, tile floors, local furniture and textiles, and rustic wood trim.

The smaller rooms in the main building have cement floors. All of the rooms are airy and cool, but feel rather bare. There's a pool and a small Internet cafe, and the family-style meals are a step up from the fare served at the *comedores* near the campground.

Tikal village. ⓒ/fax **502/7926-0065** or ⓒ 502/7926-1917. hoteltikalinn@itelgua.com. 29 units. ($120/£63) double. Rate includes breakfast and dinner. MC, V. **Amenities:** Restaurant; bar; small pool; tour desk; laundry service. *In room:* No phone.

INEXPENSIVE

Jaguar Inn *Value*   This may be the most humble and economical of the hotels right at the park, but the rooms are clean, spacious, and well-kept. Most come with two queen-size beds and a small veranda strung with a hammock. The best rooms are a couple of large, second-floor units. However, I also like bungalow no. 10, with its king-size bed and private veranda. If you're on a tight budget, you can camp here or rent one of their hammocks with mosquito netting and a locker for Q38 ($5/£2.80) per person. Since the folks out here run on generator power, be forewarned that the electricity is only turned on in the rooms between 5am and 11pm.

Tikal village. ⓒ **502/7926-0002.** Fax 502/7926-2413. www.jaguartikal.com. 14 units. Q400 ($53/£28) double. Rates lower in the off season. AE, MC, V. **Amenities:** Restaurant; tour desk; laundry service. *In room:* No phone.

CAMPING

Just off the main parking lot at the site is a marked and designated camping area with a nice lawn and some trees for shade. You can also set up your tent on concrete pads under a *palapa* (open-sided structure). The camping area has simple shared shower and toilet facilities and a communal cooking area, but there's no phone. The campground charges Q25 to Q30 ($3.35–$4/£1.75–£2.10) to put up a tent and use the facilities. You can also rent hammocks and pitch them under a *palapa* for an additional Q25 ($3.35/£2.10).

Tip: If you plan on sleeping, or just taking an afternoon nap, in a hammock, be sure to get a mosquito net, which are available from most of the places that rent and sell hammocks.

WHERE TO DINE

Most folks who stay near the ruins eat all their meals at their hotel. If you're looking for variety or staying at the campsite, there are several small restaurants *(comedores)* between the main camping area/parking lot and the gate at the beginning of the road to Flores. As you arrive at Tikal from Flores, you'll see them on the right side: **Comedor Imperio Maya, Comedor La Jungla,** and **Comedor Tikal** are the best of the bunch. All serve hefty plates of fairly tasty food at low prices. You can get a large serving of roast chicken with rice, beans, and fresh tortillas, along with a drink, for around Q40 ($5.30/£2.80).

Within the area of the ruins there are covered picnic tables and itinerant soft-drink peddlers, but no snack stands. If you want to spend all day at the ruins without having to walk back to the parking area for lunch, take sandwiches. Most of the hotels here and in Flores, as well as the *comedores,* will make you a sack lunch to take into the park.

TIKAL AFTER DARK

While you could hang out at your hotel or spend the evening swinging on a hammock, the best nighttime activity here is to visit the ruins by moonlight. Those staying near the entrance can have their admission ticket validated to allow them to roam the park until 8pm, and in some cases even later, depending on the disposition of the guards. If the moon is waxing, full, or just beyond full, you're in for a real treat. *Tip:* Before venturing into the park at night, be sure to ask about the current level of safety.

2 Flores & Santa Elena ★

488km (303 miles) NE of Guatemala City; 65km (40 miles) SW of Tikal; 136km (84 miles) NW of the Belizean border

Since accommodations in Tikal are limited, most travelers choose to (or must) overnight in the sister cities of Flores and Santa Elena, which are connected by a narrow causeway. This is not necessarily such a bad thing, since there's a lot more to do and see in these towns, plus a far wider range of hotels and restaurants.

Flores is a picturesque town with colonial-style buildings and cobblestone streets, built on an island in the middle of Lake Petén Itzá. Seen from the air, Flores appears almost perfectly round. Though most people only spend time here en route to or from the Tikal ruins, Flores is well worth exploring for a day or two. A walk around the circumference of the island is reminiscent of Venice, since buildings come right down to the water's edge. In fact, since the lake's water level has risen over the years, some of the outlying streets and alleys are flooded, and dugout canoes, kayaks, and motor launches sit at makeshift docks along the circumference of the island.

Santa Elena, Flores's mainland counterpart, on the other hand, is a ramshackle, modern boomtown with little at all to recommend it. However, Santa Elena is where you'll find the airport, bus stations, a host of hotels, and a good view of Flores. The name Flores is often used as an umbrella term encompassing Flores, Santa Elena, and San Benito, a small town to the west of Santa Elena.

Flores is the unofficial capital of Guatemala's Petén region. El Petén has always been a remote region, and it was here, on the banks of Lake Petén Itzá, that the Itzá people, descendants of the Mayas, resisted Spanish conquest until the end of the 17th century. Conquistador Hernán Cortés visited the Itzá city of Tayasal, which once stood on the far side of the lake, in 1525, but had not tried to conquer the Itzás, who had a reputation for being fierce warriors. However, in 1697, the Spanish finally conquered the Itzás, and Tayasal became the last Indian city to fall under Spanish rule. Two years after taking Tayasal, the Spanish moved to Flores, an island that could easily be defended. They renamed this island Nuestra Señora de los Remedios y San Pablo de los Itzaes, and built a fort here between 1700 and 1701. In 1831, the island was once again renamed, this time being given the name Flores in honor of a Guatemalan patriot.

Fun Fact **Horsing Around**

One of the most curious pieces of local history revolves around a sick horse that was left in Tayasal by Hernán Cortés when he passed through the area. The Itzás had never seen horses before, and as soon as Cortés left, they began worshipping it. When the horse died, a stone statue of it was made, and the worship continued until Spanish missionaries arrived in Tayasal 100 years later. The missionaries, appalled by this idolatry, proceeded to pitch the blasphemous statue into the lake. To this day the legendary horse statue has never been discovered, though searches continue to be launched from time to time.

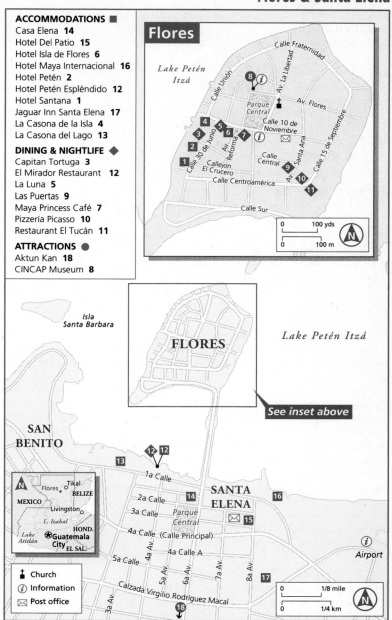

ACCOMMODATIONS ■
Casa Elena **14**
Hotel Del Patio **15**
Hotel Isla de Flores **6**
Hotel Maya Internacional **16**
Hotel Petén **2**
Hotel Petén Espléndido **12**
Hotel Santana **1**
Jaguar Inn Santa Elena **17**
La Casona de la Isla **4**
La Casona del Lago **13**

DINING & NIGHTLIFE ◆
Capitan Tortuga **3**
El Mirador Restaurant **12**
La Luna **5**
Las Puertas **9**
Maya Princess Café **7**
Pizzería Picasso **10**
Restaurant El Tucán **11**

ATTRACTIONS ●
Aktun Kan **18**
CINCAP Museum **8**

Flores

Lake Petén Itzá

Calle Fraternidad
Calle Unión
Av. La Libertad
Av. Flores
Parque Central
Calle 10 de Noviembre
Calle 30 de Junio
Av. Reforma
Calle Central
Av. Santa Ana
Calle 15 de Septiembre
Callejon El Crucero
Calle Centroamérica
Calle Sur

0   100 yds
0   100 m

Isla Santa Barbara

FLORES

Lake Petén Itzá

See inset above

SAN BENITO

MEXICO
Flores ○—Tikal
BELIZE
Livingston○
L. Izabal
Lake Atitlán
★Guatemala City
HOND.
EL SAL.

1a Calle
2a Calle
3a Calle
4a Calle (Calle Principal)
4a Calle A
5a Calle
3a Av.
4a Av.
5a Av.
6a Av.
7a Av.
8a Av.
Calzada Virgilio Rodríguez Macal

SANTA ELENA

Parque Central

Airport

✝ Church
ⓘ Information
✉ Post office

0   1/8 mile
0   1/4 km

ESSENTIALS
GETTING THERE
BY PLANE   See "By Plane" under "Essentials" in "Tikal," earlier in this chapter.

BY CAR   To get here from Guatemala City, see "By Car" under "Essentials" in "Tikal," earlier in this chapter.

The road between Tikal and Flores is well-paved, and the trip takes around an hour by car. To get to either of the sister towns from Tikal, head south out of the ruins, and turn right at Ixlú (El Cruce). Continue on past the airport, and you'll come to Santa Elena first. Stay on the main avenue into town and head toward the lake, where you'll find the causeway to Flores.

BY BUS   For information on getting to Flores and Santa Elena by bus from Guatemala City, see "By Bus" under "Essentials" in "Tikal," earlier in this chapter.

GETTING AROUND
Those in Santa Elena or Flores will most likely want to go to Tikal or explore the region around Lake Petén.

BY BUS   Very inexpensive local bus service connects Flores and Santa Elena to Tikal and several neighboring communities. However, this service is infrequent, slow, and often uncomfortably overcrowded. **Línea Dorada** (see earlier in this chapter) has three daily buses from Santa Elena to Tikal leaving at 5 and 8am and 3:30pm. The return buses leave Tikal at 2 and 5pm. Ask your hotel or around town for current schedules, as they change periodically. Duration of the trip is 1½ hours; the one-way fare is Q25 ($3.35/£1.75).

BY MINIVAN   If you don't have a car, the best way to get around this area is by minivan. Scheduled and independent minivans ply the route between Santa Elena or Flores and Tikal throughout the day. Minivans and collective taxis charge between Q30 and Q45 ($4–$6/£2.10–£3.15) per person.

Minivans from Flores and Santa Elena leave roughly every hour between 5am and 10am, and less frequently thereafter. They also meet every plane arriving at the Santa Elena airport. These minivans leave from Tikal for the return trip roughly every hour from noon to 6pm. Hotels in Flores and Santa Elena can also arrange a minivan pickup for you. It's always best to reserve your return on a minibus back to Santa Elena when you pay for your fare out. The trip usually takes an hour and costs Q30 to Q45 ($4–$6/£2.10–£3.15) per person, each way.

BY TAXI   Taxis charge between Q250 and Q400 ($33–$53/£18–£28) for the one-way trip between Flores or Santa Elena and Tikal. Between Flores or Santa Elena and El Remate (later in this chapter), the fare is around Q100 to Q200 ($13–$27/£7–£14). The higher rate is for a minivan that can hold between six and eight passengers. A taxi is your best option if you decide to explore the area around the lake, but be sure to bargain, as the first price you are quoted is almost certainly above the going rate and subject to some negotiation.

BY CAR   The road between Santa Elena and Flores and Tikal is paved, well-marked, and heavily traveled. It's about 32km (20 miles) from Flores to Ixlú, and another 32km (20 miles) on to the park and ruins of Tikal.

For information on renting a car, see "Getting Around" under "Tikal," earlier in this chapter.

ORIENTATION   The town primarily known as Flores actually consists of three smaller towns that have merged. Flores proper sits on a small island out in Lake Petén Itzá, and is connected to the mainland by a long causeway. On the mainland are Santa Elena (nearest the airport) and San Benito (closer to the bus terminal and market). Whether you arrive by air or bus from Guatemala City or Belize, you'll come into town from the east. The road in from the airport leads straight through Santa Elena to the market and bus terminal, while the causeway to Flores is a right turn in the middle of Santa Elena.

FAST FACTS   There is an information booth run by the Guatemalan Tourism Commission, **INGUAT** (© **502/7926-0533;** www.visitguatemala.com), at the Flores airport, and another one in downtown Flores (© **502/7926-0669**). Both provide basic maps to the region and ruins, as well as brochures for local hotels and tour agencies. To contact the **local police,** dial © **502/7926-1365.**

There are numerous banks in downtown Flores and Santa Elena. Most have ATMs, and many of these will work with your debit or credit card. Check with your home bank and the PLUS or Cirrus systems in advance to confirm. Downtown banks in Santa Elena include **Banquetzal,** Calle 4, between avenidas 4 and 5 (© **502/7926-0711**); **Banrural,** Avenida 3 and Calle 4 (© **502/7926-1002**); and **Banco Industrial,** Avenida 6 (© **502/7926-0281**). Most of the hotels and restaurants in Flores and Santa Elena will also exchange dollars for *quetzales,* although they may give you a slightly less favorable rate than you would get at a bank.

The **Flores post office** is on the Pasaje Progresso just off the Parque Central, or Central Park, which is in front of the church. **Santa Elena's post office** is on Calle 2 and Avenida 7. Both are open Monday through Friday, 8am to 5pm. There are a host of Internet cafes around Flores and Santa Elena. I recommend **Tikal Net,** on Calle Centroamérica in Flores (© **502/7926-0655**), with more than two dozen terminals and fast connections.

WHAT TO SEE & DO

Flores is a town for walking, and the whole island is only about 5 blocks wide in any direction. At the center is a small central park or plaza, anchored by the town's Catholic church. Be sure to check out its beautiful stained-glass windows.

To learn more about the natural history and cultural traditions of Flores and El Petén, visit the **Centro de Información sobre la Naturaleza, Cultura y Artesanía de Petén (CINCAP;** © **502/7926-0718**), which is located on the square in front of the

---

Holy Bats . . . Man!

Located some 24km (15 miles) west of Tikal is another small and relatively unexcavated Maya site, **El Zotz** ℱ. *Zotz* means "bat" in the local Mayan dialect, and that's exactly what you'll find here. Each night around sunset, tens of thousands of bats exit en masse from several caves, creating a spectacular sight. You might even see a bat falcon dive into the mass and pluck out dinner. Most of the tour agencies in Flores and Santa Elena can arrange trips to El Zotz, although these tend to be hardy overnight affairs with a fair amount of hiking involved. Rates run between Q750 and Q1,500 ($100–$200/£53–£105) per person for a 3-day, 2-night excursion.

Best in Class

Eco Escuela de Español ⊛ (© **502/5940-1235**; www.ecoescuelaespanol.org) runs a community-based language school in the small village of San Andrés, on the shore of Lake Petén Itzá. The program is Q1,125 ($150/£79) per week and includes lodging, three meals daily with a local family, and 4 hours of daily (usually one-on-one) class time. The setting allows for intensive language instruction, as well as many chances to really interact with the local culture and natural surroundings.

---

church in Flores. CINCAP operates a museum with displays on the cultural and natural history of the region. Of particular interest is the exhibit on how chicle, the substance that once gave chewing gum its chewiness, is produced. There are also exhibits on the local ecology and medicinal plants of the jungle. The gift shop has locally made baskets, woodcarvings, and carved bone reproductions of ancient Maya artifacts.

One of the most popular things to do in Flores is to **tour the lake** ⊛. You'll be approached by freelancers offering tours, or ask your hotel or one of the local tour agencies. Be sure to inspect the craft beforehand to make sure you feel comfortable with its lake-worthiness. Also, make sure your guide is bilingual. These tours last anywhere from 1 to 3 hours, and usually include stops at La Guitarra Island, which features a picnic and swimming area, as well as at the mostly unexcavated ruins of Tayasal. Here, be sure to climb **El Mirador** ⊛, a lakeside pyramid that offers a fabulous view of Flores. Many of these tours also stop at the small **Petencito Zoo** and **ARCAS** (www.arcasguatemala.com), a conservation organization and animal rehabilitation center that has some interpretive trails and displays of rescued animals either in recuperation or unable to be released. These tours cost Q75 to Q190 ($10–$25/£5.25–£13) per person, depending on the length of the tour and the size of your group. Don't be afraid to bargain.

You can also explore the lake on your own in a kayak or canoe, which are rented throughout Flores. Again, ask your hotel or one of the local tour agencies. Rates for kayaks and canoes run around Q15 ($2/£1.05) per hour. Be careful paddling around the lake; when the winds pick up, especially in the afternoons, it can get quite choppy and challenging.

If you're a spelunker, you might want to explore **Aktun Kan (Cave of the Serpent)**, a large cavern just outside Santa Elena. The cave takes its name from a legend about a giant snake living there. (Don't worry, it's only a legend.) Yet another legend has it that this cave is connected to a cave beneath the church on Flores. To reach Aktun Kan, either walk south out of Santa Elena on the road that crosses the causeway from Flores, or ask a taxi to take you there. The fare should be around Q15 ($2/£1.05). Although there are lights in the cave, be sure to bring a flashlight. Admission is Q15 ($2/£1.05).

There are a host of local tour operators that can arrange any of the tours listed above, as well as guided tours to Tikal and the ruins listed below. The best of these are **Martsam Travel** ⊛ (© **502/7926-0346**; www.martsam.com) and **Tikal Tours** (© **502/7926-4796**).

OTHER NEARBY RUINS

If the Tikal ruins in El Petén piqued your interest in Maya history, visit some of the more remote ruins of the region, which will have you traveling through uninhabited jungles and encountering a great deal of wildlife including coatimundis, howler and spider monkeys, anteaters, tapirs, and possibly even jaguars.

YAXHA   Yaxhá 🐾🐾 may be the third-largest Maya ceremonial city in Guatemala (after Tikal and El Mirador), but it wasn't until it hosted the TV show *Survivor: Guatemala* that it became one of the prime archaeological sites for visitors.

Although it's currently being excavated, Yaxhá still has the feel of newly discovered ruins. At one point, Yaxhá supported a population of more than 20,000, and more than 400 buildings, five acropolises, and three ball courts have been discovered here.

The tallest structure here, Temple 216, is located in the East Acropolis, and provides excellent views of lakes Yaxhá and Sacnab, as well as the surrounding rainforests. Yaxhá is one of the few Maya cities to retain its traditional Mayan name, which translates to "green waters." You should combine a visit to Yaxhá with a trip to the ruins of **Topoxté,** which are located on a small island in Lake Yaxhá. This small yet intriguing site is thought to have been a residential city for local elites. However, it was also a fortified city where Maya warriors put up a valiant defense against Spanish forces. Many organized tours also include a stop at the nearby ruins of **Nakum.** The turnoff for the 11km (7-mile) dirt road into the site is located about 32km (20 miles) east of Ixlú. The Q75 ($10/£5.25) admission grants you access to Yaxhá, Topoxté, and Nakum.

If you want to stay right on the lake at Yaxhá and just a stone's throw away from the archaeological site, check out **Campamento Ecológico El Sombrero** (© 502/7861-1687; www.ecosombrero.com), which has comfortable, but basic, rooms in thatch-roof bungalows. About half of the bungalows come with private bathrooms, the rest with shared bathrooms. They also allow camping, and even rent out hammocks with mosquito netting under a common shelter.

Warning: You'll probably be warned (and see the signs), but just in case, do not be tempted to swim in Lake Yaxhá—it's home to a robust population of crocodiles.

EL CEIBAL   This is another popular site to see ruins, and offers one of the most scenic routes along the way. To reach **El Ceibal** 🐾, head from Flores to Sayaxché (about 65km/40 miles), which is a good-size town with a few basic hotels. From Sayaxché, you must hire a boat to take you 18km (11 miles) up the Río de la Pasión. The Late Classic–era ruins here are known for having the only circular temple in all of El Petén. There are also several well-preserved stelae arranged around one small temple structure on the central plaza, as well as a ball court. Many of the designs at El Ceibal indicate that the city had extensive contact with cities in the Yucatán, but whether this contact was due to trade or warfare is unclear. Your best bet for visiting El Ceibal is to book an excursion with one of the tour agencies in Flores or Santa Elena. Full-day trips run around Q450 to Q600 ($60–$80/£32–£42). Overnight trips can also be arranged, combining a visit to El Ceibal to even more obscure Maya sites such as **Aguateca** and **Petexbatún.** These trips are around Q675 to Q1,125 ($90–$150/£47–£79).

If you get to Sayaxché on your own, look for **Viajes Don Pedro** (© 502/7928-6109). These folks run regular boats to El Ceibal and charge around Q225 ($30/£16) per person round-trip. However, if you have a group, be sure to try and negotiate a flat rate for the boat, which should carry anywhere from four to eight people. If you want to stay in the area, check out **Chiminos Island Lodge** 🐾🐾 (© 502/2471-0855; www.chiminosisland.com), which has six (almost) luxurious cabins in the rainforest on a small island in the waters of the Petexbatún Lagoon.

UAXACTUN   Uaxactún (pronounced "wah-shahk-*toon*") is yet another Maya ceremonial center, located 24km (15 miles) north of Tikal. Though many of the pyramids and temples here have been uncovered, they have not been restored as extensively as those at Tikal. Uaxactún also hosts what is believed to be the oldest known astrological observatory yet discovered in the Maya world. Watch the sunset from the observatory temple, located in Group E on the eastern side of the ruins, and see the sun line up precisely with other temples on the equinoxes and solstices. Your best bet for visiting El Ceibal is to book the excursion with one of the tour agencies in Flores or Santa Elena. Full-day trips cost about Q300 to Q450 ($40–$60/£21–£32), and can be combined with a stop at Tikal, although I think that's trying to cram too much into a single day. If you have your own 4WD vehicle, you can drive here yourself. The ruins at Uaxactún are open daily from 6am to 6pm, and no admission is charged. However, you must pass through Tikal National Park, therefore incurring the Tikal entrance fee of Q50 ($6.65/£3.50). Keep in mind that the dirt road between Uaxactún is sometimes not passable during the rainy season, so be sure to ask locally about current conditions before heading off.

WHERE TO STAY

There are a host of budget lodgings in San Benito, especially around the bus terminal, but I strongly advise travelers to stick to Santa Elena and Flores proper.

MODERATE

Hotel Del Patio ☼   The rooms here may be simple, but they're clean, modern, and comfortable. Opt for a second-floor unit so you can admire the tall fountain in the central courtyard. There's a midsize pool and small gym, as well as a good international restaurant. This place is run by the Camino Real corporation, which also runs the Camino Real Tikal (see later in this chapter).

Calle 8 and Av. 2, Santa Elena. ℂ 502/7926-0104. Fax 502/7926-1229. www.hoteldelpatio.com.gt. 21 units. Q490–Q600 ($65–$80/£34–£42) double. Rates include breakfast. AE, MC, V. **Amenities:** Restaurant; bar; pool; small gym; tour desk; limited room service (6:30am–10pm); laundry service. *In room:* A/C, TV.

Hotel Isla de Flores ☼   This four-story hotel in downtown Flores is intimate and charming. The decor and architecture feature a mix of modern and colonial elements. The rooms are compact, but clean and comfortable. Most come with two double beds, a good-size cable television, and a tiny balcony. The rooms on the higher floors have good views over the town and lake. A couple of rooms are set up for larger groups or families, while others have no balcony or view to speak of. This place has a helpful tour desk, and is run by the same folks who have the Jungle Lodge inside Tikal National Park.

Av. La Reforma, Flores. ℂ 502/7926-0614 or 502/2476-8775. Fax 502/2476-0294. www.junglelodge.guate.com. 18 units. Q400 ($53/£28) double. Rate includes breakfast. AE, MC, V. **Amenities:** Restaurant; bar; tour desk; laundry service. *In room:* A/C, TV.

Hotel Maya Internacional   Built on the banks of the lake more than 30 years ago, this hotel has had to contend with the rising lake waters and growing competition. In fact, some of its stiffest competition comes from its sister hotel, Villa Maya (see below), which I find to be a better option. Most of the rooms are set on a small hillside just off the lake. Despite their age, the rooms are well kept and comfortable, with clean tile floors and plenty of space; most have beautiful lake-view balconies. The setting is excellent, and a bay full of water lilies has formed between the hotel's bungalows. The pool has been built with an infinity effect that makes it appear to blend into the lake. The hotel's restaurant is in a separate, larger structure at the end of a short causeway on a patch of land that juts into the lake, and features a beautiful dining area with an impressive high-pitched thatch roof.

Calle 1 and Av. 8, Santa Elena. © 502/7926-2083 or 502/2334-1818. Fax 502/7926-0087 or 502/2334-8134. www.villasdeguatemala.com. 26 units. Q525 ($70/£37) double. AE, DC, MC, V. **Amenities:** Restaurant; pool; small gym; tour desk; laundry service. *In room:* A/C, TV, no phone.

Hotel Petén Espléndido   This modern upscale hotel in Santa Elena sits just off the causeway on the shore of Lake Petén Itzá, and offers a great view of Flores. Thanks to a complete remodel, the rooms feature contemporary decor and more modern amenities than you'll find anywhere around. There are telephones in the bathrooms (a big deal here), and four rooms are truly fitted for travelers with disabilities. The best rooms are on the second floor and have balconies directly fronting the lake. If you don't get one of these, the hotel's waterfront restaurant has a great view and serves good international and local cuisine, or there's always the pool and Jacuzzi. The hotel offers a free airport shuttle and free paddle boats for use on the lake, and also has a helpful tour desk and concierge.

1a Calle 5-01, Zona 1, Santa Elena. © 888/790-5264 in the U.S. and Canada, 502/2360-8140 in Guatemala City, or 502/7926-0880. Fax 502/7926-0866. www.petenesplendido.com. 62 units. Q525–Q750 ($70–$100/£37–£53) double. AE, DC, MC, V. **Amenities:** Restaurant; pool and Jacuzzi; watersports equipment rental; concierge; tour desk; car-rental desk; limited room service (6:30am–11:30pm); laundry service. *In room:* A/C, TV, dataport, hair dryer, safe.

Hotel Villa Maya ⚆   This is one of the most luxurious lodgings near Flores and Santa Elena. Hotel Villa Maya is located about 5 minutes from the airport, on the shores of Lake Petén Itzá, but away from the twin cities and toward Tikal. Peace and quiet, if that's what you're looking for, are an added bonus, on top of the 10 minutes of reduced travel time to the ruins. However, if you want to take advantage of the restaurants and tour options in Flores, you'll need either your own car or a taxi. Rooms are housed in a series of two-story buildings, set on the edge of the lake. Local hardwoods are used generously to trim details and furnish the place. The rooms are spacious and clean; each comes with a small triangular balcony overlooking the lake. The restaurant serves respectable but uninspired Guatemalan and international fare. The hotel also has a pool with a cascading waterfall, as well as a wonderful dock and deck area over the lake.

15 min. from Santa Elena Internacional Airport on Lake Petenchel, 4km (2½ miles) north of the well-marked turnoff on the road from Santa Elena to Tikal. © 502/7926-1276 or 502/2334-1818. Fax 502/7926-0032 or 502/2334-8134. www.villasdeguatemala.com. 56 units. Q640 ($85/£45) double. AE, MC, V. **Amenities:** Restaurant; pool and Jacuzzi; watersports equipment rental; tour desk; car-rental desk; bicycle rental; room service 7am–10pm; laundry service. *In room:* A/C, TV.

La Casona del Lago ⚆⚆   This is the newest and most luxurious hotel in the area, and is run by the same folks as La Casona de la Isla (below). Though this property isn't located on Flores proper, it's right on the shores of the lake, and has excellent views of its waters and the city. The rooms are spacious enough to fit two double beds, a few chairs, and a separate desk area, and each features white tile floors and a 21-inch television. The hotel has a pool and Jacuzzi, and even has wireless access, a rarity in this remote area.

1a Calle, Zona 1, Santa Elena. ©/fax 502/7952-8700. www.hotelesdepeten.com. 32 units. Q625–Q680 ($83–$91/£44–£48) double. AE, DC, MC, V. **Amenities:** Restaurant; pool and Jacuzzi; tour desk; laundry service. *In room:* A/C, TV, dataport, hair dryer.

INEXPENSIVE

Casa Elena ☆ (*Value*) If a business hotel existed, or even needed to exist, in this area, Casa Elena would be it. This immaculately clean, small hotel in downtown Santa Elena is conveniently located across the street from a park and taxi stand, and is just 1 block from the causeway to Flores. Rooms are a bit cozy and don't come with a balcony, but you do get a view of either the lovely interior courtyard, the park, or the hotel's pool, which is a hit with kids because of the small water slide. There's also a simple restaurant as well as an inviting rooftop terrace and bar. The hotel has a friendly air to it, and makes a good base for exploring the region.

Av. 6 and Calle 2, Santa Elena. (② **502/7926-2235**. Fax 502/7926-0097. www.casaelena.com. 28 units. Q225–Q300 ($30–$40/£16–£21) double. AE, DC, MC, V. **Amenities:** Restaurant; pool; tour desk; limited room service (7am–10pm); laundry service. *In room:* A/C, TV.

Hotel Petén From the street this hotel looks very modest, but enter the doorway, and you'll find a small courtyard with tropical plants, a tiny semi-indoor pool, and a nice brick-and-stucco building with several floors. The rooms have all been well kept and steadily improved over the years. The best rooms are those on the top two floors, and have private balconies with excellent lake views. In fact, only five rooms here don't have a lake view, so be sure to request one. There's also a popular restaurant on the ground floor. These folks have an excellent local tour company and a couple of other nearby hotels if this one is full.

Calle Centroamérica, Flores. (②/fax **502/7926-0692** or 502/7926-0593. www.hotelesdepeten.com. 21 units. Q340–Q375 ($45–$50/£24–£26) double. AE, DC, MC, V. **Amenities:** Restaurant; pool; Jacuzzi; tour desk; laundry service. *In room:* A/C, TV.

Hotel Santana ☆ (*Value*) If you're looking to snag a lakefront room at an affordable price, this is a great choice. Most of the rooms here have balconies (the third and fourth floors have the best views), but be sure you get a lake-view room and not one of the less desirable interior ones. Rooms here are cool, clean, and spacious, and are a cut above other Flores options in a similar price range. The large open-air dining room is a delightful place to sit and enjoy the lakeside setting, and there's a pool with a built-in waterfall and swim-up bar in a courtyard to the side.

Calle 30 de Junio, Flores. (②/fax **502/7926-0262** or 502/7926-0491. www.santanapeten.com. 35 units. Q300–Q375 ($40–$50/£21–£27) double. AE, MC, V. **Amenities:** Restaurant; pool; tour desk; laundry service. *In room:* A/C, TV, safe.

Jaguar Inn Santa Elena This hotel (operated by the same people who run the Jaguar Inn at Tikal) is one of the best budget hotels in Santa Elena. Guest rooms all have high ceilings and tile floors, and are decorated with Guatemalan textiles and art. Art Deco wall sconces add a touch of class here in the wilderness, and for an extra $5, you can get a room with air-conditioning. There's a garden in the courtyard and an open-air restaurant and lounge. To find the hotel, look for the sign on the left as you come into town from the airport. The only drawback here is that it's a bit of a walk to Flores, which is where most of the action—whatever action there is to speak of—is.

Calzada Rodríguez Macal 8-79, Zona 1, Santa Elena. (② **502/7926-0002**. Fax 502/926-2413. www.jaguartikal.com. 19 units. Q150–Q190 ($20–$25/£11–£13) double. AE, MC, V. **Amenities:** Restaurant; tour desk; laundry service. *In room:* TV, no phone.

La Casona de la Isla La Casona de la Isla shows the same attention to service as the other properties run by this local hotel group. The guest rooms here are all fairly small and lack much in the way of style, but they do have tile floors, ceiling fans, and air-conditioning (although some of the air-conditioning units can be rather old and noisy). Most rooms come with a private balcony, and almost all of these have good views of the lake. The L-shaped hotel is built around a stone terrace with lush gardens and a small swimming pool featuring a sculpted stone waterfall and separate Jacuzzi. The hotel's restaurant serves good Guatemalan and international fare in a small dining room off the lobby as well as on a back patio bar with an excellent view overlooking the lake.

Calle 30 de Junio, Flores. © **502/7926-0523** or 502/7926-0593. www.hotelesdepeten.com. 26 units. Q360–Q400 ($48–$53/£26–£28) double. AE, DC, MC, V. **Amenities:** Restaurant; bar; pool; Jacuzzi; tour desk; laundry service. *In room:* A/C, TV.

WHERE TO DINE

There are tons of places to eat around Flores and Santa Elena. Most are simple, serving local and Mexican cuisine and geared toward locals and the backpacking crowd. Many of the hotels listed above have restaurants serving dependable food. **El Mirador Restaurant** at the Hotel Petén Espléndido (p. 215) serves good, but far from spectacular, international fare; however, the setting is certainly the most elegant you'll find in this neck of the woods.

In addition to the places listed below, **Pizzería Picasso,** Calle 15 de Setiembre, across from El Tucán (© **502/7926-0673**), serves pretty good wood-oven pizza and a variety of pastas.

Capitán Tortuga INTERNATIONAL   This popular restaurant has a large menu with everything from barbecued ribs, pizza, and vegetarian shish kabobs to a wide range of coffee and espresso drinks, ice cream, and freshly baked desserts. Request a table on the small outdoor patio that fronts the lake or in the second floor, open-air dining room, which is reached from a stairway out back. Service can be slow at times, but if you're with a group or sharing a drink with fellow travelers, you might not mind.

Calle 30 de Junio, next to La Casona de la Isla, Flores. © **502/7926-0247.** Main courses Q30–Q120 ($4–$16/£2.10–£8.40). MC, V. Daily 11:30am–11pm.

La Luna ✦✦ *Finds* INTERNATIONAL   This hip little restaurant is the most creative and refined option in Flores. The menu includes appetizers such as stuffed pepper and falafel, while entrees include steak in pepper sauce, lobster tails, and a host of fish and chicken—and even some vegetarian—options. There are three separate dining areas—all artistically decorated—with my favorite featuring a faux ceiba tree in the center and a wild wood and mirror sculpture.

Calle 30 de Junio, across from La Casona de la Isla, Flores. © **502/7926-3346.** Main courses Q40–Q120 ($5.30–$16/£2.80–£8.40). MC, V. Tues–Sun 11am–11pm.

Maya Princess Café ✦ *Value* INTERNATIONAL   This perennially popular backpacker haunt serves hearty and well-prepared international fare. Heavy wooden tables are covered with colorful local textiles, and the walls are painted a hot pink. Portions are quite filling, and local cuisine and Mexican staples are complemented by some daring (for El Petén, at least) additions like green chicken curry and shrimp tempura. You can also catch fairly recent movies on a large screen here nightly at 9pm. Come early if you want a decent seat.

Av. Reforma at the corner of 10 de Noviembre, Flores. © **502/7926-3797.** Reservations not accepted. Main courses Q30–Q90 ($4–$12/£2.10–£6.30). AE, MC, V. Tues–Sun 7am–10pm.

Restaurant El Tucán GUATEMALAN/MEXICAN   This popular Flores restaurant serves primarily Mexican food—and large portions of it—so be sure to bring an appetite. Entrees include fresh fish and, occasionally, wild game, as well as a number of vegetarian dishes. The guacamole is a must, as is a seat in one of the two open-air dining rooms fronting the lake. There's also a small, very basic hotel here.

Calle Centroamérica 45, Flores. ℂ **502/7926-0536.** Main courses Q23–Q75 ($3–$10/£1.60–£5.25). AE, MC, V. Daily 8am–9:30pm.

FLORES & SANTA ELENA AFTER DARK

Most folks simply frequent the bar at their hotel or stick around after dinner at one of the local restaurants. Thanks to its movie showings and convivial atmosphere, the **Maya Princess Café** (see above) is probably the most happening place in town. However, it's been getting a run for its money from **Las Puertas,** at the corner of Calle Centroamérica and Avenida Santa Ana (ℂ **502/7926-1061**), which has been playing a mix of house and chill dance tunes in its hip little space, and sometimes has live music.

3 El Remate ⓧⓧ

32km (20 miles) E of Flores; 32km (20 miles) S of Tikal; 60km (37 miles) W of Melchor de Mencos

The small village of El Remate, located on the eastern shores of Lake Petén Itzá, is rapidly becoming a popular spot to stay while visiting Tikal. Its midway location between Flores and Tikal keeps you closer to the ruins but also in a much more tranquil and pristine environment than Flores or Santa Elena. Currently, you'll find budget lodgings in the village, while more upscale options can be found on the shores of the lake heading north out of the village.

ESSENTIALS
GETTING THERE
BY PLANE   See "By Plane" under "Essentials" in "Tikal," earlier in this chapter.

BY MINIVAN   Scheduled and independent minivans ply the route between Santa Elena/Flores and Tikal throughout the day. Any of these will drop you off in El Remate. For more information, see "Getting Around" under "Tikal," earlier in this chapter, and below. Fares from Flores to El Remate run around Q25 to Q35 ($3.35–$4.65/£1.75–£2.45).

BY CAR   El Remate is located about a mile north of Ixlú on the road between Santa Elena and Tikal. The road is well-paved from Flores and Santa Elena, as well as to Tikal and the Belize-Guatemala border, 60km (37 miles) to the east.

GETTING AROUND   El Remate is tiny, and you can easily walk anywhere in town. Some of the hotels listed below are located a mile or so north of the village, on the road that circles Lake Petén Itzá. If you're in El Remate, you'll most likely want to go to Tikal, visit Santa Elena and Flores, or explore the region.

BY TAXI   Taxis charge between Q150 and Q350 ($20–$47/£11–£25) for the one-way trip between El Remate and Tikal, and between Q100 and Q200 ($13–$27/£7–£14) for the trip between El Remate and Santa Elena or Flores. The higher rates are for a minivan that can hold anywhere from six to eight passengers. A taxi is your best option if you decide to explore the area around the lake. There are often taxis hanging around town. If not, your hotel can call one for you. Be sure to have your hotel set a fair price, or be prepared to bargain, as the first price you are quoted is likely to be above the going rate and subject to some negotiation.

BY MINIVAN   If you don't have a car, the best way to get around is by minivan. Scheduled and unscheduled minivans ply the route between Flores and Tikal throughout the day. All of these pass through El Remate, dropping off and picking up passengers. You can get a minivan at almost any hotel in El Remate, or walk a few hundred yards out to the main road to Tikal and flag one down. The ride takes about a half-hour to either Tikal or Flores, and the one-way fare is Q25 to Q35 ($3.35–$4.65/£1.75–£2.45) per person.

WHAT TO SEE & DO

Most people use El Remate as a base for trips to the ruins at Tikal. However, as small lodges and isolated resorts start to pop up here, so do the many tour and activity options.

Just west of El Remate is the **Biotopo Cerro Cahuí,** a small nature reserve with some trails and good wildlife-viewing opportunities. More than 180 species of birds have been spotted here. A couple of loop trails climb uphill from the entrance and offer excellent views of the lake. I recommend you visit this park with a guide, as incidents of violence against tourists closed it for a period a few years ago. The reserve is open daily from 7:30am to 4pm, and admission is Q20 ($2.65/£1.40).

One of the most popular activities in El Remate is **renting a canoe or kayak** and going out on the lake. Most of the hotels in town rent these, or can arrange it for you. Rates run around Q10 to Q15 ($1.35–$2/70p–£1.05) per hour, or around Q75 ($10/£5.25) per day.

> *Moments* **Lake View**
>
> If you're out on the lake during the daytime, scan the shoreline north-west of El Remate, and try to pick out the "Sleeping Crocodile," a silhouette formed by the shape of the forested hills as they descend toward the lake. If you can't find it, ask a local for help.

Similarly, most of the hotels in town either rent or provide **mountain bikes** for guests or can arrange one for you. The dirt road that circles Lake Petén Itzá is excellent for a mountain bike ride. Rates are about Q35 to Q75 ($4.65–$10/£2.45–5.25) per day.

If you want to explore the area by horseback, check with your hotel, or head to **Mirador del Duende** (see below).

El Remate is also gaining some local renown for its woodcarving. You'll see several roadside stands set up on the route between Ixlú and El Remate, and onward to Tikal. If you ask around El Remate, you might even be able to visit one or more of the artisans.

WHERE TO STAY & DINE

Most visitors eat at their hotels, but there are some *comedores* in the center of the village, as well as a small market. If you're looking for something different, try the restaurant at the **Hotel Mon Ami** (© 502/7928-8413).

On the route between the Petén Province and Río Dulce lies a wonderful isolated ecolodge, **Finca Ixobel** (© **502/5410-4307** or 502/7927-8590; www.fincaixobel.com), which is about 100km (62 miles) away from both Flores and Río Dulce.

Accommodations include a campground, dorm rooms, and private thatch-roof bungalows. Plus, there's an inviting lake for swimming and plenty of nearby rainforests, caves, and rivers to explore.

VERY EXPENSIVE

Camino Real Tikal ⊛   While Camino Real Tikal is no longer the only luxury option in the Petén, this modern resort, set on a hillside above the lake, is still a good choice. The bungalows are set in a long line along a ridge over the lake, and all have wonderful lake views. Inside, the rooms are spacious and feature contemporary and tasteful decor, as well as a range of modern amenities. Every room has a private balcony or porch; the third-floor units have the best views. There are two restaurants and a lovely outdoor pool area, while down by the water there's a dock out into the lake, a sandy beach area for swimming, and a wood-fired sauna. The hotel offers a free shuttle to the park and the airport in Flores.

3 miles (5km) west of El Remate. © **502/7926-0204.** Fax 502/7926-0222. www.caminorealtikal.com.gt. 72 units. Q900 ($120/£63) double. AE, DISC, MC, V. **Amenities:** 2 restaurants; 2 bars; lounge; pool; 2 outdoor unlit tennis courts; bicycle rental; watersports equipment rental; tour desk; laundry service. *In room:* A/C, TV, fridge, safe.

La Lancha Resort ⊛⊛ *(Finds)*   This is the latest addition to filmmaker Francis Ford Coppola's hotel dynasty in the Maya world. The main lodge has a commanding view of the lake, and features a soaring thatch roof oriented toward the view. The pool is located below the lodge, and a steep trail leads down to the lakeshore, where you'll find a swimming area and some canoes and kayaks. The rooms are all duplex bungalows, with the six "lake view" units more spacious than the cozy "jungle view" rooms. All are tastefully and artistically decorated, very comfortable, and feature a shared wooden veranda with views of either the jungle or the lake (hence the room names).

Lago Petén Itzá. © **800/746-3743** in the U.S., or ©/fax 502/7928-8331 in Guatemala. www.lalanchavillage.com. 10 units. Q1,012–Q1,575 ($135–$210/£71–£111) double. Rates lower in the off season, higher during peak periods. AE, MC, V. **Amenities:** Restaurant; bar; pool; bike rental; tour desk; laundry service. *In room:* No phone.

MODERATE

La Mansión del Pájaro Serpiente ⊛ *(Finds)*   Set off the main road to Tikal on a hillside overlooking the lake, this place has both standard and deluxe bungalows, beautiful gardens, and a friendly atmosphere. The bungalows feature beautiful stone and woodwork details and local textiles and crafts. The best rooms have four-poster king-size beds and a separate sitting area, and are large enough to be classified as junior suites. The small pool is set among lush gardens, and the open-air restaurant, specializing in local cuisine, has a great view of the lake.

El Remate. ©/fax **502/7926-4246** or 502/7926-0065. 10 units. Q300 ($40/£21) double; Q600 ($80/£42) deluxe double. MC, V. **Amenities:** Restaurant; bar; pool and Jacuzzi; tour desk; laundry service. *In room:* No phone.

INEXPENSIVE

In addition to the places listed below, there are a few very inexpensive options in El Remate catering to backpackers; simply walk around and see which one fits your fancy and budget. Reliable favorites include **Casa de Doña Tonita** (© **502/5701-7114**) and **Mirador del Duende** (© **502/5806-2231**), while **Hotel Mon Ami** (© **502/ 7928-8413;** www.hotelmonami.com) is a newer option.

Hotel Gringo Perdido   Three kilometers (2 miles) north of El Remate on the rough road that circles Lake Petén Itzá, you'll find one of Guatemala's oldest jungle lodges, Hotel Gringo Perdido ("the lost Gringo"). This offbeat paradise is arranged along the lakeshore, with shady hillside gardens, a restaurant, a quiet camping area, and rooms ranging from a simple dormitory to some almost-plush private bungalows. The whole thing appears to get swallowed up by the rainforest. The hotel, which borders the Biotopo Cerro Cahui nature reserve, offers good swimming in the lake, 3km (2 miles) of nature trails, and tranquillity.

3km (2 miles) west of El Remate. ℃/fax **502/2334-2305** or ℃ 502/5404-6822. www.hotelgringoperdido.com. 15 units. Q225 ($30/£16) per person with shared bathroom; Q300 ($40/£21) per person with private bathroom. Rates include breakfast and dinner. Q30 ($4/£2.10) per person to camp with meals extra. MC, V. **Amenities:** Restaurant; tour desk; laundry service. *In room:* No phone.

La Casa de Don David Hotel *(Value)*   David Kuhn was the original *gringo perdido* ("the lost Gringo") of the nearby nature lodge (see above), but left there to open this delightful place. Rooms here are clean and simple, and about half have air-conditioning. There's an open-air octagonal hammock hut for reading and resting (you can catch a glimpse of Lake Petén from here), and the hotel offers bicycles free for guest use. David and his wife Rosita have lived in this area for almost 30 years, and are a wealth of information and advice.

El Remate. ℃ **502/5306-2190** or 502/7928-8469. www.lacasadedondavid.com. 15 units. Q240–Q420 ($32–$56/ £17–£29) double. Rates include 1 meal (breakfast, lunch, or dinner). MC, V. **Amenities:** Restaurant; tour desk; laundry service. *In room:* No phone.

EL REMATE AFTER DARK

El Remate is a quiet village, and most visitors head to the small bar at their hotel or hostel to chat with fellow travelers. Some, however, head out to the lake to see the crocodiles by the light of a high-powered flashlight or headlamp. Two-hour tours, which can be arranged through your hotel, are headed by a guide, who will scan the shore and inlets for the red reflection of the crocodiles' eyes. If you're lucky, they won't submerge as you slowly approach. The cost is between Q75 and Q150 ($10–$20/ £5.25–£11).

9

Central Guatemala:
Las Verapaces, El Oriente & Copán

Verapaz translates to "true peace," but its history reveals a path of destruction blazed by the Spanish conquistadors who met unprecedented resistance in the high mountains of this region. The fierce resistance was such that the Spaniards dubbed the area Tierra de Guerra (Land of War). In the early 16th century, a groundbreaking human-rights activist, the Dominican priest **Fray Bartolomé de las Casas,** proposed the use of gentle persuasion, "evangelical love," and religious conversion instead of outright suppression. De las Casas's tactic was so successful that by 1545, Prince Phillip of Spain renamed the region Verapaz, and prohibited the use of the name Tierra de Guerra.

Today, the high mountains, dense forest, and rugged terrain offer a sense of peaceful respite from the more hectic and crowded destinations of Guatemala's Western Highlands. The Verapaz region is actually divided into two, hence Las Verapaces. This is a heavily indigenous region, and the Mayan languages of Q'eqchi and Pocomchí are dominant rather than Spanish.

Cobán, which is a budding adventure tourism hot spot, is the most important city in the Verapaz region, and makes an excellent base from which to explore Las Verapaces. The region south and east of Las Verapaces is known as **El Oriente,** or "the East." While it has no significant draw for tourists, it's home to the historic city of **Esquipulas,** near the southeastern border by Honduras. The magnificent Basílica and famous **"Black Christ"** are revered by Roman Catholics who travel from throughout Guatemala and the world on pilgrimage. Just over the border, in Honduras, lay the Maya ruins of **Copán,** one of the most important classic Maya archaeological sites yet discovered, with perhaps the best preserved and displayed collection of stone carvings and stelae.

1 Cobán ⊛

213km (132 miles) E of Guatemala City; 583km (362 miles) S of Tikal

Cobán is the most important city in the Verapaz region, and serves as the social and commercial hub for all the surrounding towns, villages, and tourist destinations. Cobán is still known as the "Ciudad Imperial," as it was dubbed by the Spanish crown when it was founded in 1538. The city sits at more than 1,300m (4,000 ft.) and enjoys a cool, yet wet, climate. (Cool mist or outright rain are common here.) Cobán is also the gateway for some of Guatemala's best eco- and adventure-tourism destinations and activities.

Las Verapaces

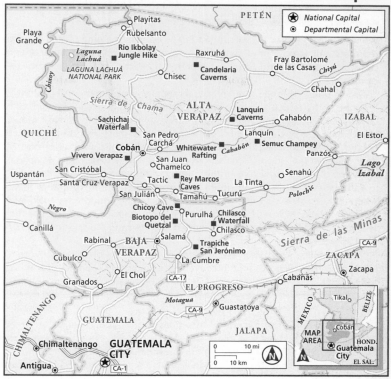

ESSENTIALS

GETTING THERE

BY BUS **Monja Blanca** (© **502/2251-1878** in Guatemala City, or 502/7951-1793 in Cobán; www.autopullmanmonjablanca.com) has buses leaving every half-hour between 1:30am and 5pm. Their station in Guatemala City is at 8a Av. 15-16, Zona 1. In Cobán, the buses leave from 2a Calle 2-77, Zona 4. The fare is Q30 ($4/£2.10) each way.

You can also use Cobán as a convenient midway point either to or from Tikal and the Petén, or Lago Izabal, Río Dulce, and the Caribbean coast.

BY CAR If you have a car, take the Carretera al Atlántico (CA-9) out of Guatemala City to the crossroads at El Rancho. The exit and road to Cobán is well marked.

GETTING AROUND

Cobán is very compact, though the very center of the city sits atop a plateau with steep hills on all sides, making walking strenuous at times. Taxis are plentiful and inexpensive. If you can't flag one down, have your hotel call you one, or try **Hilario Morales** (© **502/5561-1058**) or **Rigoberto Cermeño** (© **502/5212-3033**).

Fun Fact   Coffee & Cardamom

While Guatemala was one of United Fruit Company's quintessential banana republics and is now most famous for its shade-grown, volcanic mountain coffee, it's also the world's principal exporter of another agricultural product—cardamom.

Grown primarily in the Alta Verapaz mountains near Cobán, cardamom was brought to the region as a cash crop by German immigrants in the mid–20th century. Like coffee, this aromatic spice thrives in the area's cool, moist mountain climate. Today, cardamom is Guatemala's fourth-most-important cash crop behind coffee, bananas, and sugar. Some 200,000 people earn all or part of their wages in the industry. Small producers—farmers with less than 4 hectares (10 acres) of land—grow 70% of the country's cardamom crop.

Cardamom is an important ingredient in the curries and cuisine of India, where it's also believed to be a medicinal herb and an antidote for snake and scorpion venom. In Scandinavia, the spice is used to flavor bread and pastries, and across the Middle East, it's often added to coffee and thought to be a powerful aphrodisiac.

In Guatemala, keep your eye out for cardamom-flavored chewing gum, *chicle de cardamomo*. It's sold in convenience stores and supermarkets across the country.

If you're going to any of the nearby attractions such Semuc Champey or the Candelaria Caves, your best bet is to join a tour. Alternately, you can get to most of these places on a local bus. Ask your hotel for current times and departure locations.

Renting a car once you arrive in Cobán is also a good option. Check out **Tabarini Rent A Car** (✆ **502/7952-1504;** www.tabarini.com) or **Safari Rent A Car** (✆ **502/7952-1175**). Rates run around Q338 to Q675 ($45–$90/£24–£47) per day depending on whether you opt for a compact sedan or small SUV.

ORIENTATION   Cobán's central plaza is a long, thin trapezoid, with the Catholic church, Catedral de Santo Domingo, at the widest, eastern end. This spot has the highest elevation in town, and is also the busiest.

FAST FACTS   The **post office** is located at 2a Calle 2-02, Zona 3 (✆ **502/7951-4476**). Most hotels have their own Internet cafes, and there are many around downtown Cobán, such as the ones at **Café El Tirol** and **Hostal Doña Victoria.** (See below.)

There are several **banks** and **ATMs** within a block or two of the city's central plaza. Dial ✆ **502/7952-1225** for the **police,** ✆ **502/7952-1459** for the **Red Cross.** If you need medical attention, head to the **Centro Médico Galeno,** 2a Calle 3-08, Zona 3 (✆ **502/7951-3175**).

WHAT TO SEE & DO

While many of this region's principal attractions are outside of Cobán, the city and its immediate environs have a lot to offer visitors.

On a hill overlooking the city sits the **Templo El Calvario** ✿, an 1810 church with a beautifully restored facade. You'll have to climb a flight of steep and broad steps

Cobán

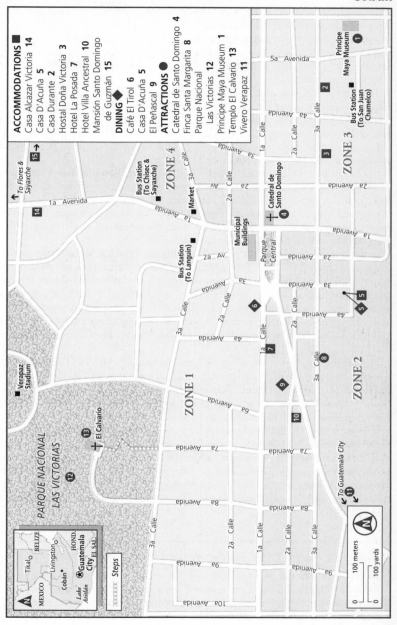

ACCOMMODATIONS ■
Casa Alcazar Victoria **14**
Casa D'Acuña **5**
Casa Durante **2**
Hostal Doña Victoria **3**
Hotel La Posada **7**
Hotel Villa Ancestral **10**
Mansión Santo Domingo
de Guzmán **15**

DINING ◆
Café El Tirol **6**
Casa D'Acuña **5**
El Peñascal **9**

ATTRACTIONS ●
Catedral de Santo Domingo **4**
Finca Santa Margarita **8**
Parque Nacional
Las Victorias **12**
Príncipe Maya Museum **1**
Templo El Calvario **13**
Vivero Verapaz **11**

before reaching the commanding view, and on the way you'll pass a series of altars used for specific prayers—health, love, wealth, success. It's believed that this site has been sacred to the local Maya for millennia, and the ongoing prayers here still bear the Maya influence. El Calvario is located at the north end of 7a Avenida. *Warning:* Avoid this area after dark or when there are few other people around, as attacks and robberies have occurred.

The city's main Catholic church, the **Catedral de Santo Domingo,** was built in the mid–16th century under the direction of Fray Melchor del los Reyes. It underwent subsequent modifications in 1741, 1792, and 1965. Today, the most interesting feature of this church is its massive whitewashed facade, which is rather plain and lacking ornamentation, but impressive in its size and antiquity. Inside you'll find a decent collection of colonial-era religious art and sculpture.

Just north of the Templo El Calvario is the **Parque Nacional Las Victorias,** a nature reserve that's a good place for a walk, jog, or bird-watching. The park has a few trails, as well as picnic tables and open-air shelters. Camping is permitted, but I don't recommend it as it's dangerous, and there have been attacks and robberies. If you want to camp, head toward Lanquin or Semuc Champey (see below). Las Victorias park is open daily from 8am to 4pm. Admission is Q5 (65¢/35p).

In the heart of Cobán sits the small, but satisfying, **Príncipe Maya Museum** *☆☆*, 6a Av. 4-26, Zona 3 (© **502/7959-2235**). This private museum has an extensive collection of pieces ranging from utilitarian pottery and ornamental burial urns to musical instruments and elegant jewelry. There are jade inlaid teeth, a full burial reconstruction, and a panel from the Cancuen archaeological site with intricate bas-relief hieroglyphics. One of my favorite pieces here is a miniature Olmec man. The museum is open Monday through Saturday from 9am to 6pm. Admission is Q15 ($2/£1.05).

Plant enthusiasts will want to visit **Vivero Verapaz** (© **502/7951-4202**), which claims to have more than 35,000 plants, including more than 650 species of orchids. You'll also be able to check out Guatemala's national flower, Monja Blanca (White Nun). This nursery–cum–botanical garden is open daily from 9am to noon and 2 to 5pm. Admission is Q10 ($1.35/70p) and includes a guided tour.

If coffee is the only species of tropical flora that interests you, you're in luck. **Finca Santa Margarita,** 3a Calle 4-12, Zona 2 (© **502/7951-3067**), is a working coffee plantation in the heart of downtown Cobán. These folks offer a 1½-hour guided tour on the history, technique, and culture of coffee growing and processing, with a tasting afterward. Tours are available Monday through Friday from 8am to 12:30pm and 1:30 to 5pm; and Saturday 8am to noon. The cost for both admission and a tour is Q15 ($2/£1.05).

(Moments Say a Little Prayer

As you drive into Cobán, keep your eye out around Km 199. You'll see a sign for Aldea Chitul, and there on your left are a couple of small caves that are actively used as sights for Maya ritual prayers and ceremonies. If you choose to stop and observe, be respectful, and do not take photos.

(*Fun Fact* **A Different Kind of Beauty Queen**

Cobán is the site of one of Mesoamerica's greatest celebrations of Maya culture. For 2 weeks in late July and early August, the city of Cobán and other towns around Las Verapaces celebrate La Fiesta Nacional Indígena de Guatemala (National Indigenous Folkloric Festival). One of the highlights of the celebrations is the selection of Rabin Ajua, the local "queen" of the festivities, chosen from representatives of the various communities around Las Verapaces. The selection of Rabin Ajua is made on July 21, and is the centerpiece of the celebrations, which include traditional local cuisine, music, and dance.

ATTRACTIONS & ACTIVITIES FARTHER AFIELD

Candelaria Caves ☞☞   This impressive cave system is sacred to the Q'eqchi Maya, and stretches continuously for some 29km (18 miles). The main gallery, **Tzul Tacca,** is almost 60m (200 ft.) high, 30m (100 ft.) wide, and 200m (650 ft.) long, and features massive stalagmites and roof windows that let in light. Side galleries hold evidence of ancient Maya rituals, and the entire system is traversed by the Candelaria River. (You can even float through the caves in an inner tube.)

You can visit the Candelaria Caves on a day trip out of Cobán, but to really enjoy them, you should stay overnight at the **Complejo Cultural y Ecológico Cuevas de Candelaria** (✆ 502/7861-2203; www.cuevasdecandelaria.com). All of the tour operations in Cobán offer guided multiday trips here.

10km (6 miles) west of the village of Raxrujá, which is north of the town of Chisec. Admission Q25 ($3.35/£1.75). Daily 8am–4pm.

Grutas del Rey Marcos and Balneario Cecilinda   About 8km (5 miles) south of Cobán sits the town of San Juan Chamelco, home to a colonial-era church and gateway to two popular local attractions: Grutas del Rey Marcos, a small cave system, and Balneario Cecilinda, a complex of natural spring–fed pools.

The **Gruta del Rey Marcos** ☞ features beautiful stalagmite and stalactite formations. Some of these are very large; one has even been dubbed the Leaning Tower of Pisa. At one point you'll have to ford a small river to get to the more impressive cave galleries.

If the weather's nice, you'll definitely enjoy a dip in the pools at the **Balneario Cecilinda,** which are very popular with locals, so expect to meet many if you come on a sunny weekend.

If you want to stay in the area, check out **Don Jerónimo's** (✆ 502/5301-3191; http://dearbrutus.com/donjeronimo), a delightful joint with a gregarious owner who knows the area well. This place specializes in ecological and spiritual vacations or retreats, and serves up tasty vegetarian cuisine. Don Jerónimo's is located 1km (less than a mile) before the Gruta del Rey Marcos.

About 8km (5 miles) south of Cobán in the town of San Juan Chamelco. Grutas del Rey Marcos ✆ 502/7951-2756. Balneario Cecilinda ✆ 502/5308-9307. Admission Q10 ($1.35/70p) for each attraction. Both open weekends 8am–5pm. The caves will open with prior reservation during the week if you come with a semi-sizeable group. It's possible, but slightly complicated, to get here by public transportation. Your best bet is to take a taxi, which should cost around Q75 ($10/£5.25). Alternatively, you could sign up for a day tour.

Kan' Ba 🎋🎋 The entrance to this new cave attraction (near the entrance to Semuc Champey) sits above the Cahabón River and features a smaller river that emerges from the cave mouth and cascades in a waterfall to the Cahabón below. Visitors see the cave in an unusual way; first by wading/swimming up to it, and second by candlelight. Candles are provided, but I recommend bringing a waterproof headlamp. The trip to the cave takes about 20 minutes each way, and at the end you can take a 15-minute inner-tube ride on the Cahabón River, which ends at the Hostal Las Marías (see below).

Near entrance to Semuc Champey, 9km (5½ miles) beyond Lanquin, a 2-hr. drive from Cobán. Tour Q30 ($4/£2.10) per person. Daily 9am–5pm, but subject to change.

Lanquin *(Overrated* The Lanquin cave is a popular destination, and while it's worth visiting if you have some extra time on a trip to Semuc Champey, I find it a little disappointing. The geological formations are more interesting at the Grutas del Rey Marcos and the Candelaria Caves, while the adventure is much greater at Kan' Ba. Leaving little to the imagination, the locals have named many of the Lanquin stalactite and stalagmite formations after the animals they resemble.

The best time to visit Lanquin is in the late afternoon, when thousands of bats exit the cave to feed. There's good swimming in the river near the mouth of the cave, and you can even camp here. The small town of Lanquin (which I prefer over the cave) has a number of churches, including one that dates to the 1500s.

About 64km (40 miles) from Cobán; the cave is located another half-mile outside of town, along the road to Semuc Champey. Admission Q20 ($2.65/£1.40). Daily 8am–5pm.

Parque Nacional Laguna de Lachuá 🎋🎋 Located in the northwest corner of the Alta Verapaz, this 9,712-hectare (24,000-acre) national park has a stunningly beautiful turquoise lake as its centerpiece. The lake, more than 5km (3 miles) across at its widest point and more than 219m (720 ft.) deep, gets its majestic blue hue from its high sulfur content, and is surrounded by lush forests of tropical flora and fauna.

Camping is available, and while there are bathrooms, showers, and basic cooking facilities, you'll have to bring your own food and drinking water. All of the tour operations in Cobán offer guided multiday trips here.

Entrance to Lachuá National Park at the town of San Marcos. ✆ 502/7983-0061. Admission Q40 ($5.30/£2.80). Camping Q20 ($2.65/£1.40) per person in a tent, with a few basic dorm beds with mosquito netting available for Q60 ($8/£4.20). Daily 8am–4pm.

Semuc Champey 🎋🎋🎋 Widely advertised as the most beautiful spot in Guatemala, this place usually lives up to expectations. A geological oddity, Semuc Champey consists

---

(Moments **Take a Break**

Touring the town can take its toll, and a coffee break is the perfect way to recharge your battery. If you want to keep your eye on the action, grab a seat at the side-street cafe at **Hotel La Posada,** 1a Calle 4-12, Zona 2 (✆ 502/7952-1495), which overlooks the west end of the central plaza. For a wide selection of exotic coffee drinks and the chance to check your e-mail, head to **Café El Tirol** 🎋, 1a Calle 3-13, Zona 2 (✆ 502/7951-4042), which is also just off the plaza but set back a bit from the action.

Staying near Semuc Champey & Lanquin

You can camp at both Semuc Champey and Lanquin. However, if you're look-ing for a little more comfort and an on-site restaurant, I recommend the **Hostal Las Marías** (© 502/7861-2209), located just before the entrance to Semuc Champey, or **Hotel El Recreo Lanquin Champey** (© 502/7952-2180), which is located just outside of Lanquin on the way to Semuc Champey. Both are sim-ple, clean, and comfortable, and good places to meet other travelers.

of a series of limestone pools and gentle waterfalls set in a narrow rainforest canyon. Aside from the stunningly beautiful waters and surroundings, what makes this spot special is the fact that these pools and waterfalls are actually a bridge of land (about 300m/984 ft. long) resting atop the raging Cahabón River. Visitors can watch the river disappear in a torrent at one end of the bridge and then, after enjoying a swim and leisurely hike, see it emerge downstream.

There are a couple of hiking trails here, including one loop trail, El Mirador, which brings you to a spectacular lookout above Semuc Champey. This loop trail takes about 45 minutes, but can take longer if you decide to hang out at the lookout. If you walk directly to the pools and falls, it's just a 15-minute hike from the parking lot and entrance.

The best way to visit is on an organized tour, which usually includes transportation, lunch, and a visit to one or more other attractions in the area, such as the town and caves of Lanquin, and/or the Kan' Ba cave. Ask your hotel, or contact **Aventuras Turísticas** ⊛ (© 502/7951-4213; www.aventurasturisticas.com).

Some guides will take you to the cave where the river emerges, which involves free climbing down the crack of the last waterfall. The reward is the sound and fury of the water as you stand underneath Semuc Champey while the Cahabón River shoots out. *Warning:* When I did this there were no ropes or protection of any kind. A slip or fall can be fatal. Moreover, your family will have absolutely no chance of successfully suing anybody on your behalf. While I count the experience of standing in this cave as one of the most amazing experiences of my time in Guatemala, keep in mind that there is very serious risk involved.

9km (5½ miles) beyond Lanquin, a 2-hr. drive from Cobán. © 502/7983-0061. Admission Q30 ($4/£2.10) adults, Q10 ($1.35/70p) children 5–12. Daily 8am–5pm. Parking additional Q10 ($1.35/70p); camping allowed for Q35 ($4.65/£2.45) per person.

ORGANIZED TOURS

The best way to see and experience the various attractions and activities around Cobán is by organized tour. While it's possible to do so via public transportation or in your own vehicle, this can be a tricky way to go for many visitors, as it's confusing, and the route is not well-marked. It's much easier and hassle-free to go on a tour. Most of the tours are small-scale operations that are reasonably priced. The guides know the area, and many of the organized tours combine two or more attractions or activities into a single day, which would be fairly impossible to do via public transportation. The best local tour operator is **Aventuras Turísticas** ⊛ (© 502/7951-4213; www.aventuras-turisticas.com). These folks offer a wide range of tour options from half-day city tours and **white-water rafting** ⊛ to bird-watching and guided visits to all of the attractions listed in this chapter. Rafting trips on the Cahabón River—which has class III and

---

Fun Fact **The Underworld**

The ancient Maya believed that caves were a mystical portal between the world of the living and the underworld of spirits and the dead, which they called **Xibalba**. From their earliest days, there is evidence that the Mayas made extensive use of caves for ritual purposes, as well as for the daily tasks of keeping dry, storing grains, and gathering water.

---

class IV rapids—are available out of Cobán for one or more days. In addition, they can arrange multiday trips to some farther-flung regions, including the Petén and Caribbean coast. Most day tours cost Q225 to Q338 ($30–$45/£16–£24) per person per day, and include lunch, transportation, and entrance fees. Prices may vary according to group size. The tour desk at the **Casa D'Acuña** (© 502/7951-0482) is also very good, and can organize just about any tour or adventure in the region.

In addition to the tour operators mentioned above, **Proyecto Ecológico Quetzal** (© 502/7952-1047; www.ecoquetzal.org) is a nonprofit, non-governmental initiative working to promote ecologically, socially, and culturally sensitive tourism in the Alta Verapaz region. They offer a number of different multiday tour options that will get you close to the people and ecosystems of this rich region.

WHERE TO STAY

In addition to the places listed below, check out **Hotel Villa Ancestral**, 6a Av. 3-11, Zona 1 (© 502/7951-1348), which was putting the finishing touches on its restored colonial home last time I visited.

MODERATE

Casa Duranta   The large rooms in this colonial-era home are spread around a very large interior garden. Most come with two queen-size beds, a large bathroom, and a small television (a couple of rooms have newer, larger televisions, and I was told all the rooms would soon have them). Intricate iron work is spread around the hotel, ranging from headboards and luggage racks to wall-size candle holders. The restaurant serves a mix of Guatemalan and international fare.

3a Calle 4-46, Zona 3. © 502/7952-4188. Fax 502/7951-4716. www.casaduranta.com. 10 units. Q350 ($47/£25) double. AE, DC, MC, V. **Amenities:** Restaurant; bar; tour desk; laundry service. *In room:* TV, no phone.

Hotel La Posada *Finds*   This atmospheric hotel is just off the city's central plaza, and parts of the building are more than 400 years old (the place has been in the same family since colonial times). The rooms are simple but rather distinct (one is housed in the residence's former chapel), and can have fireplaces, wooden floors, or antique four-poster beds. The newer annex across the street is stylistically similar, and I recommend the large and comfortable room no. 15 for couples and honeymooners, as it comes with a queen-size bed facing a beautiful built-in fireplace under a high exposed-beam ceiling. The old building has beautiful gardens and common areas, and a broad shared interior veranda with massive terra-cotta tiles. There's a semi-elegant restaurant, as well as a separate street-side cafe.

1a Calle 4-12, Zona 2. © 502/7952-1495. Fax 502/7951-3516. www.laposadacoban.com. 16 units. Q395 ($53/£28) double. Lower rates in the off season. AE, DC, MC, V. **Amenities:** Restaurant; bar; tour desk; laundry service; free Wi-Fi. *In room:* No phone.

Mansión Santo Domingo de Guzmán 🏵   Located a bit outside of downtown Cobán on the road to Semuc Champey, this may be the most modern and luxurious option in Alta Verapaz. The two-story building is done in a neo-colonial style, as well as the rooms, which feature tile floors, exposed wood-beam ceilings, wood furnishings, firm comfortable beds, and 21-inch flatscreen TVs. I like room no. 10, a second-floor corner unit with a small balcony overlooking a river valley, which is, unfortunately, across the busy rural highway. The hotel is about 10km (6 miles) outside of Cobán, and a taxi here will cost around Q30 to Q40 ($4–$5.30/£2.10–£2.80).

Km 216 Carretera a San Pedro Carchá. ℂ **502/7950-0777.** www.mansionsantodomingodeguzman.com. 14 units. Q300 ($40/£21) double. AE, DC, MC, V. **Amenities:** Restaurant; bar; tour desk; laundry service. *In room:* A/C, TV.

INEXPENSIVE

Casa Alcazar Victoria 🏵 *(Finds*   Located on the outskirts of town, this new hotel has comfortable rooms in a beautifully decorated and restored old home. There's a large tiled courtyard at the center of the building, and one interior wall is the re-creation of a church altar, with various niches occupied by antique carved religious figures. All of the rooms are different. Those on the second floor have high ceilings with exposed wood beams and old tile floors. My favorites are room nos. 12 through 15, which are large, second-floor rooms in a quiet part of the building, and have a shared veranda in front. Be careful of room nos. 31 to 35, which back on to a busy street and can be noisy. The restaurant here is excellent, and these folks have a top-notch tour operation.

1a Calle 5-34, Zona 1. ℂ **502/7952-1388.** Fax 502/7951-4265. http://hoteles.aventurasturisticas.com. 17 units. Q135 ($18/£9.45) double. AE, DC, MC, V. **Amenities:** Restaurant; bar; tour desk; laundry service. *In room:* TV.

Casa D'Acuña *(Value*   This place's popularity is disproportionate to the comfort of its rooms, which are very basic. Only one has a double bed (the rest have either one or two bunk beds), and all rooms share a couple of communal bathrooms and showers, which are kept nearly immaculate. The convivial hostel atmosphere here is a big draw, as is the large courtyard garden and the hotel's restaurant, which is one of the best in town. They also have an excellent tour operation.

4a Calle 3-11, Zona 2. ℂ **502/7951-0482.** Fax 502/7952-1547. casadeacuna@yahoo.com. 7 units, all with shared bathroom. Q100 ($13/£7) double. AE, DC, MC, V. **Amenities:** Restaurant; bar; tour desk; laundry service. *In room:* No phone.

Hostal Doña Victoria *(Value*   A former nunnery, this centrally located building is more than 400 years old and oozes character. The rooms are quite basic, but most are spacious (except the bathrooms, which are quite small), with antique tile floors, wood ceilings, carved-wood headboards, and 13-inch TVs. The central garden and surrounding courtyards offer several good spots to sit and read a book or talk with fellow travelers. There's a good restaurant and popular Internet cafe as well. These folks also run the slightly more upscale Casa Alcazar Victoria and the excellent tour company Aventuras Turísticas.

3a Av. 2-38, Zona 3. ℂ **502/7951-4213.** Fax 502/7952-1389. http://hoteles.aventurasturisticas.com. 9 units. Q95 ($13/£6.65) double. AE, DC, MC, V. **Amenities:** Restaurant; bar; tour desk; laundry service. *In room:* TV, no phone.

WHERE TO DINE

When in Las Verapaces, be sure to sample the local specialty *kac ik,* a savory turkey soup served with enough turkey, vegetables, tubers, and tamales to make a meal. *Kac ik* is either spicy or served with extra chile on the side. It's spelled a number of ways on menus across the country, so don't be surprised if you see it written as "cack ick" or a similar variation.

In addition to the places listed below, the restaurants at **Casa Alcazar Victoria** and **Hotel La Posada** (see above) are both excellent choices. For lunch or a lighter meal, try **Café El Tirol** ⊛, 1a Calle 3-13, Zona 2 (© **502/7951-4042**).

MODERATE

Casa D'Acuña ⊛⊛ *Finds* GUATEMALAN/INTERNATIONAL   The restaurant of this budget hotel is easily the best and most popular in Cobán. The menu here is quite varied. The budget clientele tend to stick to the pizzas, pastas, and Mexican fare, but there's a raging wood-fired grill, which churns out well-prepared steaks, chicken, seafood, and grilled vegetables, all of which go well with the selections from their rather extensive wine list. Lunches feature excellent salads and sandwiches. For dessert, save room for the homemade chocolate brownies.

Inside Casa D'Acuña, 4a Calle 3-11, Zona 2. © **502/7951-0482**. Reservations recommended. Main courses Q30–Q92 ($4–$12/£2.10–£7). AE, MC, V. Daily 6:30am–10pm.

INEXPENSIVE

El Peñascal ⊛ GUATEMALAN   Although their new location can feel a little too sterile, this is still one of the best places in town to get good local food. In addition to standard Chapin fare, you can get turtle soup, *tepesquintle* (a large wild rodent), and *kac ik*. The large L-shaped dining room features red tile floors and glass-topped wooden tables, while a second-floor dining area offers more seats and a view of the main dining room, where there's often live marimba music on weekends.

5a Av. 2-61, Zona 1. © **502/7951-2102**. Main courses Q40–Q80 ($5.30–$11/£2.80–£5.60). MC, V. Daily 7am–11pm.

COBAN AFTER DARK

Cobán is a quiet mountain town and shuts down early most nights. However, you can get cozy at **Milenio**, 3a Av., 1-11, Zona 4 (© **502/7951-4762**). The best bar in town, Milenio has a billiards table and a very mixed crowd. For a more elegant option, try the new tapas bar, **Bok'atas**, 4a Calle 3-34, Zona 2 (© **502/5906-6564**). Relatively late-run movies are shown at the theater in the new **Magdalena Mall** (© **502/7952-2127**) at the entrance to Cobán.

EN ROUTE TO COBAN: BAJA VERAPAZ & BIOTOPO DEL QUETZAL

South of Cobán spreads the region known as Baja Verapaz, which gets its name from its slightly lower ("baja") elevation. The principal attraction in this region is the **Biotopo del Quetzal,** a small natural reserve protecting an area of tropical cloud forest that's one of the few remaining habitats of the resplendent quetzal, the national bird of Guatemala.

Biotopo del Quetzal ⊛   Founded in 1976, the Biotopo del Quetzal covers an area of approximately 1,000 hectares (2,470 acres) of mountainous tropical cloud forest. In addition to its namesake resident (the quetzal), the Biotopo is home to an abundance of tropical flora and fauna. Sadly, due to surrounding deforestation and fragmentation, it's becoming increasingly difficult to spot a quetzal here, but you will see a wealth of epiphytic orchids, bromeliads, and mosses, as well as a host of other bird species, including the Emerald Toucanet and highland guan. If you're lucky, you might spot a howler monkey. The best time to see a quetzal in the Biotopo is February through July.

Guatemala's National Bird: The Resplendent Quetzal

Revered by pre-Columbian cultures throughout Central America, the resplendent quetzal has been called the most beautiful bird on earth. Ancient Aztec and Maya Indians believed that the robin-size quetzal protected them in battle. The males of this species have brilliant red breasts; iridescent emerald green heads, backs, and wings; and white tail feathers complemented by a pair of iridescent green tail feathers that are more than .5m (1¾ ft.) long. The females look similar, but lack the long tail feathers.

There are two different loop trails here, one marked *corto* (short); the other *largo* (long). They are about 2km (1.25 miles) and 4km (2.5 miles) in length, respectively. The short loop will take about 45 minutes to an hour; the long trail about twice as along. Several small waterfalls line the trails. Be sure to check out the information hut near the entrance to the trails, as well as the small collection of orchids and bromeliads.

At Km 160.5 on the road between Guatemala City and Cobán. Admission Q20 ($2.65/£1.40). Daily 7am–4pm. Any bus to or from Cobán (see "Getting There: By Bus," earlier in this chapter) can drop you here.

Baja Verapaz is also home to a few small towns and villages renowned for their art and craftworks. Most notable of these are **Salamá** and **Rabinal.** For tours around Salamá or Rabinal, contact Raul Fernandez (© **502/7940-0549**), a long-standing, highly knowledgeable bilingual guide.

Salamá is the provincial capital and largest city in the Baja Verapaces. At the center of Salamá is a beautiful colonial-era church with an ornately carved altar adorned with 18-karat gold. The city also has an interesting temple dedicated to the Roman goddess Minerva. This temple, built in 1916, is perhaps partly responsible for the region's renown in the realm of arts and craftworks. Salamá's market day on Monday is the biggest and best in the Verapaces.

The smaller village of **Rabinal** is named after the Rabinaleb' Maya of this region. It was founded as a Spanish colonial town by Fray Bartolomé de las Casas in 1537. The market here is held on Sunday, and in addition to beautiful *huipiles* and woodcarvings, the artisans of this town are famous for their low-fired pottery.

If you do visit Rabinal, be sure to stop in at the **Museo Rabinal Achí,** 2a Calle and 4a Avenida, Zona 3 (© **502/7979-7820**), a small museum with a collection of Maya historical and cultural displays. The museum is open daily from 9am to 4pm. Admission is Q10 ($1.35/70p).

There are no hotels or *posadas* of note in Salamá or Rabinal. If you find yourself needing or wanting to stay here, try the **Hotel Tezulutlán,** Ruta 3, 4-99, Zona 1 (© **502/ 7940-1643**), a simple and tidy option in the heart of Salamá.

Salamá and Rabinal are located off the main Ruta Las Verapaces, which runs from El Rancho north to Cobán. Marked as both CA-14 and CA-17 at El Rancho crossroads, it forks at Km 47, where CA-17 heads toward Salamá and Rabinal, while CA-14 continues on to Cobán. Salamá is another 17km (10 miles) from the fork, Rabinal another 8km (5 miles) west of Salamá.

WHERE TO STAY & DINE

Posada Montaña de Quetzal   This mountain lodge is popular with Guatemalan weekenders, and while the rooms are certainly acceptable, I find them slightly overpriced. The rooms feature red brick floors, faux-stucco walls, and simple decor. The individual cabañas are spread along a path leading down from the main lodge and rooms, and come with a separate sitting room and either one or two bedrooms. Each has a fireplace and stockpile of wood in the living room. There's a midsize pool with a diving board and a separate children's pool, though it's often too cool and cloudy to make use of them. The restaurant serves excellent local cuisine at very reasonable prices.

Km 156 Ruta Las Verapaces. (**C**) **502/6620-0709** or 502/5800-0454. www.hposadaquetzal.com. 26 units. Q269 ($36/£19) double room; Q348 ($46/£25) double cabaña. AE, DC, MC, V. **Amenities:** Restaurant; bar; pool; tour desk; laundry service. *In room:* No phone.

Ram Tzul *(Finds)*   This is by far the best choice in the area. The rooms are very spacious, with floors made from the cross section of tree trunks set in concrete. The second-floor rooms are the better bet, with large picture windows and a pitched roof with several gables. The main lobby building and restaurant are housed in a massive three-level structure with a high ceiling supported by bamboo posts and beams. The name of this place translates to "mountain heart, mountain spirit" in the Mayan Q'eqchi language. The hotel sits on its own private reserve, with a trail down to a lovely waterfall. Nonguests can hike the trail for Q38 ($5/£2.65).

Km 158.5 Ruta Las Verapaces. (**C**) **502/5908-4066** at the lodge, or 502/2335-1805 in Guatemala City. Fax 502/ 2335-1802. ramtzul@intelnet.net.gt. 12 units. Q290 ($38/£20) double. AE, DC, MC, V. **Amenities:** Restaurant; bar; tour desk; laundry service. *In room:* No phone.

2 Esquipulas

222km (137 miles) SE of Guatemala City

Esquipulas may be a relatively nondescript place along the remote eastern border of the country, but it happens to be Guatemala's most important Roman Catholic pilgrimage site. The main church in Esquipulas was upgraded to the status of basilica in 1968, and houses the city's prime treasure—*El Cristo Negro (The Black Christ),* a dark-skinned statue of Christ that's believed to have healing powers. The Basílica and Black Christ have been visited by Pope John Paul II, Mother Teresa, and Che Guevara, among others, and it's estimated that more than one million people make the pilgrimage each year.

ESSENTIALS
GETTING THERE
BY CAR   To reach Esquipulas by car, take the Carretera al Atlántico (CA-9) out of Guatemala City to the crossroads at Río Hondo. Turn south here onto CA-10. The exit will be marked for Zacapa, Chiquimula, and Esquipulas. The trip should take 3 to 3½ hours. There's a wonderful lookout located on the road into Esquipulas, about a mile before you hit the center of town. It will be on your left as you arrive, and it's worth a stop for the panoramic view of the city below.

BY BUS   Rutas Orientales, 19a Calle 8-18, Zona 1 ((**C**) **502/2253-7282** or 502/ 2251-2160), buses depart from the Zona 1 terminal every half-hour between 4am and 6pm. The fare is Q30 ($4/£2.10). Return buses leave Esquipulas from 11a Calle, just south of the Basílica, every half-hour between 2am and 5pm. The bus ride takes roughly 4 hours.

GETTING AROUND

There are scores of taxis, motor taxis, and tuk tuks in Esquipulas. Most rides around town cost Q3 to Q7 (40¢–90¢/20p–50p).

ORIENTATION

The city, and nearly all activity in it, is centered around the Basílica. The church, fronted by a park that's nearly 2 square blocks in size, sits on 11a Calle, the main road into and out of Esquipulas. All of the hotels and restaurants of interest to tourists are located within a 4-block radius of the Basílica. The north and south sides of the Basílica are packed with souvenir stands selling religious memorabilia, votive candles, and creative kitsch. There are several banks within a block or two of the Basílica, and the police station, post office, and town hall are located at western end of 6a Avenida.

WHAT TO SEE & DO

La Basílica & El Cristo Negro ⟨★★⟩   Sculpted by Quirio Cataño in Antigua, the Black Christ dates back to 1595. By 1603, it already had a miracle attributed to it, but it wasn't until 1735, when Father Pedro Pardo de Figueroa was miraculously cured while praying in front of the statue, that things really began to happen. Father Pedro was eventually elected Archbishop of Guatemala, and he used the power of this position to order the construction of a cathedral worthy of this miraculous icon. The current Basílica was finished in 1758, and is a beautiful and grand church that has withstood Guatemala's regular cycle of massive earthquakes, a miracle in itself.

The Black Christ is currently exhibited in a glass case set at the back of the Basílica's main altar. The entrance to see it is along the left side of the church. At peak periods, this line can be quite long, and it might take more than an hour to get your chance to walk around the enclosed display case.

> **Fun Fact Walk Backward**
>
> Believing it an offense to turn your back on the Black Christ, pilgrims exit the viewing area by walking backward. The going is slow at times, but the narrow pathway has no steps or railings on either side, making the task rather easy.

During Holy Week, July 21 to 27, and around January 15 (the official festival day of the Black Christ), the town is packed with religious pilgrims, including a large number of Guatemalans who bring their cars to be blessed by the priests. You'll spot these cars, decked out in colored ribbons and religious trinkets, in a specially designated parking lot and on the road on their way out of town.

Doble Vía and 3a Av. Basílica. ℂ 502/7943-1108. Free admission. Daily 6am–8pm. Mass is observed 6:30 and 11am, and 5pm Mon–Sat; 6:30, 8, 9:30, and 11am, and 12:30 and 5pm on Sun.

La Cueva de las Minas   Not far from the Basílica is the Cueva de las Minas, a natural cave that's been used for centuries for Maya ritual ceremonies. Some claim the Black Christ actually emerged from these caves, while others say that its sculptor, Quirio Cataño, got his inspiration here. The cave is about 46m (150 ft.) deep, and you'll often see local devotees lighting candles and praying.

A small zoo here holds a modest collection of local animals. I find the enclosures and displays rather inadequate and sad, particularly those for the crocodile and ocelot.

There's also a restaurant, some picnic tables, and even a basketball and volleyball court.

1km (1 mile) outside of town, off the route to the Honduran border, which heads out from behind the south side of the Basílica. www.cuevadelasminas.com. Admission Q5 (65¢/35p). Daily 7am–5pm.

Other Attractions

Most visitors to Esquipulas come solely to visit the Black Christ. However, there are a few other nearby attractions. Families with children should head to **Chatun** (✆ **502/5556-2788;** www.parquechatun.com), a family-style recreation complex with a swimming pool, sports facilities (such as a zip-line attraction), climbing wall, and children's petting zoo. Admission is Q50 ($6.65/£3.50) for adults, Q30 ($4/£2.10) for children. Chatun is located 3km (2 miles) outside of Esquipulas on the road to Honduras.

If you're looking for a day trip, the Ipala Volcano is a popular tourist spot. The crater of this 1,650m (5,400-ft.) volcano forms a beautiful blue lake, and makes a great hike. If you want to visit the volcano, ask your hotel for a reputable guide, as you shouldn't visit this remote site unaccompanied.

WHERE TO STAY

EXPENSIVE

Porta Hotel Legendario ✹ This is the largest and most resortlike hotel in Esquipulas. However, I don't think they can justify the rates they charge, especially when compared with the competition. Still, if you want a large swimming pool and some of the trappings of a modern business-class hotel, this is the place for you. The rooms are relatively simple with plenty of space, clean tile floors, and somewhat dated decor. The large pool is clearly the best feature here. The Legendario is located about 3 blocks from the Basílica.

9a Calle 3-00, Zona 1. ✆ **502/7943-1824** in Esquipulas, or 502/2361-9683 reservations in Guatemala City. Fax 502/7943-1022. www.portahotels.com. 42 units. Q1,050–Q1,125 ($140–$150/£74–£79) double room; Q1,500 ($200/£105) suite. Lower rates available weekdays and off season. Rates highest on weekends and holy days. AE, DC, MC, V. **Amenities:** Restaurant; 2 bars; tour desk; babysitting; laundry service. *In room:* A/C, TV.

MODERATE

Portal de la Fe ✹ This new hotel is on the main drag in Esquipulas, just 2 blocks from the Basílica. The rooms, spread throughout three floors, are modern and somewhat stylish, with ornate iron headboards and very firm beds. The rooms come in different sizes with various bed distributions, but all have private bathrooms and 13-inch TVs. Six of the rooms have air-conditioning, while those on the third floor have small balconies. (Room nos. 302–304 actually have views of the Basílica from their balconies.) For those who don't get these rooms, there's a rooftop terrace with good views. There's no restaurant here, but there are plenty nearby. The hotel has one computer available with free Internet usage and free Wi-Fi throughout the hotel.

11a Calle 1-70, Zona 1. ✆ **502/7943-4124.** Fax 502/7943-4262. www.portaldelafehotel.com. 29 units. Q375–Q600 ($50–$80/£26–£42) double. Lower rates available weekdays and off season. Rates highest on weekends and holy days. AE, DC, MC, V. **Amenities:** Tour desk; laundry service; free Wi-Fi. *In room:* TV, no phone.

INEXPENSIVE

Hotel El Peregrino *Value* While you could save a little by going with a basic room (a twin bed is all you'll get), I heartily recommend the slight splurge for a newer, more spacious room with a wider bed, which they call semi-matrimonial, and cable television. By far the best feature at this hotel is the pool, which has a patio with good views of the Basílica and the surrounding hills. There's also a separate children's pool and a small jungle-gym. The hotel's popular restaurant serves good Guatemalan fare, and is right in the center of the action on the side street fronting the church.

2a Av. 11-94, Zona 1. ℰ **502/7943-1054.** Fax 502/7943-1474. guatecham@gmail.com. 33 units. Q150–Q250 ($20–$33/£11–£18) double. Lower rates available weekdays and off season. Rates highest on weekends and holy days. AE, DC, MC, V. **Amenities:** Restaurant; pool; tour desk; laundry service; free Wi-Fi. *In room:* TV, no phone.

WHERE TO DINE
MODERATE
La Hacienda ℛ *(Kids* GUATEMALAN/STEAKHOUSE   This is by far the fanciest and most upscale option in Esquipulas. The food here is far more expensive than you'll find at any other restaurant in town, but it's well-prepared and filling, and includes steak, grilled chicken, and a children's menu with smaller portions. Pair your entree with a bottle of French, Chilean, Italian, or Argentine wine; the restaurant has the best wine list in Esquipulas. The dimly lit dining rooms have wooden tables and chairs, and there are even a few tables on an open-air patio in front.

2a Av. and 10a Calle. ℰ **502/7943-1748.** Main courses Q60–Q160 ($8–$21/£4.20–£11). MC, V. Daily 8am–10pm.

INEXPENSIVE
La Rotunda GUATEMALAN/INTERNATIONAL   This place rises slightly above the rest of the *comedores* and other basic restaurants in town, with its menu of Guatemalan fare, Mexican burritos and tacos, and long list of pizzas, which are actually not bad. Breakfasts here are filling and a bargain. A typical Guatemalan breakfast of eggs, tortillas, refried beans, and plantains is the forte here, but you can get an omelet or even a breakfast burrito. The second-floor dining room is shaped in a half-circle with large picture windows all around, giving you a view of the traffic, motorized and pedestrian, on the main street below.

1a Av. and 11a Calle. ℰ **502/7943-2038.** Main courses Q30–Q75 ($4–$10/£2.10–£5.25). MC, V. Daily 7am–10pm.

3 Copán ★/★
239km (148 miles) E of Guatemala City; 110km (68 miles) S of Río Hondo; 12km (7 miles) S of the Honduran border

Just past the Guatemalan border lies **Copán,** one of the most spectacular Maya ceremonial cities of Mesoamerica. The town is a small picturesque city with rough cobblestone streets and a buzzing central plaza that's the heart and soul of the place. Copán is surrounded by beautiful forests with waterfalls, hot springs, and excellent bird-watching and adventure tourism possibilities. *Note:* The currency used in Copán is the *lempira,* which at press time was about L19 to $1. In this section, prices are quoted in *lempiras* rather than *quetzales,* as *quetzales* are not accepted.

Cash Flow
The *lempira* is the official currency of Honduras. At press time, there were **18.89** *lempira* to the U.S. dollar, and approximately 2.50 *lempira* to 1 Guatemalan *quetzal.* Numerous moneychangers hang around the border crossing, but they often offer bad exchange rates. It's safe to change your money with them, but you'll have to bargain hard to get a good rate. Alternatively, you can wait until you reach Copán Ruinas and get better rates at any bank or hotel.

Crossing the Border

Crossing the border at El Florido on your way to Copán is relatively easy and cheap. If you're planning a short stay, simply show your passport, tell them you want "solo Copán (just Copán)," and fork over $3 for a stamped piece of paper that's good for up to 5 days. In this case, there's no charge to exit or reenter Guatemala, and your original Guatemalan tourist visa is still valid. The border crossing is open daily 6am to 8pm. If you plan on staying in Honduras longer, you must pay the official Guatemalan exit fee of Q150 ($20/£11). On the Honduran side you'll be issued a free tourist visa that's good for up to 90 days. If you're driving a rental car, be sure to have all your papers in order and clear the trip with the rental-car agency in advance.

ESSENTIALS

GETTING THERE

BY CAR   If you're driving to Copán, take the Carretera al Atlántico (CA-9) out of Guatemala City to the crossroads at Río Hondo. Turn south here on to CA-10. The exit will be marked for Zacapa, Chiquimula, and Esquipulas. About 10km (6 miles) south of the city of Chiquimula you'll see the turnoff for El Florido and Copán Ruinas on your left. From here it's about 38km (24 miles) to the border crossing at El Florido, and from there another 12km (7 miles) to Copán Ruinas. The road is paved the entire way, and on a good day the journey can take about 4½ hours.

BY BUS   Hedman Alas (© **504/651-4037** in Copán Ruinas, or 502/2362-5072 in Guatemala City; www.hedmanalas.com) offers daily bus service from Guatemala City, leaving at 5am from their terminal at 2a Av. 8-73, Zona 10. The return bus leaves Copán Ruinas at 1:20pm. The fare is L665 ($35/£20) one-way, L1140 ($60/£34) round-trip. The one-way trip takes about 5 hours.

GETTING AROUND

You can easily walk anywhere in Copán Ruinas, including the archaeological site. However, if you need a taxi, they are plentiful and inexpensive. Most of the taxis are small motor taxis or tuk tuks, which circulate around town and gather on the north and south sides of the central plaza. If you can't find one, call **Cooperativo Multicomer** (© **504/651-4054**) or **Lulo** (© **504/961-7823**). A taxi ride between town and the archaeological site should cost L10 to L15 (50¢–75¢/30p–45p) per person.

ORIENTATION

It may be confusing, but the actual Maya ruins here are called Copán, while the little town is officially known as Copán Ruinas. Most folks refer to it generically as Copán or make the appropriate distinction when necessary. The town is very compact, and everything of importance is located within a 4-block radius of the central plaza. No official street names are actually used, and directions are given in relation to the central plaza or some other known landmark.

FAST FACTS   **Banco Atlántida** and **Banco de Occidente** both front the central plaza and are fast and safe places to exchange money or use an ATM. To contact the local police, dial © **504/651-4060**. The post office (© **504/651-4447**) is located just west of the Copán Museum (see below). There are a half-dozen or so Internet cafes

Copán Ruinas

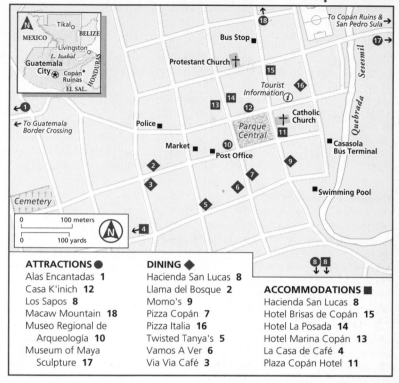

To Copán Ruins &
San Pedro Sula →

MEXICO **BELIZE**
Tikal
Livingston
L. Izabal
Guatemala City Copán Ruinas
HONDURAS
EL SAL.

← **To Guatemala Border Crossing**

Bus Stop

Protestant Church

Tourist Information (i)

Police

Parque Central

Catholic Church

Market

Post Office

Casasola Bus Terminal

Cemetery

Swimming Pool

0 — 100 meters
0 — 100 yards

Sesesmil

Quebrada

ATTRACTIONS ●
Alas Encantadas **1**
Casa K'inich **12**
Los Sapos **8**
Macaw Mountain **18**
Museo Regional de Arqueología **10**
Museum of Maya Sculpture **17**

DINING ◆
Hacienda San Lucas **8**
Llama del Bosque **2**
Momo's **9**
Pizza Copán **7**
Pizza Italia **16**
Twisted Tanya's **5**
Vamos A Ver **6**
Via Via Café **3**

ACCOMMODATIONS ■
Hacienda San Lucas **8**
Hotel Brisas de Copán **15**
Hotel La Posada **14**
Hotel Marina Copán **13**
La Casa de Café **4**
Plaza Copán Hotel **11**

around town; most charge around L20 to L40 ($1–$2/60p–£1.20) per hour. For medical emergencies, ask your hotel, or call Dr. Boqui at the **Clínica Handal** (© **504/ 651-4408**).

WHAT TO SEE & DO

Copán ✫✫✫ is one of the grandest and most magnificently preserved of all Maya ceremonial cities. Surrounded by thick jungle and set beside the gentle Copán River, the ruins are famous for their raw stone-carved hieroglyphics, massive stelae, and the impressive Hieroglyphic Stairway. Your visit here should include the extensive archaeological ruins, recently excavated tunnels, and Museum of Maya Sculpture.

The current area around Copán has been inhabited since at least 1400 B.C., and some of the earlier discoveries here show Olmec influences. The Great Sun Lord Quetzal Macaw, who ruled from A.D. 426 to 435, was the first of 16 consecutive kings who saw the rise and fall of this Classic Maya city. Some of Copán's great kings included Smoke Jaguar, 18 Rabbit, and Smoke Shell. The history of these kings is meticulously carved into the stones at the ruins.

Copán was famously "discovered" in 1839 and bought for just $50 by the adventurer John L. Stephens, who documented the story in his wonderful book, *Incidents of Travel in Central America, Chiapas and Yucatan* (1841). The book is beautifully illustrated by Stephens's companion Frederick Catherwood.

VISITOR INFORMATION

The entrance to the Copán archaeological site is located along a well-marked highway about a half-mile from the town of Copán Ruinas. The visitor center and ticket booth are at one end of the parking lot; the Museum of Maya Sculpture is at the other. The **Copán Guides Association** has a booth at the entrance to the parking area. Here, you can hire a bilingual guide for a 2-hour tour of the site for L760 ($40/£23), no matter the size of your group. These guides are extremely knowledgeable, and I highly recommend hiring one for your first visit. Admission to the archaeological site, which includes the main Copán ruins and the Sepulturas, is L190 ($10/£5.70). Admission does not include a guide. Visits to the tunnels and Museum of Maya Sculpture are extra (see below).

Museum of Maya Sculpture

I recommend you begin your visit at the new Museum of Maya Sculpture, which is located across from the entrance, a few hundred yards from the small visitor center where you pay your entrance fee. This large, two-story structure was built to protect some of Copán's more impressive pieces from the elements. Inside you'll see beautifully displayed and well-documented examples of a broad range of stone carvings and hieroglyphics. At the center of the museum is a full-scale replica of the Rosalia Temple, which lies well-preserved inside the core of Temple 16 (which you'll see later at the ruins). The museum also contains the reconstructed original facade of one of the site's ball courts. Admission to the museum is L95 ($5/£2.85).

The Ruins

The ruins are at the end of a relatively short path from the museum exit. I recommend starting at the western plaza of **Temple 16.** As you face Temple 16, the **Acropolis** will be to your left. A trail and steps lead around the back, where you can enjoy a view over the Copán River to the surrounding mountains. Follow the path to the **Patio of the Jaguars,** where you'll find the entrances to the **Rosalia** and **Jaguar** tunnels (see below). Continue on over the top of the **Acropolis** and the **Temple of Inscriptions,** and then down into the **Great Plaza,** where Copán's greatest hieroglyphic treasures were found.

> ### (Fun Fact Rodent Royalty
>
> Though Copán's illustrious 13th ruler is known in English as King 18 Rabbit, it would be more accurate to refer to him as King 18 Agouti, the rodent which is depicted in his hieroglyph.

The Temple of Inscriptions anchors the south end of the Great Plaza. To its east is the **Hieroglyphic Stairway.** This stairway, built by **King Smoke Shell,** rises up some 64 steps, each of which is carved or faced with hieroglyphs, telling the history of Copán's kings and their line of succession. To those literate in the language, the stairs once read as a giant book. Today, many of the carved stairs have fallen or faded, but enough remain to give a sense of the scale of this amazing achievement. The stairway is currently under cover, which makes it difficult to see. The lighting is poor, especially on cloudy days, but the trade-off in terms of preservation makes this necessary.

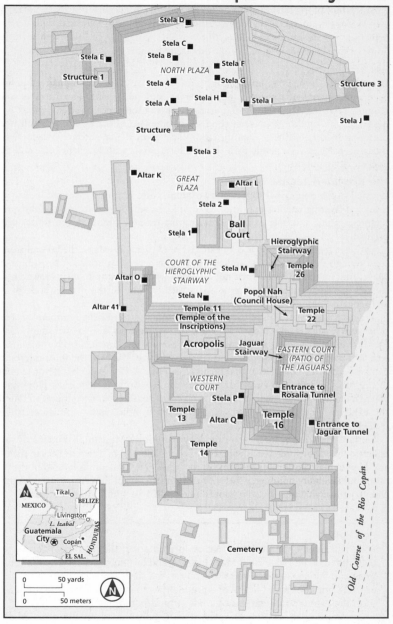

Stela D
Stela C
Stela E
Stela B
Stela F
NORTH PLAZA
Stela G
Structure 1
Stela 4
Structure 3
Stela A
Stela H
Stela I
Stela J
Structure 4
Stela 3

Altar K
GREAT PLAZA
Altar L
Stela 2
Ball Court
Stela 1
Hieroglyphic Stairway
COURT OF THE HIEROGLYPHIC STAIRWAY
Stela M
Temple 26
Altar O
Popol Nah (Council House)
Stela N
Altar 41
Temple 11 (Temple of the Inscriptions)
Temple 22
Acropolis
Jaguar Stairway
EASTERN COURT (PATIO OF THE JAGUARS)
WESTERN COURT
Entrance to Rosalia Tunnel
Stela P
Temple 13
Altar Q
Temple 16
Entrance to Jaguar Tunnel
Temple 14

Old Course of the Río Copán

Cemetery

Tikal
BELIZE
MEXICO
Livingston
L. Izabal
Guatemala City
Copán
HONDURAS
EL SAL.

0   50 yards
0   50 meters

At the foot of the Hieroglyphic Stairway, and all around the Great Plaza, are examples of Copán's carved stelae. Many of these are carved on all four sides with detailed depictions of rulers, animals, and mythic beasts, as well as glyphs that tell their stories. Some of the stelae are originals, while others are replicas.

Las Sepulturas

Located about 2km (1½ miles) from the Great Plaza, Las Sepulturas is believed to have been a major residential neighborhood reserved for Copán's elite. The site gives you a sense of what the day-to-day living arrangements of an upper-crust Maya may have been like. Las Sepulturas was once connected to the Great Plaza by a broad, well-worn causeway (which has been identified by NASA with digital satellite imaging), but today it's reached via a gentle path through lush forests with excellent bird- and animal-watching opportunities.

The Rosalia & Jaguar Tunnels

Opened to the public in 1999, these two tunnels give visitors a firsthand look at the historical layering technique of the Maya builders, who would construct subsequent temples around and over existing ones, no matter how beautiful and intricate the original.

Entrance to the two tunnels is an extra L190 ($10/£5.70) above the general admission, though these are well-lit modern excavations and not tunnels left by the ancient Maya, so it's a tossup whether or not it's really worth the extra money. However, the tunnels are fascinating and do give you a further sense of the massive scale of the archaeological undertaking.

The archaeological ruins of Copán are the main attraction here, but there are a few other sites worth visiting. **Museo Regional de Arqueología,** also known simply as the Copán Museum, holds a small collection of pottery and artifacts from the ruins, as well as a series of interpretive and explanatory displays. Perhaps the most interesting exhibit here is the complete burial niche of an ancient Copán scribe. If you're going to the ruins and the museum there, there's no need to visit this place. However, if you're hanging around town, it will only take you about 30 to 45 minutes to tour all the exhibits. The museum is open daily from 9am to 5pm. Admission is L38 ($2/£1.15).

For kids, the **Casa K'inich** ⊛, or the Maya Children's Museum, has interactive and educational exhibits that teach you how to count and add in different Mayan dialects and how to play the ancient ballgame of the Maya. The museum is located in the rear of the public library building, which fronts the north side of the central plaza. It's open Monday through Saturday from 8am to noon and 1 to 4pm. Admission is free.

Los Sapos

The small ceremonial site of Los Sapos, located across the river from Copán, is believed to be tied to ancient Maya birthing and fertility practices. This is a very small and minimally excavated site. You can see some stone carvings of *sapos,* or frogs, and the carved figure of a pregnant woman. In addition, the site features the exposed foundations of a few large structures.

Los Sapos is about 5km (3 miles) from Copán Ruinas, on the grounds of Hacienda San Lucas (see below). Admission is L38 ($2/£1.15), and several tour agencies in town offer horseback riding tours that include a visit to Los Sapos.

Read All about It

Even after more than 150 years, *Incidents of Travel in Central America, Chiapas and Yucatan,* Vols. 1 and 2 (Dover Publications, 1969), and *Incidents of Travel in Yucatan,* Vols. 1 and 2 (Dover Publications, 1963) are still the best sources on Maya ruins. These fascinating tomes were penned by American explorer, writer, diplomat, and business scout John L. Stephens, and illustrated by his British travel companion, Fredrick Catherwood. They include detailed accounts of the pair's rugged travels, a glimpse into mid-19th-century Guatemalan life, and descriptions of some recently discovered ruins.

In 1839, Stephens was appointed Special Ambassador to Central America by U.S. President Martin Van Buren. While he was there, the government of the United States of Central America disintegrated into civil war. *Incidents of Travel in Central America, Chiapas and Yucatan* describes some of the events that Stephens witnessed. Of even greater importance, it provides descriptions of either the discovery or early exploration of several major ancient Maya cities, including Tikal and Copán. Stephens actually bought the ancient city of Copán from a local farmer for around $50.

The books are lively reads and are beautifully illustrated with the extremely accurate and detailed drawings of Catherwood, an architect and draftsman. In an odd twist, these groundbreaking books were used by the Church of Latter Day Saints founder Joseph Smith as proof of the accuracy of the Book of Mormon.

Originally a lawyer, Stephens became known as the father of American archaeology. His additional writings—*Incidents of Travel in Egypt, Arabia Petraea, and the Holy Land* (Dover Publications, reprint edition 1996), and *Incidents of Travel in Greece, Turkey, Russia and Poland* (Adamant Media Corporation, 2002)—earned him the top rank in his genre. In 1850, Stephens traveled to Panama to work on the construction of a trans-isthmus railroad, but died from malaria in 1852, before the railway's completion. Stephens is immortalized in *Maya Explorer* (Chronicle Books, 1990), a detailed biography by Victor Wolfgang Von Hagan.

For his part, Catherwood published the beautiful *Views of Ancient Monuments in Central America,* with 25 watercolor lithographs he made at various ruins. While this rare book is out of print, you can see fabulous examples of his work in large format in the biography *The Lost Cities of the Mayas: The Life, Art and Discoveries of Frederick Catherwood* by Fabio Bourbon (Abbyville Press, 2000).

One of the newer attractions in Copán Ruinas is **Macaw Mountain** *ふふ* (℃ 504/ 651-4245; www.macawmountain.com), which features an extensive collection of tropical birds, primarily parrots and macaws, and some local raptors. The way the birds are displayed makes this place special. (The enclosures are quite large and well done, and you can even walk through some of them.) This attraction is spread out over a lush setting of a tropical forest and coffee plantation, with a beautiful river and well-designed trails. There's an excellent riverside restaurant and a separate coffee shop with home-roasted beans. Macaw Mountain is located about 4.8km (3 miles) west of the central plaza up a rough dirt road, and is open daily from 9am to 5pm.

Alas Encantadas (© 504/651-4133) is a small butterfly garden and breeding project with loads of winged creatures, exhibits illustrating the various stages of metamorphosis, and a botanical garden with more than 200 species of orchids. Alas Encantadas is located about 300m (⅓ mile) outside of town on the road to the Guatemalan border, and is open daily from 8am to 4:30pm. Admission is L100 ($5.25/£3) for adults, L35 ($1.85/£1.05) for children.

If you want to do some bird-watching, take a horseback ride, soak in a nearby hot spring, explore some caves, or tube on the Copán River, contact a local tour agency such as **McTours** ★ (© 504/651-4453; www.mctours-honduras.com); **Yaragua** (© 504/651-4147; www.yaragua.com); or **Xukpi** (© 504/651-4435).

SHOPPING

The streets of Copán Ruinas are often lined with young artisans selling handmade jewelry and carvings. The town is also brimming with simple souvenir shops selling T-shirts, jade carvings, and Guatemalan crafts and textiles. (However, if you're coming from or going to Guatemala, you'll want to save your purchases of Guatemalan goods for your time there.)

The **Casa de Todo** ★, 1 block downhill from the Banco de Occidente corner of the central plaza (© 504/651-4185), is an excellent gift shop with unique local crafts, a coffee shop, an Internet cafe, and a simple restaurant serving Guatemalan fare; they even have a couple of rooms for overnight stays.

WHERE TO STAY
MODERATE

Hacienda San Lucas ★★ *(finds)*   This is my favorite hotel in the area, set on a hillside across the river from and overlooking the Copán archaeological site. The rustic elegance of the rooms is a throwback to its former life as a farm and ranch, as are the high wood-beam and plank ceilings. The large rooms each are outfitted with two queen-size beds, a large shared veranda with hammocks, and a beautiful stone shower. However, TV and Internet are not available. The hotel restaurant has excellent meals, and on my last visit, they were preparing to build a yoga platform overlooking the river and ruins. The hotel abuts the Los Sapos ruins (see above), and has several excellent hiking trails on its grounds. Sunsets are taken in on a long lawn off of the main lodge building.

5km (3 miles) south of Copán Ruinas on the road to Los Sapos ruins. ©/fax 504/651-4495. www.haciendasanlucas. com. 8 units. L1,615 ($85/£19) double. Rates include full breakfast. AE, MC, V. **Amenities:** Restaurant; bar; tour desk; laundry service. *In room:* No phone.

Hotel Marina Copán ★★   The best hotel in Copán Ruinas proper spans an entire city block facing the central plaza. The rooms are all tastefully decorated and come with large TVs, while the suites have tons of space and other nice touches, such as a Jacuzzi, a kitchenette, and a view. My favorite is no. 331, a third-floor corner suite with a large balcony and a great view of town. Many of the standard rooms come with a balcony, so it's worth requesting one when you make a reservation. There's a pool in the center of the hotel and plenty of areas to relax among plants and fountains.

Parque Central. ② 877/893-9131 in the U.S. and Canada, or 504/651-4070 in Copán Ruinas. Fax 504/651-4477. www.hotelmarinacopan.com. 52 units. L1,615 ($85/£19) double; L2,280–L4,750 ($120–$250/£69–£143) suite. Rates lower in the off season, higher during peak periods. AE, MC, V. **Amenities:** Restaurant; bar; midsize pool; small gym w/sauna; tour desk; room service 6:30am–9pm; laundry service; free Wi-Fi. *In room:* A/C, TV.

Plaza Copán Hotel ⚘   This hotel has a good location on the corner of the central plaza with a good deal to boot. All of the rooms are spacious and feature red tile floors and high ceilings. I like no. 213, which comes with a king-size bed and a private corner balcony overlooking the central plaza. There's a small pool in the central courtyard and a popular restaurant. The hotel also has a helpful tour desk.

Parque Central. ② 504/651-4508. Fax 504/651-4039. www.plazacopanhotel.com. 20 units. L1,045 ($55/£31) double. Rates lower in the off season, higher during peak periods. AE, MC, V. **Amenities:** Restaurant; bar; small pool; tour desk; laundry service. *In room:* A/C, TV.

INEXPENSIVE

There are a score of budget options in Copán, and the competition for the backpacker crowd is fierce. If you have the time, you can always just walk around and see who's got the best room for the best price. My choices for real budget hounds are **Hotel La Posada,** a half-block north of the western edge of Parque Central (② **504/651-4059**); and **Hotel Brisas de Copán,** 1 block north of the eastern edge of Parque Central (② **504/651-4118**). In a town awash in budget hotels, these two have the best and cleanest facilities, while still providing good bang for the buck.

La Casa de Café ⚘ (Value   This house-turned-bed-and-breakfast, located a few blocks outside the center of town, has a good view of the Copán valley and the mountains of neighboring Guatemala. The rooms are all cheery, bright, and comfortable. Those occupying the higher ground are a little older and smaller, but they have the aforementioned view from their shared veranda. The newer rooms have exposed beam ceilings and beautiful mosaic tile sinks, with a veranda that lets out onto a small garden. The owners are extremely knowledgeable about the area, and they also rent out a few fully equipped apartments nearby.

1 block south and 4 blocks west of the central plaza. ② **504/651-4620**. Fax 504/651-4623. www.casadecafecopan. com. 10 units. L855 ($45/£27) double. Rates include full breakfast. AE, MC, V. **Amenities:** Tour desk; laundry service. *In room:* No phone.

WHERE TO DINE
EXPENSIVE

Hacienda San Lucas ⚘⚘ (Finds INTERNATIONAL/HONDURAN   The in-house restaurant at this lovely hotel is probably the best restaurant in Copán, and certainly the most atmospheric. Meals are served in an open-air patio in front of the old hacienda building. The five-course candlelit dinners are my favorite, with the choice of main courses including the house specialty of fire-roasted chicken with *adobo* sauce, a mole based on the herbs, spices, and nuts used by the ancient Maya of this area. Lunches are a bit more casual and range from homemade tamales to a salad-and-sandwich combination. The dinner hours listed below are for seatings; you can then stay and enjoy the meal, which often takes around 2 hours. A taxi here from town should run you L50 to L75 ($2.60–$3.90/£1.50–£2.25) each way.

5km (3 miles) south of Copán Ruinas on the road to Los Sapos ruins. ②/fax **504/651-4495**. www.haciendasanlucas. com. Reservations necessary. Lunch main courses L135–L285 ($9–$15/£4.05–£8.55); prix-fixe dinner L475 ($25/£14). AE, MC, V. Daily 8:30am–3pm and 7–8:30pm.

MODERATE

Twisted Tanya's ⭐ *(Finds)* INTERNATIONAL   Part upscale fusion restaurant and part itinerant party central, this place mixes together elegance and extravagance in equal doses. The lovely open-air, second-floor corner dining room has white muslin curtains and fancy table settings. The white-board menu changes daily, and may include anything from homemade curries with coconut rice to salmon in a Jack Daniel's glaze. There are always a couple of vegetarian items to choose from. Twisted Tanya's offers a L285 ($15/£8.55) prix-fixe menu of soup or salad, entree, and dessert. An early-bird backpacker special will get you soup, pasta, and dessert for just L114 ($6/£3.40). The desserts here are all homemade, decadent, and deservedly renowned.

1 block south and 1 block west of the central plaza. ℂ 504/651-4182. www.twistedtanya.com. Reservations recommended. Main courses L115–L285 ($6–$15/£3.45–£8.55). AE, MC, V. Mon–Sat 2–10pm.

INEXPENSIVE

In addition to the places listed below, you can't go wrong at **Vamos A Ver** (ℂ 504/651-4627) or **Momo's** (ℂ 504/651-3692), both serving international fare, with the latter menu including steak. For pizza and Italian fare, try **Pizza Italia** (ℂ 504/651-4172) or **Pizza Copán** (ℂ 504/651-4381).

Llama del Bosque HONDURAN   This is the place to come for simple, local fare served fast and at rock-bottom prices. Start with black-bean soup and a hard-boiled egg, and then opt for any of the grilled meat plates. For lighter meals, there are sandwiches and burritos. This is also a great choice for breakfast.

1½ blocks west of the central plaza. ℂ 504/651-4431. Main courses L30–L95 ($1.60–$5/90p–£2.85). MC, V. Daily 7am–10pm.

Vía Vía Cafe INTERNATIONAL/VEGETARIAN   I find the food at this popular spot a bit disappointing, but you can't beat it as a meeting place for locals and tourists alike. There are a few tables on a small, street-side porch, and more in a lush open-air interior courtyard. While there are some chicken dishes on the menu, this place really caters to vegetarians. One of the best dishes here is the *capela,* a homemade carrot-and-pesto lasagna. There are a host of other options, including Thai curries, Indian *pakoras,* and hearty sandwiches and veggie burgers. I'd steer clear of the pad Thai, which is a poor imitation of the real thing. This place is actually part of an extensive international chain that caters specifically to itinerant backpackers.

1½ blocks west of the central plaza. ℂ 504/651-4652. www.viaviacafe.com. Main courses L70–L90 ($3.70–$4.70/£2.10–£2.70). MC, V. Daily 7am–10pm.

COPAN AFTER DARK

Copán Ruinas is a relatively quiet town. Aside from the hotel and restaurant bars (of which Twisted Tanya's is always a good call), the most happening spot seems to be **Café Xibalba** (ℂ 504/651-4182). In addition, you might try the **Tunkul Bar** (ℂ 504/651-4410), or head to the **Vía Vía Cafe** (see above) for a more relaxed vibe.

10

The Atlantic Lowlands

Although Guatemalans, tourists, and guidebooks all refer to Guatemala's Atlantic Highway and Atlantic coast, these are misnomers—Guatemala's eastern coast actually fronts the Caribbean Sea. Nonetheless, this chapter deals with the area running northeast, east, and south of Guatemala City, which is reached via the Carretera al Atlántico (Atlantic Hwy.). With the notable exception of the Maya ruins of **Quiriguá,** there's not much to see along the highway itself until you reach the area around **Lago Izabal, Río Dulce (Fronteras),** and the coastal settlements of **Puerto Barrios** and **Livingston.**

1 Livingston ✦

318km (197 miles) NE of Guatemala City; 23km (14 miles) NW of Puerto Barrios; 40km (25 miles) NE of Río Dulce

The Garífuna are a unique race (see the box, below) with a language, culture, and cuisine all their own, so it should come as no surprise that Livingston, a laid-back Garífuna town on the Caribbean coast, is worlds apart from the rest of Guatemala. In fact, once in Livingston, you're just as likely to hear the town referred to as **La Buga,** its Garífuna name. The town's geographical isolation has helped it maintain its mellow image and lifestyle, as well as its appeal to those looking to truly get away from it all.

ESSENTIALS
GETTING THERE

There are no roads into or out of Livingston, though the town itself does have some paved streets and a few cars. You must arrive by boat, either from Río Dulce or Puerto Barrios. For directions on how to reach either Río Dulce or Puerto Barrios by bus or car, see the appropriate sections below. If arriving by car, you can find secure parking in either place near the boat docks. I recommend **Parqueo Don Augusto (© 502/ 7930-5103),** which is open 24 hours and charges just Q25 ($3.30/£1.75) per day. Don Augusto's is located just before the bridge over Lago Izabal as you come from Guatemala City.

BY BOAT   Livingston can be reached by regular boat-taxi service from both Río Dulce and Puerto Barrios. **ASOTRANSLALI (Asociación de Lancheros de Livingston; © 502/7947-0870)** is in charge of boat taxis in Livingston. The boat dock and ASOTRANSLALI office are at the end of Calle Principal, at the bottom of the steep hill leading up to the center of town.

Scheduled boats run from Puerto Barrios to Livingston at 10am and 5pm, and return at 5am and 2pm. These cost Q15 ($2/£1.05) and take about 90 minutes. However, faster boats leave for Livingston throughout the day, charging Q37 ($5/£2.60) and departing as soon as they're filled with passengers. These make the run in just 30 minutes—well worth the extra couple of bucks—and you should never have to wait more than 45 minutes or so for a boat to fill up. These faster boats also make the return trip to Puerto Barrios with fixed departures at 6:30, 7:30, 9, and 11am.

Collective boats leave for Livingston from the main dock in Río Dulce daily at 9:30am and 1pm. The fare is Q100 ($13/£7) one-way; Q160 ($21/£1.50) round-trip. Other boats will run throughout the day when full, or you can rent a boat that will hold up to 10 people to make the trip for around Q750 ($100/£53). Some of the boats arriving from Río Dulce will dock at a separate pier just upriver from the main dock in front of the restaurant Bugamama.

GETTING AROUND

Livingston is so small it's nearly a village. There are no taxis or tuk tuks, but it's relatively easy to walk anywhere in town. The town, however, is set on a very steep hill, so you may have to hoof it up or down to get where you're going.

ORIENTATION

Livingston sits on a point of land where the Río Dulce meets the **Bahía de Amatique,** which is part of the Caribbean Sea. The principal boat dock, or *muelle municipal,* lies

---

The Garífuna

Throughout the 18th century, escaped and shipwrecked slaves assimilated into the native Caribbean Indian populations on several islands in the Lesser Antilles, predominantly on St. Vincent. The West Africans were a mixed lot, including members of the Fon, Yoruba, Ewe, and Nago tribes. Over the years, the West African and indigenous elements blended into a new people, known first as Black Caribs and today as Garífuna or Garinagu. The Garífuna have their own language, traditions, history, and rituals, which celebrate the group's two primary cultural sources. For example, ritual possession ceremonies spoken in a language whose etymological roots are predominantly Arawak are accompanied by African-style drumming and call-and-response singing.

The Black Caribs were fierce warriors and frequently fought the larger colonial powers to maintain their freedom. In 1797, despite the celebrated leadership of Joseph Chatoyer, the Garífuna were soundly defeated by the British forces, who subsequently shipped several thousand of the survivors off to exile on the island of Roatan, in then British Honduras. The Garífuna began migrating and eventually settled along the coasts of what are present-day Honduras, Nicaragua, Guatemala, and Belize. The local Garífuna first settled Livingston in 1802, arriving from Roatan, Honduras. For nearly 2 centuries now, the Garífuna have lived quiet lives of farming, fishing, and light trading with their neighbors, while steadfastly maintaining their language, heritage, and traditions. Each year on November 26 (and for several days around the date), Livingston comes alive to celebrate National Garífuna Day. For an in-depth look at Garífuna history and culture, check out www.labuga.com.

Map legend:
- ◉ Departmental Capital
- ⧉ Ancient Ruins
- ♠ Park, Reserve

at the bottom of Calle Principal. The center of town is straight up the steep hill lead-ing away from the *muelle municipal,* and is where most of the hotels, restaurants, bars, banks, and shops are. Calle Principal actually runs up the hill to its crest and then back down on the other side to the sea, where you'll find the town's main beach, a few more hotels and restaurants, and the path to Los Siete Altares and Playa Blanca.

FAST FACTS   There are a couple of banks, including **Bancafe, Banrural,** and **Banco de Comercio** on Calle Principal near the center of town. To contact the local **police,** dial ✆ **502/7947-4288.** If you have any photographic needs, head to **Centro Fotográfico Amaya** (✆ **502/7947-0212**), which deals with film, digital cameras, and developing.

WHAT TO SEE & DO

There are several reputable tour agencies in Livingston that can organize tours, includ-ing those to the destinations listed below. In addition, every hotel in town can set you up. If you're looking for a reputable outfit, try **Exotic Travel** (✆ **502/7947-0049**) or **Happy Fish** (✆ **502/7947-0661;** www.happyfishresort.com).

Los Siete Altares ⧉⧉   No trip to Livingston is complete without a visit to Los Siete Altares, a series of seven waterfalls connected by a lazy jungle creek. The whole

---

Tips **Dangers & Bothers**

While I highly recommend hiking to Los Siete Altares, I'd be remiss if I didn't warn you of two serious problems. First, despite the fact that it's easy to walk by yourself, be sure to ask your hotel about the current security situation. Over the years, tourists have been attacked and robbed along this walk. Don't do it alone or in a very small group, and make sure to do the hike in the busy part of the day, between 9am and 4pm, when there will be other groups and tourists around. Second, no matter whom you go with, be forewarned that the beach between Livingston and Los Siete Altares is perhaps the most garbage-strewn stretch of sand I've ever seen. Local industry leaders have long talked about doing something about it, but on a recent trip, there was a solid band of plastic bottles, old shoes, and other assorted refuse at least 1m (3½ ft.) wide just beyond the high-tide line, running the entire 5km (3 miles) between the town and the waterfalls.

---

thing is set amid lush rainforest, and while it's a pretty spot year-round, it's best to visit during the rainy season, when the creek and waterfalls are running at their strongest. All of the local hotels and tour agencies offer guided hikes or boat trips here. The falls are located just off the beach, some 5km (3 miles) north, and it's easy to walk here by following the simple path that parallels the beach heading out of Livingston. Whether you come by yourself or with a guide, make sure you go all the way to the top and final waterfall. (Some bored or rushed guides will only bring their group to the first waterfall or two.)

There's a fabulous pool for swimming by the final waterfall—and several others along the way—and the adventurous can dive off the top of the falls into the pool. Sadly, the natural beauty is offset by graffiti, which covers the rocks.

If you go on a guided hike, it will almost certainly begin with a walk through the village of Livingston, giving you an intimate look into the daily lives of some of the locals. From here you'll climb to a promontory with a good panoramic view of the town and the Caribbean, then continue on to a small river, where a waiting canoe will take you on a short ride through the mangroves to the beach. These tours cost around Q50 to Q90 ($6.65–$12/£3.50–£6.30) per person, and include a simple lunch. A boat trip can replace the hike (a positive for some), and cost around Q100 to Q150 ($13–$20/£7–£11) per person. If you sign up for a guided tour, find out whether or not this entrance fee is included in the price. There's a small *comedor* at the entrance to the waterfalls where you can get a lunch or something cold to drink.

Just off the beach, some 5km (3 miles) north. Admission Q10 ($1.35/70p). Daily 8am–5pm.

Playa Blanca Playa Blanca is the best beach in the area, partly due to its distance from the outflow of the Río Dulce and the heavy pollution generated by the residents of Livingston. The sand here is a bit whiter and softer, and the water a bit bluer than you'll find closer to town. This is actually a private beach (hence the admission charge), and to get here, you need to sign up for a guided tour or hire a boat through ASOTRANSLALI (© **502/7947-0870**).

Located about 12km (7½ miles) northwest of Livingston. Admission Q15 ($2/£1.05).

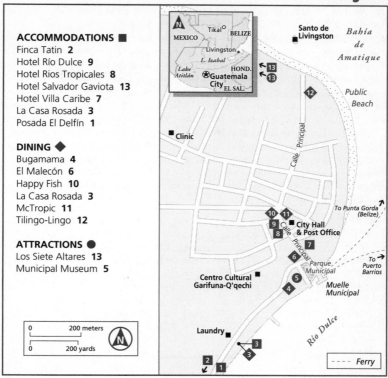

ACCOMMODATIONS ■
Finca Tatin **2**
Hotel Río Dulce **9**
Hotel Rios Tropicales **8**
Hotel Salvador Gaviota **13**
Hotel Villa Caribe **7**
La Casa Rosada **3**
Posada El Delfín **1**

DINING ◆
Bugamama **4**
El Malecón **6**
Happy Fish **10**
La Casa Rosada **3**
McTropic **11**
Tilingo-Lingo **12**

ATTRACTIONS ●
Los Siete Altares **13**
Municipal Museum **5**

Map labels: MEXICO · Tikal · BELIZE · Livingston · L. Izabal · Lake Atitlán · Guatemala City · HOND. · EL SAL. · Santo de Livingston · Bahía de Amatique · Public Beach · Clinic · Calle Principal · To Punta Gorda (Belize) · City Hall & Post Office · To Puerto Barrios · Parque Municipal · Centro Cultural Garifuna-Q'qechi · Muelle Municipal · Laundry · Río Dulce · 0 200 meters · 0 200 yards · N · ---- Ferry

Río Dulce 𝕮𝕮 A boat trip up the Río Dulce is one of the most popular area attractions. Just upriver from Livingston, the Río Dulce enters a narrow canyon known as **La Cueva de la Vaca,** which features steep walls some 92m (300 ft.) tall. One section, **La Pintada,** is made up of sheer, bright white-rock cliffs. Unfortunately, near the waterline, much of this white rock is marred by graffiti. However, beyond the graffiti is lush tropical rainforest. There are a few hot springs along the river, which form different heated pools and swimming areas. As you exit the canyon, the river broadens out into **El Golfete.** This long, wide section continues on until the river once again narrows near the town of Río Dulce.

Off El Golfete lies the **Biotopo Chocón Machacas** 𝕮, a protected area of mangroves and rainforest canals that's home to a healthy population of manatees. Often called "sea cows," manatees are massive aquatic mammals that can reach more than 3m (10 ft.) in length and weigh more than 454 kilograms (1,000 lb.). Many tours take a trip through the Biotopo, although sightings of manatees are far from guaranteed. Nonetheless, the area is quite beautiful, and the bird-watching is excellent.

Finally, some tours go all the way to the town of Fronteras, which is also simply known as Río Dulce. Fronteras sits at the demarcation point between Río Dulce and Lago Izabal. A visit here usually includes a tour of the **Castillo de San Felipe** 𝕮 (see later in this chapter). All of the tour agencies in town offer trips up the Río Dulce. Prices range from Q75 to Q225 ($10–$30/£5.25–£16) depending upon the specific tour. Try Happy Fish (see below).

Attractions in town are limited to a small **municipal museum** (© **502/7947-0070**) with a few interpretive and written displays detailing the Garífuna culture and history, and a small park just outside the museum, where you'll see a few crocodiles in a round enclosure. The large reptiles are impressive in size and menacing, but the unkempt and small pens they are kept in make this quite a sad display. The museum is open Monday through Saturday from 9am to 5pm. Admission is Q5 (65¢/35p).

While the local population lives largely off the sea, there are no major sportfishing operations in Livingston. If you're interested in a fishing outing, contact a tour agency or ask around the docks for a local fisherman who's willing to take you out. Snorkelers will need to travel out of Livingston to the nearby cays of Belize. Contact **Happy Fish** (© **502/7947-0661;** www.happyfishresort.com) about day trips. Rates are Q3,000 ($400/£210) for up to eight people.

SHOPPING

Aside from street vendors hawking handmade jewelry and simple trinkets, there's not much of a shopping scene in Livingston. One major exception, however, is the **Q'eqchi' women's craft cooperative** ⊕, run by **Ak' Tenamit** (www.aktenamit.org), a community development project that does major educational, health, and social work with the Q'eqchi' Maya of the area. Offerings include woven baskets, various textile projects, and artisanal papers made from banana and corn byproducts. They are located about a 15-minute boat ride upriver from Livingston. You can hire a boat at the docks to take you there for around Q75 ($10/£5.25) round-trip; otherwise, most of the Río Dulce tours stop there.

The local music is percussion-based with roots in West Africa. In some cases, modern electric instruments are added, and a rock or reggae influence can be heard. CDs are available in gift shops around town, and from street vendors, but be sure to take a listen first to make sure it's of reasonable quality.

WHERE TO STAY

When you arrive in Livingston, your boat will invariably be met by aggressive touts trying to steer you to a hotel where they'll get a commission. Some will even claim that the hotel you are asking about is full, or has recently closed. In general, I wouldn't believe them, especially if you have a confirmed reservation.

MODERATE

Hotel Villa Caribe ⊕⊕ *Kids*   This is easily the most luxurious hotel in Livingston, and it almost qualifies as a resort with its hillside location and views over the Río Dulce and Caribbean Sea. Rooms are large and comfortable, and all come with a private balcony. The best rooms in the house are the five individual bungalows, which are classified as junior suites. These have all been recently remodeled, and come with air-conditioning, a minifridge, and TV. My favorite of these is Punta Palma, which practically hangs off the side of the hill and has a private deck to take advantage of the view. There's a large pool and plenty of lounge chairs, which you'll appreciate given the hot and humid climate. The restaurant serves good international and local cuisine in a semi-elegant setting, often featuring live Garífuna music and dancing. There's a small beach in front of the hotel, but you'd be much better off heading to their "private" section of Playa Blanca, a 20-minute boat ride away. The hotel used to be called Tucán Dugú, and some locals still refer to it this way.

1 block up from the municipal dock. (© 502/2334-1818 central reservation number in Guatemala City, or 502/7947-0072. www.villasdeguatemala.com. 43 units. Q640 ($85/£45) double; Q825 ($110/£58) junior suite. AE, DC, MC, V. **Amenities:** 2 restaurants; bar; large outdoor pool; tour desk; laundry service. *In room:* No phone.

Posada El Delfín 🐟   Set on the waterfront west of the municipal dock, this is an alternative to Villa Caribe in Livingston's high-end market. However, I think Villa Caribe has this place beat in terms of service, comfort, and amenities. That said, the rooms here are all spacious and come with air-conditioning (which is not the case at Villa Caribe). Those on the first floor have checkerboard tile floors, which I prefer to the carpeted second-floor units, which can get a bit musty. There's a tiny pool—or giant tepid Jacuzzi—in the covered ground-floor patio. The best room by far, and one of the best in Livingston, is the honeymoon suite located at the end of a pier jutting into the bay. This second-floor room has a wraparound deck, a giant living area, a king-size bed, and a large-screen TV. Still, I think it's a bit pricey at Q1,500 ($200/£105) per night.

3 blocks west of the municipal dock. (© 502/7947-0694. Fax 502/7947-0077. www.turcios.com/eldelfin. 24 units. Q525 ($70/£37) double; Q1,500 ($200/£105) bungalow. Rates lower midweek and off season; slightly higher during peak periods. AE, DC, MC, V. **Amenities:** Restaurant; tiny pool; tour desk; laundry service. *In room:* A/C.

INEXPENSIVE

There are a host of budget options in Livingston. Many are quite stuffy, moldy, and uncomfortable, so I'd stick to Casa Rosada (below). However, real budget hounds can try either **Hotel Ríos Tropicales** (© 502/7947-0158) or **Hotel Río Dulce** (© 502/7947-0764), both of which are located on Calle Principal, near the center of town.

If you want to stay right on the beach close to Los Siete Altares, check out **Hotel Salvador Gaviota** (© 502/5514-3272; hotelsgaviota@hotmail.com), a very basic operation that boasts a decent beach for swimming and easy access to the waterfalls.

Finca Tatin 🐟   This place is a unique riverside ecolodge located about 20 minutes by boat outside of Livingston. Accommodations range from dorm rooms and private rooms with shared bathroom facilities to a few private bungalows and cabins with their own bathrooms. All are relatively basic, with minimal amenities, but they're very well kept. Most of the beds are made of soft foam, but at least they have mosquito netting. There's a relaxed, collegial vibe to the whole place, and you couldn't pick a better spot to get away from it all and explore the tropical rainforests. Kayak tours through the rainforest rivers are the specialty here, but you'll also have the chance to visit some local indigenous communities. If you're coming from Río Dulce, most of the collective and private boat taxis will drop you off here. If not, these folks will provide a boat transfer from Livingston with advance notice for Q30 ($4/£2.10) per person. A full meal plan runs around Q90 ($12/£6.30) per day.

Río Tatin, Río Dulce. (© 502/5902-0831. www.fincatatin.centramerica.com. Q75 ($10/£5.25) private bathroom bungalow; Q45 ($6/£3.15) shared bathroom; Q38 ($5/£2.65) dorm. These rates are per person. No credit cards. **Amenities:** Restaurant; tour desk; laundry service. *In room:* No phone.

La Casa Rosada *(Finds*   This is my favorite budget option in Livingston. The individual wooden bungalows all share several well-maintained common bathrooms and showers. Each comes with two twin beds, each of which is set under a fan and mosquito net. Colorful decor livens up the rooms, and the walls are mostly made of screened mesh to encourage cross-ventilation. The hotel is set on the waterfront and has a thatch-roof *palapa* built out over the water. The owners, a Belgian and Guatemalan couple, have kept the place up since they took it over 5 years ago, and run an excellent tour operation, which visits all the major tourist destinations mentioned above. This place also has one of the best restaurants in town (see below).

5 blocks west of the municipal dock. ✆ **502/7947-0303.** Fax 502/7947-0304. www.hotelcasarosada.com. 10 units. Q150 ($20/£11) double, all with shared bathroom. V. **Amenities:** Restaurant; tour desk; laundry service. *In room:* No phone.

WHERE TO DINE

In addition to the places listed below, **El Malecón, McTropic,** and **Tilingo-Lingo** are all good options. El Malecón serves local Guatemalan fare with an emphasis on seafood. McTropic also serves local fare, with plenty of seafood options, as well as some American-style dishes, including burgers and steaks. Tilingo-Lingo has a more international menu, with everything from pastas to the local specialty, *tapado.*

INEXPENSIVE

Bugamama ✿ *Finds* INTERNATIONAL   This new spot is a pleasant addition to the dining scene in Livingston. The restaurant, part of the Ak' Tenamit community development project, is a training school for local youth, and profits go to support various local community health and education projects. This is one of the best joints in town, and serves up a mean *tapado* and other local specialties, plus more familiar dishes such as chicken satay and fettuccine Gorgonzola. The old wooden building is painted in bright colors, and tables are spread through a couple of rooms and all around the veranda. Visitors and locals alike spend time here nursing a coffee, reading a book, or playing cards or backgammon.

1 block west of the municipal dock. ✆ **502/7947-0891.** Main courses Q40–Q200 ($5.30–$26/£2.80–£14). MC, V. Daily 7am–9pm.

Happy Fish ✿ INTERNATIONAL/SEAFOOD   This open-air, street-side restaurant is one of the most popular spots in town for breakfast, lunch, and dinner. Most of the tables are set in the front dining room, where a thatch roof and slow-turning ceiling fans battle the heat. However, there are a few tables right on the street under large beach umbrellas. The menu features a mix of local fare, seafood, and some international dishes. The *tapado* here is good, but a little sweet. I'd stick to the fresh fish or seafood options. They have a good espresso machine, making this a top choice for breakfast or a midday break. The restaurant also has a small tour agency, an Internet cafe, and a bar.

Calle Principal. ✆ **502/7947-0661.** Main courses Q40–Q225 ($5.30–$30/£2.80–£16). MC, V. Daily 7am–9pm.

La Casa Rosada ✿✿ *Finds* INTERNATIONAL/SEAFOOD   The food, service, and selection are consistently excellent at the intimate restaurant of this budget hotel, where subdued lighting and shell and bamboo curtains add to the ambience. The menu changes regularly, but always features a broad selection of dishes including several vegetarian options, fresh seafood, and an excellent *tapado.* Other options might include curried shrimp, a Thai-influenced special, or a spicy pasta with mixed seafood. All dinners, no matter what main dish you choose, start with a fresh salad and bread, and finish with dessert. Reservations, including your choice of a main dish, must be made by 6pm.

5 blocks west of the municipal dock, Livingston. ✆ **502/7947-0303.** Reservations required. Main courses Q40–Q85 ($5.30–$11/£2.80–£5.95). V. Daily 6:30–9pm.

LIVINGSTON AFTER DARK

By far the most happening bar in Livingston is **Ubafu** 𝒓𝒓, 2 blocks west of Calle Principal, on the road to the cemetery (no phone), which has live Garífuna, *punta*, or reggae music most nights. Traditional Garífuna drum ensembles feature a variety of conga-style wooden drums with skin heads, but one of their more interesting percussion instruments is made from several turtle shells, which are strung together and worn by the drummer like a personal trap set. For a more formal presentation of Garífuna drumming and dancing, head to the **Hotel Villa Caribe,** 1 block from the municipal dock (© **502/2334-1818**), which has presentations to accompany their dinner service several nights a week.

2 Río Dulce, Fronteras & Lago Izabal 𝒓𝒓

308km (191 miles) E of Guatemala City; 84km (52 miles) W of Puerto Barrios

Guatemala's largest lake, **Lago Izabal,** is located in an isolated, stunningly beautiful, forested section of the country, which has only recently been discovered by tourists. The river port town of Fronteras, commonly called Río Dulce, is the only major settlement in the area, and is located at the narrow section where Lago Izabal becomes the Río Dulce, which flows northeast toward Livingston and the sea.

ESSENTIALS
GETTING THERE

BY CAR   To reach Río Dulce by car, take the Carretera al Atlántico (CA-9) out of Guatemala City to La Ruidosa crossroads at Km 245. From here it's another 34km (21 miles) north on highway CA-13 to Río Dulce. Highway CA-13 also connects Río Dulce with Flores, Tikal, and El Petén.

BY BUS   **Litegua** (© **502/7930-5251** in Río Dulce, 502/220-8840 in Guatemala City; www.litegua.com), **Autobuses del Norte (ADN;** © **502/2221-2515;** www. adnautobusesdelnorte.com), and **Línea Dorada** (© **502/2232-5506;** www. tikalmayanworld.com) all have direct daily service between Guatemala City and Fronteras, Río Dulce. All have terminals within a couple of blocks of each other in Zona 1. Between the three lines, buses begin leaving around 5am and leave at least once every hour, with the last departure around 2pm. The trip from Guatemala City takes about 5½ hours, and fares run between Q50 and Q150 ($6.65–$20/£3.50–£11) one-way. Splurge for one of the "executive" or "deluxe" buses, which are more modern, comfortable, and faster. Alternatively, you can take any bus to Puerto Barrios, get off in La Ruidosa, and wait for a local bus to pass on its way to Río Dulce. Or, if you're coming from Antigua or Panajachel, all of the local tour agencies can arrange a scheduled minivan transfer to Río Dulce for Q260 to Q300 ($35–$40/£18–£21).

There's also regular bus service between Río Dulce and Flores, Petén. **Línea Dorada** and **ADN** both run this route, which takes about 3½ hours each way.

BY BOAT   Río Dulce is serviced by regular boat-taxi service from both Livingston and Puerto Barrios. The main boat dock is located at the base of the bridge on the Fronteras side. Collective boats leave Río Dulce for Livingston from the main dock at 9:30am and 1pm every day. The fare is Q100 ($13/£7) one-way; Q160 ($21/£11) round-trip. Other boats will run throughout the day once they fill to capacity, or you can rent a boat that will hold up to 10 people for around Q750 ($100/£53).

GETTING AROUND

For many purposes, boats are the preferred means of travel. Head to the main boat dock in Río Dulce, where you can catch regular service to Livingston and El Castillo San Felipe. You can also hire a small motor launch to take you around for Q375 to Q750 ($50–$100/£26–£53) for a half-day.

For land travel, taxis are readily available on the main road through Fronteras. If you can't flag one down, have your hotel call one for you.

Fun Fact Ahoy, Mate

Río Dulce is a major "hurricane hole," which means it's a safe and secure anchorage during hurricane season. Between July and October of each year, the marinas and anchorages, as well as the bars and restaurants, are packed with sailors seeking safe harbor during the Caribbean hurricane season.

ORIENTATION

There are hotels and restaurants clustered around the shores of Río Dulce, on both sides of the bridge, and farther afield. While the whole area is most commonly referred to as Río Dulce, there are more specific designations here. Approaching from Puerto Barrios or Guatemala City, the area around the base of the bridge is known as El Relleno. After crossing the bridge, you'll come to Fronteras, the larger and more important settlement.

FAST FACTS **Banco de Comercio** (© 502/7930-5141), **Banco Industrial** (© 502/5514-0888), and **Banrural** (© 502/7930-5159) can all be found on the main road in the center of Fronteras. The **Centro de Salud** health center (© 502/7390-5209) is also in this area. The number for the local **police** is © 502/5306-5873.

WHAT TO DO IN & AROUND RIO DULCE

Everything in this area revolves around its biggest attraction, Lago Izabal. Most hotels and tour agencies in town offer boat tours of the lake. Almost all of these make a stop at **Castillo de San Felipe,** and many also head to **Finca El Paraíso** (see below). Some tours head down the Río Dulce to Livingston, passing through **El Golfete** and **Cueva de la Vaca,** often making a side trip to **Biotopo Chocón Machacas.** For more details on these destinations and attractions, see the Livingston section above.

Your best bet for lining up a tour is to contact the folks at **Tijax Express** (© 502/7930-5197), which has an office just off the main street in Fronteras.

Since Río Dulce is such a popular destination with cruising yachts, there are almost always a couple of sailboats working the charter business. Ask your hotel or around the dock at Bruno's or the Restaurante Río Bravo.

Castillo de San Felipe 🜲 In 1652, Spanish colonists built this stone fort at the narrowest point of Lago Izabal, where it begins its life at the Río Dulce and flows down to Livingston. The fort was built here to dominate the waterway access into the lake and defend the Spanish from British, French, and Dutch raiders. While the stone battlements and cannons offered good protection from a water-launched attack, land attacks were a different story, and the fort was destroyed in 1686 and subsequently rebuilt.

A bilingual guide will be on hand when you enter to give you a quick 20-minute tour. The cost is included in the admission price, but be sure to tip a little (Q7–Q14/$1–$2/50p–£1 is a good amount). In addition to tours of the fort, there are picnic tables on the grounds and even a swimming area on the lake. The easiest way to get here is by boat. Boats leave throughout the day from the main dock and charge Q10 ($1.35/70p) each way.

On the shore of the Río Dulce, 3.2km (2 miles) west of the main bridge in Fronteras. Admission Q20 ($2.65/£1.40). Daily 8am–5pm.

EL ESTOR

El Estor is a beautiful community on the north shore of Lago Izabal, with forested mountains that appear to cascade into the lake. There are a couple of natural attractions of note, and many of the boat tours from Río Dulce stop here.

El Boquerón ✸   This is a stunning natural river canyon cut by the Río Sauce a few miles east of El Estor. Ride up the canyon in a boat or kayak to a small riverside beach, where the swimming is excellent.

No phone. Free admission. No official hours.

Finca El Paraíso ✸   A beautiful jungle waterfall of thermally heated water is the prime attraction at this working farm and ecotourism project. At the base of the fall you can bathe in both hot and cold water pools. These folks have a pleasant restaurant by the lakeshore, and several simple bungalows for staying overnight.

At Km 299 on the road around the lake. Admission Q10 ($1.35/70p).

WHERE TO STAY

In addition to the places listed below, **Planeta Río** (© **502/7930-5230;** www.planeta-rio.com) is a good midrange choice with ample facilities and activity options. I've also gotten good reports about the budget option **Casa Perico** (© **502/7930-5666**).

EXPENSIVE

Banana Palms ✸ *Kids*   This is easily the most luxurious option in Río Dulce and along Lago Izabal. The hotel is actually several miles outside of Fronteras, set on a lovely section of the lakeshore and very close to El Castillo de San Felipe. Each room, all very large suites, is equipped with a kitchenette, sitting room, and spacious bedroom with two queen-size beds. The second-floor deluxe units each have an outdoor Jacuzzi on their open-air deck, and some of these have excellent views of the lake. The grounds are beautiful, with lush gardens and a pretty walkway along the lakeshore. The large pool features a volleyball net and a separate children's pool. There's also a game room by the lake with a Ping-Pong table, pool table, and foosball; an outdoor basketball court; and private marina with motor boats and kayaks for hire.

Just beyond El Castillo de San Felipe. © **502/7930-5022** or 502/2334-2598 reservation number in Guatemala City. Fax 502/2331-2815. www.bananapalms.com.gt. 33 units. Q640–Q975 ($85–$130/£45–£68) double. Rates include full breakfast. Rates higher during peak periods. AE, DC, MC, V. **Amenities:** Restaurant; 2 bars; midsize pool; tour desk; laundry service. *In room:* A/C, TV.

MODERATE

Catamaran Island Hotel ✸ *Finds*   This is my favorite hotel in Río Dulce, and although it's not technically an island, you can really only get here by boat. The individual wooden cabins are relatively simple and bare-bones, but feature air-conditioning and a private porch or deck area. The best ones are either right on the edge or out over the water. At the over-water main lodge, you'll find a dark and stately, yet decidedly tropical, bar; a computer with Internet connection; and a large TV with satellite feed. The restaurant is massive, and there's a daytime bar near the pool at the center of the compound. These folks are popular with itinerant cruising sailors, and they even have a tennis court.

Fronteras. ℂ **502/5902-0831** at the hotel, 502/2367-1545 reservation number in Guatemala City. Fax 502/2367-1633. www.catamaranisland.com. 35 units. Q640–Q715 ($85–$96/£45–£50) double. Rates include full breakfast. Rates higher during peak periods. AE, DC, MC, V. **Amenities:** Restaurant; 2 bars; midsize outdoor pool; unlit outdoor tennis court; tour desk; laundry service. *In room:* A/C, no phone.

INEXPENSIVE

Bruno's There are a variety of room choices here, but the best are found in a three-story concrete building facing the river. All of the rooms come with a shared balcony, and those on the top floor have the best views. However, even the best rooms here, which come with air-conditioning and TVs, feel a bit bare and basic, so you may opt for a less expensive room away from the water or even a dorm room. The hotel is well located and offers good deals, plus it has a pool near the river and one of the most popular restaurants in town, which serves as one of Río Dulce's principal social hubs.

Fronteras. ℂ **502/7930-5721** or 502/5692-7292. www.mayaparadise.com. 17 units. Q35 ($4.65/£2.45) per person dorm room; Q100 ($13/£7) double room with shared bathroom; Q300 ($40/£21) double room with private bathroom. AE, DC, MC, V. **Amenities:** Restaurant; bar; small outdoor pool; tour desk; laundry service. *In room:* No phone.

Hacienda Tijax *(Finds* While I find the rooms here on the rustic end of the scale, you can't beat the setting and amenities. Located a short boat ride away from the main docks in Río Dulce, Tijax bills itself as a "jungle lodge." Its collection of mixed accommodations range from simple rooms and individual cabins with shared bathrooms to private cabins with air-conditioning and large two-story family-style bungalows. The rooms are fairly bare, and in some cases show the effects of the harsh and extremely humid climate. All come with the requisite mosquito netting over each bed. I recommend splurging on one of the air-conditioned cabins. The best things about this place are its pool, common areas, and the surrounding jungle. Travelers from around the world seem to converge at Tijax, and there's a friendly, hostel-like vibe to the place. The pool, which is almost always busy during the day, features two separate unheated Jacuzzis, and the soaring thatch-roof dining area and lounge is equally popular at night. A host of tour activities and hikes are available here.

Fronteras. ℂ **502/7930-5505**. www.tijax.com. 23 units. Q115 ($15/£8.05) double room; Q225 ($30/£16) double cabin with shared bathroom; Q270 ($36/£19) double cabin with private bathroom; Q450 ($60/£32) double bungalow. AE, DC, MC, V. **Amenities:** Restaurant; 2 bars; small outdoor pool; 2 Jacuzzis; tour desk; laundry service. *In room:* No phone.

WHERE TO DINE
INEXPENSIVE

Bruno's INTERNATIONAL This popular place is Río Dulce's prime meeting ground for itinerant sailors, land-based travelers, assorted expatriates, and other lost souls. There's a crowded bulletin board listing everything from tours, boat cruises, and available rooms to boats for sale, boats looking for crew, and massage therapists. The food here is well-prepared, fairly priced, and copious, so the wood tables and chairs can fill up quickly. Their fried *mojara*—a local freshwater fish—is excellent. However, service can be indifferent or bad at times. Barbecue nights on Wednesday and Sunday feature ribs, burgers, and chicken, while the great breakfasts include Guatemalan dishes and American fare such as pancakes, omelets, and home fries.

Under the bridge, Río Dulce. ℂ **502/7930-5721** or 502/5692-7292. Main courses Q40–Q75 ($5.30–$10/£2.80–£5.25). AE, DC, MC, V. Daily 7am–10pm.

Restaurante Río Bravo ✦ INTERNATIONAL/GUATEMALAN While the food here is good and served in big portions, you can't beat the setting of this place, built on a wooden deck jutting into the river. The menu features a mix of local Guatemalan fare alongside a long list of pizzas and pastas. This place is almost always bustling and the tables closest to the water are a hot commodity.

Under the bridge, Río Dulce. ⓒ 502/7930-5167. Main courses Q35–Q85 ($4.65–$10/£2.45–£5.95). AE, DC, MC, V. Daily 7am–10pm.

3 Puerto Barrios

297km (184 miles) NE of Guatemala City; 23km (14 miles) SE of Livingston; 41km (25 miles) NE of Río Dulce

Puerto Barrios is a busy, industrial port city with virtually no appeal to tourists. It is, however, a principal transit point for trips to Livingston, Belize, and the Honduran Bay Islands. Because of the difficulty of coordinating boats and buses, some tourists end up spending the night in Puerto Barrios. Just outside of Puerto Barrios, there are a few nice beaches and some wonderful tropical rainforests. You'll also see some vacation homes of wealthy Guatemalans all along the waterfront heading out of Puerto Barrios.

ESSENTIALS
GETTING THERE
BY CAR To reach Puerto Barrios by car, take the Carretera al Atlántico (CA-9) out of Guatemala City. Puerto Barrios is the end of the line some 295km (183 miles) to the northeast.

BY BUS Litegua (ⓒ **502/7948-1002** in Puerto Barrios, 502/220-8840 in Guatemala City; www.litegua.com) has direct daily service between Guatemala City and Puerto Barrios. The Litegua terminal in Guatemala City is at 6a Calle and 9a Avenida, Zona 1. The first bus leaves for Puerto Barrios at 4:30am, and they run at least every hour, often on the hour and half-hour, until 6pm. Return buses have a similar frequency, but between the hours of 1am and 4pm. The bus station in Puerto Barrios is at the corner of 6a Avenida and 9a Calle. The trip takes about 5 hours each way. Fares are between Q50 and Q100 ($6.65–$13/£3.50–£7) one-way. Splurge for one of the "executive" or "deluxe" buses, which are more modern, comfortable, and faster.

BY BOAT Scheduled boats run from Puerto Barrios to Livingston at 10:30am and 5pm. The 90-minute trips costs Q15 ($2/£1.05). Faster boats leave throughout the day as they fill capacity, and charge Q30 ($4/£2.10). These make the run in just 30 minutes—well worth the extra $2—and run roughly between 6:30am and 4pm.

   Transportes El Chato (ⓒ **502/7948-5525**; www.transporteselchato.com) runs a daily boat to Punta Gorda, Belize, at 10am. The return boat leaves Punta Gorda at 2pm. The one-way ride takes around 1 hour and costs Q120 ($16/£8.40). Before heading to Punta Gorda, you must have your passport stamped at the **Immigration Office,** 9a Calle and 2a Avenida (ⓒ **502/7948-0327**), which is located just 1 block from the dock.

   Boats to and from Livingston, as well as to Punta Gorda, Belize, use the municipal dock at the end of 12a Calle.

GETTING AROUND
Taxis are plentiful in Puerto Barrios, and cabs are always waiting to meet incoming boats from Livingston and Punta Gorda, as well as all incoming buses. Given the seediness

and relative insecurity of the city, I'd recommend taking a taxi most places. If none are readily available, have your hotel call you one.

ORIENTATION

While Puerto Barrios remains a busy port, much of the commercial traffic was shifted just down the bay to Santo Tomás de Castillo after a 1976 earthquake damaged many of the port facilities. Several banks, shops, and services are located in the compact downtown area.

WHAT TO DO IN & AROUND PUERTO BARRIOS

Most tourists use Puerto Barrios as a gateway to Livingston or Belize since there's not much to see here, but just out of town a very pretty waterfall, **Las Escobas,** has a good swimming hole at its base. You might also want to visit **Punta Manabique,** a long point of land with mangroves and swamps jutting out into Amatique Bay. There's good bird-watching and nature-viewing here, which you can enjoy on hikes or boat rides. For tours or other information, contact the **Fundación Mario Dary** (© 502/7948-0435; fundary@intelnet.net.gt), a nonprofit organization that administers this protected area.

Fishing, snorkeling, and scuba diving are popular at the nearby Belizean cays. If you want to do any tours or activities while you're in the city, contact **OGUATUR,** 16a Calle and 7a Avenida (© **502/7942-9181**), or check in with the folks at **Amatique Bay Resort and Marina** (below).

WHERE TO STAY

Although you can't beat it for atmosphere and location, the **Hotel del Norte,** 7a Calle and 1a Av. (© **502/7948-2116**) has definitely seen better days. The sea, salt air, and heavy humidity have all taken their toll on this classic waterfront hotel. Still, for a night or two, it's certainly acceptable. Another option close to the center of the city is **Hotel Valle Tropical** (© **502/7948-7084;** www.hotelvalletropical.com), which is a rather out-of-place concrete block painted an awful pale green.

EXPENSIVE

Amatique Bay Resort and Marina 🕏🕏 *(Kids*   This may be the best beach resort in Guatemala; it is certainly the most ambitious and extensive. Set on expansive grounds on its namesake bay, the resort boasts a small patch of white-sand beach and sea, as well as a full-service marina with scuba diving and fishing operations. The hotel was built on and around the ruins of a colonial-era port, and they even have an old Catholic church, lighthouse, and small fort. The rooms, however, are modern, spacious, and tastefully decorated. Many are suites or apartments with fully equipped kitchens. A wide range of tours and activities are available here, and on-site attractions include a butterfly farm and turtle hatchery.

4km (2½ miles) east of Puerto Barrios, on the Bahia de Amatique. © **502/7948-1800.** Fax 502/7948-1823. www. amatiquebay.net. 61 units. Q600–Q750 ($80–$100/£42–£53) double; Q900–Q1,275 ($120–$170/£63–£90) suite. AE, DC, MC, V. **Amenities:** 2 restaurants; 2 bars; large outdoor pool; full-service dive shop; tour desk; children's program; laundry service. *In room:* A/C, TV, hair dryer.

INEXPENSIVE

Hotel Puerto Libre 🕏   Although it's located on the outskirts just off the busy Carretera al Atlántico's crossroads into the city, this is still your best bet in Puerto Barrios. The rooms here are comfortable and well-maintained, and there's a midsize pool. The hotel also does brisk business as a local conference center, with five separate conference rooms and facilities.

Km 292 Carretera al Atlántico. © **502/7948-4738.** Fax 502/7948-4749. www.hotelpuertolibre.com. 41 units. Q210–Q295 ($28–$40/£15-£21) double. Rates almost double during Easter week. AE, DC, MC, V. **Amenities:** Restaurant; bar; small pool; tour desk; laundry service. *In room:* No phone.

WHERE TO DINE

In addition to the place listed below, the restaurant at the **Hotel Puerto Libre** (© **502/7948-4738**) is excellent, serving a mix of international and Guatemalan fare, with an emphasis on seafood.

INEXPENSIVE

Restaurante Safari ⊛ INTERNATIONAL/SEAFOOD   The best restaurant in town, Restaurante Safari has a great space jutting over the water. The open-air dining room is quite large, and can get very busy on Fridays and Saturdays, so arrive early if you want a waterfront table. Fresh fish and seafood are the best choices, although the long menu features a wide range of other options. If you're not going to make it to Livingston, be sure to try the *tapado*.

5a Av. and 1a Calle. © **502/7948-0563.** Main courses Q40–Q90 ($5.30–$12/£2.80–£6.30). AE, DC, MC, V. Daily 11am–11pm.

PUERTO BARRIOS AFTER DARK

As a port city, Puerto Barrios has its fair share of dingy bars and strip joints. Most are centered around 6a and 7a avenidas, and 6a and 7a calles. Personally, I'd recommend most tourists avoid this area, as it can be pretty dangerous, especially for foreigners. Your best bet is to head to the Restaurante Safari for some mellow drinks overlooking the water, or stick to your hotel facilities.

SIDE TRIP: QUIRIGUA ⊛

Quiriguá is a small yet important Maya archaeological site, located just off the Carretera al Atlántico some 94km (58 miles) from Puerto Barrios. Set close to the banks of the Motagua River, this UNESCO World Heritage Site was predominantly a trading city with close ties to Copán. The Late Classic city thrived from A.D. 692–900, during which Quiriguá's greatest leader, Cauac Sky (A.D. 724–784), reigned. Quiriguá was visited in 1841 by John L. Stephens, who tried to buy the site for as much as he'd paid for Copán. In the end he failed, or was too cheap, and the site was purchased by the United Fruit Company in 1910. The company built banana plantations everywhere, but fortunately spared and protected the area's Maya ruins.

To get to Quiriguá, take the well-marked exit off the Carretera al Atlántico, 1.5km (1 mile) east of the town of Los Amates. From here, it's another 3km (2 miles) on a well-graded dirt road, through working banana plantations, to the park's entrance.

When you enter Quiriguá, your first stop should be the small museum and visitor center, which features some historical information, photos, and a scale model of the site. Even though all of the written material is in Spanish, the displays will help you get a grasp of the content. The main attraction at Quiriguá is its massive carved stelae. The tallest of these, and in the Maya world, is **stela E,** which is more than 10m (35 ft.) tall and weighs more than 65 tons. In addition to the stelae, there are massive carved stones in various shapes including frogs, serpents, turtles, and mythical beasts, all covered with hieroglyphs. Most of the stelae are found in Quiriguá's **Great Plaza,** which is surrounded by low temple buildings only recently excavated. At the north end of the Great Plaza lies the **Acropolis,** which occupies the highest ground on the site and offers a good panoramic view of the plaza and surrounding forests. *Note:* Because of the landscape, bird-watching is excellent, but it also means that mosquitoes are a problem, so bring repellent.

Most of Quiriguá's stelae were erected during the reign of Cauac Sky, and his face graces seven of the nine carved stelae at the site. In A.D. 738, Cauac Sky apparently conquered Copán, captured King 18 Rabbit, and had him decapitated in the Great Plaza. This event is depicted on **zoomorph G.** After this victory, Quiriguá began converting itself from a vassal trade city into a more classic ceremonial center. Grand new stelae were erected on the Great Plaza roughly every 5 years, beginning in A.D. 751 and continuing on until A.D. 806.

While Quiriguá's stelae and zoomorphic stones are somewhat protected under tall thatch roofs, many have already been severely damaged by the ravages of time, and, more recently, by graffiti.

Quiriguá is open daily from 8am to 4:30pm; admission is Q25 ($3.30/£1.75). You can easily tour the whole site in a couple of hours or less. If you end up needing to spend the night near Quiriguá, check into the **Hotel Royal** (© **502/7947-3639**).

11

Pacific Coast

While the country's Pacific coast is popular with Guatemalans, it's often neglected—or outright avoided—by most tourists. Part of this is for good reason. Guatemala's Pacific beaches pale in comparison to those found in Mexico, the Caribbean, and the rest of Central America, and they also take a back seat to the country's cultural, historic, architectural, and natural attractions. This region is almost uniformly hot and humid, and the beaches are filled with dark, volcanic sand. The waters are often too rough for swimming, and the shores are unfortunately strewn with garbage and other bits of jetsam. There are virtually no beach resorts and very few hotels of real comfort along the entire coast.

So why go? The beach towns of **Monterrico** and **Puerto San José** are fast and easy shots from Guatemala City and Antigua, and are brimming with Guatemalan revelers and families on weekends. This area is also quickly developing a reputation for some excellent deep-sea fishing, with record numbers of billfish being raised.

The Pacific coast can be easily included in a loop trip either to or from the highland city of Quetzaltenango, passing through the towns of **Retalhuleu** and **Santa Lucía Cotzumalguapa.** The latter has several interesting archaeological sites nearby and a good museum. For its part, Retalhuleu serves as a base for visiting one of several nearby amusement parks, which are seeking to make the place a sort of mini-Orlando, at least in the minds of Guatemalans and other Central American visitors.

1 Monterrico

124km (77 miles) S of Guatemala City; 70km (43 miles) SW of Escuintla

Monterrico is Guatemala's top beach destination, but the town is tiny and accommodations are limited. The beach here is a broad swath of dark volcanic sand backed by coconut palms and mangrove. Perhaps the town's biggest draw is its other natural charms. While often inhospitable to most sunbathers, Monterrico's beaches are prime nesting grounds for several species of **sea turtles,** and the beach's backing mangrove forests have been protected as part of the **Reserva Natural Monterrico** and are home to a wide range of tropical flora and fauna.

ESSENTIALS
GETTING THERE
Both of the principal routes to Monterrico involve taking a ferry (which now takes cars as well).

BY BUS & BOAT There are no direct buses to Monterrico from Guatemala City. To get here you can take any bus from the main Zona 4 bus terminal heading to the El Salvador border, and get off in Taxisco. Several lines service this route, and buses leave at least every half-hour between 5am and 9pm. In Taxisco you can transfer to a local bus or taxi to La Avillana, where you'll pick up the ferry to Monterrico. Buses from Taxisco to La Avillana are usually waiting and leave roughly every hour. Ferries run almost constantly during daylight hours between La Avillana and Monterrico, and tend to leave whenever full. The entire fare, including the ferry, should run you around Q25 ($3.35/£1.75), slightly more if you take a cab from Taxisco to La Avillana.

From Guatemala City, Antigua, or Panajachel, any tour agency or hotel in town can book you a minibus shuttle for around Q115 to Q225 ($15–$30/£8.05–£16). Given the convenience, I think it's worth the splurge.

BY CAR If you're coming by car, you can take one of two routes. In either case, you'll head south out of Guatemala City on CA-9 toward Escuintla. The most direct route is to drive from Escuintla over to Taxisco and then down to La Avillana. In La Avillana, a car ferry should be waiting to take you across to Monterrico. The 20-minute ferry ride costs around Q50 ($7/£3.50) each way, and tends to run during daylight hours, with the occasional cushion of an hour or so on either end. These leave according to demand.

The alternate route is to head straight from Escuintla to Puerto Quetzal, and then on to Iztapa. At the end of the road in Iztapa, you'll have to take a short car ferry over the river to Pueblo Viejo, where the road picks up again for Monterrico. In Iztapa, small car ferries—some only large enough for one car—will be waiting to take you across to Pueblo Viejo. These ferries run from 6am to 9pm and charge Q40 ($5.30/£2.80) round-trip. From Pueblo Viejo it's 26km (16 miles) on a well-paved road to Monterrico.

GETTING AROUND
Monterrico is small enough that you can easily walk anywhere in town. There are no official taxi companies in town, but your hotel will probably be able to find someone who works as a freelance taxi driver if you need one.

ORIENTATION
Both routes into Monterrico will land you on the Calle Principal, which runs perpendicular to, and dead-ends at, the beach. Most of the hotels are located on a dirt road running east off of Calle Principal, just before the beach. There are a host of cut-rate budget hotels and simple *comedores* all along Calle Principal.

FAST FACTS There are no banks, ATMs, hospitals, or major services in Monterrico. Be sure to bring as much cash as you think you'll need, as very few establishments here accept credit cards. There is one Internet cafe on Calle Principal, and I expect a couple more might pop up in short order.

Moments Watching Over You

If you're driving, it's worth keeping an eye out around Km 54.5 of the highway between Guatemala City and Escuintla. As you head south, look to the right, and you should be able to pick out what locals claim to be the face of an ancient Maya in the rock and mountain formation in the distance. The lore is that he's looking toward and watching over Guatemala City.

Pacific Coast

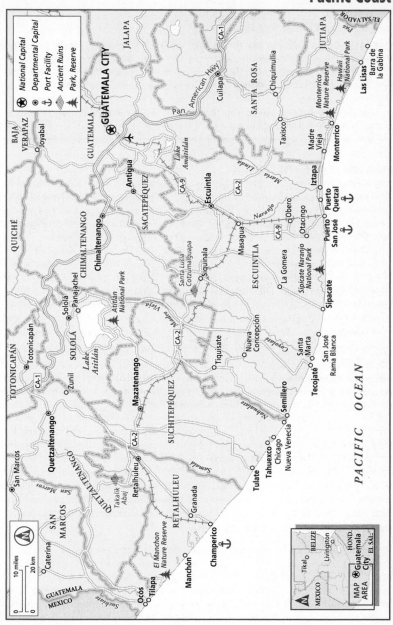

⟨Moments⟩ Off to the Races

There are no hares, but the turtles take off for the finish line every Saturday from September to December, when the Tortugario Monterrico holds a sunset race to the sea. For Q10 ($1.35/70p), sponsors pick a hatchling turtle from the facility's large tanks, place their competitor at the starting line, and wait for the signal to set their turtle into a frantic, albeit not blazing, dash to the sea. The sponsor whose turtle makes it to the water first wins. Prizes can range from a T-shirt to a dinner donated by a local restaurant.

FUN ON & OFF THE BEACH

Monterrico is the textbook definition of a laid-back beach town. Given that the surf here is often too rough for most casual bathers, the prime activities are hanging out in a hammock and reading a book. If you do decide to swim, make sure you feel very comfortable with your abilities and ask your hotel if the current surf conditions are safe. It's often best to choose a spot where you see others already swimming. Also, be sure to bring sandals, as the sand can get extremely hot under the bright sun.

A good way to stay off your feet is to take a horseback ride along the beach. Your hotel should be able to arrange a ride for around Q20 to Q40 ($2.70–$5.40/£1.40–£2.80) per hour. They can also arrange a fishing excursion with a local boat captain, which should run you Q500 to Q1,500 ($68–$200/£35–£105) for a half-day depending on the size and comfort level of the boat and the type of tackle provided.

If you want to brush up on your Spanish, check in with **El Proyecto Lingüístico Monterrico** (ⓒ 502/5978-4492) on the Calle Principal. Rates run Q550 ($73/£39) for 20 hours of study over a 5-day week.

Parque Hawaii (Hawaii Park)   Similar to but less touristy than the Reserva Natural de Monterrico (Monterrico Nature Reserve), this project is run by the **Asociación de Rescate y Conservación de Vida Silvestre** (**ARCAS;** www.arcasguatemala.com). ARCAS is actively involved in environmental protection and education, and runs several excellent volunteer programs. This protected zone is comprised of ecosystems similar to those found at the reserve. All of the hotels and tour agencies can arrange for a guided tour of Parque Hawaii. Tours usually last around 4 to 5 hours, and run between Q40 and Q90 ($5.35–$12/£2.80–£6.30) per person, depending upon the size of your group. On the trip, you'll see a wide range of bird fauna, as well as the chance to see caiman and iguanas in the wild. For more information, ask your hotel, or contact **Celso Orantes** (ⓒ 502/5236-7769; ecotoursmonterrico@yahoo.com).

About 7km (4½ miles) east of Reserva Natural de Monterrico.

Reserva Natural de Monterrico (Monterrico Nature Reserve) ⟨𝆑⟩   Sometimes referred to as the Biotopo Monterrico–Hawaii, this protected area covers some 28 sq. km (11 sq. miles), more than 70% of which are aquatic, including mangroves, canals, or estuaries. The reserve is home to a wide range of fauna, which are best seen by taking a boat tour through the canals. The visitor center on Calle Principal provides basic information and can arrange for a guide. All of the local hotels can arrange a boat tour through the reserve. One recommended local guide is **Celso Orantes** (ⓒ 502/5236-7769; ecotoursmonterrico@yahoo.com), who charges Q50 ($6.70/£3.50) per person

ACCOMMODATIONS ■
Café del Sol **2**
Dulce y Salado **12**
Hotel Isleta de Gaia **14**
Hotel Pez de Oro **9**
Hotel Utz Tzaba **1**
Johnny's Place **7**

DINING & NIGHTLIFE ◆
El Animal Desconocido **4**
El Caracol **5**
Hotel El Kaiman **6**
Johnny's Place **7**
Taberna El Pelícano **8**

ATTRACTIONS ●
El Proyecto Linguistico
    Monterrico **3**
Parque Hawaii **13**
Reserva Natural de
    Monterrico **11**
Tortuguerio Monterrico **10**

for a 2-hour boat tour. Nighttime tours to watch the turtles lay their eggs, generally between July and October, are also available.

Visitor center on Calle Principal, just east of the village center. ℂ **502/7885-0688.** Admission Q10 ($1.35/70p). Daily 8am–5pm.

Tortuguerio Monterrico 🐢🐢 The main purpose of this facility is to protect and release turtle hatchlings. Volunteers collect turtle eggs just after nesting to save them from poachers and natural predators. They then care for them and release them to sea once they've hatched. In addition to the turtle project, they raise and care for iguanas and caimans, have a short interpretive trail through the surrounding forest, and arrange boat tours through the area's mangrove canals.

A few blocks east of Calle Principal. Admission Q8 ($1.05/55p); Q25 ($3.30/£1.75) with a 45-min. guided tour. Daily 8am–5pm.

WHERE TO STAY
MODERATE
Hotel Isleta de Gaia 🐢🐢 This is perhaps the best beach hotel on Guatemala's Pacific Coast, located on the far eastern end of the country close to the El Salvador border. The piece of coastline that hosts the hotel is only reachable by boat after

crossing the Chiquimula lagoon, hence they call themselves an island. The thatch-roof bungalows are the best designed, decorated, and equipped resort rooms to be found on the coast. If you're looking for a semi-luxurious and isolated beach vacation in this neck of the woods, this should be your first and only choice.

Las Lisas. ℂ/fax **502/7885-0044.** www.isleta-de-gaia.com. 12 units. Q503–Q548 ($67–$73/£35–£39) bungalow; Q930 ($124/£65) 2-floor bungalow; Q1,080 ($144/bp]76) VIP bungalow. AE, DC, MC, V. **Amenities:** Restaurant; bar; outdoor pool; watersports equipment rental; tour desk; laundry service. *In room:* No phone.

Hotel Pez de Oro ☞

Although the hotel lacks any major amenities, the individual bungalows are my top choice in Monterrico. The spacious bungalows feature high thatch roofs, tile or polished and painted concrete floors, overhead ceiling fans, and carved-wood furniture. Each comes with a private balcony or porch. My favorite is no. 13, which is set on raised stilts, and has a good view of the ocean and more breeze thanks to the elevation. The restaurant here serves good Italian cuisine.

On the beach, about 3 blocks east of the Calle Principal. ℂ **502/7920-9785,** or 502/2368-3684 for reservations in Guatemala City. pezdeoro@intelnett.com. 10 units. Q390 ($52/£27) double. These are weekend rack rates, including tax. Rates lower midweek; slightly higher during peak periods. No credit cards. **Amenities:** Restaurant; bar; 2 small outdoor pools; tour desk; laundry service. *In room:* No phone.

Hotel Utz Tzaba ☞☞ (Kids)

If you're looking for the trappings, or at least an approximation, of luxury, this is your best bet, although it's somewhat out of town. The complex is built in a modified horseshoe around a large lawn area. The rooms are all spacious and contemporary, with high ceilings, tile floors, and relatively sparse decor, and are kept cool with modern "split" air-conditioning units. The four bungalows are two bedroom/one-bathroom affairs, each with a large sitting area, separate dining area, and full kitchenette. The pool features a swim-up bar, separate children's pool, and three unheated Jacuzzis. There's also some watersports equipment available for use, as well as a beach volleyball court and children's playground. When I last visited, I was told they may add televisions to the rooms in the future.

Km 21.8, Aldea El Pumpo. About 3km (1mile) west of Monterrico, on the road to Iztapa. ℂ **502/5318-9452.** Fax 502/7848-1479. www.utz-tzaba.com. 15 units. Q540 ($72/£38) double; Q1,043 ($139/£73) bungalow for up to 6 people. These are weekend rack rates, including tax. Rates lower midweek; slightly higher during peak periods. AE, DC, MC, V. **Amenities:** Restaurant; bar; midsize pool; 3 Jacuzzis; tour desk; laundry service; free Wi-Fi. *In room:* A/C, hair dryer.

INEXPENSIVE

In addition to the place listed below, two other good choices are **Café del Sol,** on the beach about 2 blocks west of Calle Principal (ℂ **502/5810-0821;** www.cafe-del-sol. com); and **Dulce y Salado,** on the beach about 500 yards east of Calle Principal (ℂ **502/5817-9046;** www.playademonterrico.com).

Johnny's Place

One of the most popular places in Monterrico, this American-owned joint has a variety of accommodations including dorm rooms, rustic two-bedroom bungalows, and a semi-luxurious three-bedroom "villa." The bungalows are the most common option, and feature polished concrete floors, concrete block walls, and a large, screened-in common area with basic kitchenette. The wood-frame beds all come with mosquito netting. The best rooms in the house are found in the luxury villa, with air-conditioning, television, and a hot-water shower—the rest of the rooms have cold-water showers. There are four small, mostly shallow, pools spread around the sandy grounds. A thatch-roof *palapa* on the beach is equipped with a line of hammocks, and the hotel's beach volleyball court often has a pickup game going.

On the beach, about 2 blocks east of the Calle Principal. ℂ **502/5812-0409** or 502/7762-0015. www.playde monterrico.com/johnnysplace.htm. 12 units, 1 dorm. Q45 ($6/£3.15) dorm bed; Q190 ($25/£13) double room; Q450 ($60/£32) 2-bedroom bungalow; Q750–Q800 ($100–$107/£53–£56) luxury villa. These are weekend rack rates. Rates lower midweek; slightly higher during peak periods. AE, DC, MC, V. **Amenities:** Restaurant; bar; four small outdoor pools; tour desk; laundry service. *In room:* No phone.

WHERE TO DINE

In addition to the places listed below, the restaurants at aforementioned **Hotel Pez de Oro** and **Dulce y Salado** both have respectable Italian fare, while the restaurant at **Johnny's Place** serves up good American bar food mixed with Mexican and Italian options. For Guatemalan cooking and simple seafood, try any of the *comedores* on the main road leading toward the beach.

Taberna El Pelícano 𝕽 *(Finds* INTERNATIONAL/SEAFOOD   This is easily the best and most interesting restaurant in Monterrico. The menu is longer and more creative than anything else in town, and features a variety of pastas, entrees, vegetarian dishes ("caviar" made from eggplant), desserts, and a list of daily specials. A small garden fronting the wooden tables hosts a fountain and a pair of large, almost tame, pelicans, the restaurant's namesake mascots.

Across from Johnny's. ℂ **502/5584-2400.** Main courses Q45–Q115 ($6–$15/£3.15–£8.05). No credit cards. Wed–Sun noon–2pm and 6–9pm.

MONTERRICO AFTER DARK

Monterrico is a mellow beach town, but things do pick up on Friday and Saturday nights. The most consistently popular bars in town are on or around Calle Principal, and include **El Caracol, El Animal Desconocido,** and **Johnny's Place** (see above). On most Saturday evenings, the **Hotel El Kaiman** has a raging disco.

2 Puerto San José

108km (67 miles) S of Guatemala City; 52km (32 miles) from Escuintla

Puerto San José is actually the quickest and easiest beach to reach from Guatemala City or Antigua, and therefore, it's also the most popular and developed. Still, the beach and its chaotic downtown hold little appeal for most visitors. Puerto San José was once Guatemala's principal industrial and trade port, but that role has been entirely taken over by the newly constructed Puerto Quetzal, a few miles to the east. Perhaps the greatest draw to Puerto San José is the ripe fishing grounds found just offshore. This town is developing a reputation as a major destination for sportfishing, with record numbers of marlin and sailfish being raised.

The beach right in front of Puerto San José is particularly unappealing. The best beach in the area is **Chulamar,** several miles to the west, where you'll find the Villas del Pacífico resort (below).

ESSENTIALS
GETTING THERE
BY BUS   Transportes Esmeralda (ℂ **502/2471-0327**) buses leave for Puerto San José roughly every half-hour between 6am and 9pm from Guatemala City's main Terminal de Autobuses in Zona 4. The fare is Q10 ($1.35/70p). The ride takes about 2 hours each way. Return buses follow roughly the same schedule.

BY CAR   If you're coming by car, head south out of Guatemala City on CA-9, the Pacific Coast Highway, toward Escuintla. From Escuintla it's a straight shot on a paved highway to Puerto Quetzal, where the highway ends. Follow the signs and flow of traffic for the last few miles to Puerto San José. The drive takes about 90 minutes, not including Guatemala City traffic.

GETTING AROUND
Taxis and tuk tuks are plentiful around Puerto San José, and most rides cost just Q10 to Q15 ($1.35–$2/70p–£1.05).

ORIENTATION
Puerto San José is busy and chaotic, especially considering its size. Several banks, pharmacies, Internet cafes, and *comedores* can be found in the downtown area, which is only about 6 blocks long by 4 blocks wide. The closest modern hospital, **Hospital Génesis,** 3a Av. 2-68, Zona 1 (© **502/788-0187**), is located in Escuintla.

FUN ON & OFF THE BEACH
As I said above, the beach here is rather unappealing. In fact, the beach is separated from the town by a broad canal. Small boats will take you across the canal throughout the day for around Q5 (65¢/35p). If you want to do some swimming or just hang on the beach, you're better off heading west out of town to the nearby beach of **Chulamar.**

⌒Moments Party Time

The town hosts rowdy *fiestas* from March 16 to 22, when hotels are packed with revelers, and a town fair and carnival takes over the area. Live concerts, carnival rides and games, and scores of food booths and souvenir stands are part of the festivities.

If you're looking to try your hand at landing a sailfish, marlin, or mahimahi, check in at the **Marina Pez Vela** (© **502/2379-5778**) which, in addition to serving as the new cruise ship terminal, is also home to the area's main fishing fleet. You can ask around the docks for a boat and captain. If you prefer to line things up in advance, contact **The Great Sailfishing Company** (© **877/763-0851** in the U.S. and Canada, or 502/7832-1991; www.greatsailfishing.com) or **Parlama Sport Fishing** ✠ (© **502/5704-4254** or 502/7832-2578; www.parlama.com). Rates run around Q1,875 to Q5,625 ($250–$750/£131–£394) per day, depending on the type of boat and number of people fishing. The best fishing season runs from November to May, when the sails are plentiful and the seas relatively calm. However, locals swear that the fishing is superb year-round.

WHERE TO STAY & DINE
Of the hotels listed below, only Hotel Martita is actually *in* Puerto San José. The others are several miles west of the city. I've yet to find a restaurant of note in Puerto San José, and most folks, myself included, are content to dine at the various hotel restaurants.

VERY EXPENSIVE
Sailfish Bay Lodge ✠   If you're coming to this area to fish, this dedicated fishing lodge has an enviable location on the ocean side of the canal just outside of the inlet and harbor of Iztapa. The accommodations are modern and comfortable, and the focus on fishing is apparent. In fact, all of the tours and packages offered here are for anglers, and the fishing starts early and is taken seriously. Still, while not on the water,

there's plenty to enjoy at this plush beachfront resort. In particular, the pool, Jacuzzi, restaurant, and bar are all set on the edge of the beach with excellent views of the water.

Iztapa. (℃) **800/638-7405** in the U.S. or Canada, or 502/2426-3909 in Guatemala. www.sailfishbay.com. 10 units. AE, DC, MC, V. Q17,100 ($2,280/£1,197) double for a 2-day/3-night package; Q24,375 ($3,250/£) for a 3-day/4-night package. Rates include round-trip transportation from Guatemala City, all meals and drinks, full-day fishing, and all tackle. Lower rates available in the off season. **Amenities:** Restaurant; bar; outdoor pool; Jacuzzi; tour desk; laundry service. *In room:* A/C, TV.

EXPENSIVE

Villas del Pacífico ⭐ (Kids) This large, all-inclusive resort hotel is the best option in Puerto San José, and it's equally sought after by Guatemalan weekenders and international sportfisherman. It's also the only hotel listed in this section that's right on the beach. They advertise themselves as an "All Seasons Resort," and this has led more than one confused tourist to think they were booking a Four Seasons property. It definitely is not. That said, the rooms have all the basic amenities you need, contemporary decor, firm beds, and plenty of space. All have a private balcony or patio, although none have ocean views. In fact, the rooms are set back from the beach, which is reached by a broad, arching pedestrian bridge over a mangrove canal. There is a mix of room types with various suites and deluxe suites, all of which are really family units with more sleeping options and often a full kitchenette. The hotel's main pool is very large, and on weekends and holidays there's a nightly cabaret-style show in their massive open-air amphitheater, which is followed by a lively disco. Meals at the property restaurant are adequate, but the best thing about eating here is the ocean view from the second-floor *mirador*. To reach the hotel, continue on the Carretera Vieja west out of Puerto San José until it dead-ends at the resort's entrance.

Chulamar. (℃) **502/7879-3131.** Fax 502/7879-3190. www.villasdelpacifico.com. 128 units. Q1,500 ($200/£105) double; Q2,250–Q3,750 ($300–$500/£158–£263) suite for up to 6 people. Rates are all-inclusive. These are weekend rates. Rates lower midweek; slightly higher during peak periods. AE, DC, MC, V. **Amenities:** 2 restaurants; 3 bars; 2 outdoor pools; tour desk; watersports equipment; children's program; laundry service. *In room:* A/C, TV, hair dryer, safe.

MODERATE

Aguazul This large, resort-style hotel caters to Guatemalan families and weekend revelers. It may have seen better days, but it currently shows the ravages of time and the hot, humid clime of Puerto San José. While mostly large, the rooms feel sparse and often moldy. The bungalows have enough beds for six and a basic kitchenette. On weekends there's often live entertainment and loud partying at the bars.

Km 6.5 Carretera Vieja. (℃) **502/7881-3445.** www.hotelaguazul.net. 36 units. Q390 ($52/£27) double; Q575 ($78/£40) minisuite; Q695 ($93/£49) bungalow for up to 6 people. Rates include breakfast buffet. These are weekend rates. Rates lower midweek; slightly higher during peak periods. AE, MC, V. **Amenities:** Restaurant; 2 bars; 3 outdoor pools and 2 children's pools; tour desk; laundry service. *In room:* A/C, TV.

Hotel Martita (Value) This modern, downtown hotel is your best bet in this price range, and a good option for folks here just for the fishing. This two-story place has the cleanest and most comfortable rooms in Puerto San José, and truly feels like an oasis in the midst of the clutter and clamor of this busy port town. There's a popular pool in the center of the complex, which is reserved for hotel guests, while another pool is open daily to locals and those staying at other hotels. You'll find this place just beside the train tracks that head toward the sea.

Av. de Comercio. ✆ **502/7881-1337** at the hotel, or 502/2474-1189 in Guatemala City. Fax 502/7881-2646. 38 units. Q590 ($79/£5.50) double. Rates include breakfast buffet. These are weekend rates. Rates lower midweek; slightly higher during peak periods. AE, DC, MC, V. **Amenities:** Restaurant; bar; 2 midsize pools, each with a children's pool; tour desk; laundry service. *In room:* A/C, TV.

3 Retalhuleu

192km (119 miles) W of Guatemala City; 58km (36 miles) S of Quetzaltenango; 133km (83 miles) W of Escuintla

For some inexplicable reason, the denizens of Retalhuleu have dubbed their city the "Capital of the World," which is more than a bit presumptuous. Founded in 1877, **Reu,** as it's commonly known, *is* the capital of Suchitepéquez, a rich and important agricultural region. It also makes a reasonable base for exploring some nearby archaeological sites, a couple of beaches, and IRTRA, Guatemala's large amusement and theme park complex.

> **⒯ips Tongue Twister**
>
> Retalhuleu is a bit of a tongue twister, even for native Guatemalans. This is probably why it's almost universally called Reu, which is pronounced "reh-ooh."

The city is compact, with a pretty colonial-era church and active central plaza. **Takalik Abaj** ☞☞, an important archaeological site, is just 30km (18 miles) from the city center, and several other popular sites are just outside the easily reachable town of **Santa Lucía Cotzumalguapa** ☞ (see below).

ESSENTIALS
GETTING THERE
BY BUS   Retalhuleu is serviced by regular bus service between Guatemala City and the Mexican border at Tecún Umán, as well as from Quetzaltenango. From Guatemala City, **Transportes Fortaleza** (✆ **502/2232-3643**) buses leave roughly every 15 or 20 minutes between 2am and 6pm from 19 Calle 8-70, Zona 1. The one-way trip takes around 6 hours and costs Q40 ($5.30/£2.80). Return buses run at the same frequency during roughly the same hours. The Reu bus station is located on the northern outskirts of town.

BY CAR   Retalhuleu can be reached either from Quetzaltenango or Escuintla. If you're coming from Guatemala City, the quickest route is to take CA-9, the Pacific Coast Highway, to Escuintla, and from there head west on CA-2, the coastal highway, toward Mazatenango and the Mexican border. If you're driving from Quetzaltenango, head south via Zunil to Reu.

GETTING AROUND
You can easily walk the entire downtown area of Retalhuleu. If you're too tired, or night has fallen, taxis and tuk tuks are plentiful, and most rides cost just Q10 to Q15 ($1.35–$2/70p–£1.05). A trip to Xocomil or Xetulul should run around Q40 ($5.30/£2.80). If you're having trouble flagging down a cab, have your hotel call you one.

ORIENTATION
Retalhuleu is about 4km (2½ miles) south of the coastal highway. Upon entering you're greeted by a beautiful avenue—*la calzada de las palmas*—lined with tall Royal palm trees. The entire city is centered around its popular central plaza, and just about every hotel, restaurant, attraction, and service is within a 2-block radius of this plaza.

FAST FACTS   There are several banks within a block of the central plaza, including **Banco G&T Continental** (© **502/7771-3849**) and **Banco Industrial** (© **502/ 7771-0684**). The **post office** (© **502/7771-0909**) fronts the central plaza. There are also a host of Internet cafes around Reu. One of the best, **Café Internet Antigua** (© **502/7771-4421;** www.cafeinternetantigua.com), has three separate storefronts in downtown.

The **Hospital Nacional de Retalhuleu** (© **502/7771-0116**) is located just outside of town, on the coastal highway, on the way to El Astinal.

WHAT TO SEE & DO

My favorite thing to do in Reu is to grab a seat somewhere on the central plaza and people-watch. If you're not into sitting still, you can tour the church. Like the colonial-era churches around Guatemala, **La Iglesia de San Antonio de Padua** has undergone successive rebuilding following various earthquakes. Nonetheless, it's a pretty and well-kept church with a beautiful whitewashed facade.

The city's main attraction, **Museo de Arqueología y Etnología** (© **502/7771-0557**), is quite small and relatively unimpressive. Located cater-cornered to the church and facing the central plaza, the museum has a small collection of ceramic, stone, jade, and obsidian artifacts, as well as a finely done scale model of the city's church. There's also a room with historical photographs. The museum is open Tuesday to Saturday from 8:30am to 5:30pm, Sunday 9am to 12:30pm. Admission is Q10 ($1.35/70p).

WHERE TO STAY & DINE

If the hotel listed below is full, try **Hotel Astor,** 5ta Calle 4-60, Zona 1 (© **502/7771-2559;** hotelastor@intelnett.com). If you want to eat someplace beside the Don José, try **Restaurante La Luna** (© **502/7771-0194**), which fronts the plaza.

INEXPENSIVE

Hotel Posada de Don José ☞   If you end up spending the night in Retalhuleu, this should be your first choice. The two-story downtown hotel is built around a relaxing central courtyard and pool. The rooms are well-kept and comfortable, although the decor and furnishings are dated. Some rooms come with a small balcony overlooking the street, which may be a plus or minus, depending upon whether you're more interested in local character or peace and quiet. There are a handful of suites, which come with separate sitting areas. The restaurant here is one of the best and most dependable in town.

5ta Calle 3-67, Zona 1. © **502/7771-0180.** Fax 502/7771-4176. posadadonjose@hotmail.com. 23 units. Q250–Q300 ($33–$40/£18) double; Q332 ($44/£23) suite. Rates include breakfast. AE, DC, MC, V. **Amenities:** Restaurant; bar; small outdoor pool; tour desk; laundry service. *In room:* A/C, TV, hair dryer.

RETALHULEU AFTER DARK

There is very little in the way of nightlife in Reu. Your best bet is to head to the Hotel Posada de Don José and catch the **Trío Don José.**

SIDE TRIPS FROM RETALHULEU

Retalhuleu serves as an excellent gateway to the following attractions. Alternately, you can visit any of these as a day trip out of Quetzaltenango, or as part of a route connecting Quetzaltenango to the Pacific beaches or Guatemala City.

RUINS OF TAKALIK ABAJ ☆☆

This remarkable and often neglected Maya site dates from the pre-Classic period. Its name translates to "Standing Stone" in the modern K'iche dialect, and is often incorrectly referred to as Abaj Takalik. So far, more than 80 structures built around some dozen different plazas have been discovered. Takalik Abaj also contains a wealth of carved stone sculptures and monuments, many showing clear influence of the Mexican Olmec tribes combined with prototypical and archaic Maya traits. It's even speculated that Olmec and Maya peoples may have coexisted at this site. Takalik Abaj thrived as a ceremonial and trade center from the 8th century B.C. through the 2nd century A.D., with close ties to Kaminaljuyú (present day Guatemala City). There are various well-preserved stelae here, as well as anthropomorphic carved stones. Be sure to check out the unique *barrigón*, or "fat-bellied," sculptures. There's also an early ball court, which is built in an uncommon "T" shape. One of the more remarkable finds at Takalik Abaj is the unlooted grave of an early Maya king who was buried in full regalia.

Takalik Abaj also contains a minizoo of sorts, with allegedly rescued and rehabilitating animals either found wounded or saved from poor living conditions.

The archaeological site is open daily from 7am to 5pm, and admission is Q25 ($3.30/£1.75). A guide is included with the price of admission and will accompany your group no matter what size. These guides are volunteers, and I recommend you leave a little tip of about Q7.50 to Q15 ($1–$2/55p–£1.05), even if he speaks only rudimentary English.

It's possible, yet complicated, to get to Takalik Abaj by public transportation. Your best bet is to either sign on for a guided tour or hire a taxi. Any hotel in town (or in Quetzaltanango, for that matter), can arrange a half-day tour for around Q112 to Q225 ($15–$30/£7.85–£16). The folks at **Takalik Maya Lodge** (see below) offer a day tour that visits the archaeological site and their coffee plantation, and also includes lunch, for Q210 ($28/£15) per person. If you're driving, head west out of Reu on CA-2 toward the Mexican border to the town of El Astinal. From here there are signs directly to the site.

Where to Stay

Takalik Maya Lodge ☆☆   If you want to stay right at Takalik Abaj, you'll definitely want to check out this luxurious new lodge. Taking over parts of a working coffee plantation that's also directly part of the archaeological site, this is one of the most unique hotels in Guatemala. The lodge has two types of rooms, those in the old coffee plantation, or El Paseo del Café Estancia, and Kacike Maya. I prefer the latter. The two modern suites here are very liberal interpretations of the rooms previously occupied by Maya royalty. In either case, the rooms are comfortable, with firm new beds and tasteful decor. There's also a restaurant and swimming pool, and in addition to touring the Maya ruins and coffee plantation, activity options include horseback riding, hiking, and bird-watching. The rates include your guided tours and activities, as well as entrance to the site.

Takalik Abaj Archaeological Park, Terrace 9. ℂ **502/2333-7056** or 502/5651-1094. www.takalik.com. 9 units. Q518 ($69/£36) per person in El Paseo del Café Estancia; Q645 ($86/£45) per person in Kacike Maya. Rates include 3 meals daily and guided tours. AE, DC, MC, V. **Amenities:** Restaurant; bar; small pool; tour desk; laundry service. *In room:* No phone.

GUATEMALA'S DISNEYLAND

The IRTRA provides vacation access and service to Guatemalan workers, and also runs two of the country's biggest theme parks—Xocomil and Xetulul—the first a water-themed park, the latter similar to Disney's Epcot Center. If you're traveling with children and the theme parks are your primary destination, you might want to stay at either **La Ranchería,** which has spacious, spread out bungalows, or the **Palajuno,** which continues the Epcot-like theme with units taking their design and decor from various tropical countries around the world. Both of these can be booked directly through IRTRA (℃ **502/7722-9100;** www.irtra.org.gt). Both theme parks, as well as the IRTRA hotels, are located about 12km (7½ miles) north of Retalhuleu, on the road to Quetzaltenango.

Xocomil 🎡 *(Kids)*   This is a large and well-designed water park featuring several high, fast, and exhilarating water slides, two wave pools, a "lazy river" float ride, several children's play pools, and everything else you might want or expect from a water park. I especially like some of the local touches, including the re-creations of Maya temples that are integrated into the rides and surroundings. I also like the Nido de Serpientes, a complex of seven simultaneous and intertwined water slides that let out into one common pool. There are several restaurants and snack stands on-site, which is a good thing, since the hot and humid clime of this area is quite conducive to a full day here.

℃ **502/7729-4000.** www.irtra.org.gt. Admission Q75 ($10/£5.25) adults; Q50 ($6.65/£3.50) children, students, and seniors. Thurs–Sun, plus major holidays, 9am–5pm.

Xetulul 🎡 *(Kids)*   The local version of Epcot, this park is divided into several areas devoted to the architecture of the Maya world, plus those devoted to countries such as Guatemala, France, Italy, and Spain. Amusement park rides and adventures are interspersed with, or integrated into, miniature versions of a Maya temple, a Guatemalan colonial-era town, el Palazzio Vecchio, and the Moulin Rouge. The park is remarkably well done and admirably maintained. The re-creation of the Trevi fountain is particularly impressive.

℃ **502/7722-9450.** www.irtra.org.gt. Admission Q200 ($27/£14) adults; Q100 ($13/£7) children, students, and seniors. Thurs–Sun and major holidays 10am–6pm.

THE COASTAL HIGHWAY & SANTA LUCIA COTZUMALGUAPA 🎡

As you drive from Retalhuleu toward Guatemala City or the Pacific beaches, you'll pass by the town of Santa Lucía Cotzumalguapa. While there's not much in town, there are a couple of interesting archaeological sites nearby, and one very good museum just outside of town. Perhaps feeling the pressure of Reu's naming itself "The Capital of the World," Santa Lucía calls itself "The World Capital of Happiness." However, Santa Lucía may have more of a leg to stand on. My Guatemalan friends say the town will throw a party at the drop of a hat, and quite often you'll find marimba bands playing at night in the town's central plaza.

If you decide to stay in Santa Lucía, your first choice should be the **Hotel Santiaguito** (℃ **502/7882-5435**). Located on the old Carretera al Pacifico at Km 90.4, this mini-resort has a popular restaurant, spacious modern rooms, and a large, refreshing pool.

Note: A couple of years ago a beltway, or *circunvalación,* was built to bypass the town of Santa Lucía Cotzumalguapa. If you want to visit any of the sites listed below or the hotel mentioned above, you'll want to get off the coastal highway and head toward the center of town.

Finca el Baúl   Even farther outside of the town sits Finca el Baúl. Set on a high hill in the midst of a working sugar-cane plantation, this place remains an active site of

---

⌒ Moments Big Trees

If you're driving along the road between Retalhuleu and Escuintla, keep an eye out for the many giant ceiba trees that dot the roadside, particularly around Santa Lucía. Revered by the ancient Maya, these towering trees have long, broad, and smooth trunks, and some of the specimens you'll see along this highway are more than 200 years old.

Maya ritual and worship. Still believing the site sacred, local Maya often come to a hilltop clearing here to make offerings, light candles, and perform ceremonies. Regardless of whether or not there are any practitioners on hand, you can visit the small museum and see a collection of the carved stones and stelae found on the surrounding grounds. The large stones have been carved into anthropomorphic images of crocodiles, serpents, and Maya gods. It's sort of a misnomer to call this collection a museum, as most are displayed simply in a broad open-air cleared area.

About 6km (4 miles) north of Santa Lucía. Free admission. Mon–Fri 8am–4pm; Sat 8am–1pm. Hilltop prayer site located off the main road to the Finca, about 2.5km (1½ miles) before the museum. Your best bet for getting here is to hire a taxi for around Q115 ($15/£8.05) round-trip with stops in Bilbao and prayer site, as well as time to explore.

Las Piedras (Bilbao Stones)   Just on the northern edge of Santa Lucía sits a collection of massive carved stones. The largest and most impressive of these, Monument 21, has been copied in fiberglass and is on display at the Museo de Cultura Cotzumalguapa (below). The others have been severely damaged by time, the elements, and vandals. Although it's a short and easy walk from town, you should only visit this site with a reputable guide and after checking on the current safety status, as there have been attacks on tourists here.

Just north of downtown. Free admission. There are no official operating hours.

Museo de Cultura Cotzumalguapa (Cotzumalguapa Cultural Museum) ⌖   Set just a few blocks inland from the highway on the eastern edge of town, this small museum houses an interesting collection of stelae and stone carvings gathered from nearby archaeological sites, including Bilbao (see below). The museum features an excellent replica of the massive carved anthropomorphic stone, Monument 21, from Bilbao. There are also a half-dozen or so carved stelae on the grounds outside the museum. Some of these are originals, while others are copies. It will only take you around 20 to 30 minutes to tour the museum.

The ticket booth and administration are found in a small house just beyond the museum. You may have to wake up, or shout to find, the caretaker, who will then collect your admission. The museum and its collection are part of the **Finca Las Ilusiones,** a former sugar-cane estate. If you ask politely, the caretaker may give you a quick tour of the old church across from the museum and the large manor or estate house next door.

𝒞 **502/5736-0403.** Admission Q10 ($1.35/70p). Daily 7am–noon and 2–4pm.

Appendix A:
Guatemala in Depth

A millennium of Maya civilization, 3 centuries of Spanish colonial rule, and almost 4 decades of guerrilla war have left Guatemala's economy, politics, crafts, architecture, languages, and religions with one common trait: profound variety. Home to nearly 13 million people, Guatemala is by far the most populous country in Central America, and its residents are extremely diverse. Less than a decade after the end of a long and brutal civil war, Guatemala is still writing its own history at a dizzying pace. The country seems poised between following a rising path to prosperity, democracy, and justice, and taking a precipitous fall into crime, chaos, and continued impunity.

1 Guatemala Today

Long-lasting Maya and Spanish empires produced an ethnically, linguistically, and economically divided Guatemala. Around half of the population is *mestizo* (known as *ladino* in Guatemala), or mixed Spanish-Amerindian heritage. The other half belongs to one of 23 indigenous Maya groups, each with their own language and customs. The largest group is the Ki'che, who live around Lake Atitlán and make up around 10% of the country's population. Other Maya groups include the Cakchiquel, Tz'utujil, Mam, and Kekchi, and on the Caribbean coast live the Garífuna, descendants of former slaves and Carib Indians.

Racial tensions can be strong between these groups, especially between *ladinos* and the Maya in the cities, and between *ladinos* and Garífuna on the Caribbean coast. Subsurface religious tensions also exist between the vast-majority Catholic population and the fast-growing Evangelical Protestant movement, which draws its greatest support within indigenous communities.

The Guatemalan economy is still heavily agricultural, based on the production of sugar cane, coffee, and bananas, with tourism and manufacturing playing increasingly important roles. The 2006 implementation of the Dominican Republic–Central American Free Trade Agreement with the U.S. is expected to boost foreign investment.

Despite gradual economic growth since the 1996 peace agreement, the country's war-torn past continues to cast a long shadow on its economy and society. The gap between rich and poor is wide. Up to 75% of the population lives below the poverty line, and crime continues to be a major problem. In the first 6 months of 2006, there were an almost unimaginable 30,000 armed robberies on Guatemala City buses. Lawlessness pervades many parts of the country, with vigilante groups, frustrated at the lack of police presence, often taking justice into their own hands.

The war continues to affect the political landscape as well. Most notable in this respect was the candidacy of former dictator General Efraín Ríos Montt in the 2003 presidential elections. Representing the Guatemalan Republican Front (FRG), Ríos Montt ran for president despite a constitutional amendment strictly prohibiting those who had come to power as the result of a coup d'état from holding the nation's highest office. In 2003, the Constitutional Court, packed with Ríos Montt supporters, ruled that the prohibition did not apply to the general. The decision spurred days of rioting in the capital, and Ríos Montt partisans stormed through the streets in black masks, smashing windows, torching buildings, and threatening passersby with machetes. The nation was outraged. Though he was allowed to run, Ríos Montt received only 11% of the vote, and did not qualify for the runoff elections. In the runoff of December 2003, Oscar Berger of the center-right Grand National Alliance (GANA) was elected with 54% of the vote, and his party won a plurality of seats in Congress. In addition to the FRG, the center-left National Unity for

Hope (UNE) and the National Advancement Party (PAN) also picked up seats.

In an interesting epilogue to the election, Ríos Montt's daughter Zury, a member of the Guatemalan Congress, married U.S. Congressman Jerry Weller (R-Illinois) at the general's compound in Antigua in November 2004. The union between the two legislators stirred controversy because Weller sits on the House International Relations Committee's Western Hemisphere Subcommittee, which votes on issues directly relating to Guatemala. Weller has also refused to denounce the genocidal acts of his father-in-law, whom Zury calls her "inspiration."

A decade after the end of its armed conflict, Guatemala is on the road to recovery. But that road, like so many in the country, is bumpy, winding, and steep.

2 History 101

EARLY HISTORY Before the arrival of the first Europeans, Guatemala was the land of the ancient Maya. Here, mathematicians came up with the concept of zero, astronomers developed a solar calendar accurate to a single day every 6,000 days, and scribes invented an 850-word hieroglyphic vocabulary that scholars consider the world's first advanced writing system. Some of this civilization's practices were less than civil: the Maya built extensive ball courts to play a game called "pok a tok," where the losing team could be executed.

Unlike the Incas of Peru, the Maya had no centralized ruler. Instead, the civilization consisted of a series of independent city-states, usually ruled by hereditary kings, often at war with one another. The most famous city-state is Tikal, in the northern Petén region, whose massive stone temples are the principal draw for tourists in Guatemala. In A.D. 562, Tikal was defeated in battle by the kingdom of Caracol, located in what is now the Cayo

District of Western Belize. Other city-states inside contemporary Guatemala include Quirigua, known for its detailed stelae, Kaminal Juyú near contemporary Guatemala City, Zaculeu, Iximché, Utatlán, and Petén Itzá.

Evidence of human presence in the Maya region dates as far back as the 10th millennium B.C. Maya history is often divided into several distinct periods: Archaic (10,000–2000 B.C.), Pre-Classic (2000 B.C.–A.D. 250), Classic (A.D. 250–900), and Post-Classic (900–1540). Within this timeline, the Classic period itself is often divided into Early, Middle, Late, and Terminal stages. At the height of development, as many as 10 million Maya may have inhabited what are now Guatemala, Belize, Mexico's Yucatán Peninsula, and parts of Honduras and El Salvador. No one knows for sure what led to the decline of the Classic Maya, but somewhere around A.D. 900, their society entered a severe and rapid decline. Famine, warfare, deforestation,

Maya Sites

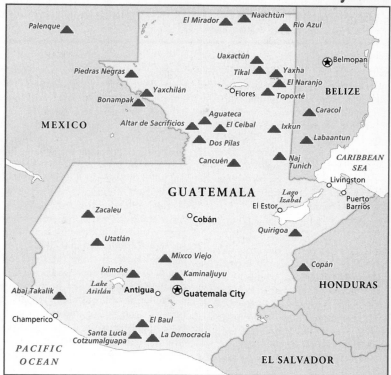

and religious prophecy have all been cited as possible causes. See Jared Diamond's bestseller *Collapse* (Penguin, 2005) for more information.

SPANISH CONQUEST On his fourth and final voyage to the New World in 1502, Christopher Columbus sailed past the Caribbean coast of Guatemala on his way to Panama, but did not land. However, his oversight did not save the area from Spanish conquest.

The conquistador Pedro de Alvarado was sent by Hernán Cortés to Guatemala in 1523. He had roughly 120 cavalry troops, about 300 infantry men, and several hundred indigenous slaves and mercenaries. In a ruthless campaign, Alvarado pitted different Maya tribes against each other, and then quickly turned on his unwitting accomplices. According to legend, when Alvarado killed the powerful Quiché king Tecún Umán at the Battle of Quetzaltenango in 1524, the quetzal (Guatemala's national bird) swooped down into the vast pools of blood and gained its red breast.

By 1525 Alvarado had completely subdued the western highlands, but the Spanish subsequently met with fierce resistance from many Maya tribes. Multiple invasions of the Petén failed, and the Kekchí in the central highlands held out as well.

Unable to control the Kekchí by force, the military allowed a group of Franciscan

---

Fun Fact What's in a Name

Spanish conquistadors named the area Goathemala, based on an indigenous word meaning "land of many trees."

---

friars under the leadership of Fray Bartolomé de las Casas to attempt the "humane" conversion of the tribe to Christianity. The friars succeeded, the population converted, and the area was given its Spanish name, "Verapaz" or "true peace." A human rights advocate until his death, Las Casas also successfully convinced the Spanish crown to pass the *New Laws* in 1542, awarding some basic protections to the *indígenas*.

COLONIAL RULE During Spanish colonial rule, Guatemala was a Captaincy General, part of the Viceroyalty of New Spain. The Spanish established Guatemala's capital at Ciudad Vieja in 1527, but moved to what is now Antigua (then called Santiago de Guatemala) in 1543 after the old capital was buried in a wave of water and mud that cascaded down from the Volcán de Agua.

For 200 years, Antigua was the center of political and religious power of the entire "Audiencia de Guatemala," including the provinces of Costa Rica, Nicaragua, El Salvador, Honduras, and Chiapas in Mexico. After severe earthquakes ravaged

Antigua in 1773, the crown decided to move the capital to safer ground. They chose the site of the ancient city of Kaminal Juyú, giving rise to Guatemala City.

In this colonial society, racial divisions were enshrined in law. *Peninsulares,* or Spanish-born Spaniards living in the New World, were at the top of the economic and political pyramid, followed by *criollos* (descendants of Spaniards born in the New World), *mestizos* (of mixed Spanish and Amerindian ancestry), *mulattos* (mixed Spanish and black), Amerindians, *zambos* (mixed Amerindian and black), and blacks. Individuals from the latter three groups were usually enslaved outright.

The Roman Catholic Church wielded enormous power, controlling vast plantations of sugar, wheat, and indigo run by forced indigenous labor. They used their wealth to construct some 80 churches, along with convents, schools, colleges, and hospitals.

There was great need for these hospitals: the diseases the Europeans brought decimated the Maya. By some estimates, nearly 90% of the Maya population was

Dateline

- **2000 B.C.–A.D. 1000** Maya civilization flourishes.
- **A.D. 200–900** Maya Classical period; Tikal at its peak.
- **562** Caracol defeats Tikal.
- **1502** Columbus sails along the coast of Guatemala.
- **1511** The Spanish conquest of the Yucatan begins.
- **1776** The capital is moved to Guatemala City after a

massive earthquake rocks Antigua.
- **1821** Guatemala gains independence from Spain, becoming part of Mexico.
- **1823** Guatemala becomes independent from Mexico.
- **1859** The border between Guatemala and British Honduras (now Belize) is established.

- **1871** Justo Rufino Barrios overthrows government, begins period of modernizing reform.
- **1948** Guatemala, laying claim to British Honduras, closes the border.
- **1954** Democratically elected President Jacobo Arbenz overthrown in CIA-sponsored coup.

wiped out after Alvarado arrived. Those who survived his violent wrath fell rapidly to diseases such as plague, typhoid, and smallpox, to which they had no natural resistance.

INDEPENDENCE Discontent with the exclusive rule of *peninsulares* reached a boiling point in the early 19th century, and a mood of reform swept across New Spain. Most of the fighting for independence took place in Mexico, where an unlikely coalition of conservatives and liberals eventually prevailed.

On September 15, 1821, Gabino Gainza, the captain general of Central America, signed the Act of Independence, breaking the region's ties with Spain. Although all of Central America initially remained part of Mexico—Mexico sent in troops to make sure that was the case—all Central American nations continue to celebrate their independence on September 15.

In 1823, an independent Central American Federation had taken shape. The Federation had a Constitution modeled on that of the U.S. It abolished slavery, religious orders, and the death penalty, and instituted trial by jury, civil marriage, and a public school system.

By 1840, the Federation had dissolved in civil war, instigated by the conservative dictators who had seized power in most of the nations, such as Rafael Carrera, a charismatic 23-year-old swineherd-turned-highwayman who, in Guatemala in 1838, raised an army, seized control, declared Guatemala independent, and promptly reversed decades of liberal reforms. With the adoption of a constitution in 1851, Carrera officially became independent Guatemala's first president.

BANANA REPUBLIC Over the course of the next century, power generally continued to change hands by military rather than democratic means. Liberal reformers traded off with conservative reactionaries, but one entity saw its influence grow fairly consistently: the United Fruit Company.

United Fruit, nicknamed "El Pulpo" (The Octopus) for its sweeping influence, first arrived in Guatemala in 1901, when it purchased a small tract of land to grow bananas. The company built its own port, Puerto Barrios, and after being awarded a railway concession leading inland from the port, it had a virtual monopoly on long-distance transportation in the country. United Fruit's rise to prominence coincided with the successive and enduring dictatorships of Manuel José Estrada Cabrera and Jorge Ubico. Collectively, these two men ruled, with great deference to United Fruit Company, from 1898 to 1941.

- **1967** Poet, novelist, and ambassador Miguel Angel Asturias wins Nobel Prize for Literature.
- **1982** General Efraín Ríos Montt seizes power in a coup.
- **1983** Rigoberta Menchú publishes *I, Rigoberta*.
- **1987** Central American presidents sign peace accords in Esquipulas.

- **1992** Menchú awarded Nobel Peace Prize.
- **1996** Guatemalan government and leftist rebels sign Accords for Firm and Lasting Peace.
- **1999** President Clinton apologizes for U.S. role in the Guatemalan conflict.
- **2002** Ex-Patrulleros de la Autodefensa Civil blockade Petén region.

- **2005** Torrential rains kill more than 1,000 people. Damage is worst around Lake Atitlán.
- **2006** Guatemala up against Venezuela for UN Security Council seat.

The Maya Calendar

While the standard Gregorian calendar is now in general use throughout Guatemala, some Maya communities and elders still rely on the ancient way of tracking time. In the Maya Calendar, each day has a hieroglyphic representation composed of numbers and pictographs, many of which can by found on stelae at most ancient Maya sites.

The Maya Calendar is actually a system of several calendars that can be combined in a number of sophisticated ways. The calendars and their accurate astronomical calculations predicting the cycles of the sun, moon, and Venus indicate the Maya had knowledge of mathematics and astronomy that was unknown to their old-world contemporaries.

The three main Maya calendar systems are known as the Tzolkin, Haab, and Long Count systems.

The Tzolkin calendar has 260 days, arrived at by multiplying 20 by 13. The numerical system was founded on a base 20 system (as opposed to our own base 10 system). Some think this came from the number of human fingers and toes, and that 13 symbolized the number of levels in the Upper World, where the gods lived. Another theory is that 260 days came from the approximate length of human pregnancy, and that midwives developed the calendar to coordinate with expected births. The Maya believed that each day of the Tzolkin had a character that influenced events. A priest read the calendar to predict a baby's future, and children were often named according to the day they were born.

The Haab was the Maya solar calendar made up of 18 months of 20 days each, plus a period of five unnamed days at the end of the year known as the Wayeb, which add up to a 365-day cycle. It was thought that if an event occurred one day during a specific Haab cycle, a similar event was likely to occur on that same day in the next Haab cycle.

The Long Count Calendar was used primarily by the priests and royalty. It tracked longer periods of time, and was based on the number of days since a mythical starting point (Aug 11, 3114 B.C.). The Long Count Calendar can be used to describe any date in the future.

In yet another layer of complexity, the Tzolkin combines with the Haab to form a synchronized cycle of 52 years, called the Calendar Round.

According to the Popol Vuh, the sacred Maya book of creation myths and predictions, we now live in the fourth world, the gods having failed in their first three creation attempts. It is believed that this age will end on December 21, 2012. While some New Age analysts have dire predictions for the date, more optimistic prognosticators foresee a day of positive human evolution. Hotels around Tikal and other major Maya ceremonial sites are already booking up for this date.

The Maya Calendar was so accurate it was adopted by other Mesoamerican societies, including the Aztecs and Toltecs.

"THE TEN YEARS OF SPRING" In 1941, a band of disgruntled military men, joined by students, labor leaders, and liberal political forces, overthrew Ubico and ushered in a period popularly referred to as "The Ten Years of Spring." Marked by moves to encourage free speech and liberal reforms, this time saw the election of Guatemala's first civilian president of modern times, Juan José Arévalo.

In 1951, Guatemala held its first-ever universal-suffrage election, bringing retired army colonel and political reformer Jacobo Arbenz to power. Confronting a vast gap between rich and poor, Arbenz fought for the passage of the 1952 Agrarian Reform Law, which redistributed thousands of acres of unproductive land to an estimated 100,000 peasant families. United Fruit was furious, having lost half its land. In 1954, the CIA, whose director sat on United Fruit's board, sponsored a coup d'état. Guatemala's new government, largely drawn from the ranks of its military, was flown into the capital aboard a U.S. Air Force plane.

CIVIL WAR & WAR CRIMES The new U.S.-sponsored regime eliminated the constitutional reforms of the previous decade, reinstituting rule by and for the *ladino* minority. In the early 1960s, a guerrilla war began between government forces and Marxist rebels, who drew their strength largely from indigenous communities and were headquartered in the highlands.

For the next 30 years, a succession of authoritarian rulers, nominally center-left or center-right, were brought to power by rigged elections or coups d'état. They largely followed the maxim of president and army colonel Arana Osorio, who said, "If it is necessary to turn the country into a cemetery in order to pacify it, I will not hesitate to do so." An estimated 200,000 people died or disappeared during the conflict, most of them indigenous. Death squads roamed the cities and highlands killing those suspected of rebel activity. Professors, students, union leaders, and priests were especially prone to attack.

In 1983, the Maya activist Rigoberta Menchú published *Me llamo Rigoberta Menchú y así me nació la conciencia* (translated into English as *I, Rigoberta*), an autobiographical tale of government massacres and the assassination of her own parents, who raised international awareness of the horrendous human rights situation in Guatemala. It won Menchú international acclaim, and in 1992, she was awarded the Nobel Prize for Peace. Some scholars later disputed factual claims made in the book, but the Nobel Committee has maintained its support for Menchú.

In August 1987, led by Costa Rican President Oscar Arias and hosted by Guatemalan President Vinicio Cerezo, the five Central American presidents met in Esquipulas, Guatemala, to sign the Accords for Firm and Lasting Peace ("Paz firme y duradera"). The Accords called for free elections, national reconciliation commissions, and perhaps most revolutionary of all in the midst of the Cold War, the rejection of foreign interference in Central American affairs. For his efforts to end the region's conflicts, Oscar Arias was awarded the 1987 Nobel Prize for Peace.

Following the recommendations of the 1987 accords, Guatemalan President Álvaro Arzú successfully negotiated a peace agreement with the URNG (as the united rebel factions were known) in December 1996. The agreement ended the 36-year-old civil war, with the government promising to support a Truth Commission led by the UN Mission to Guatemala, MINUGUA. The Constitution was also amended to allow for greater indigenous rights.

FROM PAZ FIRME TO THE PRESENT Guatemala's security situation improved after the end of the war, but great challenges remained. First, the military still wielded significant power, and did its best to cover up its involvement in the atrocities of the war. In 1998, days after delivering a report on human rights that blamed 80% of the abuses on the military, Catholic Bishop Juan Geradi was bludgeoned to death in his home in Guatemala City. Government and judicial officials were too afraid of suffering the same fate to investigate the crime.

With low coffee prices fueling economic stagnation, the crime rate soared after the 1996 accords. Murder and armed theft were commonplace. The unemployed, many former soldiers, turned their machine guns to the lucrative profession of highway robbery, pulling over buses and trucks, especially in the Petén. Kidnappings became appallingly common.

In 2002, a group of middle-aged ex-paramilitaries known as the *Patrulleros de la Autodefensa Civil* (Civilian Self-Defense Patrols, or PAC) blockaded the Petén region with clubs and machetes, demanding pay from the government for services rendered during the civil war. These services included killing Maya people suspected of rebel activities and razing indigenous villages. The group was, after all, created by General Ríos Montt, a former president widely considered to be responsible for some of the worst violence during the civil war. After 3 days, the government promised to meet the demands of the ex-PAC by levying a new national tax.

Most recently, kidnappings and highway robbery have receded somewhat, but the economic and security situation in much of the country remains precarious. Violent gangs, or *maras,* are having a noticeable impact across Guatemala, particularly in poor urban areas, and drug-trafficking and money laundering are considered to be major problems.

3 The Natural Environment

Guatemala sits at the top of the Central American isthmus, due south of Mexico's Yucatán Peninsula, between the Pacific Ocean and the Caribbean Sea. It covers an area of just more than 100,000 sq. km (40,000 sq. miles), slightly smaller than the state of Tennessee. It's bordered on the north by Mexico, on the east by Belize and the Caribbean Sea, on the southeast by Honduras and El Salvador, and on the southwest by the Pacific Ocean. Mountains cover nearly two-thirds of Guatemala, with the largest range being the **Cuchumatanes** in the northwest, really a southern extension of Mexico's Sierra Madre. South of the Cuchumatanes is **Volcán Tajumulco,** Guatemala's and Central America's highest point at nearly 4,200m (14,000 ft.). There are 32 other volcanoes in Guatemala, many of them active. Amid these mountains, Guatemala's landscape is coursed with caves, caverns, sinkholes, and underground rivers. Non-mountainous regions of the country include the narrow Pacific and Caribbean coastal plains, and a limestone plateau in the Petén, which is geographically part of the Yucatán.

Guatemala contains large expanses of lowland rainforest and highland pine forest. In an effort to combat the degradation of the rainforest brought about by widespread slash-and-burn agriculture, the Guatemalan government created the **Maya Biosphere Reserve** in the Petén Region in 1990. The reserve is the northernmost tropical forest in the Western Hemisphere and the largest contiguous tropical forest north of the Amazon, covering almost 800,000 hectares (2 million acres), or 10% of Guatemala's land area. The country is also home to rich **mangrove forest** on both the Pacific and Atlantic coasts. These saltwater-tolerant environments are major breeding and life-support grounds for a broad range of fauna.

The diversity of Guatemala's wildlife is as striking as the diversity of its people. The country is home to more than 8,000 higher plant species, 250 species of mammals, and 800 species of birds. Wildly colored butterflies swarm around the Laguna de Lachua, manatees have been spotted off the Caribbean coast, and jaguars prowl the forests of the Petén.

Revered by the ancient Maya and feared by most jungle dwellers, the jaguar is the largest New World cat, and can reach more than 6 feet in length and weigh more than 250 pounds. In addition to the jaguar, Guatemalan forests are home to four other wild cats—the puma, ocelot, margay, and jaguarundi—as well as such quintessential jungle dwellers as howler and spider monkeys, scarlet macaws, green iguanas, and boa constrictors.

The most famous resident of the Guatemalan rainforest, however, is the resplendent quetzal. Associated with the snake god Quetzalcoatl by Maya civilization, the national bird has a blood-red breast, almost electric-green feathers, and a tiny golden beak. The males of the species have tail feathers that can reach more than 2 feet in length. A good place to watch for them is in the **Biotopo del Quetzal** in the Verapaz highlands, though they can be quite difficult to spot. They are most active in the early morning.

SEARCHING FOR WILDLIFE Animals in the forest are predominantly nocturnal. When they are active in the daytime, they are usually elusive and on the watch for predators. Birds are easier to spot in clearings or secondary forests than they are in primary forests. Unless you have lots of experience in the Tropics, your best hope for enjoying a walk through the jungle or bird-watching excursion lies in employing a trained and knowledgeable guide.

Here are a few helpful hints:

- **Listen.** Pay attention to rustling in the leaves; whether it's monkeys above or pizotes on the ground, you're most likely to hear an animal before seeing one.
- **Keep quiet.** Noise will scare off animals and prevent you from hearing their movements and calls.
- **Don't try too hard.** Soften your focus and allow your peripheral vision to take over. This way you can catch glimpses of motion and then focus in on the prey.
- **Bring your own binoculars.** It's a good idea to practice a little first to get the hang of them. It would be a shame to be fiddling around and staring into space while everyone else in your group "oohs" and "aahs" at the sight of a quetzal.
- **Dress appropriately.** You'll have a hard time focusing your binoculars if you're busy swatting mosquitoes. Light, long pants and long-sleeve shirts are your best bet. Comfortable hiking boots are a real boon, except where heavy rubber boots are necessary. Avoid loud colors; the better you blend in with your surroundings, the better your chances are of spotting wildlife.
- **Be patient.** The jungle isn't on a schedule; however, your best shot at seeing forest fauna is in the very early-morning and late-afternoon hours.
- **Read up.** Familiarize yourself with what you're most likely to see. A good all-around book to have is Les Beletsky's *Traveller's Wildlife Guide: Belize and Northern Guatemala* (Interlink Books, 2004). Other relevant field guides include Thor Janson's *Maya Nature: An Introduction to the Ecosystems, Plants and Animals of the Mayan World* (Vista Publications, 2001), and the recently published *Birds of Mexico and Central America* (Collins Field Guides, 2006).

4 Guatemalan Culture

The real title of this section should be Guatemalan culture*s*. The nation is both a melting pot and a salad bowl—and in some places maybe even a melting salad bowl—in terms of its offerings in architecture, art, literature, and music. Its Maya, Spanish, and Garífuna heritages have ensured the existence of a wide array of crafts, architectural styles, and musical rhythms, as well as festivals and religious customs found nowhere else on the globe.

ARCHITECTURE In Guatemala City, colonial buildings coexist with skyscrapers and tin-roofed slums. The **Plaza Mayor, Catedral Metropolitana,** and **Palacio Nacional** are all impressive colonial structures. You might call the architectural style of the **Children's Museum** "colonial" as well—that is, if you're referring to a lunar colony. Also check out the vermilion, neo-Gothic **Iglesia Yurrita** in Zona 4, which tips its hat to Catalan architect Antoni Gaudí.

Antigua is a fabulously preserved colonial city, and many of its colonial-era churches and buildings have fortunately survived several major earthquakes. Those that didn't fully survive still add to the city's ageless air of grandeur. The **Palacio del Noble Ayuntamiento** and the ruins of the **Convento de las Capuchinas** are two of its many highlights.

If you're looking for classic monumental architecture in Guatemala, you're in luck. The creative Maya masons who constructed the stone pyramids built them to last—they've even survived the daily swarms of tourists who scamper all over them—though it's not clear how long they can endure an existence unprotected by guide ropes.

The most famous Maya ceremonial city in Guatemala is **Tikal.** With more than 3,000 mapped constructions to date and a score of impressive excavations and

reconstructions, a visit here gives you the sense of visiting a vibrant ancient city. Smaller architectural marvels dot the country, including giant stone stelae at **Quirigua,** and new sites are being discovered and excavated all the time. Those looking to see perhaps the finest example of Classic Maya hieroglyphics should head to neighboring Honduras and the ruins at **Copán,** where you'll find a staircase that holds the distinction of being the longest book written in stone.

ART Guatemalan artists range from folk artists and artisans working in a variety of forms, materials, and traditions to modern painters, sculptors, and ceramicists producing beautiful representational and abstract works.

The best-known crafts are indigenous woven tapestries and clothing. Artisans use natural dyes extracted from the *clavel* and *heraño* flowers, then mix in the crushed bodies of mosquitoes to keep the colors from running. The fabrics are woven on huge looms or simple, portable backstrap looms. Traditional dress for women includes a *huipil* (blouse) and *corte* (skirt), often fastened to the waist with a rope belt.

In recent years, mass-produced machine-woven fabrics have started appearing in markets. To spot a fake, look for gold or synthetic threads woven into the cloth, and for overly neat stitching on the back.

Other common handicrafts found in gift shops and markets across Guatemala include carved-wood masks and carved stone and jade.

Handicrafts are far from the only art in Guatemala. Mural painting is a growing form, especially works depicting emotional subjects. See the murals representing Guatemala's war-torn past and peaceful future in the church in **Rabinal** for an example.

Several galleries in Guatemala City and Antigua carry a wide range of locally produced art; see chapters 4 and 5, respectively, for more information.

LITERATURE Guatemala's literary tradition dates back to pre-Columbian Maya civilization, when Ki'che authors wrote the holy book **Popol Vuh.** The book traces the history of the Ki'che people beginning with their creation myth, linking the royal family with the gods in order to reaffirm its legitimacy. The book's exact age is unknown; the Spanish first recorded its existence in Chichicastenango in 1701.

Apart from the Popol Vuh, Guatemala's most famous literary works come from the Nobel Prize–winning poet, playwright, and ambassador Miguel Angel Asturias. Considered one of the fathers of magical realism, Asturias authored such works as *El Señor Presidente* (1946), *Viento Fuerte* (1950), and *Hombres de Maíz* (1967). A cultural center in Guatemala City bearing his name is home to chamber and open-air theaters, as well as a military museum and small art gallery. The **Miguel Angel Asturias Cultural Center** (© 502/2232-4041) is located at 24 Calle 3-81, Zona 1 (p. 108).

Literature can't be discussed without mentioning Maya activist Rigoberta Menchú, who won international acclaim with her autobiography, *I, Rigoberta,* first published in 1982. Other Guatemalan authors to look out for, both in Spanish and occasionally in translation, include the wonderful short story writer Augusto

Monterroso, as well as the poets Luis Cardoza y Arragon, Otto Rene Castillo, and Humberto Ak'Abal. See "Recommended Books, Films & Music" in chapter 2 for more details and recommendations.

MUSIC In Guatemalan folk culture, both *mestizo* and Maya, the marimba is king. *Mestizo* forms reflect their Spanish roots with marimba bands and Spanish-language folk songs influenced by the mariachi and ranchero traditions. Maya music may also prominently feature flute and drum, as with the Ki'che and Cakchiquel, or violins and harps, as with the Kekchi.

Discotheques still spin salsa and merengue, though a brash style called **reggaetón** is starting to dominate. Reggaetón is a combination of hip-hop and Jamaican dance-hall reggae, whose firmest roots are in Panama, though the music was popularized in Puerto Rico. In recent years it has skyrocketed in popularity in Puerto Rico, the Dominican Republic, most Central American nations, and among Latinos in the United States. Its biggest stars are Puerto Ricans Daddy Yankee and Don Omar.

City bars feature those rhythms as well as rock *en español.* The current darling of the genre is the Colombian-born Juanes, but not long ago, one of the brightest stars of Latin rock was the Guatemalan Ricardo Arjona, whose hits "Si el Norte Fuera el Sur" and "Ella y El" continue to grace bars' playlists.

Among the Garífuna along the Caribbean coast, you'll likely come across *punta* and *punta* rock. *Punta* is

A Word of Cultural Caution

While most Maya craftspeople are more than happy to see foreigners purchase their goods, for some indigenous people, seeing *gringos* walking the streets in native garb can be insulting—especially when women unknowingly wear traditional men's clothing, or vice versa. Use caution, and when in doubt, don't model your purchases in any but the most touristy towns or settings until you get home.

similar to many Afro-Caribbean and Afro-pop music forms, blending traditional rhythms and drumming patterns with modern electronic instruments. (*Punta* is usually more rootsy and acoustic than *punta* rock, which features electric guitars and keyboards.) *Punta* music is usually sung in the Garífuna dialect, though the latest incarnations feature lyrics in English and even Spanish.

5 Guatemalan Food & Drink

Guatemalan cuisine is similar to that of other Central American countries, relying heavily on black beans, white rice, and corn tortillas.

In addition to meat, fish, and poultry, other popular dishes include *chiles rellenos* (chiles stuffed with cornmeal, beef, and cheese) and *tamales* (a mixture of meat and cornmeal wrapped and steamed in banana leaves).

Typical fare is most often served in *comedores,* the Guatemalan version of diners, or simple neighborhood restaurants. There are international restaurants and fast-food chains in most touristy locations. Perhaps the most impressive fare is to be found along the Caribbean coast, where the Garífuna serve up a mouthwatering mix of seafood, coconuts, plantains, and spices.

Guatemalans tend to eat three meals a day, in similar fashion and hours to North Americans. Breakfast tends to be served between 6:30 and 9am; lunch between noon and 2pm; and dinner between 6 and 10pm. Most meals and dining experiences are quite informal. In fact, there are only a few restaurants in the entire country that could be considered semiformal, and practically none require a jacket or tie (they'd be in the capital), although you can certainly wear them.

FOOD

BREAKFAST   The typical breakfast in Guatemala is quite simple, usually anchored by some scrambled or fried eggs and accompanied by refried red or black beans and corn tortillas. If you order a *desayuno Chapin,* or Guatemalan breakfast, you'll also be served fresh fruit, a slice of local cheese, and some sautéed sweet plantains. Pancakes are often an option, though they might be oilier and crispier than the pancakes you're used to. Guatemalan coffee is world renowned, and you'll often get good strong coffee with your breakfast.

SANDWICHES & SNACKS   Guatemala's light menus show a heavy Mexican and American influence. Many simple eateries feature tacos, burritos, and tamales. *Empanadas,* small, deep-fried pastries stuffed with meat or potatoes, are ubiquitous. You can also get traditional sandwiches, often served on sliced white bread, as well as American-style burgers.

MEAT & POULTRY   Guatemalans eat a fair amount of meat and poultry. Chicken is the most popular, and in some remote places they'll serve it with the feet still attached. You might even get to pick the bird you'll be eating. Hunting iguanas for meat is illegal, but that does not mean it doesn't happen. *Note:* Do not order wild game unless you are certain it is farmed rather than hunted. Keep your eye out for *kac ik,* a savory turkey soup native to the Verapaz region. The dish is either served spicy or with chile on the side, and is spelled any number of ways on menus across the country.

SEAFOOD   Seafood is often available inland, though it's most plentiful and best on the coasts, especially the Atlantic coast, where shrimp, lobster, and a variety of fish are always on the menu. You're best off sticking to simple preparations, either grilled or fried.

If you're in a Garífuna region, don't miss the chance to try *tapado,* a fish stew

> **Fun Fact Men of Corn**
>
> According to the Popol Vuh, humans originally came from corn, and therefore it has special significance in Mayan culture. Corn not only plays a major role in the country's culinary tradition, it also lent its name to author Miguel Angel Asturias's 1967 Nobel Prize–winning masterpiece *Hombres de Maíz (Men of Corn)*.

or mixed seafood preparation served in a spicy coconut milk broth, often accompanied by mashed fried green plantains.

Ceviche, a cold marinade of fish, conch, and/or shrimp cooked in lime juice and seasonings, is a great treat for lunch or as an appetizer.

VEGETABLES On the whole, you'll find vegetables surprisingly lacking in the meals you're served in Guatemala— usually nothing more than a little pile of shredded lettuce topped with a slice or two of tomato. Fresh garden salads are rare and hard to come by. Most restaurant meals are accompanied by a simple slaw of grated cabbage, a potato, or beet salad.

FRUITS Guatemala has a wealth of delicious tropical fruits. The most common are bananas, mangoes, papayas, pineapples, and watermelons. Other fruits you might find include the *carambola* (star fruit) and the *guanabana* (soursop— a misleading name), whose white pulp makes for fabulous fruit shakes.

DESSERTS Guatemala doesn't have a very extravagant or refined dessert culture. Flan, a sweet custard, comes in coconut and caramel flavors, and *tres leches* is a very sweet, runny cake that almost falls into the custard category.

DRINK

BEVERAGES Most major brands of soft drinks are available, as are fresh shakes

(licuados) made with papaya, pineapple, mango, or my personal favorite, guanabana. Ask for them in milk *(en leche)* or water *(en agua pura),* and *sin hielo* (without ice) if you want to be extra sure you're not drinking tap water.

WATER Do not drink the water in Guatemala, even in the cities, as disease-causing organisms are endemic. Ask for bottled drinking water *(agua pura* or *agua purificada)* at your hotel, and whenever you can, pick up a bottle of spring or purified water (available in most markets) to have handy. You would also do well to brush your teeth with purified water.

BEER, WINE & LIQUOR The Cervecería Centroamericana's Gallo (Spanish for rooster) is the national beer of Guatemala. More than a mediocre lager, Gallo is a cultural force. Gallo T-shirts and other merchandise are everywhere. When Pope John Paul II came to Guatemala in 2002 to proclaim the first Central American saint, Gallo helped sponsor his visit. Other beers include Dorada and Moza, both produced from the same brewery as Gallo.

The region is not known for wine production, but some of the best rum in the world is distilled in Guatemala. Try the 23-year-old **Ron Zacapa Centenario** or the 12-year-old **Zaya Gran Reserva,** which have both won numerous awards and claim to be the best rum ever made.

Appendix B:
Useful Terms & Phrases

Spanish is the official language of Guatemala and the most widely spoken, but it will only take you so far. Each of the country's 23 indigenous groups has its own language, and these groups comprise almost half of the country's population.

Around Lake Atitlán you'll find speakers of Ki'che (the largest language group, making up about 10% of the population), Cakchiquel, and Tz'utujil. Mam is spoken in the Cuchumatanes Mountains near the Mexican border, while the Alta Verapaz and Petén regions are home to many speakers of Kekchi. The Garífuna people (descendants of former slaves and Carib Indians) along the Caribbean coast, have a language all their own. Many speak English as well.

Those who speak Spanish as their primary language, known as *ladinos,* are concentrated in urban areas, along the Pacific coast, and in the Petén.

Following the Peace Accords of 1996, Guatemala's Constitution was amended to "recognize, respect, and promote" indigenous languages. Children now receive instruction in their native language in school, bilingual judges and interpreters staff courtrooms, and government employees use indigenous languages when providing social services at the community level.

Guatemalan Spanish is considered one of the most pure, in terms of clarity and pronunciation, to be found in the Americas. Compared to the Spanish spoken in Mexico and the Caribbean, Guatemalan Spanish tends to be more clearly enunciated and slightly slower. It feels almost languid in comparison to, say, Puerto Rican or Cuban Spanish. This is one of the reasons language schools are so popular throughout the country. Many language schools now offer classes in Mayan languages as well as Spanish, especially in the more remote regions of the country. For a list of these schools, see chapter 2.

Below is a list of common Spanish terms and phrases. A note on pronunciation: The Spanish letter *ñ* is pronounced *ny* as in "ca*ny*on." In Guatemala, when the letter *x* appears in words of Maya origin (like "Xela"), it's pronounced *sh* as in "*sh*ell."

1 Basic Vocabulary

ENGLISH-SPANISH PHRASES

English	Spanish	Pronunciation
Hello	**Buenos días**	*bweh*-nohss *dee*-ahss
How are you?	**¿Cómo está usted?**	*koh*-moh ehss-*tah* oo-*stehd*
Very well	**Muy bien**	mwee byehn
Thank you	**Gracias**	*grah*-syahss
Goodbye	**Adiós**	ad-*dyohss*
Please	**Por favor**	pohr fah-*vohr*
Yes	**Sí**	see

Mayan Languages

① TEKTITEKO
② AKATEKO
③ SIPAKAPENSE
④ AWAKATEKO
⑤ SAKAPULTEKO
⑥ USPANTEKO
⑦ TZ'UTUJIL
⑧ POQOMAM

MEXICO

Lacandón
Tikal
ITZÁ
Flores
BELIZE
Belmopan

Sayaxché

Poptún
MOPÁN
San Luis

CARIBBEAN SEA

CHUJ
Q'ANJOB'AL
IXIL
Cobán
POQOMCHI'
Q'EQCHI
El Estor
Livingston
Puerto Barrios
Lago Izabal

MAM
K'ICHE'
ACHI'

Lake Atitlán
KAQCHIKEL
Guatemala City
Antigua
CH'ORTI'

HONDURAS

Champerico
Escuintla

PACIFIC OCEAN
EL SALVADOR

English	Spanish	Pronunciation
No	**No**	noh
Excuse me (to get by someone)	**Perdóneme**	pehr-*doh*-neh-meh
Excuse me (to begin a question)	**Disculpe**	dees-*kool*-peh
Give me	**Deme**	*deh*-meh
Where is . . . ?	**¿Dónde está . . . ?**	*dohn*-deh ehss-*tah*
the station	**la estación**	la ehss-*tah*-syohn
the bus stop	**la parada**	la pah-*rah*-dah
a hotel	**un hotel**	oon oh-*tehl*
a restaurant	**un restaurante**	oon res-tow-*rahn*-teh
the toilet	**el servicio**	el ser-*vee*-syoh

English	Spanish	Pronunciation
To the right	**A la derecha**	ah lah deh-*reh*-chah
To the left	**A la izquierda**	ah lah ees-*kyehr*-dah
Straight ahead	**Adelante**	ah-deh-*lahn*-teh
I would like . . .	**Quiero . . .**	*kyeh*-roh
to eat	**comer**	ko-*mehr*
a room	**una habitación**	*oo*-nah ah-bee-tah-*syohn*
How much is it?	**¿Cuánto?**	*kwahn*-toh
The check	**La cuenta**	la *kwen*-tah
When?	**¿Cuándo?**	*kwan*-doh
What?	**¿Qué?**	keh
What time is it?	**¿Qué hora es?**	keh *oh*-rah ehss
Yesterday	**Ayer**	ah-*yehr*
Today	**Hoy**	oy
Tomorrow	**Mañana**	mah-*nyah*-nah
Breakfast	**Desayuno**	deh-sah-*yoo*-noh
Lunch	**Almuerzo**	ahl-*mwehr*-soh
Dinner	**Cena**	*seh*-nah
Do you speak English?	**¿Habla usted inglés?**	*ah*-blah oo-*stehd* een-*glehss*
Is there anyone here who speaks English?	**¿Hay alguien aquí que hable inglés?**	eye *ahl*-gyehn ah-*kee* keh *ah*-bleh een-*glehss*
I speak a little Spanish.	**Hablo un poco de español.**	*ah*-bloh oon *poh*-koh deh ehss-pah-*nyohl*
I don't understand Spanish very well.	**No (lo) entiendo muy bien el español.**	noh (loh) ehn-*tyehn*-do mwee byehn el ehss-pah-*nyohl*

NUMBERS

1 **uno** (*oo*-noh)	16 **dieciséis** (dyeh-see-*sayss*)
2 **dos** (dohss)	17 **diecisiete** (dyeh-see-*syeh*-teh)
3 **tres** (trehss)	18 **dieciocho** (dyeh-*syoh*-choh)
4 **cuatro** (*kwah*-troh)	19 **diecinueve** (dyeh-see-*nweh*-beh)
5 **cinco** (*seen*-koh)	20 **veinte** (*bayn*-teh)
6 **seis** (sayss)	30 **treinta** (*trayn*-tah)
7 **siete** (*syeh*-teh)	40 **cuarenta** (kwah-*rehn*-tah)
8 **ocho** (*oh*-choh)	50 **cincuenta** (seen-*kwehn*-tah)
9 **nueve** (*nweh*-beh)	60 **sesenta** (seh-*sehn*-tah)
10 **diez** (dyehss)	70 **setenta** (seh-*tehn*-tah)
11 **once** (*ohn*-seh)	80 **ochenta** (oh-*chehn*-tah)
12 **doce** (*doh*-seh)	90 **noventa** (noh-*behn*-tah)
13 **trece** (*treh*-seh)	100 **cien** (syehn)
14 **catorce** (kah-*tohr*-seh)	1,000 **mil** (meel)
15 **quince** (*keen*-seh)	

DAYS OF THE WEEK

Monday **lunes** (*loo*-nehss)
Tuesday **martes** (*mahr*-tehss)
Wednesday **miércoles** (*myehr*-koh-lehs)
Thursday **jueves** (*wheh*-behss)
Friday **viernes** (*byehr*-nehss)
Saturday **sábado** (*sah*-bah-doh)
Sunday **domingo** (doh-*meen*-goh)

2 Menu Terms

FISH

atún   tuna
calamares   squid
camarones   shrimp
cangrejo   crab
ceviche   marinated seafood salad
dorado   mahimahi
langosta   lobster
langostinos   prawns

lenguado   sole
mejillones   mussels
mero   grouper
ostras   oysters
pargo   snapper
pulpo   octopus
tiburón   shark

MEATS

bistec   beefsteak
cerdo   pork
chicharrones   fried pork rinds
chuleta   cutlet
conejo   rabbit
cordero   lamb

costillas   ribs
jamón   ham
lengua   tongue
pato   duck
pavo   turkey
pollo   chicken

VEGETABLES

aceitunas   olives
alcachofa   artichoke
berenjena   eggplant
cebolla   onion
elote   corn on the cob
ensalada   salad
espárragos   asparagus
espinacas   spinach
frijoles   beans

palmito   heart of palm
papa   potato
pepino   cucumber
remolacha   beet
repollo   cabbage
tomate   tomato
vainica   string beans
yuca   cassava, or manioc
zanahoria   carrot

FRUITS

aguacate   avocado
carambola   star fruit
cereza   cherry
ciruela   plum
fresa   strawberry
limón   lemon or lime

mango   mango
manzana   apple
melocotón   peach
mora   raspberry
naranja   orange
pera   pear

piña   pineapple
plátano   banana
sandía   watermelon

toronja   grapefruit
uvas   grapes

BASICS

aceite   oil
ajo   garlic
arroz   rice
azúcar   sugar
mantequilla   butter
miel   honey
mostaza   mustard

natilla   sour cream
pan   bread
pimienta   pepper
queso   cheese
sal   salt
tamal   filled cornmeal pastry
tortilla   flat corn pancake

DRINKS

agua pura   purified water
aguas   soft drinks
batido   milkshake
bebida   drink

cerveza   beer
leche   milk
licuado   shake
ron   rum

OTHER RESTAURANT TERMS

asado   roasted
caliente   hot
cambio   change
comida   food
congelado   frozen
frío   cold
frito   fried

grande   big
la cuenta   the bill
medio   medium
muy cocido   well-done
pequeño   small
poco cocido   rare

3 Travel Terms

HOTEL TERMS

aire acondicionado   air-conditioning
almohada   pillow
baño   bathroom
calefacción   heating
cama   bed
cerradura de puerta   door lock
colchón   mattress

cuarto   room
escritorio   desk
manta   blanket
mosquitero   mosquito net
sabanas   sheets
ventilador   fan

TRANSPORTATION TERMS

Aduana   Customs
aeropuerto   airport
avenida   avenue
avión   airplane
aviso   warning
bus   bus
calle   street
cheques viajeros   traveler's checks
correo   mail or post office
cuadra   city block

dinero   money
dmbajada   embassy
entrada   entrante
este   east
frontera   border
hospedaje   inn
lancha   boat
norte   north
oeste   west
occidente   west

oriente   east
pasaporte   passport

salida   exit
vuelo   flight

EMERGENCY TERMS

emergencia   emergency
enfermo   sick
farmacia   pharmacy
hospital   hospital

ladrón   thief
peligroso   dangerous
policía   police
médico   doctor

4 Typical Guatemalan Words & Phrases

camioneta   chicken bus (You might also hear "*cheecken boos.*")
chapín   Guatemalan
chino   Literally "Chinese," but used to refer to any Asian, or anyone who looks vaguely Asian.
chulo   beautiful
codo   cheap
comedor   basic restaurant
corte   Native-style skirt
gringo   North American/European/white person
huipil   Native-style woman's top
jalón   a ride
parrandear   to party
pinchazo   Literally a flat tire, but also seen on roadside signs throughout the country to advertise tire repair operations.
¡Púchica!   excited exclamation
¿Qué onda vos?   What's up?
rebasar   to pass while driving.
típico   Native-style
tumulo   speed-bump
Vos   you

5 Traditional Maya Textiles

Some say that it's possible to take great photographs in Guatemala with your eyes closed. This is largely due to the beauty of the fabulous textiles woven and worn by Maya women, and to a lesser extent, men. The most distinctive piece of traditional clothing is the female blouse known as a *huipil*—a large shirt made of two rectangular pieces of heavy cloth, which are sewn together with no tailoring or shape other than a simple hole for the head. *Huipiles* are usually worn about waist length, but they are often significantly wider at the shoulders than the actual shoulders of the Maya women who wear them. *Huipiles* are traditionally woven on a simple backstrap loom, and feature intricate patterns and designs that may be a mix of loom technique and embroidery. These patterns and designs range from the entirely abstract to figurative, with people, animals, flowers, celestial bodies, and gods and goddesses all finding their way into the fabric of this distinctly Guatemalan art form.

It's still common to see women attend weaving classes. One of the most fascinating aspects of the *huipil* is that dozens of villages have their own style of design: Nebaj in the Ixchil Triangle of villages in the Central Highlands is famous for its tight, intricate hand embroidery with figures of horses, birds and people; the weavers from Chichicastenango embroider the neck, shoulder, and center of the chest areas with predominantly abstract designs; and those in San Lucas Toliman are known for their unique representational embroidery that resembles stick figures.

The *huipil* has been worn since long before the arrival of the Spaniards in the 16th century. However, it was the Spaniards who instituted the concept of specific village-related *huipil* styles to establish class and slave organizational structures. During the civil war of the last century, the army followed the conquistadors' lesson and used the *huipil* and other items of indigenous dress to identify people from villages thought to be sympathetic to the guerrilla cause.

Other pieces of traditional Maya dress that you will see include the *corte*, which is a large, long rectangular piece of cloth worn as a wraparound skirt. *Cortes* usually feature bright colors woven into complex patterns. Women often also wear a *tocoyal*, or headdress. These can range from pieces of cloth to long, narrow ribbons wound in a tight spiral and adorned with tassels. Highly figured and embroidered men's shirts are called *trajes*.

Today, Maya textiles are displayed on the walls of hotels and restaurants. They are sold on the streets of cities, villages, and in souvenir shops (where you'll find dolls dressed in typical dress, purses, and other accessories made of the beautiful work). In your search, it's well worth a visit to a bustling market, such as those found in Guatemala City, Antigua, Chichicastenango, or Santiago Atitlán.

Note: Please show respect for the Maya culture and remember that only women wear *huipiles*, while many of the embroidered shirts and pants are meant specifically for men. In fact, most traditional Maya are offended by any Westerner wearing traditional garb, even if it is gender correct. In many cases, the best policy is to wait until you get home before donning your *huipil* or embroidered jacket.

Index

See also Accommodations and Restaurant indexes, below.

ACCOMMODATIONS

RESTAURANTS

FROMMER'S® COMPLETE TRAVEL GUIDES

Alaska
Amalfi Coast
American Southwest
Amsterdam
Argentina & Chile
Arizona
Atlanta
Australia
Austria
Bahamas
Barcelona
Beijing
Belgium, Holland & Luxembourg
Belize
Bermuda
Boston
Brazil
British Columbia & the Canadian
  Rockies
Brussels & Bruges
Budapest & the Best of Hungary
Buenos Aires
Calgary
California
Canada
Cancún, Cozumel & the Yucatán
Cape Cod, Nantucket & Martha's
  Vineyard
Caribbean
Caribbean Ports of Call
Carolinas & Georgia
Chicago
China
Colorado
Costa Rica
Croatia
Cuba
Denmark
Denver, Boulder & Colorado Springs
Edinburgh & Glasgow
England
Europe
Europe by Rail
Florence, Tuscany & Umbria

Florida
France
Germany
Greece
Greek Islands
Hawaii
Hong Kong
Honolulu, Waikiki & Oahu
India
Ireland
Israel
Italy
Jamaica
Japan
Kauai
Las Vegas
London
Los Angeles
Los Cabos & Baja
Madrid
Maine Coast
Maryland & Delaware
Maui
Mexico
Montana & Wyoming
Montréal & Québec City
Moscow & St. Petersburg
Munich & the Bavarian Alps
Nashville & Memphis
New England
Newfoundland & Labrador
New Mexico
New Orleans
New York City
New York State
New Zealand
Northern Italy
Norway
Nova Scotia, New Brunswick &
  Prince Edward Island
Oregon
Paris
Peru
Philadelphia & the Amish Country

Portugal
Prague & the Best of the Czech
  Republic
Provence & the Riviera
Puerto Rico
Rome
San Antonio & Austin
San Diego
San Francisco
Santa Fe, Taos & Albuquerque
Scandinavia
Scotland
Seattle
Seville, Granada & the Best of
  Andalusia
Shanghai
Sicily
Singapore & Malaysia
South Africa
South America
South Florida
South Pacific
Southeast Asia
Spain
Sweden
Switzerland
Tahiti & French Polynesia
Texas
Thailand
Tokyo
Toronto
Turkey
USA
Utah
Vancouver & Victoria
Vermont, New Hampshire & Maine
Vienna & the Danube Valley
Vietnam
Virgin Islands
Virginia
Walt Disney World® & Orlando
Washington, D.C.
Washington State

FROMMER'S® DAY BY DAY GUIDES

Amsterdam
Chicago
Florence & Tuscany

London
New York City
Paris

Rome
San Francisco
Venice

PAULINE FROMMER'S GUIDES! SEE MORE. SPEND LESS.

Hawaii

Italy

New York City

FROMMER'S® PORTABLE GUIDES

Acapulco, Ixtapa & Zihuatanejo
Amsterdam
Aruba
Australia's Great Barrier Reef
Bahamas
Big Island of Hawaii
Boston
California Wine Country
Cancún
Cayman Islands
Charleston
Chicago
Dominican Republic

Dublin
Florence
Las Vegas
Las Vegas for Non-Gamblers
London
Maui
Nantucket & Martha's Vineyard
New Orleans
New York City
Paris
Portland
Puerto Rico
Puerto Vallarta, Manzanillo &
  Guadalajara

Rio de Janeiro
San Diego
San Francisco
Savannah
St. Martin, Sint Maarten, Anguila &
  St. Bart's
Turks & Caicos
Vancouver
Venice
Virgin Islands
Washington, D.C.
Whistler

FROMMER'S® CRUISE GUIDES

Alaska Cruises & Ports of Call   Cruises & Ports of Call   European Cruises & Ports of Call

FROMMER'S® NATIONAL PARK GUIDES

Algonquin Provincial Park   National Parks of the American West   Yosemite and Sequoia & Kings
Banff & Jasper   Rocky Mountain   Canyon
Grand Canyon   Yellowstone & Grand Teton   Zion & Bryce Canyon

FROMMER'S® MEMORABLE WALKS

London   Paris   San Francisco
New York   Rome

FROMMER'S® WITH KIDS GUIDES

Chicago   National Parks   Toronto
Hawaii   New York City   Walt Disney World® & Orlando
Las Vegas   San Francisco   Washington, D.C.
London

SUZY GERSHMAN'S BORN TO SHOP GUIDES

France   London   Paris
Hong Kong, Shanghai & Beijing   New York   San Francisco
Italy

FROMMER'S® IRREVERENT GUIDES

Amsterdam   London   Rome
Boston   Los Angeles   San Francisco
Chicago   Manhattan   Walt Disney World®
Las Vegas   Paris   Washington, D.C.

FROMMER'S® BEST-LOVED DRIVING TOURS

Austria   Germany   Northern Italy
Britain   Ireland   Scotland
California   Italy   Spain
France   New England   Tuscany & Umbria

THE UNOFFICIAL GUIDES®

Adventure Travel in Alaska   Hawaii   Paris
Beyond Disney   Ireland   San Francisco
California with Kids   Las Vegas   South Florida including Miami &
Central Italy   London   the Keys
Chicago   Maui   Walt Disney World®
Cruises   Mexico's Best Beach Resorts   Walt Disney World® for
Disneyland®   Mini Mickey   Grown-ups
England   New Orleans   Walt Disney World® with Kids
Florida   New York City   Washington, D.C.
Florida with Kids

SPECIAL-INTEREST TITLES

Athens Past & Present   Frommer's Exploring America by RV
Best Places to Raise Your Family   Frommer's NYC Free & Dirt Cheap
Cities Ranked & Rated   Frommer's Road Atlas Europe
500 Places to Take Your Kids Before They Grow Up   Frommer's Road Atlas Ireland
Frommer's Best Day Trips from London   Great Escapes From NYC Without Wheels
Frommer's Best RV & Tent Campgrounds   Retirement Places Rated
    in the U.S.A.

FROMMER'S® PHRASEFINDER DICTIONARY GUIDES

French   Italian   Spanish